Hybrid Warfare

The Russian Approach to Strategic Competition & Conventional Military Conflict

Curtis L. Fox

-30- Press Publishing

Published by Four Minute Men Books, a -30- Press Publishing Imprint

30press.com

Developmental editing by Ashley Franz Holzmann, Kristopher J. Patten, and V.R. Walker.

Copy editing by Addison Rop.

Cover design and formatting by V.R. Walker.

Jacket Design by Alejandro B.

Contents

Dedication

To the bearded bastards that were raised on John Wayne movies. To the snake-eaters that were born for the storm, who find comfort and leisure exhausting. To the quiet professionals that are always the first in the fight and the last home. To those soldier-diplomats that climb mountains, sleep under the stars, jump out of perfectly good airplanes, and count themselves blessed for the privilege. To all those who could not come home.

"De Oppresso Liber"

Acknowledgements

This book would not have been possible without the help of many people. My poor wife, Katie, was burdened with daily requests for advice, opinions, edits, and proofreading, and she has been a patient listener whenever I had to complain about revisions and rewrites. You are ever an enduring light and my best friend.

My constant editor, Marina Hansen, has also spent many late evenings working on revisions, prodding me to expand and expound on the connective tissues between themes and concepts. She also provided a number of the book's drawings and sketches. Your advice is greatly appreciated, and I will miss our evening discussions. This project would not be possible without your many hours of help, and I have greatly enjoyed our collaboration.

Luke Walter, Chan-hyuk Kang, and Chandler Merrill all contributed their knowledge and expertise, peer-reviewing content for historical and doctrinal accuracy. Thank you for contributing your wisdom.

Brandon Miller and my brother Joseph Fox have been faithful friends in discussing the military theory and operative concepts of this book. Your patience with my questions, the knowledge of your commentary, and your friendship are all greatly appreciated.

FOREWORD

The Global War on Terror has ended in a sigh, with both funding and operations shifting the focus of the United States and its Western Allies toward what many are calling a new era of Strategic Competition. The strategic competitors of this era—Russia, China, Iran, and North Korea—are not new to Western foreign policy. Still, few analysts predicted the Russian invasion of Ukraine coming in February of 2022.

Why did Russia invade Ukraine?

How could the attack have happened under the noses of so many international analysts?

Was it a random act of violence or a dog-eared page from the Russian playbook?

Curtis L. Fox successfully dissects the answers to those questions in this work. In an era where the nature of warfare evolves with the relentless pace of technological advancement and the complexities of global geopolitics, "Hybrid Warfare" emerges as a seminal and timely work, intricately dissecting the multifaceted dimensions of Russian conflict.

This book offers a profound exploration of the dynamic interplay between conventional military tactics mixed with facets of information warfare, cyber-enabled operations, electronic warfare, drones, surrogate forces, and myriad other emerging technologies and tactics on the modern battlefield.

Moreover, this book walks the reader through how Russia got to this point in history, where its strategies originated from, and how history and geography have shaped Russian military strategy for hundreds of years.

My journey in the realm of military operations and strategy has granted me the privilege of witnessing firsthand the transformation of warfare. From this vantage point of experience and study, I recognize this book's indispensable contribution to our understanding of contemporary military conflicts. "Hybrid Warfare" does not merely navigate the surface of its subject; it delves deeply into the intricacies of how nations, non-state actors, and coalitions adapt to and engage in this new form of conflict.

Curtis possesses a keen analytical eye, and this book dissects historical precedents, current trends, and potential future scenarios. It offers not only a thorough understanding of the strategic and tactical elements of such conflicts but also illuminates the psychological and sociopolitical dimensions that underpin them.

This book is a vital resource for military professionals, policymakers, academics, and any reader who wants to understand the "why" of the current conflict unfolding in Eastern Europe. Its detailed analysis and forward-looking insights provide readers with the tools to comprehend and engage effectively in the multidimensional battleground of the 21st century.

"Timely" is an understatement when used to describe this work, as the first draft was completed before February 2022, necessitating a page-one overhaul of the project once Russia invaded Ukraine. Real-world event after real-world event continued to push the publication date to the right as Curtis worked tirelessly on what would become something that he and our team are endlessly proud of.

As conflicts around the globe continue to evolve, works like "Hybrid Warfare" can serve as a guide for strategists and practitioners to navigate the changing terrain. The book is not only a reflection of the current state of military affairs but also a beacon, illuminating the path forward in understanding and countering the complexities of modern warfare.

Thank you for picking up the first edition of "Hybrid Warfare: The Russian Approach to Strategic Competition & Conventional Military Conflict". I can assure you that it will be an informative, entertaining, and amazing experience.

Ashley Franz Holzmann, December 2023

Chief Creative Officer

-30- Press Publishing

INTRODUCTION

THE OVERTURE

The dreaded Spetsnaz of the Cold War still exist today. Once feared as silent killers that could topple governments, they now give public demonstrations of their physical prowess. YouTube is littered with propaganda clips of Spetsnaz men throwing hatchets at targets in mid-backflip or doing leaping push-ups over a flaming jump rope.

In one video, a Spetsnaz team snow-skis downhill with AK-74s at the ready, firing massive quantities of blank ammo at an entrenched defender. In another, a Spetsnaz man disarms multiple attackers and puts them on the ground through a combination of judo and karate. There are even videos of Spetsnaz men having a concrete slab set on their abdominal muscles only to have it shattered by another soldier with a sledgehammer.

This propaganda comes off as comical, but still impressive.

Why does Moscow feel a need to telegraph the capabilities of its elite trigger-pullers? Afterall, Russia is almost always supporting some separatist group in Eastern Europe, backing a warlord in Libya, or propping up a dictator in the Middle East. Should not all these low-level military interventions demonstrate Russia's capacity to project power? And why does Russia really need to use military force to shape its strategic environment? Westerners consider this kind of thinking to be very 20th Century.

The truth is that the Russians never left the 20th Century; nor, for that matter, the 18th Century. Vladimir Putin is looking at the same geopolitical chessboard as Peter the Great, Catherine the Great, Vladimir Lenin, and Joseph Stalin. Technology and even culture may evolve, but geography remains constant and determinate.

Russia is located on the vast Northern-Eurasian plain. The land itself is mostly open steppe and tundra, making it both capital poor and devoid of geographic barriers to anchor Russia's long borders. Rather than financing armies to constantly patrol the open steppe, Russia projects subtle influence aboard to create and control buffer states and prevent rivals from building coalitions. Today, we call these strategies and activities Hybrid Warfare, and to understand them we need to first consider how the modern world developed.

The sail, deepwater navigation, maps, and the printing press, technological innovations from the High Middle Ages, laid the foundation for the Age of Exploration, leading to the emergence of the European empires. The advent of deepwater navigation enabled economic expansion, a global population boom, and the establishment of the colonial trade system.

Each Great Power in Europe established colonies in the Americas, Africa, Asia, and the Pacific. The mother country would invest in mines, farms, plantations, fisheries, foundries, and shipyards in these colonies, taking advantage of cheap labor and access to raw materials to feed the mother economy, which was connected to the colonial assets through maritime trade routes. Russia, without access to a reliable warm-water port and barred from westward expansion by entrenched adversaries, expanded east across frigid northern Asia and into the Aleutian Sea.

With the exception of Russia, each European power maintained a powerful navy to ensure that it could protect their global supply chains. The European Great Powers traded far less with each other than within these mutually exclusive empires. When a country's population reached a critical mass, thereby facilitating economic expansion, additional resources were needed to sustain the population and its underlying productive activities.

The only way to secure such resources was to seize territory from a neighboring empire. From the advent of the European Colonial Empires until World War II, European countries trained powerful militaries, cobbled together strategic alliances, and periodically went to war with one another. As European influence spread throughout the world and entrenched itself in foreign society and economies, each consecutive conflict grew to have a more profound global impact.

During the latter 18th century, France suffered several territorial losses, the most catastrophic of which was New France in North America: conceded to the British at the conclusion of the Seven Years War. The blow of losing France's colonial foothold in the New World enraged French citizens, and the reign of King Louis XV became extremely unpopular due to his mismanagement, brutal taxes, and general incompetence. His son, King Louis XVI, grossly mismanaged the Crown's crisis of legitimacy and failed to institute meaningful reforms, leading to the French Revolution.

Emerging from the bloodshed and power vacuum of the French Revolution was a young artillery sergeant who became known throughout Europe as the God of War—widely considered to be history's greatest military genius. He had an ability to understand the essentials from only a brief situational assessment, as well as a memory that could shelve subjects for days and then re-engage them as though he'd never set them down. Napoleon began his career in the ranks with no birthright and no prospects, but his brilliance soon made him a premier officer, and the French Revolution provided him many crises to resolve and many opportunities to win glory.

In 1799, Napoleon returned from Egypt to a hero's welcome and led a coup d'état against the First French Republic. The French Directory (executive council) and Council of 500 (lower legislative chamber) were both dissolved, and Napoleon and his political allies established the French Consulate government under the new "Constitution of Year VIII".

Bonaparte was careful to never seize more executive power than his popular support would permit. Through a series of electoral consultations with the French public, Napoleon secured the position of First Consul; the first among equals in government. By 1804, his numerous battlefield victories had won him enough popular support to declare himself Emperor. Napoleon would do the impossible and conquer most of Europe (with the exceptions of the United Kingdom, Portugal, and Russia). With his reign came enlightened despotism, military genius, and twelve years of global conflict.

During his conquest, Emperor Napoleon contended with a series of grand coalitions organized by the United Kingdom to prevent a permanent French hegemony. These coalitions included notable contributions of soldiers and supplies from Czar Alexander I of Russia: specifically, divisions under the direction of Lt. General Mikhail Kutuzov (he was eventually promoted to Field Marshal).

Kutuzov was present at the Battle of Austerlitz: often cited as one of Napoleon's greatest masterpieces. He saw the battlefield as Napoleon did and attempted to deny the French the strategically vital Pratzen Plateau.

Ultimately, Napoleon maneuvered Alexander into a position where he had to call on reserve troops, and Kutuzov was ordered to abandon the heights. Seeing the opening, Napoleon immediately seized the position, set his artillery in place, and fired down on the coalition's center until it broke.

Napoleon resented the Russian soldiers and supplies sent to support these anti-French coalitions. He began to plan for war: a campaign to bring Russia to the heel of the God of War. The Russians were insulated from French reprisals by vast expanses of open steppe, but Bonaparte always dared to attempt the impossible. He assembled his Grand Armée and marched eastward in 1812. The campaign was bitterly fought, and the

French were eventually able to capture Moscow, but under the advice of Mikhail Kutuzov, the Czar chose to resist through a Fabian strategy.[1]

The Russians destroyed everything of value as they withdrew eastward, preventing Napoleon's Grand Armée from foraging for supplies. Mikhail Kutuzov was appointed the leader of all Russian forces due to overwhelming public support, and, under his leadership, the Russians generally avoided decisive battles.

Instead, Kutuzov sought to whittle the French forces using skirmishes, starvation, and the cruel Russian winter. Napoleon had expected respite once he captured the Russian crown jewel of Moscow, but he found the city burned to the ground. Napoleon's weary troops weathered the winter huddling over the glowing embers of Russia's greatest city.

Less than 10% of the Grand Armée returned to France as most soldiers had died from extreme cold, starvation, and harassing Russian forces. Emperor Napoleon had subjugated all of continental Europe. The Russians were looked down on as uncultured and backwards by other Europeans, and yet they delivered the God of War a crushing defeat.

It was only Napoleon's personal charisma and mastery of the details of command that held his battered army together. Constant harassment by Kutuzov's skirmishers and cavalry, an icy winter season, and crushing starvation harried the Grand Armée through a brutal retreat to Napoleon's garrisons in Europe. When the God of War arrived, every state, duchy, and kingdom he had conquered was in revolt.

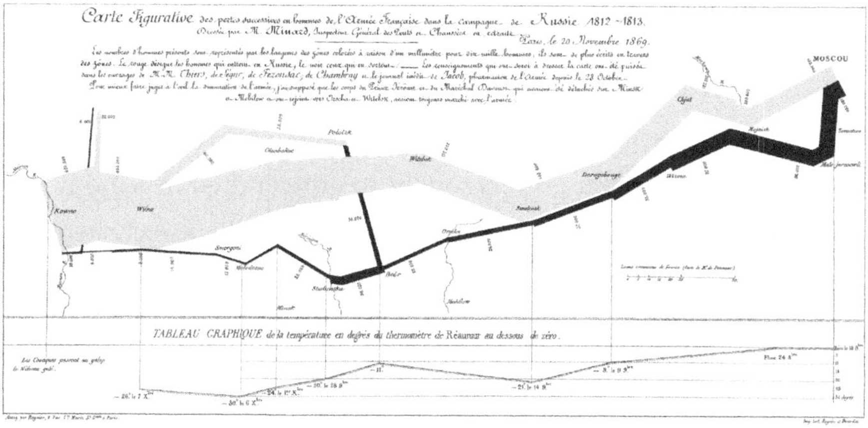

The famous drawing, Napoleon's Russian campaign of 1812, by French civil engineer Charles Joseph Minard. One may see the size of the Grand Armée as it entered Russia. The black is the size of the Grand Armée in retreat.

Russia's unique experience in repelling Napoleon engrained the necessity of strategic barriers and buffer states into the political class. Kutuzov, a star pupil of eminent Russian Field Marshal Suvorov, demonstrated the efficacy of defeating sophisticated and numerically superior armies using indirect methods. Through the Russian Campaign, Napoleon sought a decisive engagement where he could break the enemy's will to resist. That engagement never came.

Despite his military brilliance, Napoleon suffered his final defeat at Waterloo in 1815, and the British exiled him to Saint Helena, a remote island in the South Atlantic. However, even as the world breathed a sigh of relief at the demise of Emperor Napoleon, trans-European conflicts continued with alarming regularity (every 20-30 years) until the age of industrialized warfare arrived on July 28, 1914.

Prussia's Otto von Bismark master-minded the unification of the Germanic states in 1871, and Germany's populace and wealth began to grow due to the newfound political stability. A unified Germany proved itself to be an agricultural and industrial powerhouse that required new lands to feed resources into its growing economy.

Germany's rise permanently altered the balance of power in Europe, and other great powers sought to protect their hegemony through economic and military coalitions. These alliances created the powder-keg of conditions for World War I, and the assassination of Austrian Archduke Franz Ferdinand lit the fuse.

World War I was a new kind of war that pitted a country's entire economy, population, and resources against its adversary. Armies did not maneuver against one another in the field, but instead fought from the protection of trenches.

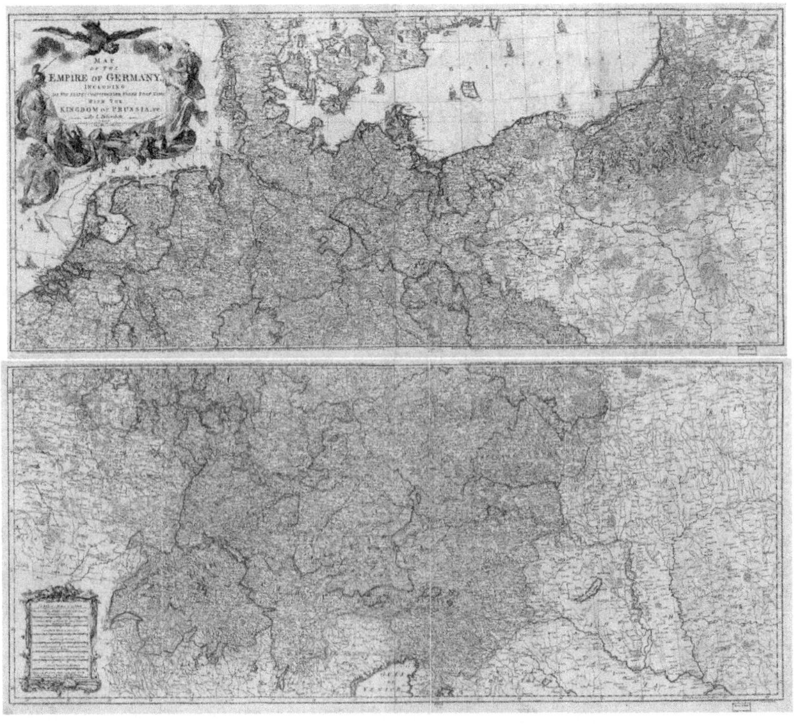

Map of the Empire of Germany, created in 1782 by Louis Delarochette.

Soldiers who attempted to run across the no-man's-land between trenches found themselves targeted by machine guns. Soldiers who remained in the trenches were at the mercy of mass artillery barrages and chemical warfare.

The United Kingdom, France, and Russia committed not just their own populations, but those of all their respective empires to hold the formidable Imperial German Army to a stalemate. In spite of the deadlock, Germany knew it was fighting the entire world; her proud people slowly starving to death.

When the United States sent another 2 million soldiers to the Western Front in 1917, the will of the German people began to fray. Germany signed the Treaty of Versailles in 1919, admitting war guilt and committing to pay the allies (primarily the United Kingdom and France) reparations for the war.

While the United States surged troops into Europe in 1917, war pressures in Russia led to the Bolshevik Revolution. Like the French Ancien Régime before it, Czar Nicholas' government was utterly blind to Russia's internal instabilities, creating space for Bolsheviks and Socialist Revolutionaries to build influence. Moreover, the Imperial Russian Army not only took egregious casualties against the Germans, but failed to make any real gains.

Reading the signs of political outrage, the German government put Vladimir Lenin on a train to Saint Petersburg in the fall of 1917, with the explicit purpose of fomenting revolution in Russia. The new government that emerged under Lenin signed the humiliating Treaty of Brest-Litovsk on March 3, 1918, removing Russia from the war while the Bolsheviks consolidated power. The Red Army was established in January 1918. Constituting the Ground and Air Forces of the Soviet Union, the Red Army was technically the military arm of the Communist Party.

Millions of Russians were killed in political purges and civil war, and the survivors were sentenced to decades of slavery and starvation under Communism. Lenin's—and later Stalin's—attempts to catapult Russia into modernity through centralized economic planning, ruthless industrialization programs, and commune farming were the impetus of several holocausts. This bitter time in Russia's history further isolated its culture and population from Western influence.

The Weimar Republic emerged in Germany as the political successor to the Kaiser. But, with the massive debts levied from the Treaty of Versailles, the German economy could not recover. Germany's industrious people were sentenced to poverty. Its currency, the Papiermark (replaced by the Rentenmark in 1924 and, soon afterward, the more permanent Reichsmark), became nearly worthless, and its proud military tradition was dismantled throughout the 1920s.

Desperate German citizens found political solutions in numerous radical parties during this period, including the communists. However, rather than egalitarian socialism, it was the promise of resurrecting Germany's economy and military that won the Nationalist Socialist (Nazi) Party the largest share of the popular vote (34%) in 1933.

Adolf Hitler refused to head a coalition government, and the Nazis paraded thunderously until President Paul von Hindenburg buckled. He appointed Hitler Chancellor of Germany in a single-party government on January 30, 1933.

As Hitler rose in Germany, the Soviet Union was enduring a series of famines. Soviet Commissars were assigned to seize farmland from the productive peasantry under a program of socialist centralization and redistribution. Replacing experienced farmers (who were sent to the gulags) with relocated commune workers had devastating consequences for Soviet agriculture.

Between 1932 and 1933, the Soviet Republic of Ukraine suffered through Holodomor, a particularly brutal famine in which Joseph Stalin instructed his Commissars to break resistance to Ukraine's Communist collectivization by intentionally withholding food distributions. It is estimated that between 6-10 million Ukrainians may have starved to death during Holodomor.

Germany rearmed throughout the late 1930s, and soon Hitler was making territorial claims on behalf of Greater Germany. Following Germany's acquisition of the Saarland and then Austria, British Prime Minister Neville Chamberlain flew to the Continent to negotiate what he later claimed as, "Peace in our time."

The Munich Agreement recognized Germany's claim over the Sudetenland of Czechoslovakia (and its other conquests), provided Hitler would make no further territorial claims in Europe. Conservative back-bencher and infamous appeasement critic Winston Churchill famously shouted across Parliament at the Chamberlain government, "You were given the choice between dishonor and war. You chose dishonor and you shall have war." For years, Churchill had warned that Berlin was rearming, and his fiery oratory stressed that Nazi Germany could never be sated.

Churchill's words were prophetic, for Hitler soon looked to Prussia (modern day Kaliningrad), which was separated from Greater Germany by a Polish corridor along the Baltic Sea. When France and Britain insisted that there would be no further territorial concessions, Hitler had every reason to believe they would back down. And so, on September 1, 1939, Germany invaded Poland, and the world went to war again.

Many forget that the Soviet Union started the war on Germany's side. The Molotov-Ribbentrop Pact was signed on August 23, 1939, declaring a mutual non-aggression pact between Germany and the Soviet Union. The Pact also established a protocol for partitioning Poland, enabling the Soviets to invade from the east while Germany invaded from the west.

In addition, the Pact was the foundation for integrating German wartime manufacturing supply chains with Soviet raw materials production. The German Panzer tanks that rolled over France and the bombers that razed London were constructed with Soviet steel and fueled with Soviet oil.

The Germans unveiled a new type of warfare that the press dubbed Blitzkrieg. Conceived by visionary general Heinz Guderian, Blitzkrieg used armored spearheads, close air support, and bold flanking maneuvers to punch through enemy lines and encircle entrenched forces. The Germans used these methods to great avail, capturing Poland, France, the Netherlands, Denmark, Belgium, and many others.

Though World War II was fought on every continent except Antarctica, 80% of the fighting took place on the "Eastern Front". After conquering France and suppressing the United Kingdom, Hitler looked to the east for "Lebensraum", a term meaning "living space". Lebensraum grew from the earlier political philosopher Friedrich Ratzen's convictions that Germany needed to seek out foreign colonies to prosper.

The surprise invasion of the Soviet Union, dubbed Operation Barbarossa, began on June 22, 1941 along an 1,800-mile front, and Hitler's Wehrmacht (German Army) made astonishing gains into Soviet territory. Several entire Soviet Army Groups were surrounded, and the Soviet Air Force was utterly shattered as the Germans sprinted to reach Russia's industrial heartland.

Soviet Premier Joseph Stalin called up all available military reserves and the entirety of the Soviet civilian population to defend the "motherland". With supply lines stretched beyond reckoning, German Army Group North stalled its advance at Leningrad (St. Petersburg). Army Group Center stalled on the outskirts of Moscow.

Army Group South stalled at Stalingrad.

The Wehrmacht, like Napoleon's Grand Armée, found itself stuck in enemy territory during the cruel winter season. Fighting on the Eastern Front gained a "no quarter asked, no quarter given" brutality. From1943 to 1945, the tide turned against Hitler's Germany. At staggering human cost, the Red Army grew into a juggernaut, pushing the Wehrmacht all the way back to Berlin. Cowering in his Furher's Bunker, Adolf Hitler and his mistress committed suicide.

Stalin's response to the German invasion was very different from the Fabian strategy employed by Marshal Kutuzov, perhaps because he lacked the patience and had far greater authority in state policy than did Czar Alexander I. Stalin's approach was ruthless, sacrificing lives and terrain for time. His commanders, most notably Field Marshal Zukov, used this time to transform the Soviet Red Army into an unassailable steamroller that crushed all resistance before it.

The same strategic lessons of the Napoleonic era were re-ingrained into the Communist leadership. The vast expanses of open space insulated Russia from invaders and made it impossible for enemies to concentrate fires or protect long supply lines. The Russian winter was a weapon in itself. In addition to the many soldiers that froze to death, there were occasions where Germans had their eyelids frozen off while looking into the wind Without eyelids, they became walking corpses—unable to blink, unable to sleep, until they slowly went insane.

World War II destroyed Europe: her cities razed to the ground, her industries broken, her populace dead or starving. The world was forced to come to grips with Germany's attempt to culturally, ethnically, and racially re-engineer Europe through eugenics and extermination.

We tend to forget that value-systems are neither universal nor self-evident. Values are anchored to geography; negotiated within the local culture over hundreds of years of shared history. What emerges from this process are behaviors and traditions that serve as lasting answers to intergenerational questions; a contract between the dead, the living, and the yet to be born.

Adolf Hitler was a procrustean "visionary" that sought to insert new values at will: guided by the light of a perverted science to improve culture and alter human nature. The final solution implemented in the Holocaust revealed untethered reason to be the torment of human society.

The Nuremberg Trials, which documented the Third Reich's crimes against humanity, were perhaps the highest moral achievement of the West in the 20th Century. But beneath the Nuremberg Trials were profound moral assumptions gleaned from Roman Catholicism, conveyed into cultural norms by the Church of England, codified over 800 years of consensual parliamentary governance, adjudicated by English Common Law, and embodied within the institutions of Germany's Anglo-American conquerors.

Germany was judged under this Anglo-American value system, and the gravity of its violations were declared "crimes against humanity". The Soviet Union embodied a collectivist value system that contrasted painfully with the Anglo-American Allies. Russia had no real history of consensual governance, sustaining monarchy and feudalism until 1917—the entire Russian serf caste was still legally bound to fiefdoms up until 1861.[2] Many of them remained in their fiefdoms in 1917.

These cultural norms enabled the Soviets to be merciless in war and draconian in peace. The mercilessness was manifested in Joseph Stalin's unflinching sacrifice of 26 million soldiers and civilians that broke the Nazi war machine and conquered Eastern Europe.

And so, for the first time since the Age of Exploration, the European Great Powers would no longer lead the world. Embodying the lessons from invasions by both the Grand Armée, Wehrmacht, and numerous other conflicts, the Soviet Union chose to conquer Eastern Europe as it pushed the Germans back. Joseph Stalin imposed egalitarian socialism on a series of buffer states that would permanently insulate Moscow from the West, and what would become known as the Eastern Bloc was formed.

New satellites like Poland, Czechoslovakia, Hungary, Romania, Bulgaria, Yugoslavia, and the German Democratic Republic (among many others) endured a systematic suppression of their cultures, economies, and national identities. Then, in 1955, the Soviet Union had these socialist "allies" sign a treaty in Poland for mutual defense and economic cooperation in what became known as the Warsaw Pact. The Warsaw Pact was the very embodiment of a foreign policy designed to promote and expand the Revolution of the Proletariat.

Alternatively, the United States and the Western Allies held the Bretton-Woods Conference to plan the post-war recovery of the world's remaining free economies. The U.S. Dollar would become the global reserve currency, all other currencies would be convertible to the Dollar, and the Dollar would be backed by gold and silver repositories.

The World Bank was established to finance economic development in the third world, and the International Monetary Fund was established to support global liquidity and currency exchange. The United States economy, the only consumer economy left intact after the war, was opened to global trade so that the devastated countries of Europe could rebuild themselves by exporting goods and services in exchange for hard currency. The United States also put the Marshall Plan into effect, channeling billions of American capital into Europe, and directly financing the reconstruction of roads, railways, ports, power grids, and more.

The United States entered World War II with the second-largest navy by ship count. By the end of World War II, the U.S. Navy was larger than all of the combined navies of the world and was commanded by battle-hardened captains and experienced crews. The U.S. Navy took responsibility for patrolling the global commons (all of the world's sea lanes) so that commerce could flourish without the Great Powers needing to fund their own large navies to protect respective overseas interests.

For the first time in history, high-value-added European firms like Mercedes-Benz could import raw materials like rubber and iron from countries like Malaysia in exchange for U.S. Dollars (by converting the Deutschmark into Dollars and then Dollars into Ringgit), produce a finished good, and then export that good to spend-thrift consumers in the United States. Shipping raw materials and finished goods from remote parts of the world to consumers in the West was protected through all phases by the U.S. Navy.

The world had a functional global economy rather than trade within mutually independent colonial empires. This incentivized European Great Powers to reduce military spending, especially on their respective navies, and relinquish their old colonies. As global supply chains increased in complexity, people worldwide were suddenly able to bring their labor to the market.

The post-World War II era, often called Pax Americana by historians and statesmen, saw the most rapid creation of wealth and elevation in standards of living for the "common man" around the globe in human history.

Pax Americana generated unprecedented peace and prosperity between the world's great industrial powers, as growth was no longer a function of securing new territories and colonial possessions. But there was a catch: nations participating in the new world economy had to cooperate in an Anglo-American alliance network designed to contain further communist expansion. Seeing how quickly Stalin had toppled and replaced governments across Eastern Europe and fearing the rise of totalitarian regimes in the advanced western economies, the Truman Administration began a policy of containment.

Countries in Europe flocked to join the North Atlantic Treaty Organization (NATO), an alliance of liberal democracies led by the Americans that served as a military deterrent against further Soviet growth. As the Americans and Soviets both developed nuclear arsenals, the stand-off later known as the Cold War had several frightening moments of brinkmanship, but the Americans were ultimately successful at containing communism and preserving their economic influence across the globe.

In his famous book *The End of History and the Last Man*, Francis Fukayama described the ascendancy of liberal democracies as the final evolution of human governance. Indeed, the Soviet collapse made many Western observers believe that history really was ending. In celebration, famous American composer Leonard Bernstein conducted the Berlin Philharmonic Orchestra, offering a triumphal Christmas Day performance of Beethoven's 9th Symphony in a soft power display of cooperation between the formerly communist controlled East Germany.

Despite professed values of egalitarian brotherhood, communism proved itself to be unsustainable without a ruthless dictator like Joseph Stalin to motivate the machine forward through terror. Mikhail Gorbachev's Restructuring (Russian: перестройка) and Transparency (Russian: гласность) removed the paranoia that allowed bloated and broken Soviet institutions to enforce compliance with policy.

In 1979, over 100,000 Soviet troops invaded Afghanistan. Soviet Ground Forces not only revealed themselves to be poorly trained and unmotivated, but entirely incapable of adapting to guerilla warfare tactics. The Soviets fought a losing struggle against Afghanistan's Mujahideen (indigenous militias fighting in a confederation under the banner of Islamic jihad) until Gorbachev authorized a humiliating withdrawal that was completed in February 1989.

By 1991, Eastern Bloc satellites were all declaring independence, and the Soviet Empire was crumbling. Meanwhile, the United States was fighting the Gulf War in Iraq. Iraq's leader, Saddam Hussein had modeled his Ba'athist regime after Nazi fascism and sought to expand his country's sphere of control after the Iran Iraq War by invading Kuwait and threatening to seize the vast oil wealth of Saudi Arabia—almost 40% of the world's oil supplies in 1991.

An American-led coalition completely destroyed the Iraqi Army—the world's fourth largest—in weeks, with trivial losses. The world bore witness: liberal democracies had won, and centrally-planned authoritarian regimes had lost. Russia re-emerged from the Soviet collapse, completely destitute. The failed nation underwent a painful decade of political restructuring and economic consolidation. Moreover, the Soviet collapse precipitated a profound decline in the Russian security environment, forcing Moscow to once again wrestle with the specter of invasion from the West.

The United States also underwent a series of transformations. Without the Soviet threat, America's allies increasingly questioned their loyalty to Washington. All the while, Washington conversely questioned why it was subsidizing the global system.

The first American transformation was the election of Bill Clinton, the first President of the modern era that considered himself a "domestic" President. He defeated President George Herbert Walker Bush, a highly capable foreign policy President, in 1993. The Clinton administration reminded the country of its own domestic challenges and Clinton's successors—George W. Bush, Barack Obama, Donald Trump, and Joe Biden—all prioritized domestic issues on the campaign trail.

The second transformation occurred after the World Trade Center attacks on September 11, 2001. The American response in Afghanistan was predictable and had international support, but no one expected the Bush Administration to advocate for "regime change" in Iraq. Iraq was, of course, a bad actor in the region. But Iraq was not an obvious threat to the United States and was a stabilizing force in the Middle East.

President Bush's national security team knew that most middle eastern states (such as Saudi Arabia, Afghanistan, Bahrain, Yemen, Oman, Pakistan, Qatar, Jordan, Lebanon, and Syria) harbored al-Qaeda-affiliated cells and training camps. They recognized that the U.S. did not have the leverage diplomatically or economically to overcome the cultural and religious sympathies for such groups among regional elites.

Removing Saddam Hussein from power with the grandiose display of American military might (dubbed the "Shock and Awe" campaign), and the deployment of heavy mechanized ground forces within reach of all the major regional powers was intended to demonstrate what would happen to any state that defied the U.S. in harboring al-Qaeda.

France and Germany, countries that the Americans had liberated and rebuilt after World War II, lobbied other NATO members against joining the war effort and went so far as to lead coalitions against the Americans at the United Nations (U.N.). Whether or not the Bush Administration was correct in deposing Saddam Hussein is beside the point. The war was important to the Americans. When they called for assistance from European allies, the Americans found themselves under diplomatic attack from multiple countries they had long considered close friends.

Washington began to question whether continental Europe collectively deserved American protection and continued economic cooperation. George Bush's doctrine of regime change terrified Moscow, and it lobbied heavily in the U.N. and abroad on the idea of non-interference in the internal affairs of other sovereign nations.

The third American transformation occurred when the Lehman Brothers investment bank collapsed in 2008, capping a subprime mortgage crisis that dragged the world economy into recession. The Bush Administration quickly passed the Emergency Economic Stabilization Act of 2008, which created the Troubled Asset Relief Program (TARP).

The Obama Administration oversaw TARP buy-outs of toxic assets off of bank balance sheets. This stabilized the financial system, but ordinary Americans were put out of work, and it took the country a decade to recover. During this crisis and throughout his presidency, Barack Obama saw foreign policy as a distraction from more important domestic issues. He frequently ignored intelligence briefings that did not support his penchant for non-interference in the larger world. His policies created opportunities for Russia to project its will into the former Soviet-sphere.

Donald Trump's presidency went beyond Obama's casual indifference to the American intelligence community and might better be described as loathing and openly hostile. This left American foreign policy somewhat rudderless, driven only by Obama's "Don't Do Stupid Stuff" and then Trump's "America First", which expanded Russia's window to influence its strategic environment. Moscow seized this opportunity by executing a bloodless annexation of Crimea and then sponsoring an insurgency in the Donbas region of Eastern Ukraine.

The Biden Administration appears to have embraced a foreign policy that borrows from the Trump Administration in policy and the Obama Administration in rhetoric. Like Donald Trump, President Biden prefers to work through ruthlessly precise sanctions and economic coercion when dealing with foreign policy problems. Like Trump, he is a trade protectionist. However, as a Democrat, Biden appeals to the authority of international institutions (U.N., World Trade Organization, and the Hague) and generally seeks consensus (or at least an exchange of warm words) with European partners before going it alone.

Russia is not a strategic competitor with the United States, except in the nuclear domain. Its economy is smaller than that of the State of Texas, and Russia is overwhelmingly reliant on oil and natural gas exports. Oil and natural gas will continue to be important energy sources for the next 50 years, even as the West is increasingly adopting wind, solar, hydro-electric, and nuclear power (where it makes sense and infrastructure permits); however, as those technologies mature, Russia's energy market is slowly shrinking.

The Americans also tapped into shale oil reserves through innovations in hydraulic fracking, so they no longer rely on energy exports from the Middle East. Therefore, Russian oil and gas exports to Europe and China must compete with the Gulf States.

The Russians are also sitting on top of a demographic crisis. Prior to 1960, having sex meant having children. Society encouraged women to marry young, preferably to husbands who could support a family that would inevitably bear 3-5 children (at least). Birth rates were not strongly impacted by economic downturns like the Great Depression. But post-1960, reliable birth control allowed families to choose when to have children, producing a profound cultural change in advanced economies.

The birth control pill enabled women to exercise economic agency at scale for the first time in history, effectively doubling the workforce. People began electing to have children after finishing college, finding adventure, building a career, paying off student debt, buying a house, and establishing a stable marital relationship. Families began having fewer children (if any), and women started spending grade school preparing for higher education and careers rather than marriage and childbearing.

This change in culture spread globally and precipitated a dramatic decline in birth rates across the developed world. The ability to control pregnancy led to a modern phenomenon where national birth rates often rise and fall with economic prosperity. People, given the choice, do not risk the additional financial burden of children if they are financially unstable.

Japan and South Korea lead the world in inverted demographics (more retirees than young workers to support them), followed by Italy, China, Russia, Germany, and Canada. The only two developed economies that have enough young people to fill out their consumer base and drive future economic growth (and a sufficient tax-base to support their pensioners) are the United States and New Zealand.

Japan offers an instructive example of the dangers of inverted national demography. In 1991, Japan's economic miracle collapsed in a catastrophic debt-liquidity spiral.[3] Following the crisis, Japan began a period of painful debt consolidation, stagnant growth, and persistent deflationary pressure known as the Lost Decade. The Japanese economy has not managed to buoy itself into real growth ever since, largely because of its inverted demography. Japan lacks a young consumer and tax base to drive growth, making the country entirely reliant on exports and foreign market access.

Russian demographics are among the worst in the world and, as oil revenues continue to fall, Moscow will have to rely on a non-existent tax base to fund the day-to-day operations of the government.

The Russians are also sitting on top of a number of public health crises. Moscow does not use public funds to collect data on public health, but Western public health officials and non-governmental organizations (NGOs) estimate that the Russian population is declining by up to 700,000 people per year.

The average life expectancy in Russia is 59 for men and 72 for women. Cardiovascular disease attributed to stress, drug habits, and alcoholism account for 52%of premature deaths in Russia. Additionally, tuberculosis and antibiotic-resistant bacteria are prevalent causes of death. There is also an HIV crisis in Russia which, due to the rampant use of shared syringes (in relation to narcotics), continues to spread rapidly. Amidst all of Russia's other public health crises, child mortality rates are also very high.

The Soviet education system produced some of the world's most capable scientists and engineers, but the system collapsed along with the rest of the Soviet regime in 1991. Moscow has not significantly invested in education since. Russian infrastructure is maintained by engineers and technicians trained during the Soviet era (who are now in their 70s). While Russia does have a small class of wealthy families who live in vibrant, highly educated cultural centers like Saint Petersburg, most of Russia's young people receive appallingly poor schooling.

Due to these crises and numerous others, Russia is in a nearly impossible position. Moscow knows it cannot compete directly with the United States or NATO militarily, economically, or diplomatically. So, President Putin and his national security cadre bide their time and seize opportunities as they present themselves.

Given that the Americans are withdrawing from the global system they created and sponsored after World War II, Putin has a little breathing room to sustain, reinforce, and improve Russia's strategic position (provided they do not go too far in offending Washington). Russia needed a method to engage its rivals that did not risk its global standing economically or diplomatically and would not commit itself to a full-scale war that is taxing in blood and treasure. Hybrid warfare fit that specific niche: a means of waging inter-state political competition below the threshold of overt warfare.

As the Americans continue to look inward, strategic competition is returning. Japan, France, South Korea, China, Italy, India, and even Germany are all beginning to understand that the Americans are no longer offering carte blanche security guarantees. So, as Moscow pursues its interests, Putin rightly understands that he has a window to reshape the Russian strategic environment. However, that window will close as numerous internal crises and the gradually declining demand for fossil fuels destabilize Russia and undermine its ability to project power.

But Russia has a few advantages.

Russia exists on the periphery of Europe, isolated from many of the political rivalries and much of the infighting between the European Great Powers. As the United States is absent to force the Europeans to be on the same side, powers like Germany and France increasingly dominate the European Union. European solidarity could fracture. Indeed, the

Russians will relentlessly target fissures between the European powers to ensure that European solidarity does fracture. Memories of World War II will not fade with the Greatest Generation.

Just as history could amplify strife within Europe, it protects Russia. The horrors of Napoleon's failed campaign against Kutuzov, and what the Soviet Union's Red Army did to Germany's elite and technologically advanced Wehrmacht are seared into the collective consciousness of Europe. No one in the West believes that they can successfully invade Russia, and Moscow still controls the world's largest stockpile of nuclear weapons. Finally, above all else, no other people on Earth are more accustomed to hardship than the Russians; the Russian people can endure any standard of living for the motherland and for victory.

This book posits that Hybrid Warfare is the Russian way of war. This book will detail case studies of the Russo-Georgian War, Crimean Annexation, and War in Donbas in order to demonstrate that Hybrid Warfare is a mode of conventional military conflict that holistically leverages all means of national power to efficiently achieve victory.

---

1. Quintus Fabius Maximus Verrucosus was a Roman Consul who was voted emergency powers as Dictator after Rome's disastrous defeat at Lake Trasimene during the Second Punic War. Fabius needed to preserve the Roman Army to keep the Carthaginians from marching on Rome, but he knew that he could not defeat Hannibal in the field. Instead of seeking a decisive battle, Fabius burned fields, raided supply lines, and killed Hannibal's foraging parties, wearing down the Carthaginian Army. Fabius' critics eventually wrested power from him, and Roman Consul Gaius Terentius Varro followed Hannibal into a trap at Cannae in 216 BC, resulting in Rome's greatest military defeat.

2. In fact, the English word "slave" is a derivation from the Eastern European ethnicity "*slav*".

3. Throughout the 1980s Japanese banks and businesses accumulated a large volume of non-performing loans and over-leveraged assets. To tame inflation, the Bank of Japan aggressively raised interest rates, which triggered a financial sell-off. Institutional investors sold assets to raise cash, which caused asset prices to fall, which in turn caused investors to liquidate additional assets, in a toxic race to the bottom.

Chapter One

The Russian Way of War

What Drives Russian Strategic Thinking and Foreign Policy?

President Putin, Security Council Secretary Nikolay Patrushey, Foreign Minister Sergey Lavrov, FSB Director Alexander Bortnikov, and Defense Minister Sergey Shoygu all had front-row seats to successive Soviet political crises that precipitated a profound decline in the Russian security environment.

Russia lost all of its satellite states and security buffers as Warsaw Pact members clamored to join NATO and the European Union (E.U.). Core Soviet Union member states like Ukraine, Kazakhstan, Armenia, Georgia, Moldova, Belarus, and the Baltic states all asserted independence. Regions within Russia like Tatarstan and Chechnya carved out autonomous enclaves from the Russian Federal government. Even Moscow's Mayor, Yuri Luzhkov, openly defied directives and policy set in the Kremlin. Russia had become inconsequential in the global matters that concerned great powers, no longer even capable of managing its own national unity. Putin himself said in 2005 that:

First and foremost, it is worth acknowledging that the demise of the Soviet Union was the greatest geopolitical catastrophe of the century. As for the Russian people, it became a genuine tragedy. Tens of millions of our fellow citizens and countrymen found themselves beyond the fringes of Russian territory. The epidemic of collapse has spilled over to Russia itself.

Lasting bitterness among Putin and his colleagues led them to seek opportunities to renegotiate the post-Soviet status quo, with ubiquitous suspicions of the West and its calls for "democracy". Moscow viewed (and still views) the United States, NATO, and the European Union as strategic threats, and Russia was and continues to be grossly outmatched by all three of these adversaries in conventional military and economic power. Russia maintains strategic nuclear parity in the nuclear domain but does not have overmatch in any other capacity. That reality informs a divide-and-conquer strategy: driving the Kremlin's agents abroad to seek out fissures between the Western allies.

Moscow constantly seeks points of leverage to support its initiatives, deploying means to pry apart emerging fissures between the Western Allies. Moscow accomplishes such objectives by providing support to populist Western leaders, conducting cyberattacks on Western infrastructure, purveying social media propaganda, and conducting assassinations, among other tactics that will be discussed throughout this book.

Russia's strategic imperatives determine Moscow's foreign policy objectives: maintain defense-in-depth, divide and conquer, dominate the approaches to the motherland from the West and South, ensure access to the Mediterranean Sea, and to dominate the Black Sea. Allowing a country like Ukraine or Belarus to enter the European Union's Eurozone would extend the presence of strategic rivals to Russia's border. The close proximity of potential enemies unacceptably compromises defense-in-depth.

Russian campaign messaging made regional autonomy for ethnic Russians in the Donbas region of Eastern Ukraine, the *casus belli* of the insurgency, but the Kremlin's intention was to destabilize Ukraine and prevent it from joining the European Union's Eurozone and eventually NATO. Whether or not the Donbas region (and specifically the Donetsk and Luhansk People's Republics) remains independent from Kyiv is only relevant to Moscow insofar as it prevents Ukraine from leaving Russia's orbit.

The industrial heartland of Russia is located on the vast Eurasian steppe and lacks any real geographic boundaries except limitless space. An invader from the west (like Germany, France, Poland, Romania, or Austria) or from the south (like Turkey or Iran) would have to extend supply lines that support an army's advance over thousands of miles.

Russian strategy goes further, attempting to extend its forward-most forces to plug strategic bottlenecks. Examples include: the Fulda Gap, the Danube River Valley, or the Caucasus Mountains. This greatly reduces the amount of ground the Russian Armed Services must cover from a 3,000+ mile front to only about 700 miles. Thus, the Soviet Union labored intensively to extend itself into Europe after World War II so it could control these critical choke points.

Russian strategic planning continues to leverage Ukraine, Belarus, Georgia, Armenia, Azerbaijan, and other Eastern Bloc countries as a buffer zone. These buffer states serve as the outer ring of Russia's defense-in-depth from invasion. Historically, they've proven vital to Russia's victories over invaders like Napoleon's Grand Armée or the Third Reich. President Putin justifies control over these buffer-states through the claim that some countries are more "sovereign" than others.

Because Russia is the self-appointed regional protector and leader, it has de facto authority over the former Soviet sphere of influence known as the Eastern Bloc. Ukraine is an independent nation, but in the eyes of the Kremlin, Ukraine is not free to advance its own foreign policy objectives in the same way that a great power like Russia is.

Moscow sees itself as equal to Washington, Brussels, Beijing, Berlin, London, Paris, and Tokyo. This belief is embodied by the 2015 Syrian intervention. Propping up the al-Asaad regime was a rare opportunity for Russia to pose as a great power on the world stage. The intervention also allowed Putin to defy American calls for "regime change" in Syria. The Kremlin sees American-led "regime change" as a direct threat to the Putin

Regime's long-term survival and seeks to undermine its practice whenever possible.

Russia's activities in Syria enabled Russia to establish itself as the key regional power broker in the Levant while further extending Russian Naval reach into the Mediterranean. The intervention also debuted many weapons systems that Rosoboronexport, the Russian state-owned arms exportation conglomerate, could sell as alternatives to expensive Western defense systems. In every way, Moscow was maneuvering to offer itself to the world as a legitimate alternative to American power.

Russian Hybrid Warfare, Defined

Western journalists and military analysts have adopted the phrase "hybrid warfare" in common parlance. It is generally used as a catch-all term referring to any shadowy attempt to meddle in the affairs of other nations, most commonly used in reference to Russia, but also sometimes China and Iran.

Recent reporting has used the term to describe Russian meddling in Western elections, the assassination attempt on Sergei Skripal (the turncoat spy who betrayed Russia's GRU intelligence service on behalf of MI6), low-intensity military operations, threats to sever natural gas exports to Western Europe, and the appearance of Putin's "little green men" in Ukraine. Though the term itself has been overused by the 24-hour news cycle (amongst related terminology like "non-linear warfare", "gray-zone activities", and "Phase Zero Activities"), hybrid warfare is the dominant modality under which Russia now wages interstate competition.

Let's ignore the hysteria surrounding Russia's shadow games and consider when, how, and why Russia leverages "hybrid" methods in warfare. Hybrid warfare is appealing to Russia as a foreign policy tool because, as a great power, the country recognizes that overt military conflict (think of Chechnya) has great cost in blood, capital, and international goodwill.

At the strategic level, hybrid warfare allows Russia to pursue its interests through military means without incurring these costs in the extreme. At the operational level, Hybrid Warfare holistically uses all levers of national influence (political, cultural, economic, military, or informational) to create asymmetric advantages in support of discrete objectives. At the tactical level, hybrid warfare deploys non-military influence to sow chaos ahead of elite troops who are tasked with swiftly seizing objectives and terrain to pave the way for conventional forces. These tactics leverage deception and ambiguity, allowing Russia to straddle the watershed between interstate political competition and overt warfare.

Military theorist Carl von Clausewitz offers us a proverb:

> ...a certain center of gravity develops, the hub of all power and movement, on which everything depends. That is the point against which all our energies should be directed.
>
> —Carl Von Clausewitz in his famous treatise On War.

When Clausewitz wrote these words in the 1830s after careful observation of the Napoleonic Wars, the readers of his day assumed the "center of gravity" to which he was referring was physical. Many envisioned it as a focal point that maneuvering regiments had to wheel around in order to form a cohesive line of battle that could muster sufficient firepower to break an advancing enemy's line of battle.

Napoleon was famous for unleashing relentless artillery bombardments on these focal points, following shortly afterward with an immediate mass assault. Some of his most astounding victories came from using this technique to break larger enemy formations in two and then defeating the respective components in detail.

Russian hybrid warfare embraces Von Clausewitz's wisdom but envisions such a "center of gravity" beyond the physical realm. Quite different from chess-like victories of maneuver and attrition, the actions taken in hybrid war are designed to achieve the deeper objective of defeating the enemy's will to resist.

The precepts of hybrid warfare were drawn from legacy Soviet doctrine, lessons learned from small wars on Russia's periphery, and close observation of modern conflicts. The Gulf War proved to be such an awesome demonstration of American military superiority that direct competition with NATO lost all efficacy.

In order to maintain its strategic position, Russia would inevitably have to fight limited conflicts in its periphery, and it could not afford to make the mistakes made in Chechnya again. Moscow needed an asymmetric tool that would allow it to not only project power, but also to do so with plausible deniability.

Though American politicians and media are vexed by Russia's guile, deception, and propaganda, these qualities are hardly unique to Moscow. As this book defines hybrid warfare's underlying doctrine and best practices, it will hopefully become clear that it is not a war in the shadows, but a conventional military conflict waged with whole-of-government support, intensive planning, great speed, and deception.

Russia does not see hybrid warfare as an independent doctrine that departs in any way from traditional military practice. To the contrary, when the Russians plan what the West has come to call "hybrid wars", they are merely deploying all available methods that maximize the chances of success for their conventional military forces. When the term "hybrid warfare" is used, the reader should imagine precisely that. The United States remains the only country in the world that announces to enemies ahead of time its intentions to invade: a benefit of being the world's undeniable preeminent technological and military power.

Maskirovka, Aktivnost, and Vnezapnost (Camouflage, Activity, and Surprise)

Russian hybrid warfare begins with the concept of Maskirovka (Russian: маскировка), or Camouflage, which refers to deception efforts that hide the Russian hand instigating the conflict. Under the cloak of Maskirovka, Russian operatives conduct Aktivnost (Russian: активность), or Activity, which encompasses all measures that prevent an enemy from bringing its military power to bear against Russia's pursuit of its objectives. Russia applies the concepts of Maskirovka and Aktivnost through several non-kinetic operations.

First, prior to a crisis, and under the cover of normal diplomatic ties, Russian operatives and informants penetrate all levels of the offending government. As Moscow sees an exploitable crisis emerging, non-military measures are deployed to generate civil unrest such as propaganda, diplomatic pressure, economic and financial sanctions, and the prodding of ideological sympathies.

These indirect influence operations are conducted to generate chaos or pressure and break down political and military resistance to the Russian narrative or objective. Russian *agenturi*(intelligence operatives) coerce, through bribery, blackmail, and intimidation, key individuals in politics, law enforcement, and military command.[1] Then, Russian operatives organize or offer material support to paramilitary groups. Paramilitary groups are deployed to engage in overt political subversion, both deepening civil unrest and curtailing the ability of adversarial policymakers to contain it. Russia shapes the operational environment through these low-cost non-military methods to prepare for kinetic military force.

The key Russian word for kinetic operations is Vnezapnost (Russian: внезапность), or Surprise. Vnezapnost refers to the speedy deployment and maneuver of forces. First, Russia implements measures of control (for example, no-fly zones and blockades of key thoroughfares), and then Moscow justifies these controls through propaganda as peacekeeping measures. Then, Russian Special Operations Forces (SOF) develop working relations with armed paramilitary units (coordinated by the *agenturi* onsite), operationalize them, and deploy them to occupy key terrain.

These advanced force operations prepare the battlefield. Then, elite Russian Ground Forces rapidly maneuver to seize objectives such as infrastructure, thoroughfares, and government buildings, relieving lighter paramilitary forces as soon as possible. Russian Aerospace Forces are deployed to achieve air supremacy and initiate close air support operations for rapidly advancing ground forces while forward observers target the remaining pockets of resistance with precision-guided munitions, artillery, and air strikes. As key objectives are secured, heavy conventional Ground Forces move in to reinforce and entrench Russian-held territory.

Non-kinetic operations create space: an opening where someone capable of organization amid chaos can make gains. Kinetic operations seize this space, using SOF to probe for footholds which can then be occupied through the rapid maneuver of elite ground forces. Once Russian feet are firmly planted, heavy ground forces follow, making the entrenchment a *fait accompli*, and for all practical purposes, irreversible.

Additional Doctrinal Frameworks for Understanding Hybrid Warfare

Though there is no universally recognized hybrid warfare doctrine, its concepts are applied across common modalities of modern warfare.

Asymmetric Warfare Warfare where the relative strength of belligerents is imbalanced and therefore necessitates a strategy in which the weaker belligerent tailors its approach to enable it to engage the stronger belligerent on near-equal terms.

Low-Intensity Conflict Conflict conducted in hostile or denied environments where there is a nominal civil government and de facto peace. In low-intensity conflict, conventional forces conduct peacekeeping operations while SOF conduct foreign internal defense, training military and police forces, and leading counterterrorism operations that disrupt insurgency networks, funding, propaganda, and recruitment.

Information Operations The deployment of measures (electronic warfare, computer network operations, psychological operations, military deception, and operations security) to disrupt adversarial decision-making while insulating and protecting the decision-making of friendly forces.

Network-Centric Warfare The deployment of advanced IT capabilities, robust computer networking, and satellite communications to give geographically dispersed forces informational superiority that enables the commander to precisely maneuver fires and forces in order to achieve relative superiority at the point of contact.

Fifth-Generation Warfare Data-driven, non-kinetic military action that leverages pre-existing cognitive biases in the population to manipulate an observer's context to achieve a desired outcome. Fifth-generation warfare is, by nature, non-attributable and is designed to create a de facto victory without the need for kinetic military force. Supporting technologies and techniques include: civil affairs, propaganda, cyberattacks, social engineering, social media exploitation, mass surveillance, electronic warfare.

Sixth Generation Warfare Warfare that deploys long-range precision-guided munitions, armed UAVs, sophisticated electronic warfare (EW) systems and cyberattacks to disable enemy infrastructure in order to create windows of opportunity for further kinetic attacks. Sixth-generation warfare leverages technology to reduce troop exposure while delivering kinetic force against enemy forces. The Russian Aerospace Forces' continuous refinement of munitions and TTPs towards increasing precision and tailored force aimed at achieving sixth-generation warfare.

Reflexive Control A sustained campaign that offers the enemy a narrative based on carefully selected information, either distributed through propaganda outlets or deliberately leaked (as though the leak was an accident), meant to mislead the enemy. Reflexive control is the art of deception and misinformation in order to create advantages on the battlefield.

Hybrid warfare applies all of these constituent elements in varying proportions to fit the requirements of any particular operation.

Interestingly enough, Russian military theorists use the term "hybrid warfare" to describe Western military and propaganda efforts, usually in Russia's traditional sphere of influence. Russian military theorist (and former KGB officer) Igor Panarin uses the moniker "hybrid warfare" when he points to the Velvet Revolution in Czechoslovakia in 1989 and the other color revolutions in former Soviet satellite states in the early 2000s as examples of American conspiratorial influence.

Moscow's *siloviki* usually blame populist uprisings on covert influence from the West (especially from the CIA). These kinds of banal explanations, which are common among the world's authoritarian regimes, absolve Moscow of any wrongdoing and place the blame squarely on Russia's traditional geopolitical adversaries.

General Gerasimov's Contribution to Pre-Existing Hybrid Practices

Valery Gerasimov, the current Chief of the Russian General Staff (as of 2021), is the man most pointedly associated with hybrid warfare (perhaps with the exception of Vladimir Putin himself). The Gerasimov Doctrine provides a framework for how Russian interventions should be understood, with guidance on the application of both military and non-military means of power to achieve outcomes favorable to the national interest.

In studying American and European forces in the Gulf War, NATO interventions in Bosnia and Herzegovina, Operation Iraqi Freedom, and the ongoing war in Afghanistan, Gerasimov noted that many factors beyond the direct application of lethal force (for example propaganda, politics, economics, culture, and financial conditions) had outsized effects on the conflict outcome.

Gerasimov offered his conclusions in an infamous article for the magazine *Military Industrial Courier* (Russian: Военно-промышленный курьер) in February 2013. The article was entitled, "The Value of Science Is in the Foresight: New Challenges Demand Rethinking the Forms and Methods of Carrying Out Combat Operations."

Gerasimov postulated that the fundamental nature of armed conflict was changing and then offered the concept of hybrid warfare as a descriptor of how great powers would compete in the future.

General Valery Vasilyevich Gerasimov was born in Kazan, Tatar SSR on September 8, 1955. He attended the Kazan Suvorov Military School (1973-1977), the Malinovsky Military Armored Forces Academy (1984-1987), and the Military Academy of the General Staff of the Armed Forces of Russia (1995-1997). In what was likely a formative command experience, General Gerasimov was appointed Commander of the 58th Army in the North Caucasus Military District during the height of the Second Chechen War.

Gerasimov then served as Chief of Staff of the Far Eastern Military District from 2003 to 2005 (where he had served his platoon, company, and battalion command time), and then Chief of the Main Administration of Combat Training and Troops' Service of the Russian Federation Armed Forces and Commander of the North Caucasus Military District from 2005 to 2006. He commanded the Leningrad Military District in 2006, the Moscow Military District in 2009, and the Central Military District in 2012.

When the Kremlin chose to dismiss Defense Minister Serdyukov, Army General Makarov was serving as Chief of the General Staff. Key political insiders perceived Makarov to be dangerously loyal to Serdyukov, which could be potentially disruptive to Putin's inner circle of national security cadre (despite being a reformer, Serdyukov was fired as Defense Minister for incredible graft and corruption). Makarov's departure opened an opportunity for General Gerasimov, who was appointed in Makarov's place.

The Western press loves to point a finger at General Gerasimov as the man who invented hybrid warfare, which is mostly fiction. As a leading Russian General, Gerasimov is expected by his peers to have theoretical knowledge and an informed opinion. As Chief of the General Staff, his opinions on the matter are of importance, but his public commentary on the evolving nature of war hardly qualifies as a radical departure from traditional Russian military doctrine. However, his article in the *Military Industrial Courier* laid out many of hybrid warfare's core concepts. He posited that from careful study of wars in the late 20th and early 21st centuries, we can conclude that the nature of warfare has changed:

"...the 'rules of war' themselves have changed significantly. The role of non-military means in achieving political and strategic goals has increased, and in some cases has exceeded the power of force of arms in effectiveness. The emphasis of the methods used in confrontation is shifting towards the widespread use of political, economic, informational, humanitarian, and other non-military measures, implemented with the use of the protest potential of the population. All of this is complemented by covert military measures, including the implementation of information operations and actions by special operations forces. The open use of force, often under the guise of peacekeeping and crisis management, is only applied to achieve ultimate success in the conflict."

General Gerasimov's remarks go further. Large-scale mobilizations and industrialized military competition faded with the Cold War, so each nation's total military and economic strength do not accurately predict the results. A brief examination of American military conflicts in Vietnam (1965-1974), Iraq (2003-2009), and Afghanistan (2001-present), the Soviet invasion of Afghanistan (1979-1989), or Russia's numerous failures to stem the tide of "color revolutions" in the Eastern Bloc offer ample evidence to support Gerasimov's thesis.

In a speech given at the Academy of Military Sciences in March of 2017, Gerasimov declared that future wars will be asymmetric in nature, characterized by undeclared conflicts that utilize smaller forces of precision with military operations that are blended with non-military influence activities:

Military conflicts at the end of the 20th century and beginning of the 21st century differ from one another with respect to composition of participants, weapons employed, and forms and methods of troop activities... New features have appeared in them such as a change in the correlation of the contribution of one type of struggle over another to the overall political success of war, the overwhelming superiority of one of the sides in military force and economic might, etc... The leading countries of the world have declared that gaining information superiority is an indispensable condition of combat operations in their concepts for the employment of armies... Today the blurring of the line between a state of war and peace is obvious. The flip side of 'hybrid operations' is a new perception of peacetime, when military and overt violent measures are not used against some state, but its national security and sovereignty are threatened and may be violated... The emphasis in the content of methods of confrontation is shifting in the direction of extensive employment of political, economic, diplomatic, information, and other nonmilitary measures, implemented with involvement of the protest potential of a population. Non-military forms and means of struggle have received unprecedented development and have acquired a dangerous, sometimes violent nature. The practical use of non-military methods and means can cause a collapse in energy, banking, economic, information, and other spheres of a state's daily activities.

Many Western security commentators have characterized Gerasimov's article in the *Military Industrial Courier* as evidence of Russia's plans to subvert the West through war in the shadows. These claims are mostly grabbing at straws. The General is merely observing the evolution of war itself and lecturing in the abstract about the future of armed conflict (with much merit to his argument). His observations could have been informed as much by American activities in Bosnia or Iraq as they were by Russia's activities in Chechnya or Georgia.

Gerasimov's Framework and Model

While Western media incorrectly points the finger at Gerasimov as hybrid warfare's progenitor, the General did develop a model entitled "The Role of Nonmilitary Methods in Interstate Conflict Resolution", which offers a logical progression of phases for understanding how a political crisis may devolve into military conflict. He discusses this model in his article for the *Military Industrial Courier.* The model is a viable framework for using military and non-military means to escalate or de-escalate a crisis at critical junctures to ensure that the outcome has a decidedly pro-Moscow slant. He postulates six stages of conflict escalation:

1. Covert Development—Information Operations are the foundation of all Russian efforts in the conflict. Intelligence operatives permeate the area of operations and aid in tailoring Russian messaging to fit specific interest groups. These operatives make contact with political parties, unions, guilds, coalitions, clubs, and any other distinguishable group that could be mobilized toward Russian foreign policy objectives. The first phase serves to create chaos and division within the conflict region and drives wedges into societal cracks that could serve as footholds for follow-on operations.

2. Escalations—Russia begins to exert pressure externally through

economic and diplomatic means. This generally consists of economic sanctions, calling outstanding debts payable to Russian creditors, throttling natural gas pipelines, and cancellation of trade agreements. Diplomatic pressure is designed to complement information operations (propaganda), driving forward a number of pro-Moscow narratives: Russia is the protector of ethnic Russians abroad, Russia defends traditional values, the current government is unjust, ethnic Russians are being persecuted, trade with Russia is preferable to Europe, and that NATO is encroaching on countries under Russian protection.

3. Start of Conflict Activities—As demonstrations and protests crescendo, *agenturi*, Spetsnaz, and SOF engage in active direct and covert action (for example, subversion, sabotage, and paramilitary operations). These limited kinetic activities prepare the area of operations for the introduction of elite forces. Large Russian Ground Forces are deployed to the periphery of the conflict zone to intimidate the offending country's political and security establishment from suppressing rampant civil unrest. Paradoxically, Russia directly sponsors destabilizing activities in order to create rhetorical justification for a heavy-handed Russian response. Cyber and electronic warfare measures are employed to inhibit coordination of crisis responders, the military chain of command, and political decision-makers.

4. Crisis—At the breaking point of the crisis, Russia commences large-scale military operations, while denying any such actions through diplomatic channels. As gaps in governmental control emerge (due to Phase 3 activities), elite forces rapidly maneuver to seize terrain and infrastructure. They seize limited, key objectives at great speed, and larger conventional forces follow

afterward to solidify gains and entrench Russia's position in the region. Information operations continue to provide a blanket to cover Russian offensive military actions and project a narrative justification for military operations once they are publicly connected to Russia.

5. Resolution—Russian leadership begins searching for potential resolutions to the conflict. Russian operatives affect a change in military or political leadership, with whom they can collaborate to enforce the desired post-conflict status quo. This leadership change places individuals who are subservient to Moscow in key roles and tasks them with establishing Moscow-aligned order and peace. Following any *coup d'état*, the region will resume routine relations with Russia. The new regime is legitimized by a continuing campaign of information operations, which doubles to ensure that the Russian presence is not resented or undermined by competing narratives.

6. Restoration of Peace (Post-Conflict Settlement)—Russia conducts peacekeeping operations and offers comprehensive economic and loan packages to stabilize the region. The assistance packages are targeted to support and entrench the group interests that align with Russia, while reducing tensions and enforcing post-conflict settlement.

In a crisis and corresponding intervention, as envisioned by Gerasimov, Russia employs a wide variety of military and non-military measures, which are closely coordinated to achieve operational objectives. It is very easy to see Maskirovka, Aktivnost, and Vnezapnost working within Gerasimov's framework. Likewise, subordinate doctrines like asymmetric warfare, reflexive control, information operations, low-intensity conflict, network-centric warfare, and fifth-generation warfare fit neatly into

Gerasimov's model as a tool kit for escalating or de-escalating a crisis as needed. So General Gerasimov's theorizing is not so much a novelty or innovation to Russian military doctrine for shadow wars, but the General's understanding and application of current best-practices in warfare.

Irregular Conflicts Before Gerasimov that Reflect the Hybrid Approach

The Russian approach to military conflict was not actually founded by General Gerasimov or anyone else currently serving in Russia's national security cadre. The development of hybrid warfare is an evolution born out of necessity—first, from observation of American post-Soviet military action (Gulf War, Bosnia, Afghanistan, and Iraq) and prior, from lessons that Russia learned in the First and Second Chechen Wars.

Given that the Soviet Union faced most of the same great power challenges as the modern Russian Federation, it should not be surprising that the Soviets also dabbled in hybrid approaches to conflict. The Soviet Union engaged in numerous interventions, military assistance programs, and irregular conflicts that passably resemble Russia's modern interventions.

In Sub-Saharan Africa, the Soviet Union fueled numerous irregular conflicts through covert action and military assistance programs, largely to export communism. The qualifications for Soviet patronage were few and simple: a desire for socialist government, ideological antipathy towards the West, permanent client-state status, and agreement to support Soviet initiatives at the U.N. (conditional on U.N. membership).

For example, during the Rhodesian Bush War (1977-1979), the Zimbabwe People's Revolutionary Army (ZIPRA) was reorganized through Soviet military assistance and logistic support. Cuban proxies trained ZIPRA guerilla forces in infantry tactics (based on conventional Soviet battalion structures) when the environment was too politically sensitive for overt Soviet military assistance. In Zaire (modern-day Democratic Republic of Congo), Soviet-backed Angolan and Cuban forces provided similar training and support to the Congolese National Liberation Front (FLNC) as it invaded the southern Shaba province.

In Namibia, the Soviets backed a similar revolution, supporting the South West African People's Organization (SWAPO). The Soviets established logistics channels and trained an elite SWAPO brigade from the relative safety of Angola. The SWAPO Brigade consisted of motorized infantry battalions with Soviet BRDM armored cars.

Even when Soviet interventions were undeniably full-scale conventional wars, these wars were usually escalations of irregular conflicts, preceded by military assistance and logistic support to irregular forces. When the Soviet Union was forced to participate in the fighting, it usually did so through client state soldiers (Cuba, Angola, or Warsaw Pact members) that were provided as proxy forces in exchange for aid packages (Castro was particularly fond of these arrangements).

Leading up to Angola's independence from Portugal (1974-1975), the Soviets provided thousands of Cuban soldiers to bolster the ranks of the People's Movement for the Liberation of Angola, ultimately leading to the Angolan Civil War. The package also included weapons, training, direct logistic support, and transportation.

Throughout the collapse of the Soviet Union, Russia was forced to frequently intervene in its near-abroad. In Transnistria, a semi-autonomous region of Moldova, ethnic-Russian separatists fought for full autonomy from the Moldovan government. Their victory was made possible by the former-Soviet 14th Guards Army, which stationed itself immediately across the eastern border in Ukraine. This force intimidated Moldovan security forces, provided material support, shared intelligence, and delivered copious artillery fire across the border on Moldovan targets. As with so many other semi-autonomous republics on the Russian periphery, Moscow supported Transnistrian autonomy to maintain control over Moldova following the Soviet breakup.

Separatists in Abkhazia, a semi-autonomous region in Georgia, attempted to break away in 1992. Though Moscow was initially indecisive in its support, Russia would eventually lend its assistance to Abkhazian separatists in the form of weapons, intelligence, and operational planning. In 1993, Moscow further supported separatist efforts by retaking the regional capital of Sokhumi through an aerial bombing campaign.

Soviet influence operations focused on limiting military, financial, and political risks by indirectly participating in conflicts from the periphery. Large-scale incursions by Soviet ground forces were the exception rather than the rule. Instead, Soviet planners lent military hardware, equipment, trainers, intelligence, and logistic support.

The Soviets left active combat roles to guerilla forces, which were usually reorganized into a conventional force structure. When conflicts did require the Soviets to play a more active role in ground fighting, the Soviets committed additional proxy forces from client states.

The Soviets preferred indirect methods of intervention that protected plausible deniability. Minimizing the exposure of Soviet personnel to the conflict by relying on proxy forces also reduced the Soviet political footprint abroad. Just as in modern hybrid wars, the Soviet-era interventions were initiated without ultimatums or official declarations of war.

There is more at work in Russian hybrid warfare than General Gerasimov. He had not yet become a leading man in Putin's National Security cadre when Moscow was interfering in the numerous "color revolutions" in its periphery, nor had Gerasimov given any relevant lectures on the topic that would have informed Moscow's approach to the Russo-Georgian War. The methods and techniques that we refer to as hybrid warfare are a legacy, and the modern Russian strategic paradigm has created the conditions for them to reemerge as a tool in foreign policy.

Hybrid Warfare as a Modality of Conventional Conflict

Russia's foreign policy objectives are defined to protect or further its strategic interests. Moscow will create crises to serve them, and Gerasimov's model offers a theoretical framework on how that process may unfold. Nevertheless, while Russia must protect its strategic imperatives, it lacks the international standing, cultural stability, population demographics, public health, education system, infrastructure, economic base, and technological sophistication to wage an intervention as costly as the First and Second Chechen Wars every couple of years.

Though military reforms have done wonders for the Russian Armed Services (as we will discover in Chapter 4), Russian military power is a paradox. Moscow balances a vast military atop a small economy that is deeply reliant on oil and natural gas exports. In fact, the Russian economy measured by GDP is more comparable to that of Canada or South Korea at approximately $1.7 trillion (for context, smaller than the State of Texas).

Measured in 2020 USD, Russia's GDP is less than 1/10th the size of the U.S. economy alone ($22.3 trillion) and less than 1/20th the size of NATO ($42.4 trillion). Russia's defense budget is the 4th largest in the world at $65.1 billion, but the American military budget is over ten times larger at $732 billion (which Congressional DoD advocates bemoan to be mere pittance) and NATO's total budget is $1 trillion. Thus,

Moscow requires asymmetric advantages that give it leverage in interstate competition against vastly superior rivals.

Given the context of Russia's military and intelligence modernizations, hybrid warfare begins to look very "conventional". The hybrid methodology is a necessary strategy that allows Russia to compete directly with Western rivals that are militarily, economically, and technologically superior.

In our exploration of hybrid warfare, Chapter 2 will examine Russia's difficulties in pacifying Chechnya, emphasizing the need for a more cost-effective approach to future military interventions. Chapter 3 will go into our first case study and examine the Russo-Georgian War. Chapter 4 will explain in-depth the institutional reforms and modernizations of the Russian Armed Forces, which were motivated by the Russo-Georgian War and necessary to support hybrid warfare.

Chapter 5 will explore Russia's intelligence services, reforms, capabilities, and role in foreign policy. Chapter 6 will discuss the elite and highly specialized units of Russia's VDV, Naval Infantry, Ground Forces, and Wagner mercenaries, without whom hybrid warfare would be impossible.

Once we understand the tools employed, two additional case studies will be presented: the annexation of Crimea in Chapter 7 and the war in the Donbas Region of Eastern Ukraine in Chapter 8. Chapter 9 will examine emerging threats in the Russian strategic environment that may incentivize a hybrid approach.

With a thorough knowledge of Moscow's doctrine and tools, an examination of real-world examples will demonstrate that hybrid warfare is best understood as an asymmetric approach to conventional military conflict that enables pursuit of strategic objectives in a resource-constrained environment.

---

1. A Russian term for "agent", usually referring to operatives of the intelligence services that are responsible for human intelligence (HUMINT), covert action, and other traditional spy craft.

Chapter Two

Russia Relearns the Indirect Approach

Hybrid warfare, and synonymous phrases like "phase-0" or "gray-zone activities" or "nonlinear conflict", became favorite talking points of the Western press and politicians. The phrases evoked nightmares of Russia's shadowy intelligence operatives and commandos. President Putin jokingly called these troops "little green men", but the dismissive title belied the dark mission to covertly insert operators into target countries, create social chaos, breakdown law and order, disrupt government services, assassinate key political figures, storm government buildings, and sponsor a shadow government's rise to power.

The reality of these troops, their mission, how they have often been deployed, their relative success, and their role in Russian foreign policy is neither well-understood nor truly novel.

Russia exists on the fringe of Europe, geographically isolated from the progress of the continent. Russia has always lagged technologically, politically, socially, and militarily behind the rest of Europe. To overcome these weaknesses, Russian foreign policy often exploited fissures to divide rival nations.

Russia maintained its strategic position by prying social cracks open, supporting dissident groups, employing propaganda, and avoiding direct and unwinnable engagements. In between the luminary leaders who fostered cultural revivals and economic improvement in Russia (Catherine the Great, Peter the Great), this approach to foreign policy preserved Russia during times of famine and economic catastrophe and in the face of technologically superior competitors. Hybrid warfare was and is the modern manifestation of this foreign policy tradition.

Russian intelligence operatives facilitated separatist movements in autonomous enclaves in Ukraine, Moldova, Georgia, Azerbaijan—all countries Moscow needs to control.

In 2016, Russian GRU operatives attempted a coup in Montenegro in order to prevent the country from joining NATO.

To enhance its economic leverage over Germany, the Kremlin brought on former Chancellor Gerhard Schröder as Chairman of the Board of Russia's state-owned oil conglomerate Rosneft in 2017. These were all attempts to enhance Russia's global strategic position by using tailored combinations of military, diplomatic, and economic means of coercion—methods beneath the threshold of overt warfare and likely to be ignored by other great powers.

Hybrid warfare is best understood as inter-state competition, competition below the threshold of overt war, that creates advantages through the tailored deployment of non-military influence and kinetic military force to achieve limited operational objectives that support a desired political outcome. Non-military tools of influence include diplomacy, economics, finance, trade, and information.

Hybrid warfare relies on meticulous pre-crisis preparation, guile, and rapid maneuverability to make up for Russia's disadvantages in economic resources, military manpower, and matériel. Through these tactics, Russia often secured its interests with limited conventional forces and without fully committing large armies to a pitched conflict that it was ill-prepared to wage.

As an approach to strategic competition, hybrid warfare's hidden hand approach also insulated Russia from bearing the backlash of diplomatic and economic isolation whenever Moscow attempted to secure strategic interests by force. Ultimately, hybrid warfare was and is an approach to conventional warfare that gives Russia asymmetric advantages to compete with vastly superior geopolitical rivals like the United States, NATO, and the European Union.

The Rise of Vladimir Putin

The exploration of hybrid warfare must begin with President Vladimir Putin, though he neither invented the doctrine nor pioneered the methods. Putin has presided over the restoration of Russia's status as a perceived great power and returned the country to a role of power broker on the world stage. In the face of formidable adversaries like the United States and NATO, this restoration created the political conditions for hybrid warfare to emerge as Russia's dominant modus operandi.

President Putin began his career as an officer in the Committee for State Security (Russian: Комитет государственной безопасности), known as the KGB, stationed in East Germany, eventually rising to the high rank of Colonel before he was 40 years old. This was a high-status career in the USSR, and established Putin as a real stakeholder in the old regime. Then, in 1991, the Soviet Union dissolved, and the Russian Federation rose to fill the void. Putin saw his country in ruins—given over to gangsters and oligarchs.

Putin entered civilian public service working in the Saint Petersburg (formerly Leningrad) administration from approximately 1991 to 1996 under Mayor Anatoloy Sobchak. When Sobchak lost reelection in 1996, Putin transitioned his career to Moscow, where he was appointed Deputy Chief of the Presidential Property Management Department.

In his new role, Putin oversaw foreign state property and managed the transfer of Communist Party assets to the Russian Federation. On March 26, 1997, Putin was appointed Deputy Chief of Presidential Staff and Chief of the Main Control Directorate of the Presidential Property Management Department under President Boris Yeltsin.

Putin was a rising star and President Yeltsin decided to groom him for senior leadership with additional authorities, roles, and duties within the Administration. In keeping with the tradition of Russian public officials publishing a dissertation to demonstrate their scholarly credentials, on June 27, 1997, Putin defended his Candidate of Science dissertation in economics titled, "The Strategic Planning of Regional Resources Under the Formation of Market Relations."

Putin was appointed First Deputy Chief of Presidential Staff for Regions in May 1998. Then, in July 1998, only two months later, Putin was appointed Director of the powerful Federal Security Service (Russian: Федеральная служба безопасности) known simply as the FSB.

In his early positions in the Russian government and intelligence services, the former KGB Colonel revealed himself to be a master of political maneuver, back door deal-making, quid pro quo, and blackmail. He has always been a pragmatic fixer, known for his discretion and results. His directorship of the FSB ushered in a revival of the intelligence agencies' role in Russian state affairs. Shortly after his appointment, Putin hosted a state dinner for the FSB and SVR (the foreign intelligence service most akin to America's CIA) officers and administrators. He communicated one simple message to the faithful *agenturi*: "We're back." His tenure, however, as the head of the FSB did not last long.

President Boris Yeltsin, weakened by a failed war in Chechnya and under immense political pressure, was looking for a successor. Yeltsin sponsored Vladimir Putin's campaign for Prime Minister. Putin was difficult for the political establishment to get the full measure of, largely because he was previously an unknown in national politics. The Duma, Russia's House of Commons, officially appointed Putin to the office of Prime Minister on August 16, 1999.

Putin enjoyed his new role as Russia's head of domestic affairs and number two man in government until December 31, 1999, when President Yeltsin abruptly and unexpectedly resigned. Under the Russian Constitution, the Prime Minister becomes the Acting-President if the President cannot continue in his duties. An election was held on March 26, 2000, and Putin won 53% of the vote, moving upward again from Acting-President to President of the Russian Federation.

The skills that enabled President Putin to rise within the Russian government would serve him well as Russia's leader. His campaign messaging focused on improving the average Russians' living standards, reducing unemployment, and restoring Russian honor as a Great Power. And, for the most part, he was true to his word. While Putin initially indulged Russia's oligarchs, he eventually played them against one another, kept them off balance, and slowly secured their fealty to the Kremlin; a feat that Boris Yeltsin could only have dreamed of.

Putin also nationalized a number of key industries so they could be reformed via top-down control, underwriting economic consolidation and revitalization through oil and gas exports. This practice was meant to leverage the advantages of profit motives and business competition while retaining some of the centralized control and economic planning inherent in communist and socialist systems.

Presently, approximately 70% of the Russian economy is owned directly or indirectly by the state, even though industries largely compete with each other on the open market. And, of course, Putin extensively overhauled and reformed the Russian Military and Intelligence apparatus, which is discussed in more detail in chapters 4, 5, and 6.

President Putin was consistently pragmatic in conducting foreign policy while ensuring Moscow got its cut. Especially during the Bush years, he recognized the U.S. as the sole superpower and did not seek to challenge that status quo directly. He even provided intelligence to U.S. mission planners for the 2001 invasion of Afghanistan to foster goodwill.

However, especially in Russia's near-abroad (defined loosely as those countries that existed within the Soviet sphere of influence), President Putin began restoring Russia's status as a great power, taking advantage of old Soviet linkages and organizations like the Commonwealth of Independent States (CIS) to bring smaller powers back into the fold as de facto Russian provinces.

Within Russia's own borders, Chechen nationalism was festering. The First and Second Chechen Wars were formative experiences for the Russian security establishment. These two wars, punctuated with a faux peace in between them, underlined the costs of the Soviet steamroller way of military interventions, and demonstrated the need for a more nuanced indirect or hidden-hand approach.

An Education in Chechnya

The Russian Empire conquered Chechnya in the Russo-Persian War of 1804-1813. Being a primarily Islamic country, Chechnya did not fit naturally into the Eastern Christian orthodoxy of the Russian Empire; however, despite successive revolts, Chechnya remained a part of Russia on the eve of the October Revolution in 1917.

In 1934, Joseph Stalin consolidated power within the Soviet Communist Party and solidified his reign as General Secretary. Never one to allow subversive elements to continue unmolested and fearing another Chechen revolt while the Soviet Union fought the Nazis, Stalin deported the entire Chechen population. On February 23, 1944, Operation Lentil commenced, and the commissars rounded up 480,000 men, women, and children in Chechnya.

According to a 1939 census, 407,690 Chechens and 92,074 Ingush (an ethnic group within the central Caucuses) were registered in the Soviet Union, indicating that nearly the entire population of Chechnya was loaded into train cars and removed from their ancestral home. Those who were deemed dangerous were sent to icy concentration camps in Siberia.

Known as the gulags, these camps were commonly used by the Communists to isolate political liabilities, dissidents, and malcontents to work them to death. Over 200,000 Chechens died, and the rest were scattered throughout Central Asia.

After Stalin's death in 1953, there was an internal competition in Moscow for who would become the new Soviet Premier. Nikita Khrushchev won the power struggle, and when he took control in 1956, he initiated a broad program of de-Stalinization in the Soviet Union. The Chechen people were allowed to return to their homeland as a part of these reforms. These events are the backdrop of modern Chechen nationalism.

When the Soviet Union began to unravel in the late 1980s, a nationalist movement called the Chechen All-National Congress surfaced, and a man named Dzokhar Dudayev rose to prominence.

During the KGB coup of August 1991, Dudayev seized the moment and declared Chechnya an independent nation. He then staged and won a faux election to become Chechnya's first President. Then Russian President Boris Yeltsin issued an arrest warrant for Dudayev and dispatched Ministry of Internal Affairs (MVD) troops to arrest him. The arrest failed, setting the stage for the First Chechen War.

The First Chechen War

On November 30, 1994, President Boris Yeltsin signed Presidential Decree 2137 to bring Chechnya back under the control of the Russian government in Moscow. The plan was for three columns of mechanized infantry originating from the towns of Mozdok, Vladikavkaz, and Kizlyar to converge on the Chechen capital of Grozny.

With the city surrounded, MVD Troops were to eliminate resistance in the countryside. Once rural areas were secure, MoD units would assault through the city on a North-to-South axis, seizing key buildings like the railway station and Presidential Palace.

The plan quickly fell apart. All three columns experienced delays and breakdowns, both due to the size and quality of local roads that had been poorly maintained. Grozny was never fully blockaded, particularly to the south, and a massive influx of some 9,000 guerillas—irregular fighters—took up residence in the city.

The Chechen resistance set up defensive fortifications in three concentric circles in the city and, almost immediately, the Russians began to experience fierce urban fighting. Foreign fighters flooded the region from all over the Islamic World to join the guerillas, bringing expertise in terror tactics and guerilla warfare.[1] The ruthless prosecution of the Soviet War in Afghanistan in the 1980s had already generated wide Muslim resentment against the regime in Moscow. The Russian invasion of Islamic Chechnya gave impoverished young Muslim men from all over the world the opportunity to channel their resentments into a war.

Russian planners had not anticipated such a tenacious defense, and commanders redoubled their air and artillery campaign to compensate, which destroyed large sections of Grozny. Yeltsin called on additional troops from the Naval Infantry, MVD Internal Troops, the 506th

Motorized Rifle Division, and the MVD's Vityaz anti-terror unit, boosting total troop numbers to around 55,000.

Yeltsin did not fully appreciate that the Chechens were waging guerilla warfare when he made these late adjustments. Russian troops proved incapable of controlling the countryside, giving the Chechens space to maneuver. Their preferred tools were the roadside bomb, the sniper, and the ambush, all of which proved effective against poorly trained and poorly led Russian armored columns, which were usually hesitant to leave the road and only patrolled during the day.

Some Chechen commanders, like Shamil Basayev, committed brazen acts of terrorism. Basayev himself led a detachment of 195 militants up the P263 highway in Stavropol Krai to the Russian border, bribing their way past checkpoints and guards. Around 70 miles north of the Russo-Chechen border he stormed the Russian town of Budyonnovsk, and the Chechen flag was raised over city hall and the police station.

Before Russian military and police forces could hem them in, the Chechens retreated to the residential district where they took around 1,800 hostages (including 150 children). After executing over 100 hostages who refused to follow willingly, Basayev and his militants barricaded themselves in the local hospital.

Russian Prime Minister Viktor Chernomyrdin was forced to negotiate with Basayev personally. After releasing women, children, and the elderly, Basayev was given free passage back to Chechnya with 120 volunteer hostages acting as human shields (who were eventually released). The siege ended with Budyonnovsk left in ruins and a total 147 dead civilians.

Seeking to imitate Basayev's raid, Salman Raduyev led 200 Chechen militants into neighboring Dagestan to attack the Russian airbase at Kizlyar. The raid succeeded in destroying two helicopters and killing

33 servicemen before withdrawing to the town itself under the pursuit of Russian troops. Raduyev took over 1,000 hostages (3,400 by some accounts) and, similar to Basayev, barricaded in the local hospital. The Chechens struck an agreement with locals to withdraw under the cover of 150 human shields back to the border, but, unbeknownst to the negotiators, Russian VDV paratroopers were flown to intercept the militants and rescue the remaining hostages. Following a heavy firefight, the Chechen raiders retreated to the village of Pervomayskoye and set up defensive positions in the school, mosque, and hospital. Locals were forced to dig defensive trenches.

The siege of Pervomayskoye lasted 8 days, and the Chechen terrorists were successful at repelling multiple assaults by Russia Ground Forces, which included tanks and elite special forces. on the eighth night, the Chechens created a breakout through the Russian cordon, and retreated towards the border. During the retreat, they managed to kill an entire detachment of the elite 22nd Spetnaz Brigade, and then linked up with a 200 to 300 man relief force from Chechnya. Together, these troops retreated back to Chechnya under intensive air and artillery harassment from the Russians.

The Chechen separatists maintained the initiative; they could strike anywhere at any time, and Russian Ground Forces could not bring decisive force down on them. On the morning of August 6, 1996, Russian forces redeployed from safe areas in Grozny to begin securing more of the southern countryside.

As Russian forces vacated the city, 1,500 Chechen militants quietly infiltrated back in. At 5:50 AM, the Chechens initiated assaults on municipal buildings, the Grozny airport, the Khan-Kala airbase, and the police and FSB HQ building. Within three hours, the Chechens had successfully captured most of Grozny, pinning down some 5,000 Russian troops, causing mass panic, and convincing many Russian soldiers to flee.

Desperate to retake the city, Russian commanders threw units at the problem in Grozny as they became available rather than organizing a coordinated response. On August 20th, Moscow recognized the hopeless disarray of Russian forces and finally ordered troops around Grozny to stand down.

A full withdrawal was ordered on August 3, 1996. Most experts agree that, by this point, Russia lacked the necessary regional forces, equipment, logistic support, and resolve to achieve anything more than a stalemate. The Chechen guerillas had won the day.

The Second Chechen War

On April 21, 1996, the self-proclaimed President of Chechnya Dzokhar Dudayev was assassinated. His cell phone was detected by an ISR aircraft during a call with a liberal Russian MP. Once positive identification was made, the Russians dropped two laser-guided bombs on his location. Though his death had little real effect on Chechnya's capacity to coordinate military resistance, it triggered a short struggle between militant leaders for overall command.

Aslan Maskhadov was eventually elected President of Chechnya following the death of Dudayev during the de facto peace of 1997-1999. The Second Chechen War ignited on August 7, 1999, when Chechen militant leader Shamil Basayev attempted to repeat his past adventure into Russian territory by leading 1,500 fighters into neighboring Dagestan.

Basayev was surprised by the vehemence with which the local police and population fought his presence. The people of Dagestan share a similar ethnic lineage with the Chechens, one that goes back to the Persian and Ottoman empires, so Basayev had expected a liberator's reception. He was surprised again by the rapid response of the Russian military.

Air attacks, the MVD 102nd Brigade, and Spetsnaz (elite Russian troops) hounded him back across the border. Unfortunately for the Chechens, Boris Yeltsin had already begun transferring power to his Prime Minister, Vladimir Putin—a man who would prove to be far more determined and infinitely more ruthless than Basayev himself. This miscalculation by Shamil Basayev had just given Putin his *casus belli*.

Russia had been intensively planning an invasion into Chechnya since July 1998. Bespoke Ground Forces units were tailored from the most trustworthy officers and reliable troops and then trained in counterinsurgency tactics during the interbellum period.

Infantry battalions were also intensively drilled in calling in regimental or division artillery support. Since the early 1800s, Russian Ground Forces have treated artillery as a special vocation, drawing top talent. Over the course of the Napoleonic Wars, Crimean War, World War I, and World War II, the Russian approach to artillery grew to feature mass bombardments.

By World War II, amassed artillery was the centerpiece of the Red Army. The Soviets used howitzers and multiple launch rocket systems (MLRSs) to blanket German field divisions and entire cities in high explosive shells and rockets. Accounts by German veterans on what it was like to receive Soviet indirect fire evoke images of the apocalypse.

Now, at the inauguration of the Second Chechen War, they were ready for a fight.

Putin ordered an escalating bombing campaign against Chechen cities, killing many civilians and destroying infrastructure alongside the Chechen militants. Much of the civilian populace was forced to evacuate. On October 1st, Putin formally declared the Maskhadov government of Chechnya illegitimate and reasserted the authority of the Russian Federal Government over Chechnya.

The three-pronged assault from the towns of Mozdok, Vladikavkaz, and Kizlyar that Russia attempted in 1994 was predictable and clumsy. This time, Putin and his advisors put a more meticulous plan in motion.

Some 50,000 troops of the Russian Armed Services and another 40,000 MVD troops sealed off Chechnya's border. By October 5th, Russian Ground Forces had advanced from the north all the way to the Terek River, occupying approximately a third of the country.

President Maskhadov made several overtures for peace, but on October 15th, Russian Ground Forces seized the strategically important Tersky Heights—a decision both Napoleon and Kutuzov would have approved—overlooking Grozny and slowly began encircling the city. Grozny itself came under heavy artillery and multiple launch rocket systems (MLRS) bombardment.

The Russian advance was characterized by slow but meticulous progress and total monopolization of force; any resistance was met with massed artillery barrages and air strikes. Once villages were secured, they were scoured for weapons and left under MVD guard before the advance continued. When surrounding Grozny, Russian forces prioritized securing the supply lines from Russia and rear areas (comparatively calm areas behind the front lines that are used to maneuver forces, station reserves, and support logistics) before making a push into the city.

The Russians expertly exploited resentment and divisions among the Chechen separatists, developing informants, turn-coats, and local allies. The city of Gudermes fell to the Russians, largely due to the defection of a powerful local family called the Yamadayevs, who funded their own private militia. Their family-sponsored militia eventually became the core of the infamous Chechen Vostok Battalion created by GRU (Russia's military intelligence service).

When Boris Yeltsin pardoned their commander, Beslan Gantemirov, and offered him the Mayorship of Grozny in the new Moscow-subordinate Chechen regime, almost 2,000 Chechen fighters changed sides to fight in the Vostok Battalion for Moscow. This reflects the community solidarity and tribalism inherent in Chechen culture—aspects that Moscow took full advantage of.

Throughout November and December of 1999, the Russians focused on securing urban centers, forcing rebels into the open countryside to endure an icy winter in the Caucasus Mountains. The alternative for the rebels was to remain in the towns and cities as they were razed by Russian firepower, as was the case in towns like Bamut, Argun, Urus-Martan, Shali, and many others. Grozny was pummeled from a safe distance with artillery, MLRS, Scud missiles, and fuel-air munitions.

On December 5th, the Russians began dropping leaflets into Grozny, urging the civilian populace to flee along a safe corridor before December 11th, after which time there would be no further leniency. Unstated in the leaflet was that the "safe" corridor contained a series of Russian checkpoints where militants fleeing the city could be identified, segregated from civilians, and arrested.

Meanwhile, some 5,000 troops of Russia's 506th Motorized Rifle Regiment and two full MVD Brigades assembled for the assault on Grozny. Alongside them were some 500 Spetsnaz troops who specialized in reconnaissance, guerilla warfare, and sniper activities. They were supported by OMON (anti-riot and anti-terror forces) and Gantemirov's 2,000 pro-Russia Chechen partisans (Vostok Battalion). These partisans would be armed with little more than the venerable AK-47, but their flexibility and fierceness were highly desirable assets for their Russian allies when fighting in the rubble of their homeland.

On December 12th, the Russians began pushing into Grozny, first infiltrating infantry reconnaissance elements to draw fire. Once rebel positions revealed themselves, Russian forward observers targeted them with artillery and air strikes. The ensuing fighting was so brutal that the Russian 506th Regiment took almost 25% casualties and had to be replaced by the 423rd Guards 'Yampolsky' Motor Rifle Regiment.

The noose slowly tightened around Grozny, forcing Chechen guerillas to maneuver on shrinking ground. The toll in casualties and munitions mounted, and their situation became increasingly dire. Two options revealed themselves: 1) sneak through enemy lines to escape the encirclement or 2) counterattack advancing Russian positions to regain the necessary space to maneuver.

On January 15th, Russian Commander Kazantsev decided the time was right and ordered an assault on the city along three axes. Advancing Russian units had to deal with an increasingly desperate resistance from an estimated remaining 2,500 defenders, as well as traps and landmines in the urban rubble.

Finally, the Chechen Commanders decided that their position in Grozny was untenable, and they moved to break out through the suburban town of Alkhan-Kala to the southwest. They hoped to retreat into the highlands, where they could regroup, rest, and rearm. After all, they had envisioned waging a guerilla campaign similar to the First Chechen War, where they had the freedom to maneuver in the rural and mountainous terrain; utilizing the ambushes, sniper attacks, and roadside bombings that had proven remarkably effective in the past.

However, internal divisions began to fester within the Chechen separatist ranks. Local defenders were at odds with foreign fighters, who were more comfortable with fighting to the death. Local Chechen Commander

Ruslan Gelayev withdrew his forces from Grozny via the planned route, while most foreign fighters chose to stay.

For the native Chechens who chose to withdraw through the Alkhan-Kala corridor, the movement turned into a route. The Chechen rebels were harried by Spetsnaz troops, artillery fire, and minefields. Of the 1,500 (mostly domestic) fighters that fled, 600 were killed or captured. The survivors dissolved into the mountains. The (mostly foreign) fighters remaining in Grozny died in combat or were captured.

On February 21st, Russian commanders formally declared the remains of Grozny to be "liberated", but OMON and Gantemirov's militias (the dreaded Vostok Battalion) continued conducting security operations for another month, dealing with isolated pockets of resistance, disarming traps and mines, and uncovering buried bodies.

After Grozny fell, Russian forces were quick to consolidate their gains. Ground Forces advanced into the southern highlands' safe-havens and strongholds. In the North, behind the frontlines, Russian Ground Forces and MVD troops established a network of strongpoints and committed to search and destroy patrols. These patrols located rebels, arms caches, and safe houses. As trickles of Chechen militants leaked out of the siege of Grozny, Russian forces were well-positioned to kill or capture them.

Though Chechen militants would continue to be able to muster forces of 100 men or more for some years to come, Russian control was immovable and irreversible. Chechen militants would take to the highlands in the South and increasingly resort to terrorist attacks, not just in Chechnya but also in Russia itself.

The Moscow Theater Crisis (October 23-26, 2002) where approximately 170 hostages were killed and the Beslan School Crisis (September 1-3, 2004) where 334 hostages were killed (including 186 children), were both attempts by Chechen terrorists to force Moscow to order a withdrawal of troops from Chechnya and recognize Chechen independence. Numerous other high-profile killings and bombings by Chechen terrorists continued with alarming regularity. They even successfully assassinated the Russian-installed Chechen President Akhmad Kadyrov in a bombing in 2004.

Russian counterterrorism operations continued to pacify Chechnya until 2009. Ramzan Kadyrov, the son of Akhmad Kadyrov, had been elected President in 2007. He functioned as a Russian Viceroy, policing the countryside with locally recruited fighters. These forces would aid in securing Chechnya alongside approximately 10,000 Russian regulars. Most separatist leaders were assassinated in one form or another, either ruthlessly hunted down in the highlands by Spetsnaz or eliminated by GRU bloodhounds when they attempted to flee abroad.

On April 16, 2009, the National Antiterrorism Committee issued a statement repealing the decree that initiated the Second Chechen War. Nevertheless, Spetsnaz GRU detachments and FSB Alfa and Vympel units are still known to frequently conduct counterterrorism operations in the Caucasus Mountains in kill-or-capture missions against surviving militant enclaves.

A Post-Modern World Watches a Pre-Modern Chechen War

In Chechnya, the Russians rediscovered the steamroller approach to warfare that was executed so ruthlessly in the Battle of Stalingrad during World War II. In accordance with Operation Barbarossa, Germany's Army Group South attacked Stalingard, a small manufacturing center on the lower Volga River, in order to shield an armored spearhead to the south that was attempting to capture oil fields in the Caucasus.

At enormous human cost, the Red Army held on to fringe pockets of the city throughout 1942, fixing the German 6th Army in place until Soviet forces could amass for a counterattack, which would be launched on November 19, 1942, encircling German forces in the city. During this counterattack, German Field Marshal Paulus was forced to surrender. The sheer mass of the Soviet tanks, artillery, and infantry formations was irresistible, and the 6th Army could not contend with the total monopolization of lethal force by the Red Army.

The Second Chechen War was fought at Stalingrad-level intensity and cruelty. The razing of Grozny also demonstrated that Russian massed artillery barrage tactics had changed little since World War II. Afterall, why risk the lives of Russian soldiers securing urban centers when shells are cheap and plentiful? This moral calculus demonstrated how callous Moscow was to the lives of Chechen civilians.

The world was appalled at the sheer brutality. Many people believed that such conflicts were a thing of the past, but modern mass media and dial-up internet delivered the fighting to the world's living rooms. Reporting on international television was relentless, and Russian censors were not as potent as they were during the Soviet era. The 1990s saw a limited emergence of independent press agents in Russian who were able to challenge official state narratives. This meant that families could watch the cruelty of the conflict their sons were fighting in every night.

Global reporting on the Chechen wars also undermined Russian troop morale. To this day, a large proportion of Russian Ground Forces are conscripted. These unwilling participants are generally considered to be less motivated and more susceptible to negative press or propaganda regarding the war effort.

There was hardly a family in Chechnya who did not lose a son to the conflict. Almost every major town in Chechnya was razed to the ground. The civilian population of Grozny suffered the worst consequences. The city of 400,000 was reduced to 21,000 inhabitants by the end of the Battle of Grozny. The rest had become refugees, died during the fighting, or fled to militant enclaves in Chechnya's southern Highlands.

Russia lost status in numerous bilateral diplomatic relationships at the U.N., including the United States. Both Presidents Yeltsin and Putin had sought to cooperate with the Americans in counterterrorism, but the Chechen Wars left little appetite in Washington for coordinated responses against al-Qaeda and other international terrorist organizations (ITOs). Moscow went so far as to share intelligence with the CIA to support the U.S. invasion of Afghanistan in 2001, but Washington could not be wooed.

Global resentment over the conflict chased away international investment and trade opportunities that would have further integrated Russia into the global economy. To this day, Russia is categorized as having an "emerging" economy on which a sophisticated modern military must balance. It depends on the export of oil, natural gas, titanium, wheat, fertilizers, and raw materials. And, of course, Moscow was responsible for slowly rebuilding Chechnya: first its political apparatus (firmly allegiant to Moscow), next its security services (utterly ruthless in hunting down political subversives), then its devastated infrastructure, and lastly, its economy.

In total, the First and Second Chechen Wars successfully maintained Russia's territorial integrity and restored Moscow's sovereignty over all of the Russian provinces and states. The wars, however, were a failure in terms of the egregious human costs and the resulting loss of status that Russia suffered abroad. They also demonstrated how little the world could do to stop a conflict if determined leaders in Moscow chose to flaunt international opinion and take military action on the Russian periphery.

Russia had to find a means of securing its strategic interests through military force while shielding itself from the costs in blood, treasure, and world opinion.

The solution was hybrid warfare. Hybrid warfare would govern the Russian approach to future interventions in numerous small-scale interventions. Chapters 4, 8, and 9 will each present a respective case study of Russian hybrid warfare in Georgia, Crimea, and Eastern Ukraine.

Russia would formulate the hidden-hand (*fait accompli*) strategy: establishing information dominance (both intelligence and propaganda), using intelligence operatives to raise friendly local partisans and militias, using special operations forces to quickly eliminate key targets and seize terrain; rapidly maneuvering heavy ground forces into the battlespace to entrench gains before the enemy can react.

These tactics, coupled with the employment of non-military influence activities, are what ultimately constitute hybrid warfare—Russia's holistic approach to conventional military conflict. It is the lessons learned of an entire nation; a culmination and evolution of the Russian way of war.

Small-Scale Hybrid Activities in Africa and Latin America

Volatile regimes in Africa and Latin America are fertile ground for Russian-sponsored hybrid conflicts. Moscow's interest in these regions had much less to do with maintaining its strategic position and more with creating diplomatic allies, client states, and export markets (particularly for military hardware).

Currently, Russia's favorite tool in Africa is the Wagner Group, a mercenary organization integrated into the Russian military's command structure. Wagner mercenaries are deployed anywhere Moscow requires a military presence but cannot send Russian troops under official status. In addition to leaving a small footprint, Wagner mercenaries require minimal military hardware and support. Training local police forces, low-key military assistance, security services, and personnel protection are typical Wagner missions. Wagner mercenaries are also frequently deployed to active combat zones and are known to engage in guerilla operations and counterinsurgency.

Wagner was deployed in Libya in 2017 and directly supported the Libyan National Army (LNA) under Khalifa Haftar. In Libya, Russia hedged its bets by supporting multiple factions. Wagner provided subtle assistance to Haftar's rivals Aguila Saleh and Saif al-Islam Gaddafi. Moscow has even assisted the E.U. and U.N.-recognized Government of National Accord (GNA), the LNA's primary opposition.

Wagner also operated in the Central African Republic, Madagascar, and Angola. Wagner assisted Sudan's President Omar al-Bashir during his failed attempt to remain in power in 2019. After the failure of French stability operations in Mali and the subsequent military coup, the new ruling junta hired Wagner to take over where the French left off.

Russia's Wagner mercenaries have also been active in Latin America. Western experts agree that Wagner was vital in stabilizing Nicholas Maduro's regime in Venezuela during the Spring of 2017. Though propping up the Maduro regime does not exactly constitute hybrid warfare, Russia's approach resembles its strategy in Africa.

Open-source reporting indicates that Russian mercenaries arrived in Caracas in May of 2018, before Maduro's Presidential election, and a second group of Wagner soldiers arrived more recently to augment Maduro's security detail. Russian Antonov-124, Il-76, and Il-96 heavy military transport aircraft, routed through countries friendly to the Kremlin like Cuba and Senegal, also arrived in December of 2019, carrying military equipment and supplies. Alongside Cuban security service operatives, Wagner ensures Maduro can rule Venezuela without looking over his shoulder.

Russia intervenes in Africa and Latin America wherever it sees an opportunity, underlining a "hybrid-light" approach. This strategy focuses on maintaining durable leverage and establishing permanent diplomatic relationships, ensuring that Russia will have a seat at the table in any negotiated settlement.

The "hybrid-lite" approach is characterized by engagement in debt diplomacy, establishing lucrative oil contracts (arbitrage), generation of customers for Russia's state-backed arms industries (especially Rosoboronexport), and negotiating permanent client-state status. In fact, many countries that reliably vote in support of Russian diplomatic positions at the U.N. are examples of this "hybrid-lite" approach: Cuba, Angola, Venezuela, Madagascar, Central African Republic, Libya, and Syria.

War in Syria with Some Hybrid Hallmarks

In 2011, the Arab Spring rolled across Africa and the Middle East. On May 15th, it arrived in Syria, triggering the Syrian Civil War. Syria's President and Dictator, Bashar al-Assad, brutally suppressed the Syrian chapter of the Arab Spring, but he gradually lost the capacity to police large parts of the country.

Given that military assistance is expensive, Russia initially supported the stability of the al-Assad regime by running diplomatic interference at the U.N. and providing logistical support to al-Assad's loyalist Syrian Arab Army (SAA). Putin vetoed U.N. sanctions and sent arms, munitions, military equipment, and supplies.

As al-Assad lost more and more ground to rebel forces throughout 2012, Russian supply convoys from the Black Sea Fleet delivered helicopters, artillery pieces, armored vehicles, electronic warfare systems, and guided munitions.

As the crisis became more intractable, Moscow was forced to send military advisors and trainers. Russia's indirect methods of support so often employed in lesser conflicts were not making gains in Syria. The SAA simply was not organizationally capable of answering the crisis, even with Russian logistics and supply. In June 2014, the ISIS "Caliphate" emerged from the remnants of al-Qaeda in Iraq and began seizing territory.

By May 2015, ISIS had captured the ancient city of Palmyra, only 134 miles away from the Syrian capital, Damascus.

Al-Assad's demise seemed imminent, and his removal from power crossed several red lines for Moscow. First and foremost, al-Assad's removal from power would cost Russia a key client state that supported Russia's regional interests.

Second, Moscow did not want to further legitimize the American policy of regime change, recently demonstrated when the Bush Administration removed Saddam Hussein from power in Iraq and again with the Obama

Administration's contributions to the NATO actions in Libya that led to the removal and death of Colonel Muammar Gaddafi.

The West—particularly the Obama Administration—originally viewed the Arab Spring as a Middle Eastern variant of the French Revolution: violent, perhaps, but perpetrated by exhausted masses after enduring decades of starvation and abuse.

Although President Obama did not follow through with his declared red line of removing al-Assad from power, his Administration continued to insist on a Syrian future without al-Assad at the helm.

This was impossible for Russia to accept.

President Putin detested "regime change", because the policy could potentially be turned against Russia and threatened his own regime's survival. Russia made its objections clear by brazenly flaunting Western moral posturing on the al-Assad issue.

The Russians also feared the potential growth of the ISIS Caliphate within the Syrian power vacuum. If Syria became an incubator and power base for ISIS, other regional governments would likely collapse under a growing populist tide.

Preventing the spread of ISIS and its virulent brand of Islamo-fascism was only a tertiary goal for Russia. Inserting itself into the Syrian Civil War established Russia as the key regional power broker. Preserving Syria's client state status and defying moral dictates from Washington were the strategic objectives. Nevertheless, Russian press releases trumpeted defeating ISIS as the primary *casus belli* for the intervention.

Russia was, once again, on the world stage.

Russia restored and expanded a Soviet-era Naval base in Syria, taking advantage of Syria's client state status—a move reminiscent of the United States' foreign basing expansion post-World War II. The Russian Tartus Naval Facility—together with the Hmeimin Air Base—provided Moscow with the ability to project maritime, air, and electronic warfare assets into the region.

Russia was mindful of the Soviet Union's failure to pacify Afghanistan in the 1980s and was careful not to commit heavy ground forces to a protracted campaign against an insurgency across the breadth of the Syrian desert. Although Moscow built up approximately 4,000 troops, composed of Spetsnaz, support troops, private military contractors, and defense industry technical specialists, these forces largely avoided direct combat in Syria.

Instead, crack Spetsnaz detachments trained and advised SAA forces loyal to al-Assad, and they conducted deep-reconnaissance missions. Most importantly, Spetsnaz detachments served in terminal guidance roles, providing critical ground intelligence for Russian Aerospace Forces (VKS) to conduct airstrikes and close air support missions.

Russian Ground Forces officers were deployed as company, battalion, and brigade command teams, effectively running command and control (C2) functions for indigenous Syrian units. Russian Aerospace Forces officers embedded in ground units to serve as a link to Russian air support.

In addition to Syrian proxies, Moscow facilitated the deployment of Quds Force operators (unconventional warfare and military intelligence experts) from Iran to coordinate Shi'ite militias to leverage key terrain. Iran's Islamic Revolutionary Guard Corps (IRGC) Major General Qassem Soleimani personally traveled to Moscow to negotiate the details of Russo-Persian cooperation in Syria.

The Russian Aerospace Forces matured in Syria, flying over 45,000 sorties in the first 4 years of the war. At the beginning of the Syrian intervention, Russian air forces flew with antiquated tactics—largely holdovers of the Soviet War in Afghanistan. Most of the munitions used were inaccurate "dumb bombs". Cluster munitions (which clear out large areas) were frequently used to compensate for the lack of precision and accuracy.

The Russians experimented with hundreds of new munitions and weapons platforms, gathered lessons, learned, retrained flight crews and pilots at home, and cyclically innovated with new tactics as their military-industrial complex delivered improved munitions.

By 2018, Russian Aerospace Forces in Syria were beginning to show real improvement and modernization. Russian pilots and flight crews were constantly rotated into Syria in two to three month shifts and, by 2020, over 90% of all Russian aviation crews had combat experience.

Russian airpower delivered overwhelming fire superiority to al-Assad's SAA on the ground, as well as a general disregard for collateral damage. Rebel opposition forces crumbled.

At the beginning of the campaign in 2015, al-Assad clung to 25% of Syrian territory, which largely constituted the urban areas to the west and along the coast, including Damascus. By 2018, he was in control of 80% of all pre-war Syrian territory.

Multitudes of Western commentators labeled Russia's participation in the Syrian Civil War as a hybrid war. To their credit, Russia deployed many "hybrid" tools in non-military and non-kinetic influence activities. The campaign itself was even led by Spetsnaz on the ground. Russia's intervention in Syria, however, would be better compared to the Second Chechen War, conducted through Syrian proxy forces.

Moscow resisted requests to deploy heavy ground forces to Syria, insisting that the majority of the ground fighting had to be conducted by the loyalist Syrian Armed Forces under the advice of Russian officers (or leadership).

Finally, unlike the United States or NATO, Russia's military, economic, and financial resources are finite—a fact not lost on Russian leadership. Russia was not willing to risk complications to its offensive momentum by wasting time on target verification or due diligence before an airstrike as the West does: at least not for something as immaterial as the moral high ground.

Thus, the Russian Aerospace Forces pounded any and all ground targets designated by ground force commanders with little regard for collateral damage or civilian casualties.

When examined carefully, Russia's participation in the Syrian Civil War was a rehash of the Chechnen Strategy: use loyalist forces to cordon the battlefield, control key terrain, monopolize the use of violence in all exchanges with the opposition, prevent over-reaching through a slow and steady advance. Despite leveraging special operations forces, information operations, military assistance, diplomatic pressure, debt diplomacy, and proxy forces, Russia's Syrian Intervention lacked hybrid warfare's three defining principles: Aktivnost, Vnezapnost, and Maskirovka.

Despite the Kremlin's belief that al-Assad would take the heat in the global court of public opinion, Russia experienced corresponding losses in soft power. This manifested as a decline in international standing, diplomatic relations, and foregone trade relations, similar to the international backlash regarding Russia's pacification of Chechnya, once again steering Moscow towards a preference of hybrid strategies in future interventions.

Hybrid Warfare

Russian hybrid wars attract much panicked rhetoric and global condemnation because they are an effective means of creating asymmetric advantages on the modern battlefield. Hybrid warfare is akin to geopolitical judo, allowing Russia to achieve foreign policy objectives without the expensive mass mobilization of forces, the painful sacrifice of thousands of young Russian troops, or the taxing backlash of public opinion—similar to the disrepute that followed the First and Second Chechen Wars.

Russia seeks to achieve its foreign policy goals through an unseen hand whenever possible, and, because Russia cannot afford to make mistakes that cause extensive backlash, the country always uses the minimum amount of force necessary and tailors it to the problem at hand.

Diplomacy is often an effective tool, but it can be coupled with a tailored information campaign to move the goalposts closer.

Boots-on-the-ground may begin with a nominal presence of Wagner mercenaries and Spetsnaz detachments, but these light forces create the conditions for introducing larger formations of elite airborne infantry. Alternatively, if Russia has viable local proxies, Russia will enable these proxies instead of risking its own troops and provide close-air support to the ground campaign.

Hybrid warfare is a unique and holistic approach to conventional warfare. It allows Russia to engage in interstate political competition at a comparatively low cost (relative to the costs of the Chechen Wars or, perhaps, the American invasion of Iraq in 2003).

In this way, Russia wages numerous small wars that advance its strategic position without exposing itself to global backlash that would accompany an overt war. Hybrid Warfare is Russia's answer to myriad threats from a geographically isolated position, and an economically and culturally moribund history, empowering it to posture on the world stage.

---

1. Military operations conducted by small groups of combatants, characterized as paramilitaries, armed civilians, irregulars, or militia, that make use of indirect or indecisive attacks (ambushes, sabotage, raids, petty warfare, hit-and-run tactics) and mobility to fight larger and less-mobile conventional forces. Guerilla warfare closely coincides with the American doctrinal mission of unconventional warfare.

CHAPTER THREE

THE RUSSO-GEORGIAN WAR

Moscow's Strategic Interest in Georgia

The Caucasus Mountains exist as the intersection of Europe and Asia, emerging from the earth as a ragged line of demarcation between the Black and Caspian Seas. The Greater Caucasus Mountains to the north serve as a geographic barrier between Georgia and Russia's southern provinces.[1]The Lesser Caucasus Mountains to the south run through Armenia and western Azerbaijan.

Georgia and Azerbaijan are cradled in the lowlands between these two ranges.

The Caucasus region has historically served as a geographic barrier between Russia and invading armies. Both the Ottoman and Persian Empires had to contend with the logistics of moving troops through the harsh terrain of the Caucasus Mountains.

Once an invader gets through the Greater Caucasus Range, there is nothing but flat terrain between them and the political-industrial heartland of Russia. This strategic imperative compels Russia to maintain a defensive buffer by dominating the north side of the Greater Caucasus Mountain Range in Chechnya and Dagestan, retaining Azerbaijan and Armenia as client states in the Lesser Caucasus range, and ensuring Georgia remains subdued in between the Greater and Lesser Caucasus Ranges.

When Georgian President Mikheil Saakashvili came to power in what became known as the Rose Revolution of 2003, he set the country on a collision course with Russia in the first hybrid war of the 21st Century.

Russia's geopolitical goals and long-term strategic objectives were well-defined from the beginning.

In a classic employment of *Maskirovka*, Russia used the pretext of defending the autonomous enclave of South Ossetia from Georgian brutality to destabilize the populist Saakashvili regime through a military intervention. Russia would provoke a conflict with Georgia and then rush ground forces into Georgia. Russian Ground Forces would achieve overmatch against the unprepared Georgians by executing a rapid armored advance, employing the concept of *Vnezapnost*. Separatist militias in South Ossetia and Abkhazia were organized and trained like Russian rifle battalions, and they were staffed with officers trained in Russian academies. These local proxy forces would employ the concept of *Aktivnost* by delaying and frustrating Georgian Ground Forces to buy time for Russia's 58th Combined Arms Army (CAA) to surge forces through the Roki Tunnel.

By employing the core concepts of hybrid warfare, Russia would destroy Georgia's ambition to join NATO and secure the strategically vital Caucasus Region. Through hybrid warfare, Moscow could deploy military force without bearing accusations from the West that Russia had unlawfully invaded its neighbor.

A long series of provocative actions by Russian-supported separatists in Georgia's breakaway regions forced President Saakashvili to commit heavy ground forces to secure South Ossetia. In the early morning of August 8, 2008, hours after Georgian Ground Forces began their advance, Russia put a carefully choreographed plan into action. When Georgia made the first move in the public eye, it created the political justification for a heavy-handed Russian response. Putin's national security cadre had skillfully maneuvered Georgia into a confrontation—hybrid warfare.

The Georgian artillery bombardment that marked the beginning of the official war was the result of three Russian strategic successes:

First, Russia placed consistently erratic external pressure on Georgia's political and military establishments, degrading Georgia's decision making.

Second, the Russian national security cadre successfully identified a gap between Georgia and the Western democracies, exploiting policy differences to corral Saakashvili into assuming he had no other choice but to fight a war.

Third, Russia successfully raised proxy forces and infiltrated troops into both South Ossetia and Abkhazia to serve as anchor points for a rapid advance south of heavy ground forces through the Greater Caucasus range via the Roki Tunnel and S10 highway.

Precursors and Historical Enmity

Georgia and its semi-autonomous region, South Ossetia, have a long history of enmity. The Red Army conquered Georgia in the 1920s immediately following the Bolshevik October Revolution of 1917.

Rumors spread through the region that many Ossetians north of the Caucasus had sided with the communists against their fellow Georgians. To maintain stability, South Ossetia became autonomous within the Soviet Union while, on the other side of the Caucasus mountains, North Ossetia became a part of Russia.

South Ossetian separatist sentiments flared after the fall of communism in 1991. The period of 1989-1992 saw numerous flashes of violence and, in 1992, South Ossetia declared an unrecognized independence from Georgia. Evidence indicates that the violence was in part orchestrated by Russia, likely in an attempt to maintain leverage over Georgia.

Russia brokered a ceasefire agreement in 1992 and installed a Georgian-South Ossetian-Russian trilateral peacekeeping force. This peacekeeping force would—in theory—jointly police the region and ensure the terms of the ceasefire were being met by all parties; but, in reality, it became a way for Russia to maintain a permanent military presence on the south side of the Greater Caucasus Mountain range (a massive obstacle to any military interference from Moscow) in South Ossetia.[2]

Abkhazia, another separatist region of Georgia along the Black Sea, fought a similar series of skirmishes in an attempt to gain autonomy from the government in Tbilisi from 1992 to 1993. Just like in South Ossetia, the conflict in Abkhazia ended with Russia playing the role of an external security guarantor, and Moscow forward stationed ground forces in the region.

On August 18, 1991, Alsan Abashidze secured an appointment as both Chairman of the Supreme Council of the Autonomous Republic of Adjara and Deputy Chairman of the Parliament of Georgia (through Russian backing). He then used ties to Moscow to create his own Adjaran "army" and leveraged influence in the Georgian Parliament to distance his regime in Adjara from the government in Tbilisi. By 1993, Adjara was effectively an independent country.

Georgia identified new geopolitical objectives when Mikhail Saakashvili was elected President in the 2004 Rose Revolution. Abkhazia, South Ossetia, and Adjara largely behaved as Russian pawns and lacked any real governance from Tbilisi. They also lacked any real economic activity outside of small-scale farming, smuggling, and other extra-legal activities (including trafficking in narcotics, sex, and weapons). Reestablishing Georgian sovereignty would not only allow the government in Tbilisi to reintegrate these regions politically and economically, but it would remove Russian influence over the Central Asian energy corridor. It would push Moscow's direct influence back to the northern side of the Greater Caucasus range, giving Georgia vital insulation from nascent threats by Russian Ground Forces.

President Saakashvili was elected on a platform of democracy, anti-corruption, and regaining Georgian sovereignty over the Russian-backed breakaway regions. Shortly after his election, Saakashvili began a populist messaging campaign in Adjara—similar to the one that brought him to power in Tbilisi (commonly referred to as the Rose Revolution). Saakashvili's messaging campaign fueled undercurrents of democracy and Georgian patriotism, triggering protests that led to a populist uprising. Saakashvili issued a one-day ultimatum to Abashidze to disband his paramilitary forces and recognize the government in Tbilisi. Realizing his "army" was already disarming and trading sides, Abashidze boarded the plane of Russian Foreign Minister Igor Ivanov and fled into exile in Russia.

Saakashvili's administration immediately appointed an acting local government and constabulary answerable to Tbilisi, and Adjara was rejoined with Georgia proper. In a phone call, President Putin curtly told Saakashvili, "Now remember, we did not intervene in Adjara, but you won't have any gifts from us in South Ossetia and Abkhazia."

Nevertheless, the preliminary success of his takeover in Adjara emboldened President Saakashvili, and he began to set his sights on more complex targets. In August 2004, Georgian Ministry of Internal Affairs special forces and police were sent to South Ossetia. The move was ostensibly to combat Russian smugglers but, in reality, it was a reconnaissance in force.

For a short time, these elite Internal Affairs troops occupied the strategic Prisi Heights overlooking a bypass road close to the de facto regional capital Tskhinvali. The Prisi Heights hold a commanding view over

Tskhinvali and all of the city's supporting road networks. Their capture by Georgian troops forced South Ossetian militias to launch a series of fierce counterattacks. The limited incursion revealed that the Georgian security apparatus could not wage conflict against an organized adversary, and they withdrew shortly thereafter.

President Saakashvili walked away from the events realizing his armed forces required a systematic restructuring.

Saakashvili's first established goal was to build a military that was not only capable of occupying South Ossetia and Abkhazia, but one that could reasonably deter Russian aggression.

To start, President Saakashvili ordered a systematic restructuring of the Army officer corps. This meant purging Soviet-era generals. While these purges were likely motivated as much by politics as by military competence, these generals were developed in the Soviet Union under the mass mobilization model of war. They had little understanding of the Western-style combined arms maneuver in which Georgian units would be training.

Unfortunately, relieving most of Georgia's ranking generals also meant that Saakashvili himself was the only person setting military policy and strategic decision-making.

Armed Forces Chief of Staff General Zaza Gogava's professional development focused on counterterrorism. He was trained in the U.S. from 1995 to 2002, and then commanded the Counterterrorism Division of the Special Operations Center in 2003 as well as the elite Police Special Tasks Division. In 2004, he was appointed Commander of Georgian Special Operations Forces of the Ministry of Defense. In early 2006, he was appointed Deputy Chief of the General Staff and then, following a shake-up of the Ministry of Defense, Saakashvili appointed Gogava

Armed Forces Chief of Staff. General Gogava was undoubtedly a skilled officer, but his command time was focused on tactical excellence and skills management, not on strategic thinking or combined arms maneuver. On the General Staff, Gogava was out of his depth.

Defense Minister Davit Kezerashvili was an entrepreneur and media tycoon, as well as one of the founding members of Saakashvili's political party United National Movement. When the party came to power in 2003, Kezerashvili began working in the Ministry of Finance until November 2006 when Saakashvili appointed him as Minister of Defense. Like General Gogava, he was an experienced manager and skilled political operative. His media connections likely helped facilitate Saakashvili's campaign and, ultimately, his election. But Kezerashvili was not a strategic planner and lacked any professional military experience to qualify his decisions.

Field grade officers (colonels and majors) were scrutinized for their nationalism, sympathies to Moscow, and understanding of the "Western way of war" (and likely their fealty to the Saakashvili regime). Saakashvili and his staff promoted many junior officers—in many cases prematurely—to fill the vacant ranks.

The most preferred candidates for command had participated in NATO training exercises or deployed in the U.S. coalition in Iraq. In fact, a select cadre of Western-trained top officers were used to fill out the ranks of Georgia's 1st Brigade, which deployed to gain combat experience in the Iraq War, training and fighting alongside NATO partners. First Brigade was still fighting in Iraq when the Russo-Georgian War began, depriving Georgia of its most capable troops.

Military expenditures rose exponentially every year from $77 million in 2004 to $923 million in 2007. Georgia procured self-propelled artillery equipment like multi-launch rocket systems (MLRS), infantry fighting vehicles, armored personnel carriers, attack helicopters, and assorted small arms (grenade launchers, mortars, sniper rifles, and assault rifles).

Russia noted that the Georgian Ground Forces bought nearly two hundred T-72 main battle tanks, Mi-24 helicopters, and a series of anti-tank missiles. Many of these systems were superior to their Russian counterparts. Night-fighting equipment was procured from Israel, giving Georgian T-72s distinct tactical advantages over Russian equipment. In addition, Georgia bought Ukrainian radar, the Buk-M1 and Osa-AK anti-access and area denial (A2/AD) systems, and the Israeli Rafael Spyder-SR SAM system.

Georgia's cooperation with the West granted it status as a prospective member of NATO. Like other former Soviet Republics, Saakashvili knew that Georgia could never escape Russia's orbit without NATO membership. However, while the Bush Administration was glad to have another partner contributing forces in Iraq, Moscow's interest in Georgia made it impossible for the U.S. or NATO to make concrete commitments to Georgia, either in security or future membership.

President Saakashvili branded himself as a budding democrat, bringing western liberalism to a country that had only known communism. Most of this was political rhetoric and maneuvering. In reality, Saakashvili had autocratic impulses and resented the inevitable dissent that resulted from political pluralism. He took steps to rein in press freedoms, realizing that ongoing critique exposed glaring inadequacies in his regime. He also micro-managed all strategic military decisions. These populist-yet-authoritarian instincts reflect a style of governance similar to that of Venezuela's Hugo Chavez.

But, while subtle details of the Saakashvili regime would be considered morally repugnant to Western democracies, Moscow was truly alarmed at Georgia's ovations westward.

A distinction must be recognized, as deterring Russia and defeating a full-scale Russian invasion are different objectives. Deterrence is based on a perception of the difficulty and cost of defeating an adversary or accomplishing a military objective. Georgia could never defeat Russia in a full-scale conventional war.

Saakashvili's plans for rejoining South Ossetia and Abkhazia to Georgia-proper never considered the possibility of a full-scale Russian invasion to preserve the separatists. It is possible that Saakashvili did not understand Moscow's strategic interests in the region.

Moscow cannot maintain real control of the Greater Caucasus (or Georgia) without its forward stationed "peacekeepers" (ground forces) in Abkhazia and South Ossetia. Moreover, the emergence of a Western-styled "democrat" in a strategically vital buffer region caused the Kremlin to take extraordinary interest. Then Saakashvili began purging Soviet-era officers from the Georgian military and establishing defense ties with the U.S. Finally, Saakashvili lobbied for NATO membership.

Russia cannot tolerate having the NATO alliance positioned on such a sensitive geopolitical artery as the Greater Caucasus. Entry into NATO was a red line for Moscow.

Russia's Objectives in Georgia

Russia's first goal was to permanently eliminate Georgia's grab for control in the breakaway regions of Abkhazia and South Ossetia. Russia generally supports breakaway regions in its former satellites, like Transnistria (an autonomous region in Moldova that also hosts Russia peacekeepers), as a means of control. Supporting breakaway regions in neighboring countries reminds Russia's neighbors of Moscow's reach and forces them to negotiate with the Kremlin. The support also delegitimizes and destabilizes populist leaders who may be hostile to Moscow.

Russia's second goal was to prevent Georgia from joining the NATO alliance. Both NATO and the European Union had been spreading steadily eastward to Russia's borders. The fact that former Warsaw Pact members like Czechoslovakia (now the Czech Republic and Slovakia) and Poland were joining western alliances and economic blocs was bad enough. Even worse was that Latvia, Lithuania, and Estonia—former Soviet Union members—also joined NATO in 2004 and one-by-one sought admittance into the E.U.

These countries had been critical Cold War allies, providing Russia not only with a strategic buffer from Western invasion, but also giving Russia a deep reach into continental Europe and the Middle East. Despite Russia's shared history with its former satellites, these states realized that Moscow would begrudge them any real autonomy.

Liberalizing their political and economic systems meant leaving Russia's orbit.

Leaving Russia's orbit meant joining NATO.

Before the collapse of the Soviet Union, Russia had effectively extended its strategic boundaries with Western Europe to East Germany (more than a thousand miles from the nearest major Russian industrial center). In modern times, however, the Baltic States have all become NATO members. The march from Narva, Estonia (a NATO member) to Saint Petersburg is a mere 100 miles, putting one of Russia's most important industrial and economic centers within easy reach of any invading army. To

Moscow's dismay, as of 2023, Georgia is still seeking NATO membership (and NATO recognizes Georgia as an aspiring member), which would further compromise Russia's defense-in-depth strategy in the Caucasus region. On multiple occasions, Vladimir Putin has stated publicly that Russia would never allow such an arrangement.

Russia's third goal in supporting South Ossetia against Georgia was to extend control over Central Asian energy exporters. The Caucasus is a nexus of critical oil and natural gas pipelines. The Baku-Tbilisi-Ceyhan oil pipeline and the Baku-Erzurum gas pipeline, key components of an energy corridor from Central Asia to the Black Sea and Europe, run through Georgia. They allow Kazakhstan, Turkmenistan, and Azerbaijan to bypass Russian-controlled pipelines by moving oil from the Caspian Sea Basin through Georgia and Turkey.

If Moscow controlled the regime in Georgia, it could ensure Russia's relative pricing hegemony on oil and natural gas. Russia could completely erode Central Asia's gains in sovereignty and economic growth overnight.

Pre-Crisis Activities and Provocations

Excellence in Russian strategic planning overcame tactical inferiority and numerous failures in lower levels of command. Russian planners created the circumstances that compelled or, at the very least, provoked Georgia's actions.

Vladimir Putin stepped down from the Russian Presidency on May 7, 2008, in keeping with the term limits laid out in the Constitution. He instead became Prime Minister (though still the most important power broker in Moscow) while his protege, Dmitry Medvedev, became President. While Putin is regarded as the principal architect of the

Russo-Georgian War, much of the preparatory work (essentially from May 7 to August 8, 2008) occurred under Medvedev's oversight.

Immediately following the rejoining of Adjara to Georgia, Putin signed a secret decree outlining Russia's goals in South Ossetia which included constructing military bases in Java and Tskhinvali near the border of Georgia, opening a military academy department in Vladikavkaz for South Ossetian cadets, and dispatching Russian military instructors. The decree also transferred Russian officers to South Ossetia to head the region's defense, law enforcement, and security ministries.

Leading up to the summer of 2008, Russian forces probed Georgian defenses, introduced new forces to the theater (as peacekeepers), and built infrastructure (fuel depots, barracks, and similar structures) to support the rapid advance of ground forces. Militias in Abkhazia and South Ossetia were trained and organized as rifle or artillery battalions.

Interestingly, Moscow did not prioritize standing up proxy forces in South Ossetia like it had in Abkhazia until after President Saakashvili reestablished Tbilisi's control of the province of Adjara. The loss of Adjara made Moscow realize that its grip on South Ossetia was perilous.

Moscow sought to turn a handful of militias into a 7,000-strong conventional army. On July 8, 2004, Georgian authorities intercepted a convoy of nine trucks loaded with weapons and ammunition driving from Russia into South Ossetia as tensions and military action increased.

The Kremlin's proxies often waged economic terrorism to provoke military action. Explosions damaged the eastern Georgian Kartli-2 and Kavkasioni high-voltage transmission lines in September 2004. Additional attacks damaged the Kartli-2 and Liakhvi transmission lines in western Georgia in October 2004. Operatives also conducted mass distributions of Russian passports to civilians in the separatist regions to further justify Moscow's stewardship of the region.

These actions entrenched Russian influence and stalled any Georgian attempts to establish order or de-escalate the brewing crisis. Russian military and intelligence officers manned almost every political and military posting in the South Ossetian defense and security establishment.

Title	Russian Background	South Ossetian Organizational Role	Date Appointed	Date Terminated
Lieutenant General Barankevich, Anatoly	Russian General Officer	Minister of Defense of South Ossetia	6-Jul-2004	10-Dec-2006
		Secretary of Security Council of South Ossetia	11-Dec-2006	3-Oct-2008
Major General Yarovoy, Anatoly	FSB Maj General	Chairman of South Ossetian KGB	17-Jan-2005	2-Mar-2006
Colonel Chebodarev, Oleg	FSB Colonel	Chief of the State Border Guard of South Ossetia	27-Jun-1905	Unknown
Lieutenant General Mindzaev, Michail	FSB Lt General Former Commander Spetsgruppa Alfa	Minister of the Interior	26-Apr-2005	18-Aug-2008
Major General Dolgopolov, Nikolai	FSB Maj General	Chairman of South Ossetian KGB	3-Mar-2006	8-Nov-2006
Lieutenant General Attoev, Boris	FSB Lt General	Chairman of South Ossetian KGB	9-Nov-2006	Unknown
Lieutenant General Laptev, Andrey	Russian General Officer	Minister of Defense of South Ossetia	11-Dec-2006	28-Feb-2008
Colonel Kotoev, Vladimir	FSB Colonel	Chairman of State Protection Guard	29-Jun-1905	Unknown
Lieutenant General Lunev, Vasily	Russian General Officer	Minister of Defense of South Ossetia Commander-in-Chief of the 58th Army of the North Caucasian Military District	1-Mar-2008 9-Aug-2008	18-Apr-2008
Major General Tanaev, Yury	Russian General Officer Chief of Intelligence Department - Urals Military District	Minister of Defense of South Ossetia	31-Oct-2008	Unknown
Colonel Bulatsev, Aslanbek	FSB Colonel	Prime Minister of South Ossetia	31-Oct-2008	3-Aug-2009
Bolshkov, Alexander	Deputy Governor, Head of Ulyanovsk oblast administration Head of Regional Staff for Presidential Candidate Dmitry Medvedev	Chief of South Ossetian Presidential Administration	31-Oct-2008	Unknown

Figure 3.1: Russian Appointees to the South Ossetian Defense and Security.

In May 2006, Russia began the construction of a new military base in South Ossetia. The chosen site was Elbachita, 2 kilometers (1.2 miles) from the town of Java and strategically located along the vital S10 road north to the Roki Tunnel—the corridor through the Greater Caucasus to Russia (North Ossetia). The facility was designed to host 2,500 personnel and was large enough to house a motorized rifle brigade. At the time of publication, this remains the only real approach for Ground Forces invading South Ossetia through the Greater Caucasus.

On September 27, 2006, Georgian Minister of Internal Affairs Vano Merabishvili announced that a GRU spy ring had been rounded up. A counterintelligence operation apprehended four GRU officers and eleven Georgian accomplices, and the Russian Ministry of Foreign Affairs immediately summoned the Georgian ambassador. As they demanded an explanation from the Ambassador, the Georgian Ministry of Internal Affairs released a series of audio and video recordings of the arrested parties confessing to cooperating with Russian intelligence and videos of Russian intelligence officers making cash deliveries to them.

Authoritarian governments never like being embarrassed, and Moscow's response to getting caught with its hand in the cookie jar was no exception. The Kremlin demanded an immediate U.N. Security Council meeting to discuss unrest in Abkhazia. Following this, the Russian Embassy began refusing to accept visa applications from Georgian citizens. Russia recalled its ambassador from Tbilisi and evacuated the families of diplomatic and security personnel in Georgia. On October 3, 2006, following Georgia's good-faith release of these GRU officers back to Russia, the Kremlin arranged a de facto embargo of Georgia.

Despite discussions between Saakashvili and Putin during the annual Commonwealth of Independent States (CIS) conference, Russian harassment, provocations, and threats would extend into 2007.[3] On March 11, 2007, Russian military helicopters strafed Georgian administrative buildings with gunfire in the Kodori Gorge of Abkhazia. The next day, Georgian villages in the Kodori Gorge were peppered with artillery fire from the Tkvarcheli district of Abkhazia. On August 6, 2007, two Russian Su-25 fighters and bombers violated Georgian airspace and bombed a radar station near Tsitelubani.

On March 6, 2008, President Putin announced that Russia would violate the standing international sanctions of weapons sales to Abkhazia. This was mostly political theater. Russian weapons had been steadily flowing into the region for years. The real difference was that Russia could now equip the Abkhazian militias with tanks, small arms, armored vehicles, and artillery out in the open without the trouble of wearing a fig leaf.

Of course, Georgia noticed the buildup; recognizing that Russian peacekeepers were merely a vehicle for entrenching Russian influence, Saakashvili and his ambassadors desperately called for internationalizing all peacekeeping forces.

The provocations continued.

Russia's actions in preparing the political environment, equipping the separatists, provoking the opposition, instituting economic sanctions, threatening reprisals, and flaunting attempts at de-escalation by third party mediators are all pages out of the hybrid warfare playbook.

The Western press has not referred to the Russo-Georgian War as a hybrid war because Russia's military incursion was overt, but the conflict had all of the hallmarks of interstate political competition below the threshold of an actual declared war—right up until Georgia made an incursion into South Ossetia. The Georgian offensive satisfied the Russian propaganda narrative, and Moscow initiated a full-scale intervention.

Actions Performed by Each Party for the First Time	Russia, Abkhazia, South Ossetia	Georgia
Air force bombing on territory of another party	23-Aug-2002	8-Aug-2008
Deployment of battle tanks into South Ossetia	3-Feb-2008	7-Aug-2008
Building of a military base in South Ossetia	1-May-2004	Never
Artillery shelling of the territory of another party	12-Mar-2007	1-Aug-2008
Exit from the Treaty on Convetional Armed Forces in Europe (CFE)	14-Jul-2007	Never
Exit from the CIS regime of sanctions on Abkhazia	6-Mar-2008	Never
De-facto recognition of the independence of Abkhazia and South Ossetia, and establishment of direct contacts with local authorities	16-Apr-2008	Never
Shooting down aircraft of another party	20-Apr-2008	8-Aug-2008
Deployment of conventional military forces not agreed to by the other party to Abkhazia	30-Apr-2008	Never
Deployment of military personnel in excess of the agreed limits to Abkhazia	26-May-2008	Never
Wounding of a serviceman of another party in 2008	3-Jul-2008	1-Aug-2008
Military aircraft violating another party's airspace in 2008	9-Jul-2008	8-Aug-2008
Obstruction of another party's Peacekeepers	27-Jul-2008	8-Aug-2008
Firing in the direction of the OSCE observers	28-Jul-2008	8-Aug-2008
Artillery shelling of the territory of another party in 2008	29-Jul-2008	1-Aug-2008
Casualty of a serviceman of another party since 2008	6-Aug-2008	1-Aug-2008
Deployment of heavy weaponry to the conflict zone, observed and confirmed by neutral observers	1-Aug-2008	7-Aug-2008 (2335)
Mass evacuation of civilians from the conflict zone	2-Aug-2008	7-Aug-2008
Mass arrival of journalists representing media of the party in the conflict zone	2-Aug-2008	8-Aug-2008
Arrival of military commanders who would be leading the operation into the conflict zone	3-Aug-2008	6-Aug-2008
Beginning of mass mobilization	3-Aug-2008	8-Aug-2008 (8:00 am)
Arrival of conventional forces medical units and commications units to the conflict zone	4-Aug-2008	7-Aug-2008 (9:00 pm)
Issue of order by a chief of military body to destroy a settlement on the territory of another party	5-Aug-2008	Never
Increase in the number of Peacekeeping forces in South Ossetia in excess of agreed limits	7-Aug-2008	Never

Figure 3.2 A timeline of significant escalations leading up to the Georgian invasion of South Ossetia, indicating the type of escalation and perpetrator.

Notably, in almost every case, Russia (or its proxies in South Ossetia or Abkhazia) was the first party to commit each violation of the status quo. Even if a strict pacifist had held the office of the Presidency in Tbilisi, the emerging conflict could not have been de-escalated without entirely relinquishing Georgian sovereignty.

Combat Operations and Campaign Execution

Russia Influences the Battlefield Through Non-Kinetic Means

Military planners in the GRU recognized that non-kinetic influence could be a force multiplier against Georgian Ground Forces. The Russo-Georgian War marked the first time in history that a major power integrated cyberattacks into its strategic planning for an invasion campaign. Russia's cyber campaign penetrated and disrupted Georgian servers and networks. The primary tool used by hackers was the Distributed Denial-of-Service (DDOS) attack.[4] This meant that when websites run by the Georgian Government could not be shut down, they were often polluted with propaganda or simply defaced.

The official government site of Georgia, the Ministry of Foreign Affairs, the Ministry of Defense, and popular news sites were all taken offline using a combination of DDOS attacks, cross-site scripting (injecting client-side scripts into web pages viewed by other users), and SQL injections (interfering with application queries made to websites' respective databases).

Russian hackers damaged or disabled 54 websites of the Georgian Government, news agencies, and financial institutions. Almost 35% of Georgian networks disappeared during peak hacking activities, which, despite Russian denials, coincided with Russian Ground Forces offensives in South Ossetia on August 8th, 9th, and 10th.

After the Russo-Georgian War, the U.S. Cyber Consequence Unit (US-CCU) reported that, even though cyberattacks were clearly employed to disrupt Georgian networks prior to kinetic operations by Russian

Ground Forces, there were no reconnaissance or mapping activities of Georgian networks by Russian hackers recorded during the August 7-12 timeframe of the war. Such activities are required for hackers to conduct effective attacks. This finding suggests that reconnaissance and mapping of Georgian networks occurred during Russia's pre-conflict preparation, several months or even years before the war. Domain names like *StopGeorgia.ru* and hosting purchases for primary hubs (web servers used to distribute malware) had been registered long before the war's outbreak (as far back as 2004, during Saakashvili's rise to the Presidency).[5]

Interestingly, while these cyberattacks were highly effective at penetrating and disabling Georgian networks and servers, they were not very effective at stalling Georgian Ground Forces or preventing them from coordinating. Due to the slower pace of infrastructure build-out, only about 20% of Georgians had internet access during the summer of 2008, and the Georgian government didn't deeply rely on its internet infrastructure.

The internet's innovations to intra-governmental management and bureaucracy, including the use of email, were relatively new to Georgian bureaucrats, and pre-internet management practices were still largely in place. Admittedly, there were a few Georgian officials who did rely on the internet to do their jobs. But, when Russian hackers shut down the government servers, these officials were able to switch to personal email accounts like Google and Yahoo to communicate.

While Russia demonstrated an impressive capacity to disrupt internet traffic, hackers were unable to delay or even marginally frustrate Georgia's military planning and coordination during the conflict.

While cyberattacks against the Georgian government were primarily meant to enable kinetic operations by Russian ground forces, they greatly aided Russian information dominance. As Russia unleashed a global barrage of propaganda, largely comprised of unsupported accusations of genocide by the Saakashvili regime, the Georgian government lacked any real means of getting their own story out.

Russia's non-kinetic influence also included a carefully crafted propaganda campaign; the world was fed a scripted narrative provided by over 50 hand-chosen reporters who accompanied Russian Ground Forces in South Ossetia. The narrative was echoed by Russian diplomats in the U.N. Security Council. Russian commanders conducted press briefings that followed the template set by American General Norman Schwarzkopf during Operation Desert Storm (the 1991 Gulf War). Georgia's inability to produce any sort of counter-narrative to Russian propaganda likely slowed any pro-Georgian international response.

Russian propagandists broadcasted loud accusations that President Saakashvili of conducting a genocide in South Ossetia. In truth, while the conflict was marred with many civilian casualties, there is little real evidence that any ethnic cleansing occurred at the hands of Georgian Ground Forces. However, ethnic cleansing against Georgian villages by separatist militias was common, and Russian commanders did little to restrain them.

On April 20, 2008, a Russian aircraft flying in Georgian airspace shot down a Georgian Unmanned Aerial Vehicle (UAV). A few days later, Russia deployed an additional 500 "peacekeepers" (a battalion of airborne infantry from the elite VDV) to Abkhazia. Russia also deployed engineers and construction troops to make repairs on a railroad in Abkhazia. The railroad happened to lead to the Russian city of Volgograd and was a vital means of moving large infantry and armor formations into Abkhazia.

Perhaps the worst provocation of Spring 2008 was the arrival of 26 shipping containers in Abkhazia carrying D30 howitzers, SA11 and ZSU 23-4 air defense systems, and BM21 rocket artillery.

The summer of 2008 was saturated with proposals for peace, mediation, and de-escalation from every great power and international governing body in the region. Georgia made proposals through July and August right up to the August 7th, escalation into war.

The United States made a peace proposal on July 8, 2008. Germany made multiple peace proposals on July 14th, 18th, 25th, 30th, and 31st, putting forward a plan for Abkhazia that was promptly rejected by the de facto Abkhazian government. The E.U. made peace proposals on July 19th and 22nd and sponsored a peace conference on Abkhazia where the Organization for Security and Cooperation in Europe (OSCE) suggested renewed negotiations.

Neither the Russians nor the de facto separatist governments even showed up. Moscow simply refused to allow outside powers to de-escalate the confrontation.

Western partners constantly reassured Tbilisi of their commitment to Georgia while simultaneously trying to avoid provoking Russia. United States, NATO, and E.U. officials implored Georgian leaders not to militarily respond to provocations by Russia's proxies. The Russian national security cadre expertly exploited this contradiction, needling Georgia with a series of violations of Georgian airspace, weapons provisions for separatist militias, economic sanctions, and diplomatic nose-thumbing.

In May 2008, Russia's 58th Combined Arms Army (CAA) began setting up assembly areas along the highway from the army's garrison at Vladikavkaz to the Roki Tunnel. The official reason for the deployment was the Kavkaz 2008 field exercise that began in mid-July 2008, but the exercise itself is now largely understood to have been a dress rehearsal for invading Georgia.

Russian combat engineers, concealed within Peacekeeping Forces, installed refueling facilities at Java, enabling the small town to logistically support a Russian offensive. On July 8, 2008, when U.S. Secretary of State Condoleezza Rice visited Tbilisi to discuss the situation, four Russian Su-24 fighters overflew South Ossetia during her visit.

By early August 2008, dozens of reporters from Russian media outlets were slowly being transported into Tskhinvali. On August 5, 2008, the 135th and 693rd Regiments of the 19th Division of the 58th CAA, the 104th and 234th Regiments of the 76th Airborne Division, the 217th Regiment of the 98th Airborne Division, and elements of the 31st Airborne Brigade were all forward staged on the north side of the Roki Tunnel.

Advanced elements of the 135th and 693rd Regiments subtly pushed south through the Roki Tunnel to establish a foothold in Georgia, and, by August 6, the command team of Russia's North Caucasus Military District had set up a local headquarters across the border in the town of Java. Volunteer forces from North Ossetia and Chechnya, including the Chechen Vostok and Zapad Battalions—feared for their ruthless and unrestrained prosecution of violence—infiltrated South Ossetia.

South Ossetian separatists continued to fire on the Georgian Ministry of the Internal Affairs Police Forces in a series of border skirmishes.

Georgian villages were peppered with intermittent artillery.

August 7, 2008

Georgian authorities reported artillery and MLRS fire on various Georgian villages from South Ossetia and responded in kind. Early in the morning, Georgian Special Forces began maneuvering toward the Prisi Heights that overlooked Tskhinvali, and reinforcements were ordered to move up from Gori and Tbilisi, arriving along the South Ossetian border at 1400.

Georgian representatives were received by Marat Kulakhmetov, the Russian Peacekeeper Commander. Kulakhmetov advised them to declare a unilateral ceasefire to draw separatist leaders to negotiations. At 7:10 pm, President Saakashvili appeared on public television to announce a unilateral ceasefire and called on South Ossetia to match his move. Shortly following this announcement, media outlets reported troop movements through the Roki Tunnel from North Ossetia, and at 11:00 pm Saakashvili received intelligence that a large Russian convoy was moving through the tunnel. The information was confirmed by western defense officials.

At 11:35 pm, after a process of constant provocation and scores of violations of territorial sovereignty, President Saakashvili ordered Georgian artillery stationed around Gori to open fire on the Russian convoys traveling south from the Roki Tunnel along the S10 highway to Tskhinvali.

Georgia's 4th Mechanized Rifle Brigade, positioned on the border of South Ossetia, received orders to immediately begin a push north along the SH24 road, which comes into the Tskhinvali city center from the south, to surround Tskhinvali from the west. The 4th Brigade followed SH196, a road branching off west before the city's southern edge, to an intersection with the SH23 road that goes east directly into the Tskhinvali city center.

Georgia's 3rd Brigade and elements of their 5th Brigade (the rest were held in reserve) were tasked with advancing north along the S10 road to the east side of Tskhinvali, following the P72 road that offers an east side loop around the city to move artillery and troops onto the Prisi Heights that overlook the city.

The main effort in securing the Tskhinvali city center came from the Ministry of Internal Affairs special forces and police units approaching on the S10 road from the south. This special police task force was armed with basic military kit, machine guns and grenade launchers, and was supported by a special forces battalion, an infantry battalion, and a tank battalion.

Both the 3rd and 4th Georgian Brigades had objectives to seize key road junctions and terrain around Tskhinvali to isolate the South Ossetian separatist militias in the city center. However, the most important objective was the Gupta Bridge and S10 north road to the Roki Tunnel, which provided Russia the means of relieving and reinforcing their militia allies.

August 8, 2008

Vladimir Putin was attending the Beijing Olympics when he received news of the Georgian offensive. He was immediately flown to the 58th CAA headquarters in Vladikavkaz.

Advanced elements of the Russian 135th and 693rd Regiments received orders to move south from the Roki Tunnel by 2:00AM to reinforce the Russian Peacekeepers in Tskhinvali. The 135th Regiment reached the Russian Peacekeeping Force HQ in Tskhinvali by 6:35AM, ensuring that Russia maintained a foothold in the city in spite of Georgian opposition.

Georgian Land Forces Command (responsible for coordinating the Georgian offensive effort) understood that the Russians were pushing forces south via the S10 highway to Tskhinvali, so Georgian artillery located on the outskirts of Gori attempted to delay the Russian advance with Grad rocket artillery batteries.

At 10:00AM, the first Russian fighter jet crossed into Georgian territory. Russian air strikes frustrated the advance of Georgian Ground Forces. The Vaziana and Marneuli airbases near Tbilisi were also destroyed.

Georgian 42nd Infantry Battalion was the first unit of 4th Mechanized Infantry Brigade that was tasked to advance towards Tskhinvali. It advanced from the west, along the P23 road, through the village of Khetagurovo. The 42nd was supported by 14 T-72 tanks and 4 BTR-80 APCs of 1st Brigade's component tank battalion (the main infantry component was fighting as a part of the American coalition in Iraq).

The Georgian tank battalion carried orders to proceed to the north-western edge of Tskhinvali on the SH23 road, placing a difficult obstacle in the way of any Russian Ground Forces approaching the city from the north. In what would prove a pivotal mistake, Saakahvili then ordered the tank battalion to assault the Tskhinvali city center from the west. This meant that the tanks would have to fight in urban terrain without the protection of flanking infantry units of the 42nd. South Ossetian fighters (supported by a few ineffective Russian airstrikes) claimed 5 tanks and their crews before the tank battalion reached Tskhinvali's western limits.

The Georgian 42nd Battalion halted at a seemingly secure position west of the city and dispatched one of its infantry companies to support the tank battalion, which was glaringly exposed without infantry support. This infantry company from the 42nd found the Russian peacekeepers' headquarters just as the left flank of the Russian 693rd Regiment and the right flank of the Russian 135th Regiment were arriving to relieve it. The Georgian company became surrounded by enemy infantry and armor.

The Georgian 43rd Infantry Battalion covered the west flank of the 42nd but met little organized resistance. Georgian 3rd Brigade mopped up resistance in several South Ossetian villages on the eastern outskirts of the city and continued to slowly secure the strategic Prisi Heights east of Tskhinvali.

Georgian Ministry of Internal Affairs special forces and police units were hounded by stubbornly dug-in militia and forced to fight block-by-block in their advance from the south towards the city center. These police and special forces units were also stalled by Russian peacekeepers, who, despite promises of neutrality, were desperately trying to buy time for Russian Ground Forces to advance.

By the early afternoon, Georgian Ground Forces occupied a large portion of Tskhinvali and several outlying villages, but resistance from South Ossetian irregulars and rapidly arriving Russian units had halted their advance. This would prove catastrophic.

At 11:00AM, the bulk of Russia's forward-staged motorized infantry regiments had passed through the Roki Tunnel and were receiving reports on the fighting in Tskhinvali as they advanced south to relieve the city.

By mid-afternoon of August 8th, all three infantry battalions of Georgian 4th Mechanized Infantry Brigade had been committed to engage elements of the Russian 135th, 693rd, and 503rd Regiments in pitched battle, moving along a southwest to northeast axis to secure Tskhinvali.

Unfortunately, the Georgians had lost sight of the key operational objective: seizing the S10 road north to the Roki Tunnel.

Georgia's 2nd Brigade served as a strategic reserve and was ordered to cover 4th Brigade's left flank west of Tskhinvali so that 4th Brigade could aid in securing the city. But Russian commanders were advancing with the full strength of their theater forces.

The Russian air campaign had refocused from strategic strikes on Georgian infrastructure by noon, hitting military facilities and harassing Georgian Ground Forces. By 2:00PM, Georgian Ground Forces were retreating from the city, having been hammered by Russian airstrikes and the 292nd Combined Artillery Regiment.

Georgian commanders finally realized that the ongoing pitched battle had given Russian Ground Forces vital time to bring up additional troops and armor. As a result, limited air attacks and cluster munitions fired from MLRS peppered advancing Russian armor and motorized infantry in several desperate attempts to disrupt their southward movement with little effect.

Overwhelming, Russian air power also forced President Saakashvili to ground the Georgian Air Force by nightfall. Georgian long-range artillery successfully damaged a bridge at the town of Didi Gupta, but the road and bridge were quickly repaired, and Russian Ground Forces continued their advance.

After a long day spent advancing south through a narrow passage on the S10 road, heavy Russian Ground Forces finally arrived at Tskhinvali and began pushing Georgian Ground Forces out of the surrounding areas. At approximately 6:00PM, the core strength of Russian 58th CAA and 76th Air Assault Division, with complements of heavy artillery and two tank columns (roughly 150 armored vehicles), passed through the Roki Tunnel into South Ossetia, and the situation became increasingly bleak for the Georgians.

Simultaneously, the Georgian Ground Forces attempted a second push into Tskhinvali with approximately 25 tanks and 30 APCs along the same axis of advance as before, again led by the 4th Brigade. The Ministry of Internal Affairs special forces and police troops concurrently attempted to push out of the villages south of Tskhinvali and back into the city center. Supported by the Georgian 41st Infantry Battalion, they slowly clawed their way into the southern outskirts of Tskhinvali. Russia's 135th Regiment had made its way around the west of Tskhinvali and was engaging Georgian 22nd and 23rd infantry battalions, using the plain to the city's west to fan out. The 693rd Regiment occupied territory in the north of the city, and the 503rd followed the SH72 road around the east of the city, bypassing the major urban fighting to put pressure on the Georgian 3rd Brigade. Remembering the difficulties of the Battle of Grozny years earlier, the Russians took deliberate care to leave urban fighting to the peacekeepers and militia proxies.

Upper estimates indicate that, by the end of the day, the remaining Georgian troops and armor may have been facing up to 120 T-72 main battle tanks and more than 250 APCs (BMP-3s and BTR-80s). By 10:00PM, Georgian troops had been almost entirely pushed out of South Ossetia. Only the 3rd Brigade and elements of 5th Brigade remained un-dislodged from the Prisi Heights to the northeast.

August 9, 2008

In the early morning, elements of the exhausted Georgian 4th Mechanized Infantry Brigade, supported by the 22nd and 23rd Battalions, began yet another push into Tskhinvali from the west, with the village of Khetagurovo set as a tactical objective for the advance. The 3rd Brigade resumed its mission of re-securing the heights east of Tskhinvali and engaged in heavy fighting.

58th CAA commander, Lieutenant General Anatoliy Khrulev, began circling around the Georgian left flank west of Tskhinvali and advanced south as his armor fanned out on the open terrain. The Russian convoy ran headlong into the Georgian 2nd Brigade.

The convoy, the bulk of which consisted of the 1st Infantry Battalion of the 135th Regiment, was forced to withdraw. Lieutenant General Khrulev himself was injured in the ambush. Spetsnaz detachments were inserted to enable the withdrawal.

With Lieutenant General Khrulev wounded, Vladimir Putin became incensed by the slow progress. Putin handed operational command over to the 76th Air Assault Division and chose to open a second front in Abkhazia.

The Georgian 43rd Battalion pressed forward to the Znauri village, but, under pressure from overwhelming Russian opposition, began withdrawing in panic. Despite some tactical successes, the 3rd Brigade was finally repulsed from the Prisi Heights, though Russian forces assaulting the heights suffered severe casualties. Georgian Ground Forces had now lost the initiative and momentum.

Despite being pushed back on the ground, Georgian air defenses also began to take a toll on the poorly coordinated Russian Air Forces. Three Russian aircraft were shot down by Georgian Buk M-1 A2/AD systems. The day ended with Georgian Mi-24 helicopters attacking separatist militia defenses near the village of Gudzabar, though little strategic success came from the actions.

August 10, 2008

Overnight, Russian troops began arriving in-force to Abkhazia. Elements of the Black Sea Fleet launched short-range missiles against Georgia's naval port of Poti. At around 5:30AM, 600 Russian marines (two battalions of the 810th Naval Infantry Brigade) and 120 vehicles arrived aboard naval vessels in Ochamchira harbor, ready to fight.

Meanwhile, in South Ossetia, the 58th CAA's 70th and 71st Regiments, elements of the 104th and 234th Airborne Regiments, elements of the 45th Special Reconnaissance Regiment, and elements of the 10th and 22nd Spetsnaz Brigades, supported by significant armor and artillery, had fully joined the fight.

Russian commanders could bring up new units to the fight with impunity, ensuring Georgian commanders faced an unassailable numeric superiority in every engagement. Saakashvili publicly announced that Georgia would be withdrawing all forces from South Ossetia.

With Russian logistic and artillery support, militias spearheaded fighting in the Abkhazian second front in the Kodori Valley. A small Georgian garrison in the Upper Kodori Gorge was bombarded with artillery, eventually forcing the Georgians to withdraw.

Russian authorities announced that the Russian Navy had sunk a Georgian patrol boat. In addition, Russian transport aircraft flew numerous sorties to Sukhumi airport, delivering over 9,000 Russian troops, 350 armored vehicles, and other military equipment to the Abkhazian campaign.

Four battalions of the Russian 7th Airborne and 76th Air Assault Divisions were airlifted to Ochamchira. Russian 20th Division deployed to the battlespace from Volgograd via a railroad line that Russian engineers, concealed within peacekeeping forces, had repaired antebellum. With the Georgian 2nd Brigade mobilized to support operations in the South Ossetian Theater, western Georgia was virtually unprotected.

By the early afternoon, remnants of Georgian Ground Forces were in full retreat from South Ossetia. The 2nd Brigade fortified Georgian villages between Tskhinvali and Gori, the most important Georgian military and transportation hub in the region. The 3rd Brigade had withdrawn from the Prisi Heights east to the village of Eredvi via the SH140 road.

August 11, 2008

Russian artillery and aerial bombardments on the town of Gori continued throughout the night, targeting airfields in both Gori and Senaki, disabling Georgia's mobile air defense system. The 76th Air Assault Division spearheaded a Russian assault south towards Gori.

Russian Ground Forces captured the village of Variani, which had served as a logistics hub for Georgian operations in South Ossetia. The 2nd Brigade fell back south to Gori via the SH24 road in an attempt to protect the vital E60 highway that connects East and West Georgia.

Russian Forces continued providing artillery support and coordinating air strikes for Abkhazian separatist militias in the Kodori Valley. Russian Ground Forces also advanced southeast into undisputed Georgian territory, capturing and destroying the military base at Senaki (2nd Brigade's home garrison and HQ) in a raid. This geographically isolated the port of Poti to the north, which began to take sporadic bombardments from Russian naval vessels. Advanced Russian troops were sighted carrying out scouting missions around the port.

Russian artillery and air forces continued to bombard Georgian positions. By early evening, Georgian Ground Forces were falling back from Gori to Tbilisi or to Kutaisi. In Saakashvili's government, fears began to mount that the Russians were going to capture Tbilisi and overthrow the

Saakashvili regime. There were even suggestions that the Russians could be interested in conquering Georgia itself.

The Russian advance halted at Variani for the night while Air Forces attempted to target Georgia's oil pipelines, international airport, construction plants, and a civilian radar station.

Fortunately, poor Russian air campaign planning and non-existing target development capabilities saved Georgian strategic infrastructure from total destruction.

August 12, 2008

President Dmitry Medvedev announced an end to Russian offensive operations; however, he ordered Russian forces to continue eliminating "hotbeds of resistance and other aggressive actions" as needed. French President Sarkozy negotiated a ceasefire.

Despite the ceasefire, Russian Ground Forces hurried further south to destroy military equipment and infrastructure around Gori. Capturing Gori severed Tbilisi from western Georgia and Abkhazia, breaking the back of any remaining Georgian resistance and guaranteeing Moscow a free hand in all territory adjacent to the Black Sea.

The advance halted at the village of Mtskheta, on the northern outskirts of Tbilisi.

A mouthpiece of the Abkhazian Militias announced that Abkhazian troops had successfully forced Georgian forces to withdraw from the Kodori Gorge. However, Russian troops took up positions around the port of Poti and paratroopers placed a bridge to the port under guard.

Operational and Tactical Performance

Maskirovka (Camouflage)

Recall, the term Maskirovka describes deception efforts to hide the Russian hand instigating and waging the conflict. The Russo-Georgian War is a monument to Maskirovka and what is possible when it is performed properly. Though the United States Government was never fooled by what was happening in South Ossetia and Abkhazia, much of the European public was. Germany in particular needed the Russian propaganda narrative. The German industrial model is fueled by Russian oil and gas, and Moscow's propaganda gave the German public (and Government) the moral rational to remain diplomatically and rhetorically neutral. This ensured that Russia would not endure harsh economic sanctions for its actions from Europe.

Russian Information Operations in Georgia conveyed three themes:

1. Under President Saakashvili, Georgia had become hostile and aggressive against ethnic-Russian populations in the autonomous regions of Abkhazia and South Ossetia.

2. Russia was driven to intervene in Georgia in order to protect ethnic-Russian citizens abroad.

3. After the NATO intervention in Kosovo, neither the United States nor the European Union had grounds to criticize Russia for intervening in Georgia.[6]

The Russian hand in instigating the conflict was effectively hidden from the global public, insulating Russia from diplomatic pressure and public backlash. Beneath Maskirovka, Russian intelligence operatives and advanced Spetsnaz elements prepared the battlespace for a rapid advance of ground forces. Pro-Russian militias were trained, supply depots were established, and the peacekeepers entrenched themselves.

Aktivnost (Activity)

The term Aktivnost refers to all measures that prevent an enemy from bringing its military power to bear, particularly on operational objectives. Russian Aktivnost was employed in a clumsy fashion, but it was nevertheless effective. Militias delayed the advance of the Georgian 3rd and 4th Brigades in securing the Gupta Bridge and S10 north road to the Roki Tunnel. Cyberattacks shut down Georgian Government websites and email. The Russian peacekeepers fought desperately against Georgian Ministry of Internal Affairs' special forces and police units, preventing the Georgians from securing the city center of Tskhinvali until reinforcements arrived (elements of the 135th and 693rd Regiments arrived early on the morning of August 8th). Russian Ground Forces had the necessary time and space to maneuver, a testament to the effectiveness of Aktivnost.

Vnezapnost (Surprise)

The term Vnezapnost refers to the speedy deployment and maneuver of forces. The application of Vnezapnost was perhaps Russia's weakest point. While activities to create space for Russian Ground Forces to maneuver were very effective, the Ground Forces and their officers proved to be professionally incapable of rapid maneuver. Traffic jams, mechanical breakdowns of all kinds, slovenly command and control, and a general lack of motivation within the Russian ranks is what gave Georgia a fighting chance.

Prime Minister Putin would eventually hand theater command to the 76th Air Assault Division to reinvigorate the offensive. However, in the early hours of the campaign, Russian commanders of the 58th CAA did push a sufficient mass of advanced elements of theater forces to stall the Georgian offensive.

Rapid advances are vital to maintaining the initiative in military campaigns, but Russia's incursion into Georgia lacked any actual rapid maneuver consistent with the definition of Vnezapnost. Regardless, the advance southward of Russian ground forces ultimately won the day, and, by August 11, 2008, Moscow was celebrating victory.

Russian Ground Forces Performance

The real masterstroke of the intervention was Russia's strategic planning, which translated into overwhelming operational superiority. Despite that, Russian Ground Forces performed very poorly at the tactical level, largely relying on Soviet-era tactics. Armored columns would advance until making contact with the enemy. When the lead elements made contact, they fought in place while the rest of the column continued the advance toward operational objectives.

Soviet-era tactics do not prioritize establishing support by fire positions or maneuver on the enemy's flanks because these actions delay the advance. The advantage to such tactics is speed and simplicity. A column can quickly advance to operational objectives if it refuses to stop for trivial things like artillery fire and enemy tanks. Moreover, the simplicity of these tactics allows them to be employed without strong command and control (C2) measures in place to maintain unit integrity. The cost, however, is high casualties.

In the final tally, the Russians suffered 351 casualties (67 dead). But oddly, it does not appear that even these Soviet-era tactics were fully rehearsed.

On many occasions in Georgia, the lead elements of a Russian armored column would take fire and the entire column would simply halt while the lead element fought in place instead of continuing the advance as doctrine dictates. The non-execution of basic tactics reflects poor training, a lack of motivation, and cowardice among junior officers and combat leaders.

Fortunately for Moscow, the Russian advance was fast enough to relieve Tskhinvali before the Georgians could capture the city center, largely because Ground Forces avoided significant engagements along the S10 road (from the Roki Tunnel through Didi Gupta to Tskhinvali).

Any enemy action on the S10 road risked bottlenecking Russian Ground Forces and preventing them from spreading out on open terrain where they could leverage their numerical superiority. Tanks simply cannot maneuver effectively in small mountain passes.

The Russian Airborne and Air Assault Forces of the VDV, particularly the 76th Air Assault Division, received general praise for their performance, largely due to the poor performance of the 58th CAA and its subordinate 19th and 42nd Motorized Rifle Divisions. Putin became frustrated enough with the lack of progress in South Ossetia to transfer theater command to the 76th Air Assault Division. Prime Minister Putin understood that rapidly advancing south into Georgia was the key to victory. After the 58th CAA stalled, he wasted no time transferring strategic command to the more competent and aggressive officers of the VDV.

The Russian Ground Forces suffered from almost a total breakdown in communications and their C2 methods were disorderly and bedraggled. Before the outbreak of hostilities, less than 20% of Russia's combat units were battle-ready and much of their measured combat capacity came from skeleton units (units with only officers and no troops).

Colonels and generals had to be handpicked from all over the Russian armed forces to participate in the Georgian Intervention (again highlighting extensive Russian preparation for the engagement). Poorly maintained tanks and armored personnel carriers constantly broke down along the S10 highway, creating traffic jams and bottlenecking the advance of Russian reinforcements in a way that Georgian artillery never could.

Russian Air Forces Performance

Russian Air Forces were inept at performing a variety of basic tasks, including suppressing enemy air defenses, reconnaissance, targeting strategic infrastructure, and close air support to ground forces. Even worse, coordination between air and ground forces was almost non-existent. The one task where air forces met expectations was in establishing air superiority.

Russian pilots enjoyed overwhelming numerical superiority and Georgian losses grew so quickly that President Saakashvili was forced to ground all planes after August 8th, lest the entire Georgian Air Force be destroyed. Georgia's most significant ground force losses were inflicted by just a few effective Russian air strikes, particularly on 4th Brigade to the west of Tskhinvali.

Russian strategic bombers were flown by pilots who needed more flight hours and pre-mission training. For example, the Tu-22 strategic bomber that was shot down by Georgian A2/AD defenses was flown by a pilot who had been on academic assignment only days beforehand. Even then, they lacked up-to-date intelligence on Georgian strategic infrastructure, often causing them to bomb targets of negligible strategic importance while neglecting active military installations. Instead of designing a comprehensive targeting plan for Georgia, Russian strategic bombers chose targets ad hoc from old Soviet-era maps.

The presence of credible Georgian air defenses (the Buk-M1) completely surprised Russian Air Forces despite years of intelligence gathering, extensive preparation of the battlespace, and advanced force operations. This elementary oversight cost the Russians several aircraft, including a Tu-22 strategic bomber. Moreover, Georgia's purchase of a Ukrainian-owned Buk-M1 (SA11) A2/AD system was open-source knowledge and publicly reported, making the Russian military intelligence failure all the more profound.

Transport aviation was the real success story of the Russian Air Forces. Fixed-wing transport aircraft flew over 100 sorties moving soldiers, vehicles, and equipment to the theater. Units were transported from as far away as Moscow and St. Petersburg to South Ossetia and Abkhazia. What's more, transport aviation flew these missions on short notice. Fixed-wing transport aircraft flew Russian troops to friendly or captured airfields due to Georgia's air defense threats, and then troops moved via ground transportation to the combat zone.

The transport helicopter fleet was largely grounded in active combat zones due to air defense threats. Frustrations brewed amongst front-line soldiers who desired close air support and aerial transport. Lingering resentments after the war generated discussions amongst senior staff that the ground forces should take over ownership of the helicopter fleet.

Russian Naval Forces Performance

The Russian Navy was not put to the test during the Russo-Georgian War, but the Black Sea Fleet dispatched a flotilla based around the cruiser Moskva and the destroyer Smetlivy. Three amphibious landing ships were used to deploy two Naval Infantry battalions (marines) on the Abkhazian coast.

Shortly after hostilities ended, Russia ordered Mistral class amphibious landing ships from France (soon to be replaced by the Priboy class program). The purchase may indicate that despite being unopposed, the amphibious landing in Abkhazia was slowed by technical challenges. The Russian vessels Mirazh and Suzdalets sank a Georgian patrol boat, but the event signifies nothing of substance about Russian surface warfare capabilities.

Georgian Armed Forces Performance

Most Georgian senior officers who understood the Soviet method of war had been purged by the Saakashvili government. Though inexperienced and primarily focused on counterinsurgency operations, the new officer corps had some training in western-style maneuver warfare. Moreover, they had purchased an array of military equipment, largely from Israel, which gave them tactical superiority, particularly in night fighting.

Georgian tanks had better fire control systems, modern radios, night vision, thermal vision, and reactive armor. Georgian soldiers were also equipped with more advanced helmets and body armor. There are numerous documented instances of Russian soldiers taking body armor off dead or captured Georgian soldiers.

The Georgian Air Force's Su-25s had also been updated and modernized with superior communications systems, avionics, night fighting equipment, and targeting systems.

The results were self-evident: in almost every engagement where Russian Ground Forces met Georgian Ground Forces in equal numbers, the Georgians gave more damage than they took. But for all the tactical successes the Georgians enjoyed, decisions made by field grade officers were reactionary and haphazard.

President Saakashvili himself, Defense Minister Davit Kezerashvili, and Armed Forces Chief of Staff General Zaza Gogava were the only strategic planners of note. Not only did Saakashvili micromanage his generals and field commanders, but his grand plan played directly into Moscow's trap—a perfect employment of hybrid warfare.

Let it never be said that Georgia's Ministry of Internal Affairs special forces and police units did not carry their weight in the company of combat soldiers. Intelligence lapses ensured the Georgians had sorely underestimated the resistance they would meet in Tskhinvali from South Ossetian irregulars and Russian Peacekeepers.

The Ministry of Internal Affairs special forces and police units were originally given the nearly impossible task of securing the city alone, with no fire support or heavy weaponry. Despite these disadvantages, they assaulted and re-assaulted the city from the south, taking heavy casualties. There is a difference between advanced tactical training in law enforcement and combat training for urban warfare.

The Ministry of Internal Affairs troops fought bravely in a role for which they were untrained and ill-equipped to perform. No reasonable commander could or should have demanded more from them.

President Saakashvili, Defense Minister Davit Kezerashvili, and General Zaza Gogava, Armed Forces Chief of Staff, were also making decisions without any real intelligence. According to General Gogava, President Saakashvili and his national security team decided to secure South Ossetia without an understanding of the extent to which the Russians were prepared to escalate hostilities.

In the aftermath, Gela Bezhuashvili, head of the Georgian foreign intelligence service, testified to parliament that intelligence indicated that the Russians began planning an incursion into Georgia as early as 2007.

However, for some reason, Georgian intelligence had been expecting the Russians to escalate tensions in September, October, and November of 2008, and were somehow surprised that escalations began in July and August.

It appears that none of this was communicated to President Saakashvili either when he gave the order to secure South Ossetia, or prior to the war when he authorized Georgia's finest combat unit, the 1st Brigade, to deploy its infantry component as a part of the U.S. coalition in Iraq. Otherwise, he might have known he was falling into a trap.

Georgian intelligence also did not expect the Russians to conduct their incursion on two fronts (South Ossetia and Abkhazia). Defense Minister Kezerashvili would later state that, had the Georgians known the extent of the invasion Russia had planned, Georgian Ground Forces would have prepared defensive positions and trenches. As it was, the Georgian military could carry on a mobile offensive campaign on a single front. Still, they were ill-prepared for heavy Russian ground formations and the full weight of the Russian Air Forces on two fronts.

Summary and Conclusions

The first hybrid war of the 21st Century is remembered as a conventional war, and yet all the hallmarks of a hybrid war were present. Russia leveraged various military and non-military means to create operational advantages. These operational advantages were acute enough to overcome a slovenly air campaign, incompetent and unmotivated commanders, extensive maintenance failures of armored vehicles, and unit-to-unit tactical inferiority.

Russian operatives trained Abkhazian and South Ossetian proxy forces to fight as conventional infantry and artillery formations and fully mobilized them to fight. Additional militia fighters were also brought in from North Ossetia and Chechnya, and Russian strategic planners leveraged the Peacekeepers already in the country to slow the Georgian advance through Tskhinvali.

The Russo-Georgian War was also the first armed conflict where cyber operations were conducted to support kinetic operations in theater. Moscow prepared the information domain well in advance, hand-picking journalists to accompany Russia's forward headquarters on the battlefield and issuing a controlled narrative.

The game board was meticulously set so that President Saakashvili would blunder into making the first offensive move. The overt military intervention that followed conforms to the general framework that General Gerasimov laid out on hybrid warfare (though the Russo-Georgian War predates Gerasimov). The war in Georgia leveraged low-intensity conflict, proxy forces, non-military influence activities, and ambiguity in interstate competition as a means for the unseen hand of Russia to gain asymmetric advantages in a conventional military conflict that was never officially declared and afterward legitimized through propaganda. That is hybrid warfare.

---

1. North Ossetia, Chechnya, Dagestan, Ingushetia, Kabardino-Balkaria, Karachay-Cherkessia, and Krasnodar Kray

2. Russia frequently uses the practice of deploying "peacekeepers" to conflict zones on its periphery as a means of establishing a forward presence in strategically vital areas. In late 2020, Azerbaijan attempted to reclaim the Nagorno-Karabakh region, an autonomous ethnic-Armenian enclave within its borders. Russia was eventually invited to arbitrate the dispute and deployed 2,500 troops (a full Brigade) to the region as peacekeepers. The presence of heavy Russian Ground Forces ensures that Russia can maintain positive control of the South Caucasus region, deterring not only local actors like Azerbaijan, but also regional powers like Turkey and Iran. Rarely do Russian peacekeepers actually keep the peace.

3. The Commonwealth of Independent States (CIS) was formed in 1991 in the aftermath of the dissolution of the Soviet Union. It consists of a core remnant of former Soviet States and Warsaw Pact members bound together in a loose political, economic, and military framework to counter-balance NATO and the E.U. Russia considers the CIS members part of its strategic buffer with the West, and thus profoundly fears its members straying from Moscow's influence.

4. A DDOS attack severs network resources from their users, disrupting host services to the Internet. DDOS attacks flood servers with false requests that overload the system and prevent legitimate requests from being fulfilled.

5. The world saw a mild preview of Russia's cyber capabilities in April 2007. In a controversial decision, the Estonian government decided to relocate a monument that celebrated the Soviet victories of World War II. The monument was a symbol of the hated communist regime instead of a celebration of shared hardship and triumph over Nazism. In response, GRU mobilized a large, decentralized network of freelance hackers against the Estonian government and economy. GRU had been building and distributing cyber tools to enable this network for years and, during its employment against Estonia, Moscow was able to claim plausible deniability. Network participants were trained on employing modular cyber tools that required little expertise to wield. Despite the lack of sophistication, the Russians proved that a distributed network of hackers deploying basic tools in volume could do formidable damage. The Estonian government, banks, businesses, and selected officials were hit with massive distributed denial-of-service (DDOS) attacks. A DDOS attack severs network resources from their users, disrupting host services to the Internet. DDOS attacks flood servers with false requests that overload the system and prevent legitimate requests from being fulfilled. By the time of the Georgian Intervention, the GRU's cyber proxies had honed their approach.

6. The Kosovo War was fought from February 1998 to June 1999 between President Milosevic's Federal Yugoslavian forces and the ethnic-Albanian rebel group known as the Kosovo Liberation Army (KLA). Ethnic-Albanian refugees had been emigrating to Kosovo for years and, after developing a super-majority in the province, sought autonomy from Yugoslavia. President Milosevic committed forces to Kosovo to expel the ethnic-Albanian majority and restore order, leading to bitter fighting and ethnic-cleansing. Led by the Clinton Administration and vehemently opposed by Moscow, NATO provided Kosovo partisans with air support and soon pushed Yugoslavian forces out of Kosovo. Russia decried Western interference in Eastern Bloc regional affairs, Moscow's traditional sphere of influence.

Chapter Four

Russian Military Restructuring and Modernization

The Russo-Georgian War was a potent reminder of Russia's military preeminence in the Eastern Bloc. The Russian Ground Forces and Spetsnaz showed monumental improvements over their performance in Chechnya just a decade earlier. Clearly, President Putin's modernization efforts and military reforms were effective. But there were glaring problems brought to light during the Russo-Georgian war that also needed to be addressed.

Many Ground Forces officers were either slow to take the initiative or incompetent in basic leadership tasks. Vehicles, especially tanks and infantry fighting vehicles (IFVs), frequently broke down, stalling the advance.

The Russian Air Forces demonstrated almost total incompetence in strategic bombing and close air support roles. Russian military intelligence also inexplicably overlooked the presence of Buk M-1 air defense systems in Georgia. These failures gave President Putin and his National Security Cadre the political justification to bulldoze the remaining institutional resistance in order to modernize the Russian Armed Services. The military that would emerge would be a potent tool for supporting Russia's foreign policy objectives.

The Kremlin prioritizes nuclear deterrence, submarine-based maritime denial, an air force that can provide air superiority and support to ground forces, heavy ground forces that can deploy long-range precision-guided munitions, and electronic warfare (EW) systems to create asymmetric advantages.

Russia was planning for conventional war, not just conflict in the shadows. As discussed in previous chapters, Chechnya created the need for a new approach, the development of new tools (Aktivnost, Vnezapnost, and

Maskirovka), and the use of deception and targeted messaging, but hybrid warfare is not codified or defined in Russian doctrine.

The Russians do not conceptualize hybrid warfare as a separate or independent methodology. Moscow is innovating hybrid warfare tactics and tools as they actively plan new military operations. The Kremlin then deploys these new methods as needed to create strategic and operational advantages.

Russia's military modernizations are transforming the Armed Services from a Soviet-style mass mobilization conscript model into an American-style professional force capable of combined arms maneuver and foreign interventions. Moscow has spent billions of dollars transforming its Army, Navy, Aerospace Forces (formerly the Air Force and Air Defense Force), and Strategic Rocket Forces to ensure that Russia remains competitive with NATO's technological innovations.

As the Russian Armed Services continue to reach technological and organizational maturity, Moscow is regaining the ability to shape its strategic environment through foreign interventions, grudgingly termed hybrid wars by the West.

Procurement of new equipment would be meaningless without a complete overhaul of the military education system, officer corps, command and control (C2), as well as an infusion of professional soldiery. Defense Minister Anatoly Serdyukov led the fight against entrenched interests in the Armed Services to make these reforms a reality. He is the man most singularly responsible for Russia's restored capacity to wage war.

But, to understand why these modernizations and reforms were necessary and how they enable Moscow to wage hybrid warfare, we must first understand what forces, equipment, platforms, structure, and leadership Russia inherited from the Soviet Union.

We will briefly discuss the Soviet Ground Forces, Navy, Air Forces (and Air Defense Forces), and Strategic Rocket Forces, and then move into the transformational Serdyukov reforms nicknamed "The New Look".

The Rusted Soviet Inheritance

Russia inherited the lion's share of the Soviet military, including armaments, military systems and platforms, ships, soldiery, force structure, officer corps, military academies, and most of the military-industrial complex. While the Soviet military tradition was a point of pride for Russia, its sheer size in manpower and equipment was impossible to support in the post-Soviet era.

By the mid-1990s, post-Soviet upheaval had caused the Russian economy to contract to approximately half the size of the United Kingdom's (in 1992 U.S. Dollars); and yet, Russian strategic planners envisioned forces large enough to compete with the entire NATO alliance.

Stuck in the past, military planners failed to give direction to inevitable force reductions, and such reductions came without a realistic vision for the role of Russia's Armed Services in domestic and foreign policy. Throughout the 1990s, planners refused to shed the goal of conventional parity with NATO, so the Russian Armed Services kept much of their bulk and traditional force structure, resulting in chronic underfunding.

Soldiers could not train.

Pilots did not have air-worthy planes let alone adequate flight hours.

A once formidable blue-water navy rusted in the shipyards.

Thousands of tanks were parked in permanent storage with locked-up engines and weeds growing in their tracks.

So, what exactly did the Russian Federation inherit?

Ground Forces—The Heart of Soviet Power

The Soviet Union was first and foremost a land power, so, while it maintained a blue water navy, its true conventional strength came from massive ground forces. In the event of war with NATO, the Soviet Union and Warsaw Pact members planned a mass mobilization (envision the massive armies of Field Marshal Zhukov in World War II).

Soviet Ground Forces were the centerpiece of this planned mobilization. The role of the Ground Forces was to deploy massive tank armies to achieve a breakout into Western Europe, shattering NATO frontlines and driving Anglo-American forces into the Atlantic Ocean.

Most military planners thought that Soviet Ground Forces would attempt a breakout into Western Europe by passing through the German Volgelsberg Mountains, traversing south-west along two corridors that converge on the city of Frankfurt, and lead to crossings on the Rhine (commonly referred to as the Fulda Gap).

When the Cold War ended, allied strategists revealed that Soviet Ground Forces' superiority in forces and firepower was so great that when NATO military planners ran wargame simulations of a potential Soviet Ground Forces invasion of Western Europe, the results were catastrophic.

Most scenarios ended with Allied Ground Forces being immediately overrun in West Germany. The remnants of shattered Allied lines would be pushed backward into France, then trapped against the Atlantic.

The most likely outcome would have been either encirclement and surrender or a mass evacuation by Allied navies reminiscent of the German encirclement of British Expeditionary Forces at Dunkirk in WW2.

To save the British Army, Prime Minister Winston Churchill was forced to initiate Operation Dynamo, calling on all civilian shallow-draft vessels to cross the channel and evacuate 338,000 British and French troops trapped on the beaches of Dunkirk. NATO planners calculated that, in the event of war, Soviet Ground Forces would drive backward and ultimately trap NATO troops in a similar manner.

While the Soviet forces were a danger to all of mainland Europe in the event of a Soviet attack, NATO strategists also viewed Soviet Ground Forces as an insurmountable obstacle to any conventional invasion of the Eastern Bloc. The Soviets effectively plugged key strategic choke points that would have allowed for a breakout into Soviet territory.

The Soviet Union bequeathed Russia a force structure in which the army was the operational level unit, organized into Combined Arms Armies (CAAs) and Tank Armies (TAs). The division (Soviet divisions were approximately 10,000 men) was the unit of maneuver with a combined arms structure and a plethora of combat support units and service elements.[1]

There were three division types: motorized rifle, tank, and airborne infantry.

At the strategic level, Soviet Ground Forces were organized into theaters of war (continental geographic territories with their bordering maritime areas and airspace), theaters of military operation (fronts where military forces are deployed within a theater of war), and military districts (geographic subdivisions that constitute all of the landmass that Soviet Ground Forces were responsible for defending).

At the zenith of operational capabilities in the 1980s, Soviet Ground Forces maintained a standing forces total strength of approximately 1,825,000 men with 191 maneuver divisions (134 motorized rifle divisions, 50 tank divisions, and 7 airborne divisions). These figures do not include the increase in force size from conscriptions that would have occurred at the outbreak of World War III.

The Soviet Ground Forces did not offer the precision instruments needed to wage hybrid warfare. On the contrary, the Soviet Red Army was more akin to a steamroller. During the 1930s and leading up to WW2, Germany transformed its Wehrmacht (Army) into the most sophisticated fighting force the world had ever seen, with the best equipment and training, an ultra-modern air force (dubbed the Luftwaffe), lightning-fast panzer divisions, and a frighteningly professional officer corps inherited from the Prussian aristocracy.

The Wehrmacht seemed invincible when Hitler ordered his generals to initiate Operation Barbarossa, the invasion of the Soviet Union. But, despite catastrophic Soviet losses during the early invasion deep within the heart of the motherland, Soviet Ground Forces (also known as the Red Army) proved immovable.

They stopped the German advance at Stalingrad in the south, Moscow in the center, and Leningrad in the north. The Wehrmacht killed 9 Red Army soldiers for every single German soldier, but the massive tank armies of Soviet Field Marshal Georgy Zhukov rolled westward over all organized resistance with a macabre inevitability. Even 80 years later, the horrors of what the Red Army did to the Wehrmacht are seared into the collective consciousness of Europe.

Russia, however, was sorely incapable of sustaining this massive war-fighting capability. Moscow was forced to leverage hybrid warfare to compete directly with the West, necessitating a massive overhaul of the Russian Ground Forces (Army and VDV).

Naval Forces—A Submarine-Based Blue Water Navy

While the Soviet Navy was a true blue-water force that could project power globally, strategic planners viewed it as a "blue belt of defense". Its primary purpose was to deny access to Soviet coastal waters and undermine NATO's free traverse of the world's oceans, especially in the Northern Atlantic.

Admiral Gorshkov, appointed Soviet Naval Commander-in-Chief in 1956, sired late- and post-Soviet naval doctrine. Gorshkov realized that the backbone members of NATO (United States, United Kingdom, and France) were all seafaring powers with sophisticated blue-water navies.

To even the odds, he designed a navy where the nuclear submarine served as the backbone and primary strike tool.

Ballistic missile submarines would serve as the naval component of the Soviet nuclear triad (alongside strategic bombers and missile silos). Hunter-killer submarines (attack and cruise-missile subs) would hunt NATO's ballistic missile submarines, hound carrier battle groups, and strike at transatlantic supply convoys supporting the European Theater.

Because of the key role that naval aviation plays in hunting submarines, Gorshkov understood that contesting NATO air supremacy would be vital to any campaign that relied on submarine warfare. Soviet submarines would therefore have to be protected by naval aviation (land and carrier-based) and supported by the surface fleets, creating a doctrinal paradox for the Soviet Navy.

For Soviet hunter-killer submarines to stalk American ballistic missile submarines, carrier battle groups, and supply convoys, Soviet hunter-killer submarines would have to operate in the open ocean, far from the protection of land-based Soviet naval aircraft. This meant that Soviet submarines would fall under the protection of the Soviet carriers and surface warfare fleets, which were grossly outclassed by their NATO counterparts.

Thus, Soviet hunter-killer subs would be vulnerable to NATO carrier-based anti-submarine warfare (ASW) aircraft. Without massive capital expenditures towards creating a credible carrier battle group with multiple operational air wings, Soviet submarines would be dangerously exposed when operating anywhere but in Soviet coastal waters, which is incompatible with their primary mission. The problem remains quite intractable in Russian naval strategy today.

One does not usually consider the Navy's role in Russia's hybrid conflicts and military interventions, but the Navy is an important pillar. For Russia to credibly extend its reach to places like Syria, Africa, or Latin America, it would need to revise its doctrine of using the Navy as a "blue belt of defense" and move towards a Navy more capable of open ocean dominance.

Such a transformation requires extensive modernization and shipbuilding and is still underway at the time of publication. Moscow envisions a blue-water navy reemerging from the rusted Soviet legacy that can guarantee access to foreign markets and resources and can support the deployment of troops abroad like the American Navy does.

The Air Forces—Oddly Similar to Soviet Ground Forces

Germany's Luftwaffe demonstrated to the Soviets how important air superiority was to supporting advancing ground forces. The Soviets applied this lesson in the same way they approached land warfare: with a mission to maintain a massive overmatch in forces and firepower. The Soviets maintained an Air Force and a separate Air Defense Force.

While the Air Force had an offensive role, the Air Defense Force was responsible for protecting Soviet air space.

The Air Defense Force maintained squadrons of fighter aircraft that could race to intercept approaching strategic bombers. Soviet military planners considered the Air Defense Force to be the third-ranked strategic funding priority behind Strategic Rocket Forces and Ground Forces. Alternatively, the Soviet Air Force was assigned three tasks: establish and maintain air superiority, destroy enemy nuclear delivery capabilities, and support ground forces.

The Soviets assumed there would be time to mobilize their air forces during a short crisis preceding any hostilities. Following the mobilization period, the Soviet Air Force would initiate an enormous theaterwide air campaign against enemy nuclear delivery systems, airfields, and air defense installations. Following this, the air forces would transition to supporting the advance of Soviet Ground Forces in a breakout into Western Europe.

Russian military planners were eventually forced to fold the legacy Air Defense Force into the Air Force, creating the unified Aerospace Forces. The Soviet-styled mass mobilization of aircraft to overwhelm the enemy was far too imprecise and wasteful. Hybrid warfare requires a sophisticated air force that can deliver precision-guided munitions ahead of advancing armored ground forces or independent detachments of special operations forces.

A new joint command structure would also have to be established so that a single joint force commander could coordinate air and ground operational capabilities to the greatest effect.

Strategic Rocket Forces—Mutually Assured Destruction

The Strategic Rocket Forces constituted the silo, rail, and mobile truck-based strategic deterrent of the Soviet Union. The Strategic Rocket Forces complement the Air Forces' strategic bombers and the Navy's submarine-launched ballistic missiles (SLBM) pillars of the Soviet nuclear triad. All of the Soviet strategic nuclear forces as well as the Soviet Union's treaty commitments and permanent status in the U.N. Security Council were inherited by the Russian Federation.

In 1990, the total Soviet nuclear complement was estimated to be 1,398 Inter-Continental Ballistic Missiles (ICBMs) with 6,612 accompanying warheads, 940 submarine-launched ballistic missiles (SLBMs) with 2,804 accompanying warheads, and 160 strategic bombers with 855 accompanying warheads (Total: 2,500 launchers and 10,271 warheads).

The tragic reality is that the Earth will most likely never be free of nuclear arsenals, and Moscow considers modernizing its inherited nuclear deterrent to be its highest strategic priority.

American General Matthew Ridgeway wrote a number of compelling papers while working in the Pentagon before the Korean War in which he postulated that, because the world has nuclear arsenals, the inherent risks of a nation committing itself to a full-scale war are too high to contemplate. He concluded that future conflicts would often be undeclared and fought in small engagements at a comparatively low scale, preferably through proxy forces.

While Ridgeway accurately prophesied future American conflicts in Korea, Vietnam, and Afghanistan, his predictions also apply to the emergence of Russian hybrid warfare. As Russia modernizes its nuclear arsenal, hybrid warfare and other forms of limited conflict may be the only forms of warfare that Moscow is willing to risk.

Russia Begins to Reshape Its Soviet Inheritance

The massive military capability that Russia inherited from the Soviet Union steadily crumbled into a rusted mess of incompetence and corruption. Worse, Russia's generals and military planners maintained enough political leverage to nullify most attempts at reform by the Yeltsin Administration throughout the 1990s. The real impetus for reform would only come from the embarrassing defeat during The First Chechen War (1994-1996).

Russian Ground Forces were shown to be top-heavy (too many officers for too few soldiers), incompetently led, poorly supported, unable to coordinate, inadequately trained, and unmotivated. Russian Air Forces revealed a complete inability to coordinate with Ground Forces during the conflict. Planes were undermaintained, functioned poorly in combat, and lacked precision-guided munitions for close air support.

In the end, Russian Air Forces were often forced to resort to carpet bombing as the only means available to support ground operations.

As Vladimir Putin rose to power, restoring Russia's prestige became the highest national priority. Putin ran for President (keep in mind that, as Prime Minister, he was promoted to "acting President" after Yeltsin resigned) on a simple message: he would restore Russia to its rightful place among the world's great nations and increase the common standard of living. Putin would pursue these tasks by reinvesting oil and natural gas revenues from state-owned enterprises like Gazprom and Rozneft.

Though the public did see some modest standard of living increases during President Putin's early years (aided by rising oil prices), reforming the Russian Armed Services and intelligence apparatus became the cornerstone of restoring national honor. All other campaign promises were secondary.

Russia's success in the Second Chechen War, where the Ground Forces adopted a Soviet-style steamroller approach against Chechen partisans, was discussed in Chapter 2. The tactic of monopolizing violence within the battlespace worked extremely well, especially considering it was executed by poorly funded forces and led by incompetent and corrupt officers. But the downside for the Russian government was that mass artillery barrages, carpet bombing campaigns, city razing, and brutal assassinations by Spetsnaz-led kill teams generated horrific images of war for world newspapers. In the aftermath of the wars with Chechnya, Russian military analysts realized that such barbaric approaches were untenable in an increasingly connected world.

The overwhelming costs in blood, treasure, and public opinion necessitated a different approach in the future, creating the impetus for abandoning the Soviet Inheritance in exchange for a modern force capable of waging hybrid warfare.

Military reform began with the basics. Pilots received additional flight hours. Soldiers spent more time on the rifle range. The officer corps was subject to a series of anti-corruption campaigns that resulted in surreptitious purges. Line unit tanks and APCs were put on consistent maintenance schedules. The size of standing Russian armed forces was reduced from the Soviet levels of over 3 million in 1990 to 1.1 million by 2008.

State Armaments Program (GPV) 2020 and 2027

President Putin and his entourage knew that resurrecting the Russian Armed Services would require modernizing force structures, improving training, and promoting professionalism; however, these reforms also needed to be accompanied by modernized combat systems and equipment.

Hybrid warfare requires precision-guided munitions, sophisticated command-and-control (C2) infrastructure, mobility, digital communications, and advanced air forces to support highly aggressive offensive actions effectively. To this end, Putin and his national security team initiated the State Armaments Program 2020 (GPV 2020) at the tail end of 2010.

At a staggering cost of approximately ₽20.7 trillion ($700 billion U.S dollars), Russian authorities planned for GPV 2020 procurements to run through the next decade. It was an extraordinarily large expenditure for an economy smaller than the State of Texas, indicating just how seriously President Putin and his national security cadre took modernization efforts. About ₽19 trillion was allocated to support spending on procurement, and the remaining ₽1.7 trillion was allocated to modernizing the military-industrial complex.

The funds themselves were backloaded in disbursements. One-third was disbursed from 2011 to 2015, and two-thirds disbursed from 2016 to 2020 (after much of the military-industrial complex had undergone an overhaul). GPV 2020 focused heavily on procurements for the decrepit Navy, the Aerospace Forces (the new service formed from consolidating the Soviet-era Air Forces and Air Defense Forces), and the Strategic Rocket Forces. Despite being a point of pride, the Russian Ground Forces had the least ground to cover in modernization and received the remaining funds.

In September 2014, President Putin convened a high-level meeting to begin drafting the next decade-long state armaments program, intended to be initiated in 2015. Due to Western sanctions in response to the Russian annexation of Crimea and corresponding constraints of the Russian economy, the program, eventually known as GPV 2027, would not be approved until late 2017.

Funds allocated to GPV 2027 closely resemble GPV 2020: approximately ₽19 trillion for the procurement of military equipment, modernization, and research & development, and ₽1 trillion allocated to invest in military-industrial infrastructure.

GPV 2027 inverted the priorities of GPV 2020 to evenly round out support for the capabilities of each of Russia's Armed Services. The Ground Forces received a much larger share of the budget for new tanks, to include IFVs and APCs, and Electronic Warfare systems (equipment that is particularly useful for hybrid warfare). Naval procurements for large surface ships were put on hold until port infrastructure and naval shipyards could be modernized.

The bulk of Naval procurements focused on advanced submarines (a bright spot in the military-industrial complex's otherwise moribund production of naval vessels) and small but advanced surface ships. Military industries were also unable to produce new fighters like the Su-57 in sufficient volume for the Aerospace Forces.

Aerospace Forces planners directed firms like Mikoyan and Sukhoi to produce modernized variants of legacy aircraft like the Su-35 (an updated variant of the venerable Su-27) and Mig-35 (an updated variant of the world-renowned Mig-29). As Russia's most credible deterrent, the Strategic Rocket Forces continued to be the highest priority in Research & Development.

In 2008, only 10% of Russian military armaments were categorized as "modern". The primary goal of GPV 2020 was to update or replace Soviet legacy armaments and systems. The target that planners set in 2008 was to increase the "modern" share to 30% by 2015 and 70% by 2020.

From the beginning and for much of the program's life, the Russian military industrial complex has appeared insufficient for such a massive undertaking.

In 2017, the Defense Ministry announced that 79% of Strategic Rocket Forces, 45% of Ground Forces, 53% of the Navy, and 73% of Aerospace Forces were modernized. Moreover, Russian industries met these production targets despite Western sanctions. Taking such assessments of the modernization of equipment with more than a little salt, it would still seem that GPV 2020 was a resounding success.

GPV 2027 (initiated in 2018) builds on the success of GVP 2020, focusing on mobility, the ability to deploy rapidly, C2 systems, improved logistics, and service branch integration and interoperability (joint operations, as an example). Procurement will continue the "quality over quantity" trend, shifting away from the Soviet-era focus on mass production and instead towards technical sophistication. The question is: what does Russia mean by "modern"?

"Modern" in the Russian parlance certainly does not mean that a system is equal or superior to Western counterparts. "Modern" as used by Moscow is more proximate to "good enough" or "effective in its purpose", or maybe "credibly competitive". Very little GPV 2020 and 2027 expenditures relate to research and development (R&D) of new systems (approximately 10-15%).

Instead, due to fiscal and production constraints, the focus is on updating legacy platforms rather than procuring entirely new ones. It is easy to dismiss such an approach, but the Russians have been wildly effective at controlling costs while delivering capable combat platforms.

Procurements continue to be obstructed by the limitations of the Russian military-industrial complex, which is in dire need of an overhaul itself. This is why President Putin and Defense Minister Serdyukov (and his successor Sergey Shoygu) have specifically allocated funds towards modernizing defense industries.

At the core of most Russian defense-industrial firms are Soviet-era engineers aged into their mid-70s, antiquated manufacturing facilities, and a corrupt corporate executive using personal ties and bribery to win state contracts. It is a miracle that any production targets were met for GPV 2020, let alone early: indicating just how effective the program has been.

GPV 2020 and 2027 have transformed the warfighting capacity of the Russian Armed Services, giving them the necessary technology to wage hybrid warfare. In addition to modern combat platforms, Russian R&D and procurements have focused on advanced Electronic Warfare systems and anti-access and area denial systems (A2/AD).

Capabilities in Electronic Warfare and A2/AD create asymmetric advantages for Russian Ground Forces in combat, ensuring that enemies cannot muster organized resistance to rapid Russian advances. Their use has been integrated into Russian tactics, techniques, and procedures (TTPs), and these new platforms are ideal for hybrid warfare.

Despite the successes of GPV 2020 and GPV 2027, President Putin could not stop at buying the Russian Armed Services a bunch of fancy new tools. He had to ensure that these new systems were in the hands of a competent chain of command and trained soldiers. This meant painful reforms in military structure, education, planning, and finances, for which he set his new Defense Minister Anatoly Serdyukov to the task.

Anatoly Serdyukov's New Look

Anatoly Serdyukov was one of many public officials in Saint Petersburg that President Putin remembered when he became influential in Moscow. In 2004, Putin appointed Serdyukov head of the Tax Ministry (at the lobbying of Serdyukov's father-in-law, Prime Minister Viktor Zubkov), which, under Serdyukov's supervision, would be reorganized into the Federal Tax Service.

Many of Serdyukov's staff from Saint Petersburg were appointed to the Federal Tax Service as he pushed out or intentionally over-worked the old guard. One of his favorite practices was rotating personnel between the Federal Tax Service in Moscow and the regional tax service departments, which kept public servants on their toes and prevented them from staying in influential positions long enough to develop any inappropriate or corrupt relationships.

In February 2007, Anatoly Serdyukov was appointed as Russia's first civilian Defense Minister by Vladimir Putin. The explicit purpose of his appointment was to impose reforms on a stubborn and corrupt military establishment. The military establishment, particularly the General Staff, considered the appointment of a civilian with no real military experience a slap in the face.

Chief of General Staff at the time Yuri Baluyevsky personally led the public criticism of Serdyukov's appointment. When Victor Zubkov became Prime Minister, Serdyukov offered Putin his resignation (which was promptly rejected), as Zubkov was his father-in-law, and their working relationship would represent a conflict of interest. General Baluyevsky crowed to the press that next maybe Putin would appoint a woman in Serdyukov's place (this was not meant as a progressive suggestion, but as a derogatory and insulting remark).

Serdyukov retaliated by auditing how the members of the General Staff performed in the military's mandatory physical fitness tests. Most of the Generals failed, creating a media firestorm. Interestingly, failure to meet physical fitness standards soon became one of several justifications used to dismiss disruptive, corrupt, or incompetent senior officers.

In June 2007, General Yuri Baluyevsky was dismissed as Chief of the General Staff (he was given a consolation position on the Security Council), and General Nikolay Yegorovich Makarov was appointed to replace him on the General Staff.

For whatever legitimate reservations the General Staff had voiced about reform, the Russo-Georgian War demonstrated that Putin's efforts from 1999 forward had resulted in tangible improvements in military planning, leadership, professionalism, and coordination.

The war also revealed glaring weaknesses in operational execution, command and control, close air support (which was non-existent), antiquated military equipment, communications, logistics and supply, and more. Thus, Russia's first hybrid war of the 21st Century in Georgia gave Putin the political justification to compel deeper reforms despite the General Staff's stubborn institutional resistance.

Serdyukov brought unparalleled energy and fastidiousness to his job, forcing the General Staff into a subordinate position simply through his persistent oversight and mastery of finance. The General Staff was most likely grateful that he chose not to involve himself in day-to-day administration or strategic planning, but Serdyukov brought along a cadre of experts from the Federal Tax Service and created a financial control department for the Ministry of Defense.

Under the old system, the General Staff had managed the defense budget on its own. For years, the Kremlin had been increasing defense funding, and somehow all that money never seemed to make its way into new programs or combat systems.

After the implementation of the financial control department, generals began to walk to budget meetings like they were walking the last mile to the chair, knowing they would have to account for every kopeck.

Following Serdyukov's new budget oversight measures, as though by magic, defense spending began to have the desired effect. Programs began to slowly lurch forward. Numerous R&D projects made marked progress. Infantry companies discovered they had training funds and maintenance crews began slowly receiving new inventory of replacement parts.

The Ministry of Defense has been quiet about the number of generals and senior officials that were caught misallocating funds for personal gain. Of course, there were numerous high-profile cases that caught fire in the media, but those cases were most likely the tip of the iceberg. Serdyukov would eventually purge over one third of the officers in the Central Military Administration.

Serdyukov also championed severe cuts in personnel redundancies amongst the operational forces. When "New Look" reforms began, the Russian Armed Services had 1 officer for every 2 soldiers. He set a goal for 1 officer for every 15 soldiers. His personnel cuts would eventually relieve the armed forces of over 200,000 jobs (mostly officers).

Serdyukov also directed his small army of auditors to examine defense procurement corruption. Military industrial firms had to account for failures in delivering new systems that were ordered years ago. They were also asked hard questions about expensive R&D projects that were decades in the making with no tangible results.

Interestingly, the reforms championed by Serdyukov were not titled "reforms". A career bureaucrat would have been unlikely to win public support for military innovations if the public was aware that the generals, who presumably would have had some subject matter expertise, were universally opposed to his vision for the armed forces.

The solution to institutional opposition against reform was simply to call his program a "New Look", a deliberately ambiguous phrase that wouldn't immediately provoke backlash.

The New Look focused on six pillars: restructuring the officer corps, reorganizing command and control structures, eliminating skeleton units, reshaping military education, building a Non-Commissioned Officer (NCO) Corps, and professionalizing the force.

New Look structural and institutional reforms ran parallel to military modernization programs for armaments, systems, and hardware in GPV 2020 and its successor GPV 2027.

Despite being forced out of office before his plans could be fully implemented, Serdyukov's reforms had a profound impact on the overhead, professionalism, readiness, and financial footing of Russia's Armed Services.

Restructuring the Officer Corps

Restructuring the Officer Corps began with eliminating the excessive bloat from superfluous staffing requirements. The number of officers had to be cut from 355,000 to approximately 150,000. This reduction in the top-heavy nature of Russian military leadership was complemented with new, bottom-up subject matter expertise and the creation of a professional non-commissioned officer (NCO) corps.

The Russo-Georgian War shed light on a troubled officer corps that had proved itself incompetent, corrupt, and insubordinate. Indeed, there are many anecdotal stories of careerist colonels interviewing for brigade command only to admit in the interview that they did not know how to command a brigade at all.

The lack of a performance- or competence-based system of promotion was identified as the causal factor in the lack of officers' initiative towards mission accomplishment. Senior military leaders continue to rely on systematic purges, and personnel cuts to rid the system of outstanding instances of incompetence, but there remains no permanent institutional system in Russia for developing the kinds of officers that are requisite for a modern military.

Moreover, the Russian Armed Services have few institutionalized means for senior leaders to identify and retain outstanding junior officers for guided career development. The Soviet era was notorious for patronage-based career progression, and the Russian Federation continues the practice today.

Circumventing further institutional opposition to reforms, particularly from the General Staff, senior leaders have elected to use the interventions in Eastern Ukraine, Crimea, Syria, and other external conflicts in Russia's near-abroad as a substitute. Officers earmarked for advancement, particularly in the VDV, Ground Forces, and Aerospace Forces, are baptized in modern combat (combined arms maneuver and joint operations), giving them superior credentials for higher command.

Though it is not a permanent solution to the question of which officers to promote, a core cadre of Russian officers destined for higher command have been shaped by real combat experiences. As Russia engages in additional interventions in its near-abroad, it is likely that those conflicts will also serve as a proving ground for young top performers.

Russia will continue to have trouble promoting the most qualified officers, but the system of sending earmarked junior officers to combat zones for experience is effective at breeding the kinds of talent that hybrid war requires. Military bureaucracies are good at managing the status quo, but they are bad at innovation and risk-taking.

Officers groomed in peacetime to manage the day-to-day activities of the force are unlikely to engender such qualities. By selecting Russia's best officers through relevant combat experiences, Russia is tailoring the command structure towards modern warfare.

They are officers who are not afraid to seize the initiative or advance rapidly, and they are intimately familiar with combat systems and troop leading procedures.

Reorganizing Command and Control Structures

The Russo-Georgian War exposed the inefficiencies of the previous system of command and control (C2). The legacy Soviet-style C2 had four successive levels: military district, army, division, and regiment. Reform led to a new, more flexible system with only three levels: military district, joint operational command, and brigade.

The antiquated Soviet system relied on armies as the operational level unit and divisions as the unit of maneuver. Russian Ground Forces' new operational unit became the smaller, lighter, more flexible brigade.

Since Serdyukov's time, Russian planners have had second thoughts on fully committing to independent brigades with maneuver and line battalions, choosing to maintain a few independent divisions with maneuver regiments in several instances, as well. These divisions usually consist of regiments with the same number of line battalions as an independent brigade, but these regiments each have a larger proportion of their support and logistics assets concentrated at the division level.

The Russian Armed Services are taking a joint approach to the modern battlefield. The service branches and military districts provide forces to joint operational commands established for specific missions or interventions. Russia's six military districts were reorganized into four military districts (called Western Military District, Central Military District, Eastern Military District, Southern Military District) and one military command (the Northern Fleet Joint Strategic Command). Generals have command of all formations within their respective military districts (except for Strategic Rocket Forces) and serve as force providers for external conflicts. The new National Defense Management Center (NTsUO) was founded, leveraging innovations in Information Technology (IT) to connect Moscow to joint operations and military district commands. The NTsUO unifies and integrates all Russian C4ISR (command, control, communications, computers, intelligence, surveillance, and reconnaissance) into a single center.

The Russians continue to use a General Staff system that follows the Prussian model of military administration (rather than the Anglo-American), meaning that most officers will never rise above the rank of major or lieutenant colonel (field grade officers). But the field grade officers that show the aptitude (criteria varies, but promotees usually come from the top 10% of military academy graduates, have combat experience, have politicians that are personally invested in their careers, and have spotless records) are promoted to serve as permanent staff officers on the General Staff where they are groomed for higher command.

The Russian General Staff, which has powers similar to the American Office of the Secretary of Defense and subordinate geographic combatant commanders, conducts all military planning, establishes doctrine, and oversees all procurements.

Officers on the General Staff specialize as planning assistants to the Generals, and officers in the service branches can permanently specialize in leading their units without concern for future career progression or staff officer duty. In layman's terms, an infantry battalion commander will always be an infantry battalion commander.

Rather than transitioning through broadening assignments, higher education opportunities, and staff officer time (the way Western officers do), Russian field grade officers focus strictly on excellence in leading their troops.

Alternatively, as selected officers take their place on the General Staff, they become responsible for planning in their previous specialties. For example, an infantry officer will serve in planning as an infantry subject matter expert, while a signals officer will serve as a signals subject matter expert.

Hybrid warfare is not possible without sophisticated C2 systems (hence the emerging term C4ISR to better describe advanced command and control processes), and C2 begins with capable officers. Still, as stated in Chapter 2, Russian hybrid warfare uses network-centric warfare (the deployment of advanced IT networks and communications) to achieve informational superiority.

Moscow has created a central command center called the National Defense Management Center (NTsUO) that unifies and integrates all Russian C4ISR, supporting enhanced political awareness and control over Russia's military engagements. NTsUO gives the General Staff and the Kremlin the ability to coordinate intelligence activities, SOF, forward ground and air components, and numerous indirect influences on the battlefield with greater precision and decisive action.

The General Staff also provides persistent planning in doctrine, procurements, and oversight, binding these elements together to support a sophisticated war machine that wages hybrid conflicts.

Reshaping Military Education

Serdyukov correctly assessed that building a highly professional military would mean modernizing the military education system. The "New Look" reduced the number of military education centers from 65 different institutions of varying types to just 10, consisting of 6 academies, three joint centers, and one university.

The curriculum is now focused on practical training (as opposed to a more theoretical or managerial approach to education common to Western military academies) and all officers are required to learn a foreign language.

One anecdotal example of the new prioritization of a "quality over quantity" mentality emerging in the Russian military education system is the revised General Staff Academy, which admitted only 16 officers in 2009, compared to 100 officers in 2008, before the "New Look" had been initiated.

Another educational innovation worthy of note was the establishment of a permanent NCO training center at the Ryazan Higher Airborne School. The VDV (Russian Airborne) retained its status as Russia's premier fighting force, demonstrating superior readiness and fighting spirit over the Ground Forces, first in Georgia and later in Crimea and Donbas. The VDV's accomplishments prompted the idea that new NCOs should draw from traditions of the Airborne and Air Assault infantry.

Hybrid warfare requires capable officers who understand how to maneuver their units on the battlefield, not just to defeat an enemy formation and achieve the desired political end-state. To this end, Russia's reformed military education system no longer seeks to churn out large numbers of officers indoctrinated in the communist ideal, but practical problem-solvers willing to lean forward in their respective tasks.

Building a Non-Commissioned Officer (NCO) Corps

The Russian General Staff is against building a professional cadre of sergeants (non-commissioned officers) to fill the Russian armed forces' junior leadership roles, and such proposals remain extremely controversial. Institutional resistance also comes from the Officer corps in general, which views empowered NCOs as a challenge to their authority and prestige. But the Russo-Georgian War made it clear that the Russian Armed Services, especially the Ground Forces, required competent junior leadership.

There is evidence that Serdyukov envisioned a Western-style NCO corps: something that both the collective consciousness of the Officer corps and General Staff had long ago decided against. Some Western defense analysts believe that, as Serdyukov delegated resources to building a professional NCO corps that could enforce discipline and oversee training the General Staff actively undermined implementation. Whatever the truth in the Ministry of Defense's intrigue, Serdyukov's vision was almost certainly blunted by the size of the task at hand.

Building a competent NCO corps from scratch, at least in the Anglo-American model, is not a trivial task. Good NCOs are not taught in academies so much as grown organically through field and combat experience. Even junior NCOs (corporals or sergeants) in the United States Army typically had one or two combat deployments from the last two decades of conflict, as they must have been soldiers for 3 to 5 years before becoming junior leaders. The free societies of the West lend well to delegating leadership tasks to subordinates.

First, soldiers obey their sergeants because of force of personality. There is a reason sergeants are known for being mean, hard bastards. Second, soldiers follow leaders who demonstrate competence, hence why being a sergeant requires practical knowledge and experience.

Lastly, officers usually bestow on sergeants a formal promotion above their peers, indicating that the newly minted NCO has the Commander's full trust and confidence as a leader. Good sergeants are trained in their units over many years. Outstanding instances of informal leadership are identified by superiors and then officers invest in these individuals through development opportunities until they are ready to be formally promoted and given real responsibilities.

Rather than create a new class of junior leaders, the Russian General Staff seems to have subverted Serdyukov's original intent to navigate this tedious developmental process. Instead, after some haphazard experimentation, the General Staff implemented a system where Russian NCOs train to be technical experts rather than true "leaders".

In the Ministry of Defense's first attempt to create an NCO corps, planners founded an academy within the Ryazan Higher Airborne School that offers curriculum in 17 areas of military specialization. Originally, the Ministry of Defense recruited civilians and soldiers for almost three years of NCO training at the academy. After that time, they were supposed to take on responsibilities in their units. This method did not work very well, principally because too few NCO candidates could be forced through such a long training pipeline and, after new NCOs completed their training, they arrived at their new units without any prior relationship to the soldiers under their charge.

The second attempt to create an NCO corps was a stopgap measure insisted upon by Serdyukov. Five thousand military academy graduates who were slated to be commissioned as Junior Lieutenants were inserted into NCO positions as sergeants (with lieutenant's pay) and promised a commission as soon as a platoon commander (or deputy platoon commander) position opened up. Though these measures at least filled vacant NCO billets, these academy graduates had neither the practical experience nor gravitas necessary for junior leadership roles as envisioned by Serdyukov, and they lacked the technical expertise for subject matter expert roles as envisioned by the General Staff.

Moreover, the young men who had endured years of hard study at the Russian Military Academy must have been livid when they discovered they were not going to receive an officer's commission out of the gate. The controversial practice of appointing junior officers to NCO billets was phased out after Serdyukov was ousted from office in 2012. By 2016, the Ministry of Defense had fewer than 1,000 such academy graduates assigned to sergeant and petty officer (Naval NCOs) positions.

Finally, in 2017, the General Staff released standardized training guidelines for personnel, including career pathways for contract soldiers seeking NCO billets (billets that fit the technical expert role more than the leadership role). The new system set a tiered NCO rank progression and training requirements at Ryazan at each new rank. This offered professional soldiers career progression with increasing authority and pay at each level, and it harnessed the academy to augment the practical experience that prospective sergeants receive in their respective units as soldiers.

Tier-1 contains newly recruited contracted soldiers who serve in entry-level positions. Their training includes 6 weeks of basic training and 3-10 months of Military Occupational Specialty (MOS) training.

Conscript soldiers are also at the Tier-1 level but, because they fill menial roles, they cannot advance and do not require MOS training.

Tier-2 contains squad leaders, tank commanders, crew leaders, and other junior leadership positions. Candidates for Tier-2 receive 3 months of additional leadership training (at Ryazan Higher Airborne School) and must have demonstrated technical proficiency while serving a minimum of 2 years in Tier-1.

Tier-3 contains platoon and deputy platoon leaders (a billet filled by junior officers). Candidates for Tier-3 require service in a Tier-2 position for 3-5 years and must undergo an additional 3 months of training.

Tier-4 contains NCOs serving on staff at regiments, brigades, and divisions. Candidates are Tier-3 NCOs who have served at least 10 years, and they must undergo 3-5 months of staff training at the Ryazan Higher Airborne Command School (RVVDKU).

Tier-5 contains NCOs serving on staff at the Army Group level or higher. Candidates are Tier-4 NCOs who have served at least 15 years. They receive 3-5 months of staff training at the Ryazan Higher Airborne Command School (RVVDKU).

By the end of 2017, all Ground Forces and Airborne Forces NCO positions had been filled by professional contract soldiers.

The introduction of a professional NCO Corps of subject matter experts (and pseudo-leaders) bodes well for the performance of Russian units in future hybrid conflicts. Having experts that are intimately familiar with their jobs, the combat systems, and the inner workings of the military bureaucracy greases the wheels of military operations.

Units in garrison maintain a higher standard of readiness and are more capable of rapidly deploying. Units in combat perform with greater efficiency. The Russian General Staff refused to support a Western-style NCO Corps; however, given Russia's dearth of young talent (Russia has low-quality public education, numerous public health crises, and few qualified young people), the Russian system may actually be better served by a cadre of NCO technical experts that can be retained in their respective roles over the course of their careers. Time will tell.

Professionalization of the Russian Armed Forces

The foundation on which the Serdyukov New Look reforms are built is the overall professionalization of Russian Armed Services. Contract soldiers are generally considered to be more motivated than their conscript counterparts; however, when the New Look reforms were first initiated, contract soldiers were still considered an unnecessary personnel expense.

By 2012, Serdyukov was slowly changing this mentality amongst Russian military planners, and he set goals to achieve a 5:4 ratio of contract soldiers to conscripts by 2017 (meaning approximately 420,000-450,000 contract soldiers would have to be recruited). This component of Russian military modernization was mostly successful.

All Russian men under the age of 27 are liable for 2 years of mandatory military service. They are usually chosen by lottery, as the Russian armed forces are not large enough for every young man in the country to join (unlike the Soviet armed forces), but young men can be exempted for a variety of reasons (higher education opportunities, political connections, and technology-oriented career fields).

As the Ministry of Defense scales up the recruitment of contract soldiers who can choose when, where, and how they serve, conscriptions scale down. By 2015, the number of contract soldiers exceeded the number of conscripts.

Since 2017, all NCO vacancies have been manned by contract soldiers. Although experience and authority remain problems for NCO leadership, positions are now filled by a more motivated pool of talent.

In 2017, conscripts numbered 276,000 with 384,000 contract soldiers. Military planners sought to achieve a manning of 499,200 contract soldiers by the end of 2020 (Western analysts believe they came just short of their 2020 goal), but the Ministry of Defense continues to offer recruits wages that stack up well against the average Russian annual salary.

Eliminating Skeleton Units

The elimination of "skeleton units" proved to be one of Serdyukov's most controversial reforms. It not only purged the military of thousands of officers, but also effectively ended the enduring Soviet concept of mass mobilization.

Under the old system, surplus officers were given command of "skeleton units", which in the event of a national mobilization to war, could be immediately filled out with a massive influx of conscript soldiers. During peacetime, the skeleton units sat still, and the officers assigned to manage them did very little because they had no troops or equipment to manage.

It is easy and boring leading a military unit that does not have any soldiers, breeding incompetence and corruption. So, while Serdyukov preserved some components of mobilization plans like weapons storage facilities and equipment, Russian Ground Forces were reduced to a trim 172 active divisions and brigades. The small number of divisions deeply offended generals old enough to remember the vast forces of the Red Army, but Russia's 172 remaining units would be fully manned with professional soldiers called "kontraktnik" (Russian: контрактник) and would maintain a permanent status of readiness.

To put these force reductions in perspective, of the Ground Forces' 22,000 non-antiquated tanks, which were either inherited from the Soviet era or constructed from Soviet-era designs, only 2,000 would be kept in a state of readiness for operations.

The old Soviet mass-mobilization approach to waging war is dead, and hybrid warfare has become the dominant Russian modus operandi. Serdyukov's New Look reforms created a greatly reduced, but much more battle-ready force structure. All officers would command troops. All units would receive annual training and modern equipment.

Excess units (skeleton units) were discarded. Surplus (under-performing) officers were retired. An army that relies on drafted conscripts and inexperienced officers is hardly capable of rapid combined arms maneuver, precise coordination of close air support, or any of the other activities that are part and parcel to hybrid warfare.

Battalion Tactical Groups

Western analysts frequently categorize the emergence of Battalion Tactical Groups (BTGs) as another solution to the Russian Armed Services' chronic man-power shortages. Despite great efforts made to fully professionalize the force, the Russian Ground Forces still rely heavily on conscripts who, by law, cannot be deployed to combat unless there is a national mobilization.

BTGs are constructed around a regiment's or brigade's contract soldiers, who are concentrated into a single line or maneuver battalion (typically a motorized rifle battalion that is based on the BMP-3 or BTR-M infantry fighting vehicle). This single infantry battalion is complimented with up to the entire regiment's or brigade's armor, fire support, ISR, and support assets. This gives Russian Ground Forces a basic tactical unit that is legally deployable and, at least on paper, is capable of out-gunning and destroying units of much greater size by engaging their components in detail.

As a hybrid warfare tool, the BTG's operational priority is to control terrain. It does this by concentrating strike assets and leveraging extensive ISR resources to inform precision fires and maneuver against enemy forces. BTGs deployed in hybrid warfare also leverage local paramilitary proxies to provide security and deny key terrain.

This frees a BTG's limited maneuver companies from security tasks and allows them to be concentrated on designated points of attack. The performance of a BTG is highly dependent on executing a sophisticated scheme of maneuver for forces and fires through advanced C2 (and therefore requires an excellent command staff).

BTGs are generally thought to have two Achilles Heels. First, they are extremely vulnerable in the field (especially without supporting proxy forces) because there are only three infantry companies available to protect an entire regiment or brigade's worth of support assets. Second, BTGs must coordinate a regiment or brigade's complement of support assets with a mere battalion's C2 assets (HQ and Command staff and signals platoon).

Dedovshchina—Abuses in the Armed Forces

One of the most subversive problems facing the Russian Armed Services is the system of dedovshchina (Russian: дедовщи́на). Dedovshchina is an informal system of brutally hazing newly recruited conscript soldiers, usually committed by experienced conscript soldiers with more than a year in service.

In Soviet times, when almost all junior leadership roles were performed by officers, the abuses would occur once a platoon's lieutenant had gone home for the night. The Russian Armed Services have done little over the past thirty years to reform these practices.

Dedovschina has made the Russian public very fearful of having its sons serve in the military. It hampers recruitment efforts for contract soldiers and creates profound problems in retaining experienced soldiers once their contract or conscription terms are over.

Hazing is a very light word for the abuses that occur under dedovshchina. While some abuses are relatively trivial, like requiring junior soldiers to do chores and basic housekeeping tasks of barracks life, soldiers are also routinely beaten, humiliated, sexually abused, raped, and tortured.

In 2006 alone, the New York Times reported that violent physical abuse claimed the lives of 292 Russian soldiers, either by accidental death during the abuse or by suicide after the abuse.

In one particularly appalling case, a soldier was ordered by a drunken senior to squat on the balls of his feet for hours on end. Despite pleas that he could not feel his legs, the senior would not relieve him. Eventually, the soldier was able to return to bed, but he was diagnosed with blood clots in both his legs the next day, likely due to an extended lack of circulation from his squatted position. As the clots became infected, the soldier was transferred to a civilian hospital where eventually the doctors were forced to amputate both his legs and his genitals.

Russian psychologists have documented hundreds of instances where conscript soldiers suffered from serious psychopathy for the rest of their lives after completing their term of military service (further contributing to the Russian public's chronic problems of alcoholism and opiate abuse).

The prison-like conditions of the military barracks drive low retention rates of experienced soldiers, and they are undermining the overall professionalization of the Russian Armed Services. And because Russia's NCOs lack any real authority by design, they have not been very successful in putting an end to these abuses.

Ultimately, dedovshchina is the result of a closed-off system. The Russian public does not know what happens in the barracks except what their sons relate to them after getting out of the service. The Russian press publishes particularly egregious abuses on the rare instance that the incident cannot be silenced.

Strong NCOs would help rein in abuses, but the best cure is transparency, something the Russian government has never tolerated. Open investigations in dedovshchina embarrass battalion officers, the General Staff, and the Russian Armed Services as a whole. Conditions are slowly improving, particularly with the increased use of contract soldiers, but dedovshchina remains a persistent problem in the ranks.

The End of Anatoly Serdyukov

To better understand the problems that the Russian Federal Government faces in instituting real reforms in the Ministry of Defense, it is worth a brief detour to examine the intrigue that led to the demise of Anatoly Serdyukov.

Defense Minister Serdyukov seemed a gifted and determined reformer who cracked down hard on corruption in the military establishment. Implications by Russian attorney and tax advisor Sergei Magnitsky, however, revealed that Serdyukov was highly corrupt himself, even before he was appointed Defense Minister.

Sergei Magnitsky represented the American investment firm Hermitage Capital Management against allegations of tax fraud by the Russian government. On June 4, 2007, Russian tax investigators raided Hermitage's Moscow office under a warrant to investigate underpaid taxes and seized hundreds of documents that had nothing to do with the audit. Magnitsky was commissioned by Hermitage Capital Management to investigate the claims made by Russian tax authorities.

Magnitsky discovered that the police had given the confiscated materials to an organized criminal tax ring. The police had accused Hermitage of underpaying taxes in order to create a justification for the raid. After the raid, with Hermitage's internal finance documentation in hand, the Russian tax investigators (read: organized criminals) then forged a change in ownership of Hermitage's holdings in three Russian companies. Following this, they forged contracts to falsely indicate that Hermitage owned $1 billion in shell companies through these primary three companies.

The tax investigators and their police, judicial, and Ministry of Interior Affairs co-conspirators hired and bribed attorneys to file in court against these shell companies for payment of outstanding debts, and then hired and bribed more attorneys to "represent" Hermitage's fake shell companies in court. Without Hermitage's knowledge, these attorneys pleaded guilty on the company's behalf to judgments for debts that did not exist.

After there was a binding court ruling in place against the company for outstanding debts, Hermitage was no longer profitable on paper and could therefore receive a tax write-off for the interest on its outstanding debts and expenses. This criminal tax ring filed a tax return on behalf of Hermitage with the Russian Federal Government in the amount of $230 million. The refund, which was the largest in Russian history, was issued on December 24, 2007.

Because Magnitsky's investigation implicated the Ministry of Internal Affairs, police, judges, numerous attorneys, federal tax officers, auditors, bankers, and the mafia, Russian authorities arranged for Magnitsky to be arrested under the false charges of conspiring to perpetrate tax fraud with Hermitage in November 2008.

After 11 months of squalor living conditions, beatings, starvation, and genuine torture (far exceeding the magnitude of Western water-boarding practices), Sergei Magnitsky died without a trial. The conspirators simply could not compel Magnitsky to confess to crimes he had not committed. Despite their drastic attempts to keep it under wraps, outside eyes began to pry, and the story became too sensational for the conspirators to contain.

Magnitsky had implicated Defense Minister Serdyukov as the apex of this $230 million tax corruption pyramid. Serdyukov's mistress, Yevegeniya Vasileyva, was implicated in Magnitsky's investigation as well. She was eventually charged with stealing over $100 million from Oboronservis, a state-owned (Ministry of the Defense and Ministry of the Internal Affairs) holding company that was originally established to run the Russian military's non-core operations (logistics, repairs, and maintenance), but gradually transformed into a military property real estate company.

Vasileyva served as director and Serdyukov had recently served as chairman. Vasileyva had been liquidating State assets to pay kickbacks to government officials. The police raided her home and found Serdyukov there in a bathrobe.

It is an open question whether Serdyukov was fired for overseeing a massive grift in his personal time while hypocritically purging grifters in his day job, or whether he was fired for having an affair. He was married to Yulia Pokhlebenina, the daughter of Prime Minister Viktor Zubkov, one of the most powerful men in Russia and one of President Putin's closest friends (today Zubkov is the chairman of Russia's state-owned energy conglomerate Gazprom). In 2000, the year Serdyukov married Yulia, Zubkov was serving as the head of the Saint Petersburg Tax Office. Zubkov appointed Serdyukov, then a furniture salesman, to be his deputy and gave Serdyukov career guidance that eventually led to the Defense Ministry.

In either case, once Serdyukov's enemies realized that he was vulnerable, sharks began to circle, and President Putin was forced to accept his resignation. He left office on November 6, 2012, handing over the reins of the Ministry of Defense reform to Sergey Shoygu.

The Russian system is plagued by this kind of corruption, and it tragically infects not just the military but all attempts to deliver meaningful reform to the public. Infrastructure continues to atrophy. The education system has not been rebuilt since the Soviet collapse. The average Russian citizen lives on a scant $635 per month and, due to a dearth of tax revenue, the government must be propped up by oil and natural gas revenues.

Russia also has inverted demographics, with more retirees than working people, making it impossible to have a consumption-led economy. These challenges continue to frustrate President Putin's vision for the country and, even though Russian military reforms continue to gain ground, systemic corruption will always be present behind the headline successes. This means that, when Russia wages hybrid warfare, it is always fighting with one foot in a bucket.

The Russian Armed Forces Without Serdyukov

Despite the fact that Serdyukov was ousted from office in November 2012, his "New Look" has had a profound impact on the force structure, financial sustainability, procurement programs, discipline, and training regimes of the Russian Armed Services. His reform agenda outlived his tenure in office and transformed the Soviet steamroller conscript force of mass-mobilization into a professional force with a joint command structure.

The next Minister of Defense Sergey Shoygu was simultaneously the leader of United Russia (Putin's political party), Governor of Moscow Oblast, and Minister of Emergency Situations. At first, Shoygu was supportive of the New Look reforms, and he protected the funds that were earmarked for procurements and research and development.

Professionalization of the Armed Services remained a high priority for Shoygu and he is supportive of efforts to create an NCO Corps (albeit not so much for leadership as for technical expertise). He also retained the structural changes made to the military education system and C2. Most importantly, Shoygu followed through with the implementation of GPV 2020 and GPV 2027 procurement programs that would transform Russian military systems, platforms, and hardware. Shoygu has insisted on combat readiness through snap inspections (made personally) and training drills.

However, Shoygu has also tried to heal the rift between the Office of the Defense Minister and the General Staff. He chose to wear a military uniform to show that he is a team player despite having never actually served in the ranks. Most troublingly, Shoygu brought back many individuals that Serdyukov fired due to corruption or incompetence, and he dissolved the Financial Control Department.

Serdyukov's reforms may exist on paper, especially through headline grabbing procurement programs like GPV 2020 and 2027, but the deep institutional rot may have returned.

Summary and Conclusions

The Soviet Union bequeathed the Russian Armed Services an underfunded, undermaintained, rusted, and incompetent mess. However, following the "New Look" reforms and GPV 2020-2027 modernization programs, Russia has re-emerged as a formidable conventional military power. Anatoly Serdyukov's "New Look" has restructured the officer corps, reorganized command and control structures, eliminated skeleton units, reshaped military education, and formed a proto-NCO corps. The Russian Armed Services are also rapidly transitioning from using conscripts to a force of professional contract soldiers.

GPV 2020-2027 modernizations indicate that Moscow's priorities are credible nuclear deterrence, open oceans denial through a submarine-based navy, a long-range precision strike capable air force, defense-in-depth through advanced ground forces, and the conduct of limited interventions abroad through joint operations.

These focus areas ensure Russian strategic imperatives remain secure and indicate that strategic thinking in the Kremlin has not significantly changed, even as the Russian government increasingly adopts hybrid warfare practices. Russian military reorganizations are preserving and expanding the role of conventional forces in national strategy, while hybrid warfare will continue to be Russia's dominant modus operandi.

---

1. An army's unit of maneuver is the basic building block of combat power. It is the basic level at which units are managed by theater commanders and contains all of the internal intelligence, logistics, support, and combat capabilities that enable it to function on the battlefield. The Brigade Combat Team, commanded by a Colonel, is the unit of maneuver in the United States Army.

CHAPTER FIVE

REMAKING THE RUSSIAN INTELLIGENCE SERVICES

The intelligence services play a central role in Russia's practice of hybrid warfare. They enable information dominance through clandestine collection activities and propaganda and deploy covert operatives to prepare the battlespace for a military intervention. These intelligence activities support campaign planning and create a chaotic environment ripe for exploitation, paving the road for kinetic military operations.

Operatives provide critical information on military and political objectives, political figureheads, national sentiments, and enemy forces, informing Moscow on how to shape the environment to support foreign policy objectives.

Elite troops and special operations forces (SOF) are deployed to coordinate proxy forces and strike at key targets to shape the environment. Elite troops rapidly seize key infrastructure, terrain, and government buildings; conduct terminal guidance (for close air support) against entrenched enemy forces; secure politically sensitive objectives; and pave the way for larger conventional forces. Without a sophisticated intelligence service and SOF complement, hybrid warfare would not be available to Russia as a foreign policy tool.

Chapter 1 discussed the doctrinal underpinnings of hybrid warfare and Chapter 4 discussed Russia's attempts to reform a Soviet-era steamroller into a modern military. This chapter explores the Russian intelligence services and the tools they wield to support Russian foreign policy.

Their intimate involvement in Russian foreign policy and military interventions causes the press to associate hybrid warfare with the shadowy workings of Russian operatives and, as we will see, there is some truth to the perception. Ultimately, Russia's intelligence services support conventional military conflict by creating conditions that maximize the chances of success when combat operations commence.

Main Intelligence Directorate (GRU)

GRU (Russian: Гла́вное разве́дывательное управле́ние), now known in Russia as just the GU, is the military intelligence agency of the Russian Federation. Unlike the FSB or SVR, which report directly to the Kremlin, GRU is subordinate to the General Staff of the Armed Services and the Minister of Defense.

GRU is Russia's most active foreign intelligence service, deploying almost six times more foreign agents abroad than its sister service SVR. This makes GRU Russia's most important and capable intelligence service. GRU was the lead institution for the planning and execution of interventions in Georgia, Crimea, Donbas (Eastern Ukraine), and Syria. With a global network of intelligence operatives, agents, cyber specialists, and Spetsnaz troops, GRU is the intuitive lead agency for planning and executing hybrid wars.

GRU is also Russia's oldest intelligence service and the only such service to survive the collapse of the Soviet Union relatively unchanged. Founded in 1918, and subordinate to Leon Trotsky's Soviet General Staff, the early institution that would become GRU was the primary foreign intelligence service of the early Soviet Union.

GRU developed a fierce rivalry with the feared secret police counterpart NKVD, which was eventually replaced by the Committee for State Security (KGB), and successfully maintained its independence from the KGB and survived the Soviet collapse intact.

GRU uses a more military-derived approach to its missions than its sister intelligence services; it identifies objectives, determines the preferred action tool, calculates the necessary application of force, and executes. There is much less concern for the sensitivities involved in international relations or diplomatic norms than there is in the more sophisticated and risk-averse SVR. There is also a competitive nature between the primary Russian intelligence services (GRU, FSB, and SVR), which likely drives some of GRU's recent risk-taking. The attempted assassination of Sergei Skripal, the attempted coup in Montenegro, and many other high-profile activities abroad are good anecdotal examples.

Even though GRU has been a leading agency in Russia's recent military interventions, it is not clear which of GRU's clandestine activities abroad were approved by the Kremlin. GRU's inability to stay out of international headlines has infuriated the General Staff. In a 2018 Ministry of Defense crisis meeting; defense policy heads and ranking generals accused the agency of, "complete incompetence" and "unbridled sloppiness".

Unit 29155

GRU stands up "units" as needed with experienced personnel who have the appropriate training to perform covert or clandestine missions. Unit 29155 was one such secretive unit, despite receiving absurd levels of public visibility for a team of highly trained covert operatives. Unit 29155 is a covert action, political interdiction, sabotage, and assassination team that operates in Europe, and it just cannot seem to stay out of the news.

The New York Times reports that Major General Andrei Averyanov leads the unit. British Security Services identified and indicted unit members Colonel Anatoly Chepiga and Colonel Alexander Mishkin for the attempted assassination of Sergey Skripal with Novichok nerve agent. Unit members were also indicted for the attempted assassination of Bulgarian arms dealer Emilian Gebrev in 2015, an attempted coup in Montenegro intended to prevent the former Yugoslavian country from joining NATO, and supporting the Catalan Independence Movement in Spain.

It is worth noting that, while the press has played up the cloak-and-dagger nature of Unit 29155, it is not immediately obvious that they have a good performance record. Sergey Skripal was a former Russian intelligence officer who turned informant for British MI6 (after a long career he eventually defected to the U.K.). He is now enjoying retirement in exile from Russia in Salisbury, U.K. On March 4, 2018, GRU operatives from Unit 29155 attempted to assassinate him by spraying Novichok nerve agent on his front door. Following the assassination attempt, an MI5 (the domestic security service counterpart to James Bond's fabled MI6) investigation released a detailed report of the assassins' activities in the U.K.

From the official and public reports on the Skripal job, the mission appears to have been a ham-fisted attempt at a covert operation—analogous to using a hammer for spinal surgery. Ironically, the report also revealed the impressive counterintelligence and criminal investigative capabilities of the U.K.'s MI5.

GRU agents Chepiga and Mishkin flew in from Moscow to Gatwick Airport in England on Aeroflot Flight SU2588. They arrived in the U.K. on March 2, 2018, took a train to Victoria Railway Station in Central London, and took public transit from Waterloo Station to the City Stay Hotel in Bow Road, East London.

On March 3rd, they took public transit back to Waterloo Station and boarded a train to Salisbury for what investigators suspect was a reconnaissance trip. Then they returned to their hotel in London later that day.

On March 4th, they returned to Salisbury. CCTV videos identified them in Sergey Skripal's neighborhood at 11:58 am. This is when they spread the nerve agent on Skripal's door. They headed for the train station and arrived at Waterloo Station at 4:45 pm. By 7:28 pm, they had made it back through passport control at London Heathrow Airport and, by 10:30 pm, they were on Aeroflot Flight SU2585 back to Moscow.

The Unit 29155 members entered the U.K. under aliases with false passports. The cover story for their travels was one-dimensional and implausible. Moscow claimed they were on holiday to visit the Salisbury Cathedral and made the counter-accusation that the West was persecuting innocent Russian citizens when they traveled abroad.

Colonel Anatoly Chepiga (alias Ruslan Boshirov) and Colonel Alexander Mishkin (alias Alexander Petrov) were senior GRU operatives with extensive time abroad, particularly in combat zones like Chechnya, Ukraine, and Syria. In fact, Colonel Chepiga was awarded the title "Hero of the Russian Federation" (the Russian equivalent of the Congressional Medal of Honor) for leading a team to extract Viktor Yanukovych from Ukraine during the Euromaidan Crisis.

Ultimately, the Skripal assassination attempt created a diplomatic crisis for Russia. The use of chemical nerve agents on British soil was an egregious red-line violation of international norms. Before the nerve agent was neutralized, Skripal, his daughter Yulia, police officer Nick Bailey, Charlie Rowley (a neighbor who discovered the bottle used to transport the nerve agent), and Dawn Sturgess (Charlie's girlfriend) were exposed. Tragically, Dawn mistook the bottle Charlie had discovered for perfume and sprayed it on her wrist.

Both Charlie and Dawn were admitted to the Salisbury District Hospital. While Charlie recovered, on July 8, 2018, Dawn was pronounced dead after doctors decided to switch off her life support. Officer Bailey was also exposed but recovered.

When the assassination attempt became public knowledge, the U.K. immediately summoned the Russian ambassador and expelled a large number of Russian diplomatic and intelligence officers from the country. Over 20 other countries followed suit in a massive show of solidarity. Over 150 Russian diplomatic and intelligence officers were expelled from their host countries in the United Kingdom, the United States, Germany, France, and elsewhere.

The losses to the collective intelligence-gathering capabilities of Russia's SVR, FSB, and GRU must have been too staggering for the Kremlin to digest. Moreover, Russia's diplomatic establishment was also dealt a serious blow from both the damage done to their reputation and the sudden loss of experienced personnel to carry diplomatic engagements forward.

Following the summer's expulsions in September 2018, GRU head Colonel, General Igor Korobov, was summoned to the Kremlin for an intense "dressing down". Korobov collapsed at home and died a little over a month later. A public release claimed that his sudden collapse and death was due to "stress".

GRU Rises

GRU made several errors during the Russo-Georgian War in 2008, including underestimating the strength of Georgian resistance and failing to identify anti-access and area denial (A2/AD) systems as a threat to Russian air power. Following the war, GRU became a favorite whipping boy of the Russian national security establishment. GRU was effectively branded incompetent by senior leaders in Moscow until the 2014 Crimean Intervention gave it a chance at redemption.

The Kremlin considered the Crimean Annexation a textbook opportunity to make good use of their variant of "military intelligence". GRU's Spetsnaz Brigades, in-house cyberwarfare capabilities, and extensive infiltration of ethnic-Russian nationalist and Ukrainian opposition movements would all play in an impressive *fait accompli*.

The ongoing conflicts in Eastern Ukraine and Syria have become a proving ground for hybrid warfare techniques; similar to the Germans perfecting blitzkrieg tactics in Franco, Spain, prior to World War II. With a worldwide network of spies, hackers, and Spetsnaz troops at its disposal, GRU has emerged as the panzer division of Hybrid Warfare.

GRU has invested deeply in its in-house cyber capabilities since the 1990s, recruiting young talent in grade school and steering them toward related courses like cryptography or software engineering. GRU also sponsors computer hacking competitions to identify capable young recruits.

The shadowy Unit 54777 (or the 72nd Special Service Center) is a "center of gravity" for Russian psychological operations through cyber activities. It is financed through a series of federal grants to front organizations offering public-facing policy and diplomacy services. GRU uses these front organizations to engage with Russian expatriates abroad. Good examples of such organizations are InfoRos and the Institute of the Russian Diaspora. Unit 54777 is also thought to be connected with the CyberCaliphate, publicly a cyber arm of Islamic State but, in reality, a probable GRU front.

It is unclear where exactly such units fall under the GRU hierarchy. Indeed, the crowd-sourcing approach to hacking-based espionage is specifically intended to give GRU a degree of separation and plausible deniability, but they may receive taskings from the 6th Division of the 2nd Directorate, which is responsible for "electronic intelligence". Other suspected GRU-funded and supported hacktivist organizations include APT 28, Fancy Bear, Sofacy, Pawnstorm, Sednit, Cyber Berkut, Voodoo Bear, BlackEnergy Actors, STRONTIUM, Tsar Team, and Sandworm.

GRU is also peculiar in that all Russian Armed Services' information gathering and analysis units are subordinate to GRU and its independent intelligence activities abroad. This is a characteristic that is different from both other Russian agencies and their Western counterparts. All of the intelligence sections, officers, and detachments of the Russian Armed Services answer to intelligence chiefs managed by the 5th Directorate of GRU.

Spetsnaz GRU—ISR and Direct Action Specialists

Finally, GRU has its infamous Spetsnaz brigades and reconnaissance units—the boogeymen of the Cold War. Spetsnaz is the tool of choice for kinetic operations. Military districts, armies, and flotillas are supported by respective intelligence departments, which are subordinate to GRU.

Each Ground Forces division or brigade contains a reconnaissance battalion or company at the operational level. Reconnaissance units contain signals intelligence squads, technical intelligence squads (radar and seismic observation), motorized reconnaissance units, and observation squads (physical reconnaissance). Just like these reconnaissance elements are designated ISR assets of their respective Ground Forces brigades or divisions, Spetsnaz Brigades are strategic ISR assets to their respective military districts.

Generally, each Spetsnaz Brigade contains between 900-1,500 soldiers and comes equipped with a brigade HQ, signals company, special weapons company, support company, logistics company, engineering and sapper platoons, medical center, in-house training unit, and three line (operations) battalions.

Each line battalion contains three Spetsnaz companies (200 Spetsnaz soldiers each), a communications company, an engineering and sapper platoon, and a medical platoon. Spetsnaz troops operate in teams of eight to fourteen, usually performing deep reconnaissance or direct action behind enemy lines. Likewise, the Special Reconnaissance units of the Naval Infantry serve as strategic ISR assets for their respective fleets. Naval and Marine Reconnaissance Stations (MRSs) consist of 120-200 men (basically a company-sized equivalent to their land-based sister units). GRU's Spetsnaz may number close to 17,000 total personnel.

During the Cold War, Spetsnaz teams were given an additional function. In the event of a war with NATO, Spetsnaz teams were designated to penetrate deep behind enemy lines to eliminate forward-deployed tactical nuclear weapons, particularly before they could be used to mitigate the superior numbers of Soviet Ground Forces.

Spetsnaz are well-regarded as fighting troops in Russia but do not conduct full-spectrum Special Operations like their Western counterparts. Rather, they are a specialized component of the Ground Forces tasked with meeting commanders' priority information requirements (PIR).

This is not to say that GRU Spetsnaz are not frequently in the thick of combat, but they are often entrusted with missions of a more sensitive or sophisticated nature (comparable in function to America's Marine Force Recon or maybe the 75th Ranger Regiment). Additionally, they have earned a certain macabre renown in austere places like Afghanistan and

Chechnya and are among the Russian Federation's most trusted troops. But first and foremost, they are ISR assets, which is why all Spetsnaz brigades are operationally controlled by the 5th Directorate.

As of 2013, Spetsnaz recruits are primarily contract soldiers, but each Brigade usually hosts a small fraction of conscript soldiers; albeit conscripts that have demonstrated the necessary intelligence and physical fitness. Spetsnaz men undergo a brutal training regime that revolves around extreme physical conditioning and mental dexterity. Instructors go to great lengths to "surprise" recruits. This is meant to ingrain formulaic responses to the unexpected through the proper execution of tactics and technical skills.

Like the Ground Forces, GRU's Spetsnaz Brigades are each commanded by a Colonel. As the GRU's upper ranks are dominated by *agenturi* (intelligence collection specialists), it can be challenging for Spetsnaz officers to climb the ranks. Many of Spetsnaz's most talented leaders often transfer to the VDV to keep close to military-oriented special operations.

Spetsnaz is a proving ground for GRU *agenturi*, training men in reconnaissance, direct action, sabotage, explosives, and infiltration. Those with the aptitude are selected and sent from their units to train in HUMINT and foreign languages as *agenturi* (intelligence operatives).

While serving in Spetsnaz is highly beneficial to an officer's career, insiders within the GRU hierarchy tend to see the Brigades themselves as outside help, perhaps because the Spetsnaz Brigades technically belong to the military districts and Ground Forces. Nevertheless, because so many GRU men came from the hard-hitting Spetsnaz, the agency itself has a reputation as a blunt instrument that lacks finesse, as opposed to the chic and sophisticated operatives of the SVR.

Foreign Intelligence Service (SVR)

SVR (Russian: Служба внешней разведки) came into existence from a simple renaming of the KGB's First Chief Directorate (Russian: Пе́рвое гла́вное управле́ние, known by the English acronym PGU). Like its predecessor, SVR is responsible for conducting foreign intelligence. SVR's headquarters is at Yasenevo (a district of Moscow), conveniently distanced from many of the other political centers that spar for influence in Moscow.

SVR is generally reputed as a very capable foreign intelligence service, but it is an order of magnitude smaller than its GRU or FSB counterparts. Directly subordinate to the President of Russia, the SVR enjoys a far more intimate relationship with the Kremlin than the other special services.

SVR went to great lengths to stay out of the post-Soviet power games within the Russian government, frequently pointing to its mission of gathering information abroad rather than at home as evidence of its political neutrality. As a result, SVR provides the President of Russia with a weekly intelligence briefing and daily informational updates.

The privilege of directly providing intelligence and analysis to policymakers in the Kremlin is truly unique among the Russian special services, reflecting the high level of trust placed in SVR. The Soviet Politburo would never have dared bestow such policy-shaping influence on the KGB for fear it might get too powerful and take over (which the KGB attempted in August of 1991).

The First Chief Directorate of the KGB (PGU) was on the sidelines for the failed August Coup of 1991. When Mikhail Gorbachev and Boris Yeltsin fully regained control of the government, the disbandment of the KGB and a shakeup of the entire Russian intelligence apparatus immediately followed. Lieutenant General Shebarshin, the head of the First Chief

Directorate, kept his staff and operatives as far away from the crisis as possible.

The KGB's patronage of PGU had been generous. PGU's intelligence networks covered the Earth in a profound fashion. Intelligence priorities were determined by a country's proximity to the USSR, proximity to the United States, attitude towards the USSR, scientific development, natural resources, attitudes towards Socialism, regional American influence, and a country's usefulness as a recruiting ground.

PGU pulled in massive volumes of information. While most of this information was vetted and filtered poorly, it delivered insights into politics, economics, technology, and social trends regarding friends and enemies alike. PGU and fellow Warsaw Pact special services would work to stand up over 50 intelligence agencies and secret police forces in the Third World, generating assets that would be useful for decades.

The downside of KGB patronage was that PGU could not actually report the truth, nor was it permitted to directly analyze the information it collected. PGU officers in Yasenevo were required to route all information to the Communist Party of the Soviet Union (CPSU) through the dreaded Lubyanka (KGB headquarters). Any information reported could not contradict Communist ideology and was expected to confirm the preconceived leanings of Soviet leadership.

Following the August Coup of 1991, Shebarshin would be hounded out of the PGU by Foreign Minister Boris Pankin. His replacement, Yevgeniy Primakov, a career foreign intelligence officer with expertise in the Middle East, would become the father of the modern SVR. He had extensive contacts and relationships throughout the PGU and was widely expected to take a central leadership role.

After a series of bureaucratic shake-ups and renamings, Primakov was named Director of the newly minted SVR by Boris Yeltsin via Presidential Decree. He would eventually succeed in promoting his preferred candidate, General Trubnikov, to the position of First Deputy Director, ensuring Primakov's service would live past his own tenure.

Primakov's background in bureaucratic maneuvering and manipulation would prove invaluable in saving SVR from the post-Soviet chaos in the Russian government. His most immediate priority was to tourniquet the systematic hemorrhaging of SVR's personnel and talent pool, many of whom had traded invaluable state secrets to Western intelligence services to flee and retire in the West.

It had also become difficult to fund intelligence operations abroad. All of the agency's financial couriers had been recalled, and the KGB's front companies had closed their doors.

Additionally, Primakov altered SVR's "look" and tried to give the service a facelift. He reoriented SVR from a geographically oriented perspective that suited inter-state competition (primarily with NATO) towards international issues that occupied the attention of all governments, namely: the proliferation of weapons of mass destruction, transnational organized crime, international drug trade, and global terrorism. Below the facelift, however, the mechanics remained the same: spy on the opposition. SVR was also intended to appear research oriented—a fact-finding organization staffed by experts and professionals.

On January 28, 1993, SVR published the first ever public release by any of the Russian special services entitled the "New Challenge After the Cold War: Proliferation of Weapons of Mass Destruction". A series of similar exposés followed; all to create an aura of legitimacy (similar to the annual publication of the CIA World Factbook).

SVR reached out to its Western counterparts for cooperation. Though it is easy to scoff at Russia's foreign intelligence service seeking détente, it is possible that Primakov did have altruistic hopes for what could be. Primakov deliberately appointed deputies that were seen as Western or liberal in orientation.

The Russians proposed that both sides reduce spying on one another in "bad faith" through coercive recruitment and instead rely on strictly "psychotropic means", deliberately ambiguous terminology that probably alluded to creating agents through ideological sympathies.

Lieutenant General Kirpichenko led a group of SVR advocates to visit the CIA, insisting that the agencies at least set up a few contacts. CIA leaders were unimpressed, finding SVR generally unreformed and vehemently anti-Western. However, CIA Director Robert Gates visited Moscow in October 1992 and soon followed up with "working contacts" between the first deputy heads of the CIA and SVR.

SVR went so far as to send a three-man delegation to the United States to explain Russia's security changes and discuss with congressmen, journalists, and academics the need to cooperate in combating organized crime and WMD proliferation.

Any real gains from this attempt at détente were shattered by the arrest of Aldrich Ames on February 21, 1994. Ames, a career CIA intelligence officer, had become frustrated and resentful that his supervisors saw him as a problematic drinker and chronic underperformer. He turned over dozens of American informants in Russia to the KGB and subsequent SVR and FSB, people who were either tortured in the Lubyanka or unceremoniously shot.

Ames was the most devastating spy in American intelligence history until the arrest of Robert Hanssen in 2001. SVR was running Ames, Hanssen, and others, all while making overtures of cooperation and "good faith" spying. At the time of publication, Ames is serving a life sentence in a maximum security facility. Robert Hanssen was sentenced to 15 life terms and died in prison on June 5, 2023.

SVR's Dark Arts

SVR's core competency is HUMINT (human intelligence), the oldest and purest form of spy-craft. SVR operatives spy under diplomatic protection from Russia, usually working legitimate jobs as a Russian citizen with a Russian passport abroad. Additionally, Russian operatives are not required to career progress every few years like their Western counterparts.[1]

The SVR keeps its most talented people in positions where they can have maximum impact. This often allows successful operatives to remain in the field for 15-20 years. These operatives are known for playing the long game when they recruit agents, targeting them not only for their present duties, but for how they might be promoted in the future. Prospects' passions, weaknesses, faults, and resentments are carefully examined over many years.

CIA officer Aldrich Ames' motivations for working as a Russian mole were resentment over a series of negative performance evaluations and a desire for a lavish lifestyle. Subjects with large outstanding debts and sensitive private "issues" are likely candidates (because they are susceptible to blackmail).

SVR operatives observe prospects for many years before determining the opportune time to make a proposition (likely when the prospect is at a low point). Once an individual has fed the SVR information, their handlers have leverage over them, and the operative can never return to normal life.

In the event that an SVR agent suddenly grows a conscience and refuses to cooperate further, their handler has the power to publicly expose them as a traitor and provide evidence of their activities to domestic authorities.

Russian expatriates and citizens abroad are also likely targets for SVR operatives. While the Soviet-era KGB and PGU often recruited spies in academia where intellectuals held sympathies for Marxism (or at least resentments against Capitalism), SVR often appeals to ethnic Russians abroad on the grounds of patriotism or sense of duty. If that does not work, then blackmail is equally permissible.

In the case of Aldrich Ames, he quietly contacted the Russian Embassy on his own (his offer to turn informer was so unexpected that at first the Russians did not believe him).

Ames' duplicity as a Russian agent has only been rivaled by that of Robert Hannsen, an FBI agent and counterintelligence officer. Hannsen used official duties at the FBI as a pretense to establish a point of contact with the GRU, KGB, and, eventually, SVR. Ames and Hannsen sold thousands of classified documents and national secrets (for example, identities of American agents abroad, nuclear strategy, counterintelligence operations, or defense policy information) in exchange for cash.

Despite past attempts at cooperation, SVR carries on the KGB's shadow games with the West. The United States and NATO remain the primary opponent, though the rise of the European Union is equally problematic to Russia. Primakov and his successors emphasized analytical work and envisioned a think tank-like atmosphere at SVR. Political intelligence (insider knowledge on a country's policymaking) is also a primary focus.

Successive modernization programs for the Russian Armed Services (GPV 2020 and 2027) have created a dire need for advanced military technologies, and the Russian military-industrial complex lacks the necessary talent and intellectual depth to meet these demands.

In addition to its other priority intelligence requirements, SVR continues to carry forward the KGB's old mission of stealing (and reverse-engineering) Western military technology to reduce research and development costs in Russia. Even if Russia had a vibrant university system, business community, capital markets, and workforce (it does not), espionage is much cheaper and faster than financing domestic technology development.

SVR is also responsible for controlling the public narratives on Russian activities abroad. This may include targeted messaging campaigns, blackmailing journalists, regulating a friendly press corps in Moscow, and outright disinformation campaigns. SVR also focuses intelligence collection activities on international terrorism, transnational crime, and drug trafficking.

SVR and the Illegals

The "illegals" are another Soviet legacy item. During the Cold War, the KGB sent its operatives abroad to become citizens in target nations. Within the KGB's First Chief Directorate was a small and highly secretive sub-unit, Directorate S, responsible for the Illegals program. Directorate S was eventually inherited by the SVR's Department of Operations subgroup "Illegal Networks".

Unlike conventional spies who operate under diplomatic protection, these "illegals" had no official status as Soviet citizens and no official sanction. KGB "illegals" were infiltrated into target countries and tasked with assimilating the culture and speaking the language. They established elaborate cover identities as either native citizens or immigrants from countries unaffiliated with Moscow.

Many Soviet "illegals" stole identities from dead children in the West. Soviet operatives would steal or forge a birth certificate and then fabricate a history for the child as though it had grown up, creating a paper trail for a false identity that one of their operatives could assume. "Illegals" even trained as couples, getting married in Russia and then moving to the West where they could "meet for the first time" and fall in love in the presence of Western friends.

They would have children, who would be raised as Americans, Canadians, or Europeans, and then over decades, attempt to maneuver their careers towards positions of influence. They often sought admission to the Ivy League, where networking opportunities would enable them to climb into positions of political influence. The ultimate goal was to land in policy-making circles or even in the American and British intelligence community.

This practice developed from the older use of Com-Interns. The Com-Interns consisted of American, French, British, and German Communist sympathizers, mostly from elite universities, who came to Soviet Russia in the 1920s and 30s to witness the experiment in Marxism. These individuals were recruited to emigrate back to the West as informants. However, Stalin's purges in the late 1930s had most of these individuals arrested and killed, along with most of the foreign intelligence apparatus.

The "illegals" arose out of a Soviet foreign intelligence school that was founded to train peasants into spies capable enough to replace the Com-Interns as informants in the West. By 1968, the school had evolved into an academy called the Krasnoznamennyi Institute (KI), which ran three-year courses in foreign languages and taught practical classes on basic intelligence tradecraft (examples include covert meetings with agents, safehouses, undercover operations, agent recruitment, surveillance, and dead drops).

Classrooms and training sites were scattered around Moscow and the forests outside the city. Students were privately tutored by retired intelligence operatives, using the city as a training ground. After the fall of the Soviet Union, Primakov convinced Boris Yeltsin to sign Secret Decree No. 1999-S dated October 17, 1994, which re-enshrined the Soviet tradition of the Foreign Intelligence Academy.

Since Vladimir Putin came to power, numerous high-profile incidents have occurred concerning Russian deep-cover spies. Russian spies have not been this active since the Cold War. In the spring of 2001, the United States, United Kingdom, and Germany all simultaneously reported an increase in Russian intelligence activity. In 2010, the FBI conducted one of history's largest roundups of Russian spies. Twelve Russian "illegals" were arrested resulting from an FBI counterintelligence investigation that began back in the Clinton Administration.

The Russian agents were living quiet lives in the American suburbs. Some of them had been operating in the United States for 20 years. Eight of those arrested were married couples who were using false identities and spoke multiple languages (English, Spanish, Russian, and Mandarin). The spy ring had been attempting to penetrate policy-making circles of the Washington Beltway, seeking contacts and employment at NGOs, activist organizations, think tanks, and Congressional lobbying groups.

For whatever successes the various iterations of Russia's "illegals" program have produced, the consensus of Western national security experts is that it has had a meager return on investment. The "illegals" program draws

Russia's top talent, puts them into years of intensive training, and then sends them under deep cover to foreign countries where they may have to remain dormant for decades. Russia's greatest intelligence successes have come from spies that operate abroad under official sanction and diplomatic immunity—not from the Illegals program.

The 2010 round-up of Russian "illegals" by the FBI cost the SVR at least a dozen highly trained operatives as well as their networks and contacts. Among the arrested were the infamous Anna Chapman (formerly Anya Kushchenko before she married a British national), Mikhail Anatolyevich Vasenkov (alias Juan Lazaro) and Vicky Peláez (his wife and a Peruvian immigrant to the U.S.), Andrey Bezrukov and Yelena Vavilova (aliases Donald Heathfield and Tracey Lee Ann Foley), Vladimir and Lidiya Guryev (aliases Richard and Cynthia Murphy), Mikhail Kutsik and Nataliya Pereverzeva (aliases Michael Zottoli and Patricia Mills), Mikhail Semenko (who operated under his real name, Alexey Karetnikov (who operated under his real name), and Pavel Kapustin (alias Christopher Metsos). All of these arrested operatives, except Pavel Kapustin (who escaped custody) and Alexey Karetnikov (who was arrested separately), were traded for American and British agents who had been apprehended in Russia.

The beautiful Anna Chapman is now a celebrity in Russia, and has cultivated a persona as a national icon, model, public speaker, and recruiter for the spy agencies. However, none of the other agents have been so resilient. Vladimir and Lidiya Guryev had two sons who were born and raised in Canada, and never knew of their family's connection to Russia until their parents were arrested. These boys were deported to Russia and have since sued to regain their Canadian citizenship.[2]

None of these operatives will ever be able to serve abroad again, but, worse, Moscow cannot be sure of their loyalties now. Any or all of them may have cut a deal with American intelligence to spy against Russia once they return home, so SVR cannot risk giving these operatives jobs as analysts. They must collect a meager pension and live quietly in Russia where they are likely under surveillance by the government they used to serve.

Pavel Kapustin is an interesting case because he was one of the most experienced and capable deep cover operatives ever apprehended. Kapustin was a money man and go-between for this spy network. He remained on the move and contacted Illegals operatives sporadically to interview them about their performance, hand-off cash, and give them new procedures from Moscow. He operated under the alias Christopher Metsos and traveled with a Canadian passport. At the behest of the FBI, Metsos (Kapustin) was arrested by Interpol at the Larnaca International Airport in Cyprus where he had bought a ticket to Budapest.

It is possible that the judge was under political pressure from the Cypriot government (who was in-turn under pressure from Moscow) to allow Kapustin to post bail. Bail was set at €27,000, despite enormous objections made by Interpol and the Americans. Kapustin immediately posted bail (apparently producing €27,000 was trivial for this man) and then disappeared in the night. However, despite avoiding extradition to the U.S., Kapustin's cover was blown, and his face became known to every spy agency in the world. It is anyone's guess where he is now. Perhaps working a desk job for SVR in Moscow. Or perhaps he is living quietly in the Canary Islands or Scotland or maybe Montana (Russian intelligence operatives often choose to retire in the West rather than Russia itself). But Kapustin, a highly valuable clandestine intelligence operative with at least 35 years of foreign service experience, can never work for Russia again in the same capacity abroad.

The Illegals program is sexy on paper, but, despite being active in the U.S. for over a decade, these operatives did not accomplish their mission of penetrating Congressional policy-making circles. A dozen highly gifted individuals sacrificed "normal" and probably "successful" lives amongst family and friends in the place they called home. It is not clear what exactly the SVR gained in return.

SVR and the Commonwealth of Independent States (CIS)

The PGU (First Chief Directorate of the KGB) had not maintained a significant presence in the Soviet member states before the fall of Communism. These countries had all been seen to by the 2nd Chief Directorate of the KGB, as well as their own respective KGBs. After the fall of communism, SVR was forced to stand up new intelligence stations and establish networks in these places. In fact, many former Soviet and Warsaw Pact countries were seen as an even higher priority than the United States or NATO due to their geographic proximity to Russia.

Few challenges have troubled Russian leadership more than losing control over the CIS countries (Armenia, Azerbaijan, Belarus, Kazakhstan, Kyrgyzstan, Moldova, Russia, Tajikistan, and Uzbekistan). After the Soviet Collapse in 1991, Russia founded the CIS and coerced participation from its current members to reestablish some measure of control over these countries' respective economies and security apparatuses.

Many former Soviet-sphere countries were eager for Russian intelligence cooperation after sampling Western alternatives. Western intelligence services often offered "entry-level" cooperation to potential partners in Eastern Europe by training intelligence operatives and analytical personnel. In practice, these offers of cooperation often fanned resentments.

Western intelligence instructors refused to teach anything but the most rudimentary of methods to unproven partners (lest these methods be applied against Western interests). The basic skills taught usually contradicted the old Soviet approaches already in use.

In a March 1992 press conference, Russia announced they were laying the foundations for cooperation with the CIS member states. CIS consists of a core remnant of former Soviet States and Warsaw Pact members bound together in a loose political, economic, and military framework to counter-balance NATO and the EU. The general framework extracted commitments from all members so they would not spy on each other. Russia considers the CIS members part of its strategic buffer with the West and, thus, profoundly fears its members straying from Moscow's influence.

Director Primakov claimed that SVR already exchanged information in good faith with CIS partners, and there was little need for establishing SVR's agent networks within the CIS. The first CIS intelligence agreement was signed on April 5, 1992 by Armenia, Belarus, Kazakhstan, Kyrgyzstan, Moldova, Russia, Tajikistan, Turkmenistan, and Ukraine.

All signatories pledged not to spy on each other (although there is no honor among thieves) and to assist in mutual training of personnel. This agreement would be expanded in 1995 to allow for cooperation on combating organized crime, international terrorism, and the drug trade.

FSB, Russia's lead law enforcement and domestic intelligence agency, became Russia's leading agency in the CIS member states, rather than SVR. While Russia's CIS intelligence agreements preclude SVR from conducting collection activities within the CIS, the agreements contain ambiguous enough language to allow FSB to fill the void in a "law enforcement" capacity.

This arrangement with the CIS members also yielded an unexpected benefit. Turncoats, double agents, political exiles, and disgraced intelligence operatives from the CIS members often flee to Russia, where their respective intelligence services and law enforcement agencies cannot pursue them. This gives Russia an extraordinary amount of leverage over the ruling parties of the CIS members.

The FSB is well aware of all passports checked by Russian customs and any country (or dictator) that wants its fugitives back must negotiate for them, and this arrangement only goes one way. Because FSB operates within the CIS, Russian exiles seek safe havens in the CIS at their own peril.

Zaslon—The Unseen Men

Zaslon (Russian: Заслон) is the in-house special mission unit of SVR. Russian authorities deny the existence of Zaslon, but the consensus among security experts is that the unit performs Russia's most sensitive missions abroad. The world may never know exactly what Zaslon's classified mission statement includes but, functionally, the unit is a multi-purpose tool kit that Moscow uses when strategic assets or personnel are at risk. The unit is often deployed to protect Russian diplomatic personnel and clean out Russian embassies in war zones (Zaslon closed down the Russian Embassy in Baghdad before Operation Iraqi Freedom in 2003). Zaslon is also tasked with HUMINT collection activities, working in intimate proximity to host-nation government officials as it operates out of Russian embassies abroad.

Zaslon was founded in 1997 by secret Presidential Decree and is subordinate to the SVR's 7th Department—Center for Self-Security. Reports have trickled out that Zaslon was deployed to Syria in 2013, causing speculation that Russian leaders may have feared sensitive military technologies were at risk of being exposed or diplomatic documents were at risk of being captured. It's also possible the Kremlin was concerned about military personnel being abducted by Iranian-backed militias or captured by small bands of ISIS-affiliated fighters.

The unit is estimated to consist of approximately 250-300 highly experienced operatives with extensive service records in other secretive Russian units. National security experts also believe that Zaslon operatives must maintain proficiency in several foreign languages.

On the few occasions where Zaslon personnel have been identified abroad, they usually wear plain olive, khaki, or black uniforms with a Russian Flag or embassy patch instead of a specific unit patch. They reportedly prefer the old AK-47's 7.62mm ammunition to the current 5.45mm ammunition used by most Russian troops due to the AK-47's preeminence in the world's conflict zones (leaving less evidence of Zaslon's presence).

While operating abroad, the unit reports to the Russian embassy rather than military commanders or even GRU. The Kremlin directly tasks Zaslon through the Russian diplomatic communication channels, bypassing any military chain of command operating within a given region.

SVR In Closing

SVR does not play the same role in hybrid warfare as GRU. Where GRU often takes the lead in campaign planning, has operational control over Russia's Spetsnaz Brigades, and is subordinate to the General Staff (which oversees the Armed Services), SVR only answers to political leadership. As an agency, SVR is responsible for strategic intelligence, primarily from human sources. For example, SVR is responsible for helping the Kremlin understand how Poland will react to Russian activity in Eastern Ukraine, or whether the American Senate Foreign Relations Committee considers

Georgia a vital national ally, or whether the European Union will sanction Russian oil and natural gas exports for supporting a conflict in Donbas.

SVR informs President Putin's strategic decision-making. As a leader, it's vital to know how global political conditions will tolerate a military intervention before committing troops. Clumsy applications of military force have triggered world wars (consider Austria's reaction to the assassination of Archduke Franz Ferdinand and the beginnings of World War I).

Federal Security Service (FSB)

FSB is the primary inheritor of the Soviet KGB and has taken over residence of the dreaded Lubyanka, the former KGB Headquarters building in Moscow where the secret police interrogated political prisoners. FSB descended directly from the KGB's Second Chief Directorate, responsible for domestic security and counterintelligence.

One of Russia's historical paradoxes is that maintaining a unified state has always required a secret police. Russia is located on the vast North-Eurasian steppe, and its geography does not lend to a long growing season or fertile farmlands. Russia's few major rivers like the Volga run north and remain frozen for much of the year. These factors have limited Russian urbanization and capital creation since the time of feudalism.

Russia's distant provinces and localities have had little to tie them to the regime in Moscow beyond a common language. It would have taken an army many months to march from Moscow to any other major Russian cities and years to march from Moscow to distant eastern provinces like Kamchatka.

From the High Middle Ages to the present, the Russian State has held itself together through a ruthless secret police that keeps political dissidents and disruptors in check. This unfortunate fact of geography that dictated the manner of the rule of the Czars left a status quo of authoritarian governance that conveniently suited Soviet Communism. Following the best-kept traditions of the Czar's Secret Police, Stalin's feared NKVD, and the Politburo's powerful KGB, FSB has taken up the mantle.

Following the dissolution of the USSR, the KGB was deliberately partitioned into independent agencies with mutually exclusive functions. The First Chief Directorate became the Foreign Intelligence Service (SVR).

The 8th and 16th Directorates, responsible for electronic intelligence, would become the core of the Federal Agency for Government Communications and Intelligence (FAPSI).

The 15th Directorate, responsible for protecting priority strategic facilities, became the President's Main Directorate of Special Programs (GUSP).

The 9th Directorate of the KGB became the Federal Protective Service (FSO), responsible for protecting government VIPs, including the President. The KGB Border Troops became the Border Service. The largest fragment consisting of the Second Chief Directorate and all of the remaining smaller directorates and departments formed what came to be known as FSB.

In midwifing the new system of intelligence services, Boris Yeltsin wisely ensured that each independent special service had mutually exclusive realms of authority that created a system of checks and balances on power. No one service had a monopoly on the information that flowed into the Kremlin.

Interestingly, similar to the Soviet Politburo's arms-length and fearful treatment of the KGB, President Yeltsin frequently played the special services off one another to ensure that no one service could infringe on the Kremlin's supremacy in setting policy. Then came Vladimir Putin. He was appointed Director of FSB in 1998, then served as Prime Minister in 1999, and became President in 2000.

Putin eliminated FAPSI, the Federal Tax Police, and the Federal Border Service as independent agencies in 2003. The Federal Border Service was placed under FSB, and FAPSI was divided between FSB and FSO. FSB officials were also reassigned to key posts in the powerful Ministry of Internal Affairs (MVD) (organizations such as the Minister of Internal Affairs or the Chief of the Directorate of Internal Security). Thus, MVD effectively came under FSB control.

An Ivy League for a New Russia

When Putin became President, it began an era of generous funding and expanded influence for FSB. Yeltsin had worked to decentralize the Russian intelligence services in the 1990s, understanding that each service had extensive resources to leverage in political influence if it was not confined to a discrete domain of responsibility.

Putin, on the other hand, saw FSB as an ideal breeding ground for competent senior leaders. An empowered FSB was useful in controlling Russia's powerful oligarchs and removing resistance to Putin's reforms.

Putin heavily concentrated power in FSB, hoping the institution's leadership would evolve into a cadre of senior statesmen invested in Russia's future. The institution would play the role of America's Harvard, Yale, and the other Ivy League schools, bestowing approved orthodoxy on future national leaders. Aspiring members of this nobility would be identified as outperformers early in their careers, and those people would receive guided development as intelligence officers or administrators, like Putin himself.

The Russians call these military and intelligence-groomed statesmen *Siloviki (Russian:* силовики). Patriotism and competence are requisite for continued advancement. These FSB elites would eventually constitute their own caste, separate from the rest of Russia, and were expected to collectively hold a stake in the regime and protect the long-term interests of Russia. Though this strategy delivered Putin a great deal more power and personal influence than Boris Yeltsin, FSB proved to be a disappointing source of noblemen.

FSB In Practice

FSB officials amassed large sums of personal wealth and began to use the agency's resources against other government institutions. FSB, the Federal Drug Control Service (FSKN), and the Presidential Security Service (a service within FSO) were actively fighting one another, spying on each other, and jailing each other's personnel.

FSB also had many intelligence and operational failures. For instance, it failed to predict the Moscow protests of 2011 and was powerless to stop them beyond obtusely intimidating and arresting the ring leaders.

From 2013 to 2014, FSB grossly underestimated the Euromaidan protests in Ukraine and, when sent to protect puppet-President Victor Yanukovych, FSB operatives failed to realize that he was losing his nerve. When Yanukovych fled the country, Moscow was caught completely off-guard.

During the 2011-2013 protests against President Putin's announcement to re-seek the Presidency in 2012 (he stepped down to be Dmitri Medvedev's Prime Minister from May 2008 to May 2012), sometimes called the Snow Revolution, the FSB could do little to quell the populist challenge to Putin's regime except fumble through a series of heavy-handed and entirely ineffective high-profile arrests. FSB's coordinated efforts to intimidate critics of the Kremlin amounted to a drop in the bucket. Ultimately, a series of laws that limited protest activity to certain hours in certain areas had to be passed, giving local law enforcement more tools to break up large groups.

In 2015, Putin decided to rein in the FSB and untangle the mess. He began by dismissing several prominent political appointees who came from FSB. To stop some of the bureaucratic infighting, the FSKN was dissolved as an agency. Putin ceased using FSB as a recruitment base for any further key positions in the government. He then began to institute "discipline".

Anti-corruption campaigns began to ensnare provincial governors, mayors, mid-level public officials, and even problematic scientists. Though FSB was the key instrument in implementing these probes, it was also the biggest loser in political influence. Anecdotal examples include Andrei Gerasimov, who was forced to retire as head of FSB's Information Security Center, and Major General Vladimir Podolsky, who was put on public trial for fraud and sentenced to four years in prison. Podolsky had previously served as commander of the legendary Vympel counter-terrorism unit.

These reforms indicate a titanic shift in the future stability of Russian political leadership. Putin's elevation of FSB occurred in search of a dedicated cadre of senior officials who understood and advocated for Russia's long-term interests. FSB briefly served as a proving ground for Russia's highest caste; however, Putin realized FSB had adopted this role kleptocratically, without having any real stake in the regime or in Russia itself.

Putin's new political strategy is to keep everyone in the government off-balance. The intelligence services, especially FSB, are now on a short leash. This is a return to similar practices of the late Soviet Politburo, who understood just how dangerous an autonomous KGB could be. FSB remains an important tool of state control, but its influence in state policy is waning.

Much of FSB's expansion under Putin as Director was enabled through the strategic emplacement of loyalists in other branches of government coupled with the annexation of smaller offices that once belonged to KGB. However, FSB's power derives from more than clever political maneuvering.

In 1998, FSB formally adopted a role vacated by the 5th Directorate of the KGB. A subunit, one independent of the larger FSB bureaucracy, called the Directorate for Protecting the Constitution, was founded to combat internal sedition.

The secret police were back.

Interestingly, in 1999, the Directorate to Combat Terrorism and Political Extremism was also formed. The Directorate was the first service in Russian history created exclusively to combat terrorism, and it was originally distinctive and independent from the Directorate for Protecting the Constitution (where agents of the state investigate subversion against the Kremlin).

In the view of the Russian government, political sedition and terrorism are separate issues. But these two distinct Directorates would eventually be combined into one entity and renamed a "Service"—the Service for Protection of the Constitutional System and Combating Terrorism.

It is not a coincidence that within this dual-function service is FSB's Center for Special Operations, containing special mission units Alpha, Vympel, and Smerch. This sub-section within FSB independently investigates sedition (defined broadly as unapproved political activities) and terrorism and has three elite units to conduct extrajudicial arrests or targeted killings as needed.

Activities Abroad

By Russian Law and a series of bilateral agreements, SVR cannot conduct intelligence activities in the Commonwealth of Independent States (CIS). Instead, FSB owns intelligence gathering activities in the CIS, where the Russian defense apparatus deeply fears "color revolutions". The Velvet Revolution of Czechoslovakia (1989), the Rose Revolution of Georgia (2003) that resulted in Mikhail Saakashvili winning the presidency, the Orange Revolution of Ukraine (2004), and the Tulip Revolution of Kyrgyzstan (2005) are all regional examples of populist uprising that unseated a Moscow-aligned authoritarian regime through democratic (and sometimes violent) means.

In addition to CIS, there is evidence that Russia maintains extensive intelligence assets in Germany. Many of these assets are legacy informants of the disbanded but feared Stasi (the secret police of former East Germany).

It is unclear whether such assets would belong to SVR or GRU as Russia's foreign intelligence services or whether FSB may claim jurisdiction due to East Germany's status as a former satellite state of Russia.

FSB conducts "anti-sedition" and "anti-foreign intelligence" activities in CIS and the Russian near-abroad, including intelligence collection and covert special operations in Crimea, Donbas, and Kiev. The Directorate for Current Information and International Relations serves as the lead component. FSB's Federal Border Service is also responsible for countering foreign intelligence in Russia and the CIS through its Intelligence Department.

FSB Analysis Capabilities

A persistent myth followed the collapse of the KGB. Former KGB officers propagated rumors of legendary analysis capabilities performed by highly trained staff within the depths of the Lubyanka. In truth, the KGB founded the Current Information and Analysis Service, its first in-house analysis unit, in 1989. Before then, the KGB employed no analysis staff.

This was an additional measure of control placed over the KGB by the Politburo. In practice, the KGB delivered raw information to the other government departments, and then each department would refine this raw information into intelligence and draw their own conclusions. This prevented the KGB from setting policy through manipulated intelligence flows into the Kremlin.

Comparatively, the American CIA has always separated the collection of information from the fusion of raw information into intelligence. The CIA's Directorate of Analysis and National Clandestine Service (formerly known as the Directorate of Operations) are both independent and mutually exclusive so that analysts can distil intelligence products dispassionately without interference or pollution by the collector.

FSB inherited the KGB's proto-analysis apparatus and resolved to remedy its deficiencies. In 1991, FSB founded its own analysis department, which would eventually bear the name Current Information and International Relations Service. Within this Service are the Department of Current Information, the Directorate of Analysis, the Strategic Planning Directorate, the Department of Unclassified Information, and the Directorate of International Cooperation.

Collectively, these departments refine intelligence, draw conclusions, and provide a distilled product to political leadership. This relationship is unprecedented in Russian intelligence. The Kremlin trusts FSB to inform policymakers in a way the all-powerful KGB was never privileged (though FSB is not as trusted as SVR).

Spetsgruppa Alfa—Russia's Boogeyman

FSB's Spetsgruppa Alfa (Special Group Alpha) is perhaps the most famous special mission unit (SMU) of Russia. Founded in 1974, Alfa served as an elite counterterrorism force directly subordinate to the KGB Chairman. Spetsnaz GRU brigades were already tasked with deep reconnaissance and the destruction of enemy infrastructure, weapons, and facilities. However, KGB Chairman Yuri Andropov wanted a similar tool that he could wield in a wider set of domestic geopolitical problems.

The first Alfa team consisted of 30 handpicked men tasked with the official mission of counterterrorism. While counterterrorism was the political justification for Alfa's existence (much at the behest of the Politburo), Alfa's first missions were all related to interdicting foreign intelligence operations in the Eastern Bloc.

While Alfa was tasked with kill or capture missions against Western intelligence operatives and their agents throughout the Soviet Union, Andropov had bigger plans. He postulated that, in the event of a war with NATO, covert operatives and SMUs from the West might be tasked with assassinating Communist Party leadership and Soviet High Command. Alfa was then tasked with protecting Party leaders and VIPs.

The 15th Chief Directorate of the KGB was responsible for managing nuclear bunkers that ensured the continuity of the Soviet government in the event of nuclear war. Alfa frequently ran fire-drills with the 15th Directorate, securing and escorting VIPs to their bunkers. This crucial role gave the KGB Chairman enormous political leverage due to Alfa's intimate proximity to senior Party leaders.

In practice, Alfa's missions were universal direct and covert action, special reconnaissance, personnel protection, counterterrorism, political interdictions, and counterintelligence. The Soviet Ministry of Defense lacked a Spetsnaz unit with equivalent tactical training, so when leaders began planning the invasion of Afghanistan, they tapped the KGB to lend Alfa group for a special tasking. In December 1979, Alpha conducted Operation Storm-333—the first action of the Soviet-Afghan War. Alpha led the assault on the Afghan Presidential Palace with orders to kill every Afghan in the building, assassinating President Hafizullah Amin and his family.

Alfa also holds the trophy for history's most ruthless hostage rescue. In 1985, Alfa was dispatched to Beirut, Lebanon to respond to the kidnapping of four Soviet diplomats. Local KGB agents identified, by name, the hostage takers as members of a radical offshoot of the Muslim Brotherhood.

When an Alfa team arrived on site, they immediately began rounding up members of the hostage-takers' families.

The team cut off body parts of the male family members, placing them in a cardboard box that was then delivered to the hostage takers. The message was clear: more would follow if the hostages weren't released.

The hostage takers capitulated and surrendered. They were then unceremoniously placed on their knees and executed in the street.

The validity of this tale has been disputed by numerous regional leaders. Some sources claim the crisis was resolved through back-channel negotiations. Regardless, it is indisputable that, following the incident, citizens of the Soviet Union and, later, Russia enjoyed a 20-year hiatus from political kidnappings both in Lebanon and the wider Middle East.

In 1990, the Supreme Council of Lithuania voted to secede from the Soviet Union and Alfa was dispatched to quell political dissidents from one of the key Soviet Baltic satellites. In an attempt to control public messaging and information, Alfa eventually seized the Vilnius TV Tower. This attempt to eliminate Lithuanian dissent would ultimately fail, as public messaging was hardly the root cause for frustrations with Soviet Communism; however, the seizure of the Vilnius TV Tower was a textbook demonstration of Alfa's role within the KGB.

Alfa also played a pivotal role in the infamous August Coup of 1991. That year, Communist hardliners in the KGB attempted to overthrow Soviet President and General Secretary Mikhail Gorbachev to prevent his liberal market reforms and decentralization from breaking up the Soviet Union.

Alfa received orders to storm the White House (a government legislative building in Moscow that, at the time, housed the acting Parliament of Russia) and eliminate Russian President Boris Yeltsin. Yeltsin had been attempting to rally support behind Soviet President and General Secretary Gorbachev.

The consensus of present military commanders was that Alfa (alongside its sister unit, Vympel) could have cleared the Russian White House of all organized resistance within a half hour. Still, an assessment of potential casualties of Russian civilians ultimately led Alfa operatives to refuse to storm the building, dooming the KGB coup.

Yeltsin, realizing Alfa's pivotal role in sparing his life and the new regime, removed Alfa from its chain of command in the KGB and brought it under his direct control immediately following the crisis.

When the USSR collapsed, the KGB was disbanded. Alfa and its sister unit Vympel were transferred under the authority of the Main Guard Directorate (the predecessor of the FSO), responsible for protecting government officials. Yeltsin's government feared the threat of shifting allegiances in specialized units like Alfa to the regime's continued existence. Eventually, Yeltsin moved Alfa and Vympel to the MVD, re-designating them as "anti-terrorism" units.

For Alfa operatives, being re-tasked as a subordinate unit to the federal police forces was one humiliation too far. A large number of Alfa's most gifted officers quit the unit. Russian oligarchs and organized crime offered them lucrative opportunities that likely paid far better than their state salary and pension. It wasn't until after the catastrophic 1995 Budyonnovsk Hospital Hostage Crisis (Chechen separatists attacked the southern Russian city of Budyonnovsk), in which Alfa played a leading role, that Yeltsin realized that Alfa and Vympel could not perform their mission if the units remained chronically underfunded and under police authority.

Following the crisis, the small remnant of the original Alfa and Vympel units were transferred to FSB, joining what would eventually become the Center of Special Operations. FSB finally funded Alfa's reorganization, retraining, and, ultimately, their rebirth as a leading SMU in the Russian arsenal.

Today, Alfa likely has approximately 300 operatives. Alfa's primary force is stationed in Moscow, and its secondary units are spread between strategically important population centers such as Krasnodar, Yekaterinburg, and Khabarovsk to provide anti-terror coverage to as much of Russia's vast breadth as possible.

Alfa and Vympel are estimated to contain four or five assault groups of 30 men each. Modern Alfa operatives are all officers and must undergo nearly constant training for approximately five years before being fully qualified.

Prospective Alfa officers endure a ruthless training regime (a regime that would never be tolerated in the West). Their training encompasses not only conventional military skills (such as small unit tactics, combat communications, fieldcraft, weapons training and marksmanship, and demolitions) and counter-terrorism skills (like close quarters battle, urban combat, explosive breaching, and offensive driving), but also intelligence tradecraft and special activities. Alfa operatives may engage in espionage, personnel protection, counterintelligence, counterterrorism, universal direct and covert action, military assistance, and irregular warfare at the behest of Russian political leadership.

Western analysts do not fully understand Alfa's jurisdiction. In the days of the KGB, Alfa was a shield protecting Soviet leadership. However, the unit also specialized in counterterrorism missions and counterintelligence interdictions (capture or kill missions on foreign agents operating in Russia), all while engaging in political interdictions abroad.

Under FSB, the unit remains oriented toward internal security, counterterrorism, and counterintelligence concerns of the Kremlin. Yet Alfa is also active in the Donbas region of Ukraine, managing and disciplining the militias of the Donetsk and Luhansk People's Republic.

Russia has never published precisely what Alfa's jurisdiction encompasses, but Alfa divides its workload with its sister unit, Vympel, conducting operations throughout the Russian Federation and CIS countries. Given the unit's function and organizational history, Alfa may prioritize internal missions within the Russian Federation while Vympel prioritizes missions in the CIS, both units working under the direct control and sanction of Russian political leadership. However, these domains are certainly not binding or mutually exclusive. It is well understood that Alfa and Vympel train and deploy together and frequently exchange personnel.

Spetsgruppa Vympel—The Boogeyman's Twin Brother

If Alfa was the KGB's shield, then Vympel was its sword. KGB Chairman Andropov desired a unit that could infiltrate foreign countries to conduct universal direct and covert action, including sabotage and assassinations. Andropov wanted the ability to short-circuit a war with NATO by eliminating the political chain of command before military action could be authorized; particularly the release of nuclear ordnance.

The "illegals" are deep-cover operatives of Directorate S (which now belongs to the SVR) who maintain a permanent presence managing clandestine networks in the West under fabricated identities. KGB heads believed that the "illegals" could also serve as support infrastructure for commando units to aid their infiltration into a target country during a crisis. Vympel would then be able to conduct sabotage and assassinations with a network of contacts, safe houses, vehicles, weapons caches, and money at their disposal. This pool of intelligence officers from the "illegals" of Directorate S eventually became the primary recruiting ground for Vympel.

Although the value of decapitating an enemy government was self-evident to Soviet leadership, the process of creating Spetsgruppa Vympel was slow and driven largely by necessity. A school called the Officer Corps Development Course (KUOS) in Balashikha was founded in 1969 to train KGB intelligence officers in basic combat tactics and irregular warfare. Directorate S acquired KUOS in 1976 and founded the "8th Department", an ambiguous name for a subunit responsible for conducting assassinations and sabotage in foreign countries.

In addition to running an irregular warfare school, tailored task groups of KUOS cadets (strictly, cadets who were advanced in their training) were assembled to address specific crises, tensions, or problem areas abroad on an as-needed basis. For Operation Storm-333, Directorate S created Special Operations Task Group "Zenyth" to aid an Alfa detachment (GROM detachment) in eliminating the leadership of Afghanistan. Following the full-scale invasion of Afghanistan, KUOS assembled Special Operations Task Groups Kaskad-1, Kaskad-2, Kaskad-3, and Kaskad-4.

The mission of the Kaskad task groups was to support KGB counterintelligence operatives in Afghanistan, suppress insurgent activities in local villages, and hunt down enemy agents. Kaskad task groups also trained indigenous operatives to take over duties from their Soviet counterparts when they rotated out of the country.

Later in the war, KUOS deployed Special Operations Task Group Omega to Afghanistan to build, train, and mentor the Afghan counterintelligence service (KAM) and its Special Operations Tasks Battalion. KAM was designated to take over all KGB activities.

In August 1981, Spetsgruppa Vympel (Russian for "Pennant") was born within Directorate S—8th Department, using combat-experienced intelligence officers from the Zenyth and Kaskad (and later Omega) Special Operations Task Groups. Vympel would become the KGB's darkest instrument. It was sanctioned to conduct irregular warfare, military assistance, political interdictions, counterintelligence, universal direct and covert action, special reconnaissance, HUMINT and other intelligence collection activities, and any other mission under the umbrella of full-spectrum special operations.

Despite the many uses KGB leadership found for Vympel, the unit's foundational purpose was to infiltrate and paralyze the leadership of hostile nations (political assassinations and sabotage). Vympel grew as it proved its value, forcing recruitment to expand from the ranks of elite intelligence officers to the larger ranks of the Soviet Armed Forces. Soldiers with relevant experience from elite units such as GRU Spetsnaz or the VDV were likely common prospects.

During the August Coup of 1991, when Spetsgruppa Alfa refused the order to storm the Russian White House, Vympel was also on-site. According to some reports, Vympel was on-deck to take the White House immediately after Alfa; however, given Alfa's insubordination and cited concerns of civilian casualties, KGB leadership considered the coup over and never gave the order for Vympel to execute.

During the 1993 Russian Constitutional Crisis, Vympel and Alfa were again ordered to storm the White House, but this time by Boris Yeltsin. President Yeltsin and Soviet-nationalist hardliners in the Federal Assembly (Parliament) had extra-constitutionally declared each other illegitimate, triggering a constitutional standoff.

Alfa and Vympel would again hesitate in following the order. This open insubordination in the face of an order directly from the President so disgraced the Ground Forces Commander that he reportedly considered placing a gun in his mouth at his command post.

The on-site Alfa and Vympel teams refused to follow orders to storm the White House until Alfa Lieutenant Sergeyev was mortally wounded by sniper fire. There is some confusion about from who and where the sniper fire came, but the rank and file of Vympel and Alfa were outraged. Their concern of civilian casualties was repaid with the death of a comrade. They took President Yeltsin's side and stormed the building.

In the aftermath of the crisis, Alfa was transferred to the MVD, and the old KGB Vympel was dissolved. A fraction of the estimated 300 Vympel officers were transferred to the MVD to establish the Vega Group as specialists in counter-sabotage. The rest chose to end their time in service rather than become a glorified swat team in support of federal police.

Like its sister unit, Vympel was finally transferred to FSB following the bloody 1995 Budyonnovsk hospital hostage crisis. Under FSB, the unit regained its old name and heritage. Vympel's official missions became counterterrorism, nuclear safety enforcement, and the defense of strategic infrastructure.

While these publicly recognized missions seem to indicate that Vympel has moved out of the shadowy world of covert operations and into the light, Vympel is one of the few Russian units that is authorized to employ tactics considered to be "terrorist in nature".

Vympel's authorization to use terrorist tactics allows the unit to conduct sabotage and assassinations. The unit is also authorized to work with insurgencies, enabling local partisans to deploy such tactics.

In March 2000, Vympel deployed to Chechnya and arrested or captured Chechen militant leader Salman Raduyev who led the Kizlyar Hostage Taking Raid into Dagestan (see Chapter 2).

Vympel has been involved in managing Ukrainian militias in the Donbas region. There is evidence that Alfa and Vympel operatives have been dispatched to eliminate separatist militia leaders in Donbas on the occasion that these leaders refuse to obey directives from Moscow. Accounts of these activities are anecdotal, but they provide at least some evidence of a mission portfolio far wider than the Russian government will admit.

As mentioned earlier, it is possible that both Alfa and Vympel now perform similar duties, with Alfa prioritizing activities within Russia and Vympel prioritizing the CIS. But neither unit appears to be hindered by jurisdictional barriers in performing their respective missions.

Vympel's training is very similar to Alfa's, and its recruiting base likely includes intelligence officers, the VDV, and other elite units of the Ground Forces. Vympel has also been known to send operatives abroad to pick up new tactics and techniques. Some sources allege that some Vympel operatives have actually embedded themselves under deep cover into Western SOF units to steal training secrets.

Vympel's highly experienced operatives are expected to speak 2-3 foreign languages, again hinting at Moscow's intent to wield Vympel beyond Russia's borders. Like its sister unit Alfa, prospective operatives are also relentlessly trained over 5 years before they are considered fully qualified Vympel officers.

FSB In Closing

Like SVR, FSB has not historically played the same central role in hybrid warfare as GRU. However, FSB offers Moscow many important tools of political influence and coercion. FSB's policing and intelligence activities in the CIS countries give Moscow the ability to collect intelligence on emerging threats in the countries it considers most vital to its strategic security.

Moscow also accepts CIS political exiles with open arms, forcing CIS members to negotiate with the Kremlin for overturned dictators and strongmen (most of whom are loyal to Moscow). FSB also offers Spetsgruppa Alfa and Spetsgruppa Vympel terrifying Swiss Army knife units that can carry on highly sensitive missions in the Russian periphery.

FSB proved to be a disappointing source of senior statesmen for President Putin, but it has assumed many of the old roles of the KGB. FSB is not only a secret police and counterintelligence service, but it also has foreign intelligence roles in the CIS that are invaluable to Russia when it wages hybrid warfare.

Summary and Conclusions:

Even while Russia adopts hybrid warfare as its approach to armed conflict, the Russian way of war remains conventional. The American Military has been fueled by intelligence in every major conflict of the post-World War II era, with an increasing centricity of SOF in each subsequent intervention.

The difference between America's use of intelligence services to support combat operations and the respective roles of their counterparts in Russian hybrid warfare is that the Russians place enormous emphasis on a dual concept of informational superiority; the concepts of Maskirovka, Aktivnost, and Vnezapnost.

The Russians use information superiority, both in collecting information to guide combat action and in the deployment of targeted messaging and propaganda to create a viable narrative, enabling the seizure of critical objectives in an atmosphere of orchestrated chaos.

In chaos there is profit.

When opportunities open, SOF and elite ground forces can rapidly maneuver to secure key terrain and infrastructure. Such tactics serve as a means for Russia to create asymmetric advantages in conventional military conflict.

---

1. Career progression is a hallmark of the American system. Whether in civilian agencies, the military, or politics, American government employees are encouraged to progress between roles and positions so that they can develop broad experiences and gain wider institutional knowledge. This also prevents corrupt or incompetent individuals from remaining in influential positions indefinitely and ensures that there is always new incoming talent. The downside is that career progression does not engender subject matter expertise in government leaders and personnel as much as it creates generalists.

2. Anna Chapman was a Russian operative who worked in the West until the FBI arrested her in 2010. Anna Kushchenko immigrated to the United Kingdom from Russia and married Alex Chapman in 2001, gaining British citizenship. Anna first began working her way into elite circles in London, but eventually divorced Alex and permanently relocated to New York City in 2009. Under the guise of working in real estate, Anna Chapman worked hard to meet wealthy and powerful people around Manhattan in order to reach into political circles. She had a reputation for enjoying New York's high society and nightlife. She's now a celebrity in Russia.

Chapter Six

Russia's Elite Forces

Hybrid warfare is only made possible through intelligence services. Intelligence supports informational superiority and non-kinetic preparation of the battlespace. Non-kinetic preparatory operations must create space for elite forces to maneuver on the battlefield during the kinetic phase. In Russia, the intelligence services each have elite units at their disposal to shape the battlefield, and these forces allow the Kremlin to act abroad with a delicate touch from an unseen hand.

However, forces subordinate to the intelligence services are simply too specialized and too few to conduct an entire campaign on their own. Even though special mission units (SMUs) are necessary for highly sensitive and complex taskings, eventually, hybrid warfare requires more kinetic force than the intelligence services can provide. This is where Russia turns to elite units like the VDV which can deploy rapidly and in large numbers.

Russian Airborne Infantry—The Premier Combat Force of the Russian Federation

Russia's Airborne Forces, pronounced Vozdushno-Desantnye Voyska (Russian: Воздушно-десантные войска) or known simply as the elite VDV, are the backbone of Russia's elite forces in manpower, esprit de corps, prestige, and combat readiness. The VDV has spearheaded operations in Chechnya, Crimea, Donbas, Syria, and Georgia.[1] It also features prominently in Russia's annual military exercises (Vostok and Zapad), evidence of their continued status as Russia's premier combat force.

In most armies, elite Airborne infantry units are tasked with parachuting behind the line of contact to secure key objectives (such as airfields, crossroads, bridges, villages, and other structures of significance that yield a military advantage). The somewhat heavier Air Assault infantry leverage helicopters to achieve greater mobility. These units airlift troops ahead of advancing ground forces in order to tie up enemy reserves and secure key infrastructure. Air Assault forces typically utilize airfields seized by their Airborne counterparts to push mechanized infantry companies behind the line of contact.

Like GRU, the VDV is directly subordinate to the General Staff under the command of a Colonel General (currently Mikhail Yuryevich Teplinsky). They are recognized by their distinctive sky-blue beret and the blue-striped telnyashka (Russian: тельня́шка) undershirt. VDV receives Russia's top officers, preferred enlisted recruits, and best equipment so that it can act as the personal crisis response force of the President of Russia.

Russia continues the Soviet organizational practice of maintaining the airborne infantry as an independent armed service branch, apart from the Ground Forces. During the Soviet era, the VDV was designed to deploy behind enemy lines to cause enough chaos to enable a Soviet Ground Forces breakout. The VDV might also be tasked with securing strategically important infrastructure, tactical nuclear weapons sites, and airfields. After the fall of Communism, the VDV was reorganized into an air-mobility-based mechanized infantry force.

From the bottom-up, the Airborne platoon consists of three infantry fighting vehicles (IFVs) (BMD-2s or BMD-4Ms), each containing a squad of 7 paratroopers. Typically, these squads consist of a squad leader, driver-mechanic, gunner, two riflemen, a machine gunner, and assistant machine gunner. The platoon will have a maximum of 14 paratroopers that can dismount for ground combat. VDV platoons are formed around the BMD family of IFVs (either BMD-2 or the updated BMD-4).
The BMD is a tracked IFV with a turret, a 100mm cannon, a 30mm auto-cannon, and a secondary armament of 7.62mm PKM machine gun.

Three platoons constitute an Airborne company, accompanied by a company headquarters element (two IFVs) and a grenadier-machine gun section transported in an APC. Three infantry companies form the core of a VDV battalion, which also includes a headquarters and command staff that is transported by a motorized signals platoon, one reconnaissance platoon (2-3 IFVs), one support platoon, and one medical section.

Air Assault battalions differ in two ways from their Airborne-paratrooper counterparts. First, Air Assault support platoons and medical sections are transported by air-droppable trucks (KamAZ-43501 and GAZ-66). Second, they include a motorized 6-tube 82mm mortar battery for mobile indirect fire-support. Three VDV battalions constitute either regiments, which are subordinate to a division, or independent brigades.

Air Assault regiments generally contain one command and control (C2) Company, one signals company, three Air Assault line battalions, one anti-tank battery, one A2/AD battery, one self-propelled artillery battalion, one sniper company, one sapper company, one Nuclear-Biological-Radiological (NBC) Defense company, one medical company, one maintenance company, one airborne support company, and one material support company.

Air Assault divisions are, in-turn, outfitted with a C2 company, signals battalion, three Air Assault line regiments, one tank battalion, one artillery regiment, one anti-access and area denial (A2/AD) regiment, one reconnaissance battalion, one sapper battalion, one material support battalion, one medical detachment, one airborne support company, one electronic warfare company, one unmanned aerial vehicle (UAV) company, one NBC Defense company, and one military police (MP) company.

Airborne divisions have two primary differences apart from their Air Assault brothers. They do not include a tank battalion, and their primary combat power consists of two Airborne line regiments (rather than three Air Assault line regiments).

The VDV contains two Airborne divisions (98th and 106th Guards Airborne Divisions), two Air Assault divisions (7th and 76th Guards Air Assault Divisions), and four independent Air Assault brigades (11th, 31st, 56th and 83rd Guards Airborne Brigades). Brigades resemble regiments in forces and fires, but they have all the internal support units necessary to maneuver independently.

Regiments are subordinate to a division and maneuver as a part of the larger unit. Independent Air Assault brigades consist of one Airborne line battalion, two Air Assault line battalions, one artillery battalion, one reconnaissance company, and several other specialty companies (engineers, signals, air defense, maintenance, anti-tank, support, and medical).

In the West, Airborne and Air Assault infantry are generally considered to be "light" infantry units. This means that they are trained for intimate close combat (especially in urban terrain), maintain a high level of combat readiness, and are foot mobile (or light-skinned vehicle mobile).

In Mother Russia, VDV battalions are fielded as mechanized infantry, similar to a typical motorized rifle regiment, but they achieve increased mobility through transport aviation via the 61st Air Army, the unit designation for Russia's Military Transport Aviation Command.

On paper, this allows VDV divisions, brigades, regiments, and battalions to bring much more firepower and mobility to the fight than their direct Western counterparts. However, despite being employed as mechanized infantry, the VDV's BMD-2s and BMD-4Ms offer little more protection than the American Mine Resistant Ambush Protected (MRAP) or High Mobility Multipurpose Wheeled Vehicles (HMMWVs are known in the United States as the "HUM-V" or "Hummer"). This means that VDV battalions are often employed in a mechanized infantry role despite more closely resembling Western light infantry.

Like the Ground Forces, the VDV is also increasingly operating in battalion tactical groups (BTG), a task-organized heavy battalion capable of independent combined arms maneuver and fires. In September 2012, the General Staff issued a general order instructing every line regiment and independent brigade in the Russian Ground Forces and VDV to establish at least one BTG within the regiment or brigade itself.

BTGs fielded by the VDV are uniquely vulnerable. VDV companies are designed around air mobility through the IL-76 transport aircraft, which can each carry one platoon (three IFVs). This means that an entire Airborne or Air Assault company can be transported to the battlefield by 4-5 aircraft depending on the load configuration.

Due to the need for an IFV platoon that can be transported by a single IL-76 transport, VDV platoons are significantly smaller than companies of the Russian Ground Forces. VDV platoons have approximately 42-46 dismounted infantrymen per company compared to the Ground Forces' 66+. Additionally, as was explained in Chapter 4, the professionalization of Russia's Armed Services is an ongoing process and contract soldiers are at a premium. The VDV is a priority destination for contract soldiers, but there are insufficient numbers to completely fill the ranks. In fact, most Russian units are only at 75% of full manning. The average VDV company may be fielding closer to 30-35 dismounted soldiers, meaning VDV companies more closely resemble NATO platoons in manpower.

BTGs usually have three infantry line companies (essentially a motorized rifle battalion) accompanied by a large portion of the regiment's firepower and support assets, including one signals platoon, one anti-tank battery, one A2/AD battery, one self-propelled artillery battalion, one sniper platoon, one sapper platoon, one NBC Defense platoon, one medical platoon, one maintenance platoon, one airborne support platoon, and one material support platoon.

Protecting a regiment's worth of support assets is usually a task for three line battalions, but BTGs must make do with three line companies: a problem greatly exacerbated by the small nature of VDV companies, which must be air-mobile through the IL-76 transport. So, despite being Russia's most aggressive, most well-trained, and most well-equipped fighting men, the VDV's combat capabilities are catastrophically undermined by the limitations of their basic fighting units and the inherent weaknesses of the battalion tactical group formation itself.

The VDV has an estimated strength of 45,000 soldiers, but the Ministry of Defense has set a goal to grow the force to 60,000. Air Assault divisions are likely to become "heavier", with expanded force structure, tanks, and air defense assets. Each division (7th, 76th, 98th, and 106th divisions) is to receive an additional Airborne regiment, and, due to its success, the 31st Guards Airborne Brigade will be expanded into the 104th Guards Airborne Division (a numerical designation revived from the Soviet-era VDV). Combat training for the VDV now also includes battalion-level firing exercises, rather than just company level, so that the VDV can increasingly shift towards fighting in large formations.

Despite an aging vehicle park and chronic under-maintenance, Transport Aviation has been a bright spot in otherwise moribund Aerospace Forces operations. And, while the IL-76 transport aircraft is increasingly viewed as inadequate for large airborne operations (a correct assessment), each VDV division retains its own aircraft, which are permanently assigned to support rapid deployment.

Western observers estimate that, following post-Soviet reorganizations, each VDV division can theoretically deploy in two and a half lifts via organic air transport assets (primarily the IL-76). The independent Air Assault brigades are increasing operational mobility by leaning on helicopters.

The VDV owes a great deal to Colonel General Vladimir Anatolyevich Shamanov. He served as Chief of Staff for the 7th Guards Airborne Brigade during the First Chechen War in 1994 and then held a series of senior leadership positions in the VDV throughout the Second Chechen War (1999-2000). Known as a butcher both by his own men and the enemy, his reputation for a certain macabre ruthlessness eventually led to his forced retirement from command in 2000.

Shamanov joined Vladimir Putin's entourage and gained assignments to top political roles. Due to his overall success, Shamanov was appointed Commander of VDV in 2009. Shamanov's political success and connections within Putin's regime gave the VDV immunity to most of the major budget cuts, purges, and reorganizations of the Russian Armed Services during the Serdyukov Reforms. In comparison, the Spetsnaz Brigades were temporarily removed from GRU authority and given to the Ground Forces. VDV would remain a privileged reserve force of the President of Russia, a status it enjoys today.

45th Guards Spetsnaz Brigade (or Special Reconnaissance Brigade)

The 45th Guards Spetsnaz Brigade (often referred to as 45th Special Reconnaissance Brigade) is an independent Spetsnaz brigade within the VDV. While the 45th retains traditional Spetsnaz roles like deep reconnaissance and direct action, it is also tasked with several missions that are more in keeping with the Western conception of Special Operations, including special reconnaissance, universal direct and covert action, counterinsurgency, military information support operations, and irregular warfare. In 2016, the unit strength was an estimated 700 men plus support personnel.

The 45th Special Reconnaissance Regiment was originally formed as a regiment following the union of two Soviet-era Airborne battalions (218th and 901st Battalions) that had managed to maintain a highly competent core cadre of officers after the Soviet collapse and subsequent reorganizations. Most of these officers trained in the Spetsnaz GRU system, and they had a free hand to make the 45th Special Reconnaissance Regiment their own.

While the 45th fills many of the same roles as the other Ground Forces Spetsnaz brigades, they specialize in counterinsurgency (COIN). They have also developed tailored psychological warfare (PSYWAR) assets and advanced unmanned aerial surveillance (UAS) capabilities to support irregular warfare. The 45th also supports Russia's premier SMU, the Special Operations Forces Command (KSSO), in conducting what in the American lexicon would be considered Advanced Force Operations (AFO) taskings. This allows KSSO teams or elements to become kinetic immediately following their insertion into the battlespace.

When the First and Second Chechen Wars created a demand for practitioners of COIN, the 45th debuted as one of Russia's premier COIN specialists. Like other Spetsnaz units, the 45th is often operationally controlled by the GRU. Indeed, the 45th is perhaps GRU's most professional and capable Spetsnaz brigade, benefitting from top-notch contract-soldier recruits from VDV line units, always receiving the latest equipment, pioneering new tactics, and enjoying a preferred status due to its position within the VDV itself.

The 45th gave the Kremlin a good look at its capabilities in Crimea and Donbas; thus, in 2016, the decision was made to expand the regiment into a full brigade by tripling its Spetsnaz line companies from 6 to 18. Conceivably, this would allow the 45th to conduct combat operations in three independent regions. While there is reasonable doubt that the 45th can maintain the same unit-to-unit quality through such a rapid expansion, the 45th SRB is likely to be in the vanguard of future Russian interventions abroad, particularly in missions where psychological warfare, proxy forces, or counterinsurgency capabilities are required.

Russian Naval Infantry (Marines)

Russian Naval Infantry (referred to as Marines in the West) receives far less press attention than the renowned VDV, but it is an elite force that has played a critical role in all of Russia's recent military endeavors. Consisting of about 8,000-9,000 personnel, the Naval Infantry is responsible for both offensive and defensive coastal actions.

Unlike the U.S. Marine Corps, the Russian Naval Infantry lacks the size, firepower, and equipment required to conduct large amphibious landings. Oddly, the force is also not exactly designed as an elite light infantry and special operations capable force like the United Kingdom's Royal Marines. Russia's Naval Infantry is a light mechanized force and has a very different doctrine for amphibious missions, preferring to use air assault and parachute forces to neutralize coastal defenses.

Russia's Naval Infantry have a shared heritage with the prestigious VDV and often train at the Ryazan Training Center alongside VDV troops. In fact, many Naval Infantry officers are VDV officers. The force is broken up into Naval Infantry brigades (much smaller than a typical VDV brigade) and independent battalions, respectively, assigned to the major Russian fleets and flotillas.

Alongside the VDV, Russia's Naval Infantry have a reputation for being among the most capable units in Russia's conventional military forces. In fact, 61st Naval Infantry Brigade is considered one of the best-trained and most experienced combat units in the entire Russian armed forces. The 61st has deployed to combat zones in Crimea, Donbas (Luhansk), and Syria in front of many other conventional forces units that were, at the time, in a higher state of readiness to deploy, specifically because of its sterling reputation.

The Naval Infantry's Spetsnaz components are the Naval Special Reconnaissance. They are divided into four "Naval or Marine Reconnaissance Stations" (MRSs), each a subordinate component of a Naval Infantry Brigade which, in turn, is attached to a Naval Fleet or Flotilla. These units of combat reconnaissance divers are informally known as the Russian "commando frogmen". Naval or Marine Reconnaissance Stations are company-sized elements (120-200 men) that are operationally subordinate to GRU.

The MRSs fill the same primary roles as Ground Forces Spetsnaz GRU units in direct action and deep reconnaissance, but they have a maritime reconnaissance focus for ports, naval facilities, offshore platforms, and inland waterways. They have also been known to train for boarding and seizing enemy warships as well as counter-sabotage missions for the Russian surface fleet.

The Russian Naval Infantry also offers another type of "commando frogman" called the Counteraction Underwater Diversionary Forces and Facilities (Russian acronym: PDSS). These combat swimmers are trained to conduct land and sea operations behind enemy lines, like their reconnaissance diver brothers, but were created for a more defensive purpose.

The PDSS conduct underwater patrols, counter-mining operations, and clearance diving in order to protect Russian vessels, inland waterways, and port facilities from sabotage by enemy "frogmen" and special operations forces (like perhaps the British Special Boat Service). The PDSS combat swimmers operate in numerous detachments of 50-60 men, each stationed at one of Russia's many port facilities.

The Russian Special Operations Forces Command (KSSO)

The very generic sounding Russian Special Operations Forces Command (KSSO) (Russian: командование силами специальных операций) is an independent command that trains, deploys, and supports Russia's leading special mission unit (SMU). Within KSSO are several operational elements developed on the Western model (pioneered by the British Special Air Service).

Where Spetsnaz brigades are operationally controlled by the GRU, KSSO is a strategic command led by a Major General that answers directly to the Chief of the General Staff. KSSO began training in 2009 and became active in 2013, born out of the need for the Russian General Staff to have a "Tier 1" SMU that could conduct full-spectrum special operations in support of foreign interventions.

Why Not Just Use the Existing Spetsnaz Units?

Strategic foreign interventions require national-level intelligence assets, sophisticated planning, high degrees of specialization, and extensive support infrastructure. These requirements simply outstrip the GRU Spetsnaz brigades' capabilities. In fact, it is the troops of the VDV that are actually seen by Russians as Russia's elite "trigger pullers", and they have a much higher degree of prestige in the Russian Armed Services than the Spetsnaz GRU.

While Spetsnaz brigades are certainly a cut above the rest, their manning remains subject to a twice-yearly turnover of personnel. Spetsnaz brigades are primarily manned by professional soldiers who volunteer to sign three-year contracts. These contract soldiers are recruited from Russia's civilian workforce (or high schools), similar to enlistments in the United States. However, not all Russian contract soldiers are really "volunteers".

Russia makes up for its recruitment shortfalls every year by conscripting (drafting) civilians into the Armed Services to perform many of the more menial jobs for two years in service. Many conscripted soldiers choose to sign a three-year contract as though they were volunteers, trading a year's extension of their 2-year conscripted service requirement for better pay and a degree of choice about where they serve.

Despite efforts to fully professionalize the force, approximately 20-30% of the Spetsnaz brigades' manning is still done by conscript soldiers. New soldiers join the unit every six months, and soldiers who have finished their two or three years of service depart. Comparatively, members of FSB's Alfa and Vympel can expect five years of training before they are even considered fully qualified. Interestingly, as KSSO has become operational, GRU Spetsnaz units have come to resent the new force for their obvious decline in institutional standing.

Russian and Soviet planners have historically relied on elite KGB (or FSB) units to conduct unusually complex foreign interventions. The textbook example is Operation Storm-333, where Alfa and Vympel conducted a joint mission to eliminate Afghan President Amin and his entourage. The raid on the Presidential Palace was supported by a company of 345th Guards Airborne Regiment and a battalion of the 154th Separate Spetsnaz

Detachment, but the storming of the Presidential Palace itself had to be outsourced to more specialized practitioners of the Dark Arts: Alfa and Vympel.

However, tasking Alfa and Vympel to conduct foreign interventions also creates new institutional challenges. Both units belong to FSB, so the Chief of the General Staff must request them, rather than deploying them freely. Alfa and Vympel also have minimal support assets, which limits their capabilities. Both units may be ordered to conduct a variety of highly sensitive missions (such as espionage, personnel protection, counterintelligence, counterterrorism, universal direct and covert action, military assistance, or irregular warfare); however, in 2009, Russian military planners looked abroad and surveyed best practices. They discovered the extent to which talented support staff, infrastructure, sophisticated training regimes, team development, individual career management, and customized equipment were being employed in the U.S. Special Operations Command (USSOCOM).

KSSO Gets Started

In 2009, the "Directorate of Special Operations" was established with a core cadre from Unit 92154 at Solnechnogorsk training center, near Lake Senezh. Rumor has it that Unit 92154 was a Spetsnaz detachment that was specially assembled from highly experienced Spetsnaz GRU troops to engage in guerilla fighting in Chechnya and the Caucasus mountains. A second training center was established at Kubinka-2 on the outskirts of Moscow. These centers received extensive infrastructure overhauls to support training, command and control, logistics and support, and deployment.

In April 2012, the new command was renamed "Special Operations Forces Command" or KSSO. The KSSO consists of the Special Purpose

Center (Kubinka-2), the Center for Special Operations Forces (Senezh), the Center for Training Specialists (Senezh), the 561st Emergency Rescue Center, and several operational line teams with varying specialties.

Russia has not merely taken a Spetsnaz unit and re-designated it. The methodology of bringing in new personnel to KSSO is unique, extensive, and distills thoroughly vetted top-notch operatives. KSSO recruiters seek out the very best performers in conventional forces, especially in reconnaissance units, and offer them positions in Spetsnaz GRU brigades where they can gain relevant experience. Their performance in Spetsnaz GRU is tracked until they are deemed ready for KSSO, at which point they are reassigned to begin specialized training at Senezh and Kubinka-2.

Training of "officer recruit special operators" begins at the Ryazan Higher Airborne Command School and the Novosibirsk Higher Military Command School. Advertisements are also placed in military enlistment offices, and monthly tryouts are offered. Minimum qualifications for candidates include running 3 kilometers in 12:00-12:30, sprinting 100m in 13.0-14.0 seconds, completing at least 18 pullups, and passing a physical.

Selected officers and enlisted candidates are sent to Senezh where they undergo further rigorous examinations in physical conditioning, personality, and teamwork. The Senezh experience is not intended to produce capable individuals but teams that can work together to complete complex objectives. All candidates are vetted and tested for their ability to band together as a team to solve problems, and teams themselves are constructed from mutually complementary individuals. KSSO is not looking for the strongest, fastest, or smartest soldier. They are looking for the correct soldier with the right experience.

At Senezh, recruits are trained in freefall parachuting, mountaineering, swimming, scuba diving, and urban and close-quarters combat (CQC). At

Kubinka-2, recruits learn reconnaissance and maritime operations. There is also a mountain warfare center called "Terksol" in Kardino-Balkaria. After receiving the mandatory qualifications for all unit members, newly minted operatives may be sent to a variety of schools for special skill sets. KSSO is estimated to have 2,000-2,500 personnel under its command, while the operational line teams may have around 250 operatives, organized into 5 squadrons of approximately 50 men each.

KSSO has also embraced the way Western militaries support SOF, operating independently as a rapidly deployable force. The Command has a dedicated "special aviation brigade" that controls combat aviation assets as well as a squadron of IL-76 transport planes. The Command also has extensive combat support and combat service support functions. In fact, the Senezh compound has a helipad large enough to accommodate three Mi-26 heavy transport helicopters (each with a carrying capacity of 70 soldiers).

The Russian Ministry of Defense defines Special Operations as:

> A complex of special actions of troops (forces), coordinated by objectives and tasks, time and place of execution, conducted according to a single concept and plan in order to achieve certain goals. Special actions of troops (forces) are activities carried out by specially designated, organized, trained and equipped force, which apply methods and ways of fighting not typical for conventional forces (special reconnaissance, sabotage, counterterrorism, counter-sabotage, counterintelligence, guerilla warfare, counter-guerilla warfare and "other activities").

KSSO Begins Deploying Forces

Although KSSO almost certainly played a security role during the Sochi Olympics, their first real use was in Crimea. By early 2014, the GRU had conducted extensive intelligence preparation of the battlespace, with constant monitoring of Ukrainian force postures and communications. Alongside the 45th Special Reconnaissance Regiment (not yet a brigade) and the 431st Naval Reconnaissance Station (eventually reorganized into the 388th), KSSO teams were likely deployed to Crimea on or around February 24, 2014. The bloodless, irregular war that followed would have impressed Sun Tzu.[2]

Russian Forces seized power and then disarmed, blockaded, and converted over to their cause all organized military resistance on the peninsula. GRU-controlled proxy forces (consisting of local rabble-rousers, would-be-politicians, and ethnic Russians) began seizing infrastructure, transportation hubs, and government buildings in black uniforms.

A single KSSO detachment deployed to Crimea dressed like a similar motley crew of Russian proxies and seized the building of the Supreme Council of Crimea.[3] Sergei Aksanov, a Russian politician with links to organized crime, was brought in as the new Prime Minister of Crimea, and he initiated an "emergency session of the Supreme Council". The Crimean MPs walked into the building under armed guard. Aksanov then claimed the men in black uniforms were under his direct control as Crimea's Self-Defense Forces. Aksanov held a vote for Crimea to hold (stage) a referendum on whether to rejoin Mother Russia.

Russia surprised the world in September of 2015 when it launched an intervention in Syria. The mission to prop up Bashar al-Assad's regime would be very different from Russia's operations in Crimea and Donbas.

Using al-Assad's Syrian Army as a well-armed and motivated partner force, Moscow dusted off old methods of high-intensity conflict through proxies, harkening back to the old Soviet military assistance missions in places like Angola, Zimbabwe, and Zaire (modern-day Democratic Republic of Congo).

Whenever possible, Russian Ground Forces were kept clear from direct ground combat in Syria, deferring instead to Syrian loyalist forces and Russia's Wagner mercenaries. Proxy forces were supported by Russian air power, which formed the primary contingent of Russian military assistance. Russian advisors had been present in Syria for some time, training al-Assad's forces on Russian weapon systems (purchased with loans from Russian state-owned banks).

After the Russian intervention was launched, GRU Spetsnaz detachments and KSSO operatives were called upon primarily for intelligence-surveillance-reconnaissance (ISR), military assistance, and special security missions. Special reconnaissance and military assistance are core functions of KSSO. GRU Spetsnaz detachments were likely delighted to have a classic ISR mission.

As one Spetsnaz officer noted to military theorist Mark Galeotti, "This is the kind of war Spetsnaz have been training for thirty years." Russian close air support and battlefield intelligence would prove to be the deciding factor between al-Assad's loyalist forces and the plethora of rebel groups trying to depose him.

At the peak of the intervention, approximately 250 GRU Spetsnaz soldiers were in-country. They were drawn from several Spetsnaz brigades and the 431st Naval Reconnaissance Station (eventually reorganized into the 388th MRS). While KSSO was a part of every major operation in Syria, press reporting only singled out a team of KSSO operatives reportedly in-country for sniper and scout missions. KSSO operatives were used to lead Syrian Ground Forces, perform deep reconnaissance, and conduct terminal guidance for close air support.

KSSO was also trusted with many missions of higher complexity, like hostage rescue and personnel recovery.

In November 2015, KSSO operatives received and executed a dual tasking: recover the flight recorder from a downed Su-24M and rescue survivors from a downed Mi-8AMTsh helicopter.

On August 16, 2017, a 5-man KSSO element on deep patrol in the abandoned town of Akerbat was ambushed by 40 Islamic State terrorists (platoon strength). After all other members of the patrol were wounded, Lance Corporal Denis Portnyagin mounted a lone defense, killing 14 terrorists single-handedly and protecting his comrades until they were rescued.

On September 20, 2017, ISIS jihadists attempted to capture a Russian military police platoon that was stationed in Idlib to observe a ceasefire. KSSO served as the ground element of a rescuing task force, coordinating dozens of airstrikes on organized opposition as they advanced to rescue the lost platoon. It is estimated that the ISIS elements suffered heavy casualties, and all military policemen survived. During Operation Dawn of Idlib, KSSO conducted several raids behind enemy lines that killed several dozen ISIS fighters. ISIS losses included factional field commanders of Ahrar al-Sham, Jaysh al-Nasr, Suqour Al-Sham, Hurras Al-Din, and others.

The KSSO's Senior Lieutenant Alexander Prokhorenko was killed during the Palmyra Offensive. He was in a forward observer position, identifying targets for airstrikes, when he was detected by ISIS fighters. Completely surrounded and realizing that there was no way to make the evacuation position and knowing he would either be killed or captured, he requested an airstrike on his own position to kill as many enemy fighters as possible. President Putin declared him a Hero of the Russian Federation.

Although audio of his last words was never released, the Russian government released a transcript to his family and the public.

> *Prokhorenko:* They are outside, conduct the airstrike now please hurry, this is the end, tell my family I love them, and I died fighting for my motherland.
>
> *Command:* Negative, return to the green line.
>
> *Prokhorenko:*Unable command. I am surrounded. They are outside. I don't want them to take me and parade me. Conduct the airstrike. They will make a mockery of me and this uniform. I want to die with dignity and take all these bastards with me. Please, my last wish. Conduct the airstrike. They will kill me either way.
>
> *Command:* Please confirm your request.
>
> *Prokhorenko:* They are outside, this is the end commander, thank you, tell my family and my country I love them. Tell them I was brave and I fought until I could no longer. Please take care of my family, avenge my death, good bye commander, tell my family I love them.
>
> *Command:* {No response. The Commanding officer presumably authorized the airstrike.}

> #OTD in 2016 Russian officer Alexander Prokhorenko was posthumously declared a Hero of Russia for courage and heroism in the performance of his military duties. Near the city of Palmyra, being surrounded by ISIS, he ordered an airstrike on his position to destroy the terrorists.
>
> Though Moscow has used Syria as a proving ground for young officers who have been earmarked for higher command, Russia never intended to use either KSSO or Spetsnaz as a "tip of the spear" for assault missions or conventional ground combat.
>
> President Putin's national security team was adamant about not getting sucked into desert ground combat that might damage domestic public opinion or consume scarce resources. Thus, KSSO has played the role of an enabler for Syrian loyalist forces, particularly through training, deep reconnaissance, and terminal guidance.
>
> Embassy of the Russian Federation in Sri Lanka. Facebook Post. 11 April 2020.

What Comes Next for Russia's Newest Elite Force?

KSSO is the future of Russian special missions and will continue to take a leading role in hybrid warfare. Its operational teams constitute Russia's most well-funded, well-resourced, well-supported, and well-trained elite forces. As KSSO continues to build institutional standing, it will increasingly draw Russia's top talent and justify investment of scarce resources into infrastructure, aviation, specialized equipment, and support personnel.

It is also likely that GRU Spetsnaz, Alfa, Vympel, and the VDV will adopt practices pioneered by KSSO. In the way that British SAS is often supported by detachments of elite Paratroopers or Royal Marine Commandos, KSSO may also be institutionalizing support relationships with a select cadre of Spetsnaz and VDV detachments. KSSO already has a working relationship with GRU Spetsnaz in Syria.

Wagner Group

Private Military Contractors (PMCs) have long been illegal in Russia. The Kremlin fears paramilitary forces that are under the control of singular individuals. The high corruption level within the regime and the numerous influential oligarchs who retain enormous personal resources make PMCs a deep political liability. However, despite the illegal status of PMCs in Russia, the Kremlin has embraced Wagner.

Wagner Group is a mercenary organization in the worst sense of the word; it has been integrated into Russia's military chain of command and takes its orders from the Ministry of Defense. Because Wagner is more of an unofficial branch of the Russian military than a conventional mercenary company, fears of an oligarch-funded coup via PMC have historically been mitigated, at least to the point that Wagner's benefits outweigh the dangers.

During the Soviet era, Moscow made extensive use of "military advisors" abroad, though they were functionally little more than mercenaries. Moscow recognizes that it cannot always deny the existence of Russian-speaking operatives abroad, so it adopts the narrative that these mercenaries are "volunteers or soldiers on extended leave".

The Soviets deployed unofficial personnel to Egypt (1967-1973), Syria (1967-1974), Lebanon (late 1970s), Angola (1975-1991), and numerous other countries and respective conflict zones. These military advisors were

Soviet citizens acting ostensibly on their own behalf while receiving a salary from a Soviet proxy. These "volunteers" were mercenaries in all but name, and they were usually disavowed by the Kremlin and disbanded at the conclusion of the conflict.

Wagner was founded by Dmitry Utkin, a former Lieutenant Colonel and GRU brigade commander, sometime in 2013. An ultra-nationalist, Utkin embraced "Russkiy-Mir", the notion of a Russian World (mostly the former Soviet Union and its Warsaw Pact allies) beyond the actual geographic boundaries of Russia. The ideology is akin to pan-Slavic identity and harkens to Russia's cited role of protecting Slavic ethnicities in Eastern Europe.

Utkin's nationalism may have aided in gaining the Kremlin's trust for Wagner's first real deployments to Eastern Ukraine and then Syria. Russian oligarch Dmitry Prigozhin is on Wagner's Board of Directors and is heavily involved in promoting the organization to policymakers in Moscow. Prigozhin owns, among many other enterprises, the Concord-M catering corporation which supports catering contracts for the Moscow and St. Petersburg school systems.

Wagner in Ukraine

First reports of Wagner operating in Ukraine date back to the early 2014 Annexation of Crimea. At the time, Wagner was merely a patchwork of local volunteers, Cossacks, and remnants of the Slavonic Corps (a Hong Kong-registered predecessor to Wagner that saw little real success).[4] However, Wagner's first real heavy lifting took place in the Luhansk People's Republic (LPR), one of the Russian-supported separatist states in the Donbas region of Eastern Ukraine.

Lacking a social media presence and seldom mentioned by local authorities, Wagner's mercenaries were nevertheless deeply involved in the regional conflict, serving as force multipliers, trainers, and separatist officers. In Donbas, Wagner served a similar function to American Green Berets (U.S. Army Special Forces), enabling a resistance movement under covert sanction and plausible deniability. The operations were marked by a high level of competence, indicating that Wagner may have been receiving direct tasking and support from the GRU at the time.

Wagner was also responsible for ensuring that Russian-sponsored separatists did not grow too independent from Moscow. These activities included assassinating the LPR's Defense Minister, Alexander Bednov; assassinating the leader of the Prizrak Brigade, Aleksey Mozgovoy; disarming the Odessa Mechanized Brigade; and many other repressive actions against any separatist leaders who refused to follow directives from Moscow.

Wagner in Syria

Wagner enjoyed a high degree of initial success in Syria. Its mercenaries played a central role in the recapture of Palmyra in the Spring of 2016 and were also tasked by GRU and FSB with duties around Latakia and Aleppo. Wagner provided personnel embedded within Syrian ground units as a vanguard, force multipliers, security specialists, and C2 nodes. And, unlike Western PMCs, Wagner played no role in logistics or support.

Whatever initial success Wagner had is likely attributable to the lack of a well-organized opposition; Syrian rebel militias and ISIS forces were untrained, without any real leadership, and put in the field without effective C2. The conflict with U.S. SOF at Deir al-Zour shined a very bright light on Wagner's inadequacies.

On February 7, 2018, approximately 500 pro-al Assad Syrian forces, complete with T-72 main battle tanks, infantry fighting vehicles, and artillery, lined up on the western bank of the Euphrates River. The river served as the dividing line between Russian and American zones of influence.

As the pro-Syrian forces began crossing the river and maneuvering towards a small American outpost at Deir al-Zour, American officials made use of established deconfliction lines, warning Moscow to call them off. Secretary of Defense Mattis even called Chief of the Russian General Staff Valery Gerasimov directly, who claimed that these ground forces were not Russian and were outside of his control. American officials knew this to be a falsehood due to active monitoring of the communications traffic where everyone was speaking Russian.

A team of 30 Americans (a mix of SOF and Rangers) hunkered down and, as incoming artillery and mortar fire began to pound their small compound, returned fire while coordinating a series of ruthless airstrikes on the hostile forces. The compound was soon reinforced by a team of Green Berets supported by a Marine platoon, and American air support began arriving in waves.

Reaper drones, F-15E fighters, F-22 fighters, AC-130 gunships, and even B-52 strategic bombers pounded these mysterious Russian-speaking fighters until a few survivors abandoned the wreckage of their armored vehicles and limped back across the Euphrates.

In the aftermath of the battle, the New York Times estimated that 200-300 enemy combatants had been killed. Many of these casualties were soldiers of the al-Assad regime, but best estimates assert that between 100-200 of them were Wagner mercenaries.

The general consensus is that these Wagner-led forces crossed the Euphrates hoping to secure a Conoco natural gas rig near Deir al-Zour. Wagner assumed that the civilian-led American chain of command would be indecisive in authorizing the direct use of force against Russian troops, creating a small window for Wagner and its Syrian proxies to overwhelm the small American garrison, provided the Wagner-backed convoy could advance fast enough. These tactics bring to mind Maskirovka (Camouflage) and Vnezapnost (Surprise): bread and butter practices in hybrid warfare.

Secretary of Defense (ret. General) Mattis was not so accommodating. The decisiveness of his leadership, the appropriate delegation of authorities to the theater commander and ground force commander, the stubbornness of the American garrison, and the extensive kinetic assets that were stacked on-site for a fight at Deir al-Zour revealed the formula for defeating hybrid warfare.

The Wagner forces leading the assault were, for the most part, militarily inexperienced. Prior to 2017, with trivial exceptions, Wagner had strictly recruited men with formal military experience. However, as the need for additional personnel increased, Wagner was forced to loosen recruiting standards, hiring ethnic Ukrainians, Cossacks, and other civilian volunteers with no proven military background. And, while pre-deployment training for Wagner personnel had been excellent, many of these practices were abandoned to increase numbers. The casualties at Deir al-Zour notably lacked veterans, especially former Spetsnaz or VDV men.

Wagner Abroad

Russia has found uses for mercenaries far beyond Ukraine and Syria. Russia is deploying Wagner abroad to former client states of the

Soviet Union, countries with low-intensity conflict zones, countries with resources in petroleum or minerals, and countries that could potentially buy Russian military hardware.

When dispatched, Wagner trains host nation forces in military tactics, organizes militias, protects state officials, and guards key infrastructure. These skill sets are often used to stabilize pro-Moscow regimes. Client countries with a reported Wagner presence include the Central African Republic, Libya, Sudan, Mali, Madagascar, the Democratic Republic of Congo, Ethiopia, Chad, Zimbabwe, and Kenya. President Nicolas Maduro of Venezuela is also suspected of being a Wagner client.

As Venezuela destabilized into a failed state in 2016, Maduro came under increasing pressure to go into exile. Reports indicate that he called on Moscow for protection. Russia now guides Venezuelan oil exports around American sanctions, channeling hard currency back to Caracas to keep Maduro in business. This lucrative arrangement allows Moscow to profit from oil arbitrage, arms sales, and loan interest payments. To protect this relationship Moscow sent personnel, most likely Wagner, to ensure Maduro stayed in power.

Command and Control, and Training

Wagner maintains a linear and concise chain of command that is designed to interface with Russian Ground Forces. At the top of the Wagner pyramid are the "Commander-in-Chief" and Managing Director. Middle leadership consists of an administrative group (estimated to be 390 personnel), general staff (estimated to be 20 personnel), and control group (estimated to be 35 personnel).

The Department of Military Preparation also manages pre-deployment training in firearms, combat engineering, tank and IFV driving, artillery,

A2/AD systems, and other military specialties. Routine training regimes include almost constant practice on the rifle range, and deployment preparation usually includes a two-month comprehensive training package in mission-relevant skill sets.

Wagner mercenaries deploy under a unit structure that resembles either conventional formations or Spetsnaz (depending on the mission), allowing seamless integration with battlespace command and control structures.

Wagner's training center is co-located with GRU's 10th Spetsnaz Brigade at Molkino, Krasnodar Krai, and the Ministry of Defense has spent several million dollars modernizing the Molkino training facility. Because Wagner's mercenaries have the institutional buy-in of GRU, they have access to many of the same training facilities and techniques used by Spetsnaz brigades. GRU has also been known to supply Wagner personnel with alias passports to better enable travel abroad.

Recruitment

Given Russia's hollow economy and overwhelming economic dependence on oil and natural gas exports, it is not difficult to understand why so many young men see Wagner as a valid career path. The ideal targets for Wagner recruiters are former soldiers from elite units like Spetsnaz or VDV, but these recruits are rare. Wagner's primary recruiting base consists of men who have completed their mandatory service as conscripted soldiers and are finding it difficult to adjust to civilian life. As long as they have retained basic military skills or useful specializations, Wagner offers great wages.

The average citizen of Russia earns a salary of approximately $635 a month. Wagner paid its operatives well during the Crimean Annexation and War in Donbas. In 2014, Wagner offered recruits $1,300 a month while training at Molkino, $1,900 a month while deployed to Ukraine, and $2,900 a month while serving in the Luhansk People's Republic. In addition to base salaries, Wagner paid bonuses of $960 a week to men while they were in combat.

Pay during the Syrian Intervention started out very high. In 2015 and 2016, Wagner mercenaries in Syria earned as much as $3,800 a month. By early 2017, wages had increased to $4,800 a month with some sources reporting figures as high as $8,000 a month. Then, Russia handed over Wagner's financing responsibilities to the Syrian al-Assad Regime.

Under Syrian management, top-tier specialists could receive a highest possible salary of $3,300 a month, while lower-ranking men received $2,200 a month. These wages would have been entirely adequate for maintaining qualified personnel had they been paid on time and in full, but consistent payment scheduling was not a strong point for the Syrian Government. This almost certainly contributed to Wagner's poor-to-incompetent performance late in the Syrian campaign.

Wagner's Role in Russian Foreign Policy

Wagner is a mercenary organization, but, in function, it is an unofficial branch of the Russian Armed Services. The Kremlin deploys Wagner to conduct irregular warfare when the job requires a fig leaf of deniability. Wagner also offers Moscow another opportunity to put trained veterans to good use after they have left the Armed Services.

This unofficial tool of foreign policy gives the Kremlin a remarkably effective unseen hand with which to reach abroad. However, when Wagner fails to recruit experienced soldiers, fails to train its personnel, or when Russian special services fail to provide adequate support, Wagner flounders.

Summary and Conclusions

Elite forces are required for hybrid warfare, as they offer limited but tailored kinetic force. In the Russian system, the elite units of the VDV, Naval infantry, KSSO, and Wagner share functionality with units that are operationally controlled by the intelligence services, such as GRU's Spetsnaz brigades. Russia's elite forces provide a kinetic force that is highly maneuverable and capable of high precision.

The VDV and Naval Infantry form the vanguard of Russian Ground Forces. KSSO is Russia's new national mission force, designed for highly sensitive and specialized foreign interventions. Wagner serves as a deniable force multiplier, training and leading proxies, protecting key VIPs, assassinating problematic or uncontrollable local leaders, and conducting sabotage.

Almost all conventional wars are preceded by intelligence-gathering activities, special reconnaissance, and the like. Russian hybrid warfare differs from Western practices in that after non-military methods are used to create chaos (or a de facto power vacuum), elite forces win the day before an enemy can organize any real resistance.

Heavy Russian Ground Forces complete the *fait accompli*, entrenching themselves on the gains made by elite units. But, while the Russians make innovative use of elite forces coupled with non-military and non-kinetic influence activities, these are all still tools of conventional warfare. Propaganda, economic coercion, guerilla operations, and covert action are methods that conquering armies have deployed throughout history.

Numerous martial luminaries deployed them, including Julius Caesar, Alexander the Great, Hannibal Barca, Vlad the Impaler, Sir Arthur Wellesley Duke of Wellington, William Tecumseh Sherman, Lucius Cornelius Sulla, and many others. Hybrid warfare is more correctly characterized as a holistic approach to conventional war that relies on skillful planning and more than a little guile.

---

1. A feeling of enthusiasm, strong regard, mutual care for the honor and reputation of a military unit.
2. Sun Tzu was an ancient Chinese general (544-496 BCE) who wrote *The Art of War*, one of history's most famous military treatises. In it, Sun Tzu discusses strategy, indirect tactics, spy craft, alliances, deception, and leadership. He also offers generals alternatives to chess-like battles of attrition, believing that the perfect victory was a victory obtained without having to fight at all.
3. The Autonomous Republic of Crimea was a self-governing parliamentary republic within Ukraine. It was governed under the Constitution of Crimea in accordance with the laws of Ukraine. On January 20, 1991, Crimea became an Autonomous Soviet Socialist Republic after a referendum, gaining independence from Ukraine within the Soviet Union. On May 15, 1992, following the Soviet collapse, Ukraine voted to annul Crimea's referendums for independence. A negotiated settlement led to the 1998 Constitution of Crimea.
4. An ethnic group composed of Slavic-speaking Orthodox Christian people, known for living in autonomous militaristic communities on the vast open steppes of Eastern Europe.

CHAPTER SEVEN

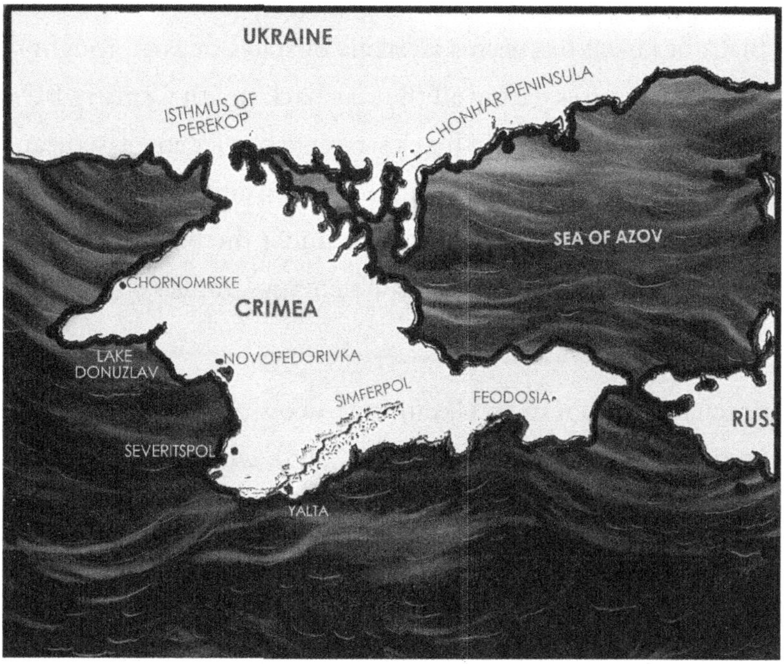

THE CRIMEAN INTERVENTION AND ANNEXATION

Like Georgia, Russia feels it must dominate Ukraine. Geographically, Ukraine has numerous advantages in agriculture, navigable waterways, oil and natural gas resources, and minerals as well as proximity to the Black Sea. These factors made it the agricultural and industrial heart of the Soviet Union. Most of the steel used to build the Soviet Navy (and later, the Russian Navy) came from Ukraine.

The Black Sea itself has been a strategic obstacle or asset, fought over by numerous empires dating all the way back to 5th Century BC. Russia uses the Black Sea both as a strategic barrier and as a means of projecting power. Additionally, numerous oil and gas pipelines from Central Asia and the Middle East cross under the Black Sea, giving Russia greater influence over Europe's energy supplies and global energy prices.

With such deep interests in Ukraine, Moscow could not stomach the Orange Revolution in Kyiv (2004-2005), which fundamentally reoriented Ukraine away from Russia. The Kremlin feared that Ukraine would integrate itself economically with the E.U. and that Ukraine might seek NATO membership to remain free of Russia's tentacles (like so many other Eastern Bloc nations).

Russia bore witness to NATO's expansion eastward after the Cold War, admitting Poland, the Czech Republic, Slovakia, Hungary, Romania, Albania, Bulgaria, Montenegro, Croatia, Lithuania, Latvia, and Estonia; most of which were under Russian influence if not under direct control from Moscow.

As Putin stated in April 2014, "Our decision in Crimea was partly due to... considerations that if we do nothing, then at some point, guided by the same principles, NATO will drag Ukraine in and they will say: 'It doesn't have anything to do with you.'"

Dominating the Black Sea is almost as important to Moscow as keeping Ukraine out of NATO and the E.U. The Russian Black Sea Fleet is domiciled at the Sevastopol Naval Base and the Russian economy needs Crimea's deep-water ports to ship goods and raw materials. Rival powers like Turkey would almost certainly take advantage if Russia's military presence in the region diminished.[1]

Annexing Crimea both created additional political chaos, ensuring Ukraine would not be accepted for NATO or E.U. membership, and ensured Russia's continued dominance of the Black Sea. With the lessons of Chechnya and Georgia in mind, the GRU and their masters in Moscow had to figure out how to annex Crimea without Russia looking like the aggressor, eliminating the possibility of a conventional military invasion.

The Euromaidan crisis from December of 2013 to February of 2014 had paralyzed the government in Kyiv and the military chain of command. In fact, both Ukrainian President Victor Yanukovych and SBU (Ukrainian Security Service) Director Oleksandr Yakymenko had already fled to political exile in Russia. With the Ukrainian political apparatus decapitated, the public raged at corruption in Kyiv. Amid a general atmosphere of chaos that helped cloak already deceptive practices, and with its strategic imperatives in mind, Russia executed a hybrid war in Crimea.

Precursors and Historical Relationship

The Russo-Ukrainian relationship has been characterized by either stalwart alliances or brutal coercion, depending on the historian. The Ukrainian story itself is a tragedy by Western standards, with the country constantly dominated by larger powers to the East or West.

In 1654, Cossack hetman Bohdan Khmelnytsky signed the Treaty of Pereyaslav that allied Ukraine with the Russians against Poland, and Ukraine has remained entangled with Russia in one form or another ever since.[2]

Ukraine's Crimean Peninsula is of great strategic importance. Between 1853 and 1856, France, Britain, Sardinia, and the declining Ottoman Empire fought a bitter conflict with Imperial Russia over the Peninsula in what became known as the Crimean War. As the Ottoman Empire slowly disintegrated and lost control of the Balkans, Tsar Nicholas III looked towards the Black Sea's ports with envy.

Russian deep-water ports are frozen for much of the year, and access to the Black Sea through Crimea would have proven highly beneficial for projecting naval power and establishing new trade relations. Russia needed to make Turkey subservient to ensure dominance in the region, triggering France and Britain to come to the Ottoman Empire's aid in order to maintain the balance of power. While Russia would eventually capitulate to the Western alliance, the war cost the lives of over 350,000 soldiers.

When the Soviet commissars arrived in Kyiv, promising Marxist egalitarianism, the first item on the agenda was communicating the Communist Manifesto to the *proletariat,* those members of society whose only economic value was derived from their labor.[3]

In 1917, the majority of rural peasants in Eastern Europe were only a generation out of full serfdom, and most of them were still economically bound to the land they were born on—an arrangement akin to sharecropping in the American South. The nobleman that owned the land received the vast majority of the surplus and paid his farmers a subsistence wage in coin and produce.

Those peasants that left the farm, the landless poor, often sought factory work in the cities, but frequently subsisted as vagrants or criminals between work (envision the character Rodion Raskolnikov from Feodor Dostoevsky's Crime and Punishment).

The Ukrainian "bourgeoisie" (called kulaks), the property-owning class, consisted mostly of productive peasants who had risen far enough out of poverty to own a small family-sized farm. In 1929, Joseph Stalin pronounced, "Now we have the opportunity to carry out a resolute offensive against the kulaks, break their resistance, eliminate them as a class and replace their production with the production of kolkhozes and sovkhozes."[4]

These farmers were arrested, either by commissars leading angry mobs or later by secret police. The kulaks were broadly charged with hoarding or controlling the "means of production". Many were simply executed during the process of arrest, and the survivors were sent to the Siberian gulags in a process that Stalin called dekulakization.

Gradually, the Soviet commissars found replacement labor for Ukraine's new farming collectives. Unfortunately, candidates eligible for commune farming (mostly members of the underclass) seldom had any knowledge of basic farming and, as a result, historians estimate that between 6-10 million Ukrainians starved to death in a series of famines. The period known as Holodomor (during the winter of 1932-1933), which can loosely be translated as "killed by starvation", was particularly brutal.

Subsequent mass starvations became so dire that the Soviet commissars were forced to post signs in Ukrainian towns reminding citizens that, "To eat your own children is a barbaric act." Over 2,500 individuals were convicted of varying acts of cannibalism during Holodomor (the practice was more widespread than is reflected by the paltry number of prosecutions, and the commonality of flesh markets has been well documented). Stalin's "Great Terror" (1937-1938) further purged any Ukrainians bold enough to air resentments regarding Communism's many downplayed genocides. This is the backdrop to modern Ukrainian nationalism.

Realizing Ukraine's vital role in the Soviet economy, consecutive Soviet Premiers encouraged the migration of ethnic Russian nationals to Ukraine to lay a blanket of seeming unity over simmering resentments. The Kremlin made many public shows of solidarity and encouraged the development of numerous heavy industries in Ukraine. Soviet Premier Nikita Khrushchev made sure to preserve his Ukrainian accent and even seemed to embellish it in radio addresses. But, despite Moscow's goodwill, the Ukrainian public was exhausted with Communism and rule by Moscow. On December 1, 1991, Ukraine voted for independence from the USSR.

Following the Soviet collapse, both Russia and Ukraine fell into political and economic disarray. Factions of oligarchs, corrupt politicians, civil servants, and organized crime bosses ran roughshod over Ukrainian institutions.

Moscow exploited this chaos to maintain control over Ukrainian foreign policy.

Ukrainian leaders attempted to balance Russian influence with growing European economic relations. Moscow saw the European Union as a direct threat to its traditional sphere of influence and repeatedly attempted to compel Ukraine's membership into the Russian-dominated Eurasian Economic Union (EEU) as an alternative to the E.U.

This status quo was finally disrupted when Ukraine's pro-Russia president Leonid Kuchima was replaced by populist Viktor Yushchenko in the hotly contested election of 2004. In what became known as the Orange Revolution, Yushchenko defeated the Russian-supported candidate Viktor Yanukovych. The election was immediately followed by mass protests and strikes until the courts mandated a recount. During the campaign, Yushchenko became seriously ill, generating rumors that Russian operatives had poisoned him with dioxin, a poison that disfigured his face and resulted in a stay in an Austrian hospital. The method of delivery and perpetrators have never been positively identified.

Prime Minister Yulia Tymoshenko led Yushchenko's new administration. She attempted to maneuver Ukraine towards the European Union (E.U.), World Trade Organization (WTO), and NATO, sparking a national debate about how Ukraine should be externally oriented. The election also inspired Moscow to begin investing more deeply in Ukrainian politics.

The Orange Coalition would not survive long due to infighting and corruption, much of which was orchestrated by Moscow. In February 2010, pro-Russia candidate Viktor Yanukovych, who had run his campaign with Russian financial support and was suspected of electoral fraud, won in a run-off with Prime Minister Tymoshenko to become President.[5]

Yanukovych assembled a government made up of ethnic-Russian parties with voting bases in Eastern Ukraine. Former Prime Minister Yulia Tymoshenko was eventually arrested by the Yanukovych administration and charged with a litany of crimes to ensure she could never be politically active again.

It seems that President Yanukovych, despite being a Kremlin puppet, did sincerely attempt to make concessions to appease Ukrainian nationalists. For example, he continued to court European economic integration. His coalition government, however, included the ethnic-Russian Party of Regions which had merged with the oligarch-controlled Ukrainian nationalist party Strong Ukraine.

The need to balance the political coalitions seems to have dictated to Yanukovych his practice of balancing East and West economic ties. His foreign policy addresses in 2010 expressed a vision for a neutral Ukraine that cooperated with both the West and Russia.

While Yanukovych sought closer relations with the E.U., he simultaneously negotiated more advantageous natural gas agreements with Russia and extended Russia's lease on the Black Sea port facilities, including the Sevastopol Naval Base. Ukrainian nationalists were told that these revenue-producing (but pro-Russian) measures were necessary to secure loans from the International Monetary Fund (IMF) and to control budget deficits for future E.U. admittance.

Yanukovych's rationalizations for close relations with Russia kept Ukrainian nationalists at bay because there was an element of truth in them. And, despite underwriting Yanukovych's career, Moscow seems to have tolerated his distancing act because Putin understood that Yanukovych's ruling coalition was balancing a unicycle on the point of a pyramid. Make no mistake, while Kyiv was given latitude in rhetoric and diplomacy, Moscow had the final say on the end-state.

Russian Strategic Motivations

Russia has deep strategic interests in Ukraine. As mentioned in previous chapters, following the Soviet collapse and chaotic 1990s under Boris Yeltsin, President Putin promised the Russian people order. While order originally came with an authentic desire for participation in an American-led global community, Putin soured on congenial relations as the E.U. and NATO continued to absorb former Eastern Bloc members.

In Ukraine's Orange Revolution, Kyrgyzstan's Tulip Revolution, and Georgia's Rose Revolution, each country's respective public chose to elect a government that would reorient the country towards the West.

In Moscow's view, the incremental progression of Western military and economic institutions towards Russia's borders directly threatens the existing regime.

As Eastern Bloc states join NATO, Russia loses its strategic buffer with its geopolitical rivals. Moscow is also keenly aware that, as Russian citizens are exposed to Western culture, they assume new standards of normative behavior, which has the potential to manifest in demands for state reforms and regime legitimacy through clean electoral processes, outcries for free speech and open journalism, and numerous other pressures for liberal change.

President Putin began his time in office rhetorically open to "small" liberal reforms, largely to develop good relations with the United States and E.U. However, as color revolutions removed and replaced pro-Moscow regimes in the Russian periphery, Putin began casting himself as a stalwart defender of Russia, ethnic Russians abroad, and traditional Russian values. He also indulged nationalist hardliners by increasing military spending, leading to the "New Look" Reforms, GPV 2020, and GPV 2027, which sought to modernize and professionalize the Russian Armed Services. Putin's national security cadre was convinced that the West sought to overturn his regime and concluded that only a revitalized military could deter further eastward expansions of the E.U. and NATO.

Aside from Russia's ongoing chess match with the West, the Kremlin must control Crimea in order to fully dominate the Black Sea. The naval base at Sevastopol, and its domiciled Black Sea Fleet, allows Russia to project naval power into the Mediterranean and even the Indian Ocean.

Sevastopol itself offers a deep-water port, natural harbor, and extensive infrastructure. The Black Sea Fleet is being upgraded and modernized with new submarines (mostly of the Kilo and Lada classes), frigates (Grigorovich class), and amphibious landing craft. Even without modernization, the Black Sea Fleet remains a potent reminder of Russian power.

Like other Russian fleets, the Black Sea Fleet's warships are equipped with advanced anti-ship cruise missiles, air defense systems, and torpedoes. The 11th Coastal Defense Missile Brigade is stationed in Crimea and is currently being upgraded with an integrated air defense system based on the S-400 platform. A complement of advanced combat aircraft are stationed at Crimea's Kacha and Gvardeysk air bases, capping Russia's formidable regional ground and naval forces with credible airpower. Russia will go to war to preserve these strategic advantages.

Non-Military Influence and Covert Action Prepare the Battlespace

The Euromaidan Crisis

Pro-E.U. and Ukrainian nationalist opposition parties pressed hard against austerity measures implemented by Yanukovych (tax increases coupled with reductions in state services and benefits), which eventually forced him to make concessions in order to maintain his ruling coalition.

In November 2013, Viktor Yanukovych announced his intention to sign an Association Agreement with the E.U., laying out the roadmap and legal framework towards Ukraine's membership in the E.U. This was an enormously popular measure in Ukraine but, as Yanukovych pushed forward a requisite free trade agreement in the legislature, he came under withering pressure from Russia.

Later that month, Yanukovych attended a meeting of the Eastern Partnership in Vilnius, Lithuania, but refused to sign a political association and free trade agreement with the E.U. Yanukovych's actions signaled to the public that he was intentionally slow-walking the proceedings.

Shortly thereafter, Yanukovych confirmed the public's worst fears when he announced that he would pursue closer relations with Russia. He rushed to Moscow where, on December 16th, President Putin rolled out the Ukrainian-Russian Action Plan. Putin agreed to cut Ukraine's natural gas prices by 33% and guaranteed that Russia would purchase $15 Billion in Ukrainian sovereign bonds to help alleviate its growing debt crisis.

What became known as the Euromaidan protests erupted throughout November and December of 2013 and was largely centered in Kyiv's Independence Square (Maidan Nezalezhnosti). Angry demonstrators hoped to blockade ratification of the treaty.

Demonstrations simmered over Christmas and re-erupted after police injured an opposition leader on January 12, 2014. Rioters in the hundreds of thousands began demanding that Yanukovych resign. The Minister of Internal Affairs authorized police forces to use physical force and firearms to contain the riots, causing hundreds of injuries and several deaths.

By early February 2014, Euromaidan protests had spread from Kyiv throughout the country. Protestors began occupying government buildings, particularly at the Ministry of Justice, in spite of new anti-protest laws. President Yanukovych made a last-ditch effort to negotiate with protestors by offering to release arrested opposition leaders and reestablish limits on presidential power. He promised to share power with a bipartisan parliamentary coalition under the 2004 Constitution and to facilitate a special presidential election by the end of the year.

It was too little, too late. Yanukovych was forced to flee Kyiv overnight on February 21, 2014, eventually resurfacing in Moscow to lead Ukraine's "Government in Exile".

The Ukrainian Parliament voted to impeach President Yanukovych and return to the 2004 Constitution. On February 22nd, Yulia Tymoshenko was released from prison. Oleksandr Turchynov became interim President and Arseniy Yatsenyuk became Prime Minister. Presidential elections were set for May 25, 2014 in which billionaire Petro Poroshenko was elected. Poroshenko would sign the E.U. Association Agreement on July 27, 2014.

Moscow's Non-Military Influence Activities

Contingency planning to capture and annex the Crimean Peninsula likely began in the early 1990s. The Orange Revolution in Kyiv almost certainly inspired new urgency in the planning. GRU and FSB used time and patience to penetrate policy-making circles within the Orange Coalition and subsequent administrations, generating opposition to reforms and pro-Western agendas.

Members of the opposition were offered patronage to disrupt the legislative agenda and civil servants were bribed to disrupt implementation. The Kremlin's influence eventually brought Viktor Yanukovych to the Presidency, ensuring that Moscow could exert direct influence over Ukraine's chief executive.

Moscow brought down enormous personal, political, and diplomatic pressure on President Yanukovych when he announced that Ukraine would sign an Association Agreement with the E.U., and he was forced to delay any concrete commitment in Vilnius.

The Ukrainian military remained under-funded, poorly trained, and led by weak and corruptible officers. Yanukovych appointed Russian loyalists to high-ranking positions throughout the Defense Intelligence of the Ministry of Defense of Ukraine (DIU). Rather than managing the institution, these appointees promptly began dismantling DIU's intelligence collection and analysis capabilities. SBU, Ukraine's primary security service and domestic intelligence agency, was penetrated by Russian agents from top to bottom.

Yanukovych's SBU Director, Oleksandr Yakymenko, was a Moscow loyalist and appointed FSB-connected officials to run SBU's byzantine system of directorates. Shortly following Viktor Yanukovych's exile, Yakymenko showed up in Russia with a boatload of intelligence secrets.

Yanukovych had ordered the SBU Director to raid SBU headquarters. After destroying Ukraine's most important intelligence offices and archives, Yakymenko defected with four other top spies, a dozen subordinates, a treasure trove of state secrets, and all of the files documenting SBU's cooperation with FSB activities in Ukraine.

Russian Information Operations—A Means of Chaos, Deception, and Legitimacy

Since the 1990s, Russia has been very careful to conduct information operations (IO) in Ukraine subtly. This policy of caution has yielded moderate influence over public sentiments while remaining subtle enough to avoid public criticism from political leaders. However, as President Yanukovych's December 2013 about-face on E.U. membership sparked the Euromaidan protests, the Russian IO campaign kicked into high gear. The Russian narrative first sought to generate domestic support for Yanukovych's pivot to Moscow by trumpeting the benefits of the debt relief and natural gas deals.

By late February 2014, realizing that the Ukrainian public was done with Yanukovych and irreparably against a realignment with Russia, IO pivoted to new narratives that generated popular support amongst ethnic Russians for an intervention in Crimea. Propaganda also sought to raise doubts internationally about the legitimacy and popular support of the Euromaidan protests.

After Yanukovych fled Kyiv, Russia diplomatically recognized him as the leader of Ukraine's government in exile and legitimate head of state. Propaganda was again tailored to complement that narrative.

Putin's IO agents denied Russia's involvement in destabilizing Ukraine at all times, while warning the world not to provoke Russian military might. The Kremlin even threatened potential reprisals in nuclear diplomacy in response to Western "aggression" and outside interference.

Propaganda also targeted proxies in Ukraine, preparing them to mobilize as a separatist insurgency in support of Russian annexation. Russian messaging also promoted Slavic ethnicity and the Russian diaspora (coined by some as "Russkiy Mir"), and basic appeals to nationalism.[6] Related segments of Slavic ethnicities were encouraged by Russia's propagandists to engage in a post-liberal struggle in defense of traditions, morals, and Russian sovereignty.

In the Ukrainian case, the narrative called on ethnic Russians to stand up to bullying by the E.U. and WTO, who insisted Ukraine implement painful austerity measures before the country could be a member of their respective systems. Moscow also directed messaging towards the home front, informing Russians that the United States was leveraging Ukraine to get a foothold near the Russian border.

The Russian Cyber Campaign—Creating Space to Maneuver

Russian IO leaned heavily on cyber operations to propagate their own narratives and prevent Ukrainian officials from challenging Russian propaganda. However, Russia's cyber campaign also inhibited coordination for Ukrainian responders. As protests devolved into riots, cyberattacks on Ukrainian servers and government websites increasingly undermined the ability of political leadership to communicate instructions to military and law enforcement officials.

The disruption of Ukrainian communication not only served Russia's desire for chaos but created space for Russia's elite forces to seize key objectives and terrain.

Russian cyber actors penetrated Ukrainian cellular networks, including Ukrtelecom, which provided cellular services to Crimea. Cyber agents sent threatening messages to Ukrainian troops and their families and monitored or disrupted the cellular traffic of Ukrainian Parliament Members.

The Crimean Peninsula was also hit with numerous distributed denial-of-service (DDoS) cyberattacks, reminiscent of Georgia in 2008. Ukrtelecom reported that Crimean telecoms facilities were seized by "unknown parties" in late February of 2014. Physical damage to fiber optic trunk cables in Crimea further throttled communications between the peninsula and mainland Ukraine.

Research performed by the malware research firm FireEye indicates an aggressive acceleration of Russian malware attacks between February and March of 2014. "Callbacks", messages sent back to Russian servers from malware-infected computers in Ukraine, jumped 40% in March 2014. The leap in malware callbacks in March versus the February baseline is profound.

Brute force attacks are not the only cyberwarfare tools Russia can muster. Russia has been deploying cyber tools against Ukraine and Western adversaries for years. A noted example codenamed "SNAKE", was designed to penetrate secure servers running Windows operating systems all over the world. It applies complex methodologies to evade host defenses and gives an attacker covert communication channels. One method "SNAKE" uses to bypass security protocols is to hide outgoing DNS and HTTP requests in the victim's web traffic so that malware scanners cannot detect when the virus is reporting its status or requesting instructions.

A sub-component of "SNAKE" is the Uroborun rootkit, a Russian cyber weapons program that began development sometime around 2005 and has likely been active since 2011. It attacks high-level targets by setting up rogue peer-to-peer networks to steal data. It is designed to reach air-gapped subsystems through enterprise networks of large organizations.

According to G Data analysis (a German security firm):

> Uroborun is a rootkit, composed of two files, a driver and an encrypted virtual file system. The rootkit is able to take control of an infected machine, execute arbitrary commands and hide system activities. It can steal information (most notably files) and it is also able to capture network traffic.

> Its modular structure allows extending it with new features easily, which makes it not only highly sophisticated but also highly flexible and dangerous. Uroborun's driver part is extremely complex and is designed to be very discrete and very difficult to identify.

Uroborun has been active on servers in Ukraine, likely giving GRU further privileged access to policy-making circles and military planning. Though Russian intelligence services had already extensively penetrated all levels of the Ukrainian government, security service, and military, Ukraine has become a Russian cyberwarfare testbed for reconnaissance procedures and infiltration tools.

The Crisis in Crimea Escalates into the Kinetic Phase of Hybrid Warfare

The Euromaidan Crescendo

From late January into early February of 2014, Euromaidan protests in Kyiv against President Yanukovych became increasingly violent, forcing Yanukovych's ruling coalition in Parliament to pass legislation that declared the movement to be illegal and subversive. They authorized security services and police to contain further protests.

Vladimir Konstantinov, the Speaker of the Sevastopol City Council, met with Russian leaders in Moscow and publicly called on Kyiv to bring opposition leaders to justice. The public widely saw Konstantinov's actions as an open invitation for Russia to intervene in Ukrainian politics directly.

The crackdown authorized by Parliament largely backfired, and protests continued to intensify. President Yanukovych, under immense domestic pressure, hosted negotiations with Euromaidan leaders. He promised to return to the 2004 Constitution, release arrested activists, form a national unity government as early as March, and facilitate a special presidential election by the end of the year. This was a deep political setback for Moscow, causing the Russians to alter their strategy from supporting Yanukovych in Kyiv to supporting pro-Russian separatists.

On February 20, 2014, violence in Kyiv peaked in a bloody crackdown by Ukrainian security services under order from President Yanukovych. Berkut, a special police unit of the Ministry of Internal Affairs with a reputation for acting as a cudgel against political dissidents, was particularly heavy-handed. The unit killed over 60 people and injured dozens more, forcing the Parliament to order a ceasefire.

Moscow dispatched the 45th Special Reconnaissance Regiment (SRR) to Crimea with orders to generate public momentum behind a popular uprising that would facilitate Russian annexation. GRU Agents began an aggressive campaign of organizing ethnic Russian communities to rally against the regime in Kyiv, laying the foundation for an intervention.

Sometime during the night of February 21st, President Yanukovych fled Kyiv to his voter base in Eastern Ukraine. Shortly thereafter, he reemerged in Moscow to lead Ukraine's government-in-exile. Yanukovych's flight was a complete surprise to the Kremlin, which had dispatched GRU and FSB personnel to see to his personal security.

Russia pivoted from offering generous economic aid to Ukraine to applying heavy economic and diplomatic pressure to further destabilize the regime. Vladimir Konstantinov and other Crimean MPs publicly proposed that Crimea appeal to Russia to be a guarantor for Crimean autonomy.

The next day, as it became apparent that Yanukovych was missing, the Ukrainian Parliament impeached him as President. Yanukovych's Party of Regions then began to distance itself from the ousted leader as his political allies were arrested by the emerging new regime in Kyiv.

These high-profile arrests added fuel to pro-Russian protests in Crimea and Eastern Ukraine. Russia's Southern Military District was ordered to mobilize and deploy forces to the Ukrainian border as a warning to Kyiv not to interfere with the nascent insurrection.

Protestors succeeded in releasing former Prime Minister Yulia Tymoshenko from prison. Tymoshenko was jailed by Yanukovych's regime in order to permanently remove her from the political chessboard.

President Putin convened an all-night meeting of his national security team and diplomatic officials on the night of February 22nd. The council concluded that diplomatic pressure, political influence, and economic coercion were exhausted. Moscow no longer saw the Yanukovych regime as a viable means of supporting Russian foreign policy objectives.

Putin's team planned the deployment of forces to secure Crimea and set a timeline for annexation. Sevastopol and its Black Sea Fleet facilities would be a critical launching point for special operations forces and reconnaissance units.

The 3rd Spetsnaz Brigade and two battalions of the 16th Spetsnaz Brigade received orders to transfer from their base in Tambov, Russia, to forward staging areas in the Southern Military District close to the Black Sea, foreshadowing an impending intervention.

On February 23rd, Ukraine's interim government appointed Oleksandr Turchynov as acting President. Parliament then immediately voted to stick a finger in Moscow's eye by repealing Russian as an official state language. This mistake served Moscow's new agenda by further alienating the Russian-speaking regions of Crimea and Eastern Ukraine from the interim government in Kyiv.

Russia's Black Sea Fleet dispatched the 431st Marine Reconnaissance Station (MRS) to conduct reconnaissance missions in the Kherson Isthmus. Highway E97, which runs from mainland Ukraine through the isthmus to Krasnoperekopsk, is one of two main avenues of approach to Crimea. The 45th SRR conducted targeted messaging (propaganda efforts), organized pro-Russian separatist protests throughout the region, and began coordinating militias to secure key terrain and infrastructure.

Elements of the 810th Naval Infantry Brigade supported and blended into the emerging militias and "Crimean Defense Forces". Reports surfaced of large Russian military convoys emanating from Sevastopol and moving freely throughout Crimea.

Euromaidan protests continued in Simferopol but, in Sevastopol, support for new autonomy from Ukraine gained momentum. With the enthusiastic support of thousands of demonstrators, Sevastopol's City Council voted to establish a parallel administration and "civil defense units". Similar units were declared active in Simferopol, leveraging propaganda to portray Russian troops as local civil defense auxiliaries shielding a movement of the people from outside interference. These civil defense units intimidated and ultimately suppressed Euromaidan support in Simferopol.

Demonstrators in Sevastopol chose Aleksei Chalyi, a Russian politician, as de facto mayor on February 24th. Sevastopol had never had a mayor before, having previously operated under a governor chosen by the President of Ukraine. Mechanized units of the 810th Naval Infantry Brigade (NIB), stationed at the naval base in Sevastopol, rapidly seized numerous highways, crossroads, and airfields throughout the Crimean Peninsula, and then set up blockades and checkpoints.

President Putin finally broke a long silence from the Kremlin by announcing support and recognition for the concerns of the Crimean People on February 25th. In a rally hosted by the activist organization "Crimean Front", hundreds of pro-Russian protesters blockaded the Crimean Parliament in Simferopol, calling for a referendum on independence.

Infantry fighting vehicles (IFVs), likely from the 810th NIB, began appearing at intersections and government buildings in Sevastopol. Elite Russian Ground Forces secured Nakhimov Square in the city center by the end of the day. Troops arrived on the outskirts of Yalta, surrounding the 50th Anti-Aircraft Missile Regiment garrisoned there, effectively sealing off the city from outside reinforcement.

At 1400 on February 26th, President Putin ordered snap military readiness exercises for the Western, Southern, and Central Military Districts. These exercises included over 150,000 troops across Russia but covered the movement of over 40,000 soldiers to the Ukrainian border in Russia's Southern Military District adjacent to the Kerch Strait.

Russian Ground Forces (likely elements of VDV) were airlifted to the naval base at Novorossiysk and the airbase at Anapa on the Russian coast of the Black Sea. These massive military readiness drills are indistinguishable from mobilizing for a full-scale invasion, and they absolutely paralyzed decision-making processes in the Ukrainian government and military.

Outside the Supreme Council of Crimea in Simferopol, thousands of ethnic Tatars and Euromaidan supporters confronted several hundred pro-Russian demonstrators.[7] Volodymyr Konstantinov, Chairman of the Supreme Council of Crimea, announced that the Crimean parliament refused to discuss a secession vote from Ukraine.

Protests in Simferopol continued, and, by nightfall, most Tatars had returned home while pro-Russian demonstrators' numbers had swelled into the thousands. Russian proxy forces seized control of the Highways P27 and P23 that connect Sevastopol to Simferopol. The Black Sea Fleet began positioning ships outside militarily relevant harbors and naval facilities such as Sevastopol, Balaklava Harbor, Lake Donuzlav, Feodosia, Kaffa Bay, and the Kerch Strait.

Little Green Men Seize Crimea

Masked gunmen in unmarked green uniforms began appearing throughout the Crimean Peninsula, seizing airports, closing off border crossings, setting up checkpoints on major highways, and securing government buildings. IL-76 transport planes began rapidly moving VDV troops directly into Crimea. Landing ships delivered elements of 10th Spetsnaz Brigade and 25th Spetsnaz Regiment into Sevastopol Harbor, to be reinforced by elements of the 3rd and 16th Spetsnaz Brigades throughout the week.

These newly introduced Spetsnaz units, which were mobile through APCs, IFVs, and helicopters, quickly advanced to secure tactical objectives pre-identified by GRU, FSB, 45th SRR, and 431st MRS during their advanced force operations (AFO). President Putin famously quipped, "...the heavily armed, tightly coordinated groups who took over Crimea's airports and ports at the start of the incursion...they were merely spontaneous self-defense groups who may have acquired their Russian-looking uniforms from local shops."

On February 27th at approximately 0400, a KSSO detachment, dressed in the same unmarked green uniforms, seized the Crimean Parliament and Council of Ministers buildings. A platoon of 30 KSSO men conducted the initial raid and seizure, reinforced by a bus containing another 30 men of 45th SRR with heavy weapons and supplies.

Moscow-approved MPs were then escorted into the building for an "emergency session". Votes were submitted under gunpoint to dissolve the existing Crimean government, replace Prime Minister Anatolii Mohyliov with Sergey Aksyonov, and hold a referendum on autonomy from Kyiv. A referendum on secession from Ukraine was announced for May 25, 2014, but was soon rescheduled for the much closer date of March 16, 2014 by Sergei Aksyonov.

Berkut units, both stationed in Crimea and arriving from other parts of Ukraine, established checkpoints on the Isthmus of Perekop along Highway E97 and the Chonhar Peninsula along M18/E105, effectively cutting off traffic to the Crimean Peninsula from mainland Ukraine.

Early in the morning of February 28th, a company-sized element of men in green uniforms, likely the 431st MRS, seized the complex targets of Simferopol International Airport and the local TV tower. The assault was conducted via Mi-8 "Hip" transport helicopters and supported by Mi-35M "Hind-E" gunships.

A dozen Russian IL-76 transport planes began unloading VDV troops from the 7th Air Assault Division at a local military airfield close to Simferopol. The additional motorized troops maneuvered quickly to blockade the entrances of other Ukrainian military installations throughout Crimea, effectively bottling up Ukrainian forces and confining them to the garrison.

Ships from the Black Sea Fleet blockaded Ukrainian Sea Guard vessels stationed in Balaklava Harbor from putting to sea. The roads to Balaclava Bay were seized by a motorized rifle battalion traveling in a dozen military trucks and five IFVs.

The Night Wolves biker gang, an ultra-nationalist group of which President Putin himself is a member, posted on their website that they were guarding administrative buildings in Sevastopol and blocking the local roads supporting Crimean independence. The gang, led by a man named Aleksander Zaldostanov, who goes by the nom de guerre "Surgeon", has chapters in Russia, Ukraine, Latvia, Belarus, Serbia, Macedonia, Romania, Bulgaria, and Germany, which advocates (or agitates) for the concept of pan-Slavic ethno-nationalism. Pan-Slavic ethno-nationalism is in keeping with the idea of Russkiy-Mir (Russian World), a favorite propaganda point in Russian information operations.

On March 1st, elite Russian units, likely from the 431st MRS, rendezvoused with Berkut defectors to fortify the border checkpoints on the Isthmus of Perekop along Highway E97. Russian Spetsnaz units surrounded Ukrainian forces garrisoned in Kerch.

The Parliament of the Russian Federation approved President Putin's official request for rendering military assistance in Crimea. Russia's political support emboldened the de facto Mayor of Sevastopol, Aleksei Chalyi, to declare continued support for ousted President Viktor Yanukovych's government in exile. The new regime in Crimea announced that it no longer recognized the legitimacy of orders coming from Kyiv.

The newly installed Prime Minister of Crimea, Sergey Aksyonov, sent a signed letter to Moscow requesting military assistance. Aksyonov also introduced Crimea's "Defense Forces" to the public, claiming that the troops and militias in Crimea were under his control and operating with his authority. The announcement also accepted the defection of the officially-disbanded Berkut Special Police units and established Berkut as an elite unit of the Crimean Defense Forces (all members would soon receive Russian passports and citizenship).

Dozens of Ukrainian military installations came under siege by fast-moving and aggressive Russian forces in the early morning of March 2nd. Feodosia, a small naval installation and port town, was completely cut-off from the outside by Russian Ground Forces, isolating Ukraine's 1st Marine Battalion. To obstruct Kyiv's awareness of highly vulnerable Russian transport aircraft on approach to Crimea from the Southern Military district, Spetsnaz units disabled a radar station in the small coastal town of Sudak on the southeast coast of Crimea.

Russia used diplomacy to stall for time by leveraging the opportunity for talks in Paris; however, Russian Foreign Minister Sergei Lavrov refused to even meet with his Ukrainian counterpart Andriy Deshchytsia, claiming he was a representative of an illegal government. Simply showing up in Paris allowed Moscow's propagandists to claim that Russia was seeking a diplomatic compromise with Kyiv. Meanwhile, elite forces continued to make kinetic gains on the ground.

On March 3rd, Russian Spetsnaz units seized the Kerch Strait ferry, securing an additional means to transport in Russian troops from the Southern Military District. After several days of blockade, the Ukrainian 204th Fighter Wing surrendered the Belbek Airbase to Russian Spetsnaz units. The garrison was disarmed, removed from the base, and told to walk home.

Underlining the catastrophe of surrendering the Belbek Airbase for Ukraine, the Russians seized 39 Mig-29 fighters. Russian warships of the Black Sea Fleet further isolated the garrison at Feodosia by blockading the small port town from the sea. Additionally, Russian elite forces seized airfields southeast of the town of Dzhankoi along the E97 Highway from Kerch.

Approximately 200 servicemen of the 204th Fighter Wing returned to the gates of the Belbek Airbase. These troops were apparently overwhelmed with the shame of surrendering the base without firing a shot. As a single group, they marched unarmed on the Russian Spetsnaz units guarding the base entrances on March 5th.

The Ukrainian officers knew that, if the Russians opened fire on unarmed soldiers, the massacre would get world press coverage, which did, indeed, restrain the Russians. The standoff eventually ended with the Russians agreeing to a token unarmed Ukrainian security presence on the Belbek base alongside occupying Russian Forces.

March 5th also saw 700 soldiers from the 50th, 55th, and 147th anti-aircraft missile regiments who were stationed at Yalta, Feodosia, and Fiolent (southern outskirts of Sevastopol) respectively, defect to Russia's proxy "Crimean Defense Forces". Feodosia's only remaining garrison was the 1st Marine Battalion.

Officers of the Ukrainian 10th Saki Naval Aviation Brigade saw the writing on the wall. They ordered all flight-capable aircraft at Novofedorovka Airbase to be put in the air and flown to other bases before they could be seized by the Russians or surrendered by defectors.

Moscow again displayed its high prioritization of information dominance. On March 6th, Russian troops seized the Simferopol Radio and Television Transmitting Station, discontinuing Kyiv-friendly channels and replacing them with the Moscow-based Rossiya 24 news channel. The decommissioned Kara class cruiser Ochakov was scuttled at the entrance to Lake Donuzlav in western Crimea in order to blockade Ukrainian naval facilities at Novoozerne. Seven Ukrainian combat vessels, including a Ropucha I class landing ship, Kostiantyn Olshansky, were bottled up in port.

On March 7th, in a brazen disregard for Ukrainian sovereignty, Russian forces seized a customs station in the village of Chonhar in the Henichesk region of Kherson Oblast (mainland Ukraine). The act firmly closed that avenue of approach to Crimea for any relief forces (particularly armored units and motorized infantry) sent from the mainland.

A checkpoint on the border crossing was first established on February 27th by Berkut defectors and then reinforced by Russian Naval Infantry detachments. Russian state-owned energy giant Gazprom announced that it was suspending gas services to Ukraine unless the government in Kyiv could pay off all of its existing debts to the company and forward pay for incoming supplies.

In the most alarming escalation of the entire campaign, on March 8th, Moscow threatened to suspend nuclear weapons inspections required under the Strategic Arms Reduction Treaty (START) in reprisal for American and European "meddling and interference" regarding Ukraine. This sent a clear message to the United States and NATO that Russia considered Ukraine such a vital strategic interest that it was willing to jeopardize nuclear diplomacy if the West inserted itself into the crisis.

Another decommissioned vessel, a rescue and diving support ship, was donated by the Black Sea Fleet to scuttle next to the Ochakov, further sealing in vessels stationed at Ukrainian naval facilities at Novoozerne on Lake Donuzlav.

In what can only be described as a military catastrophe for Ukraine, on March 9th, the naval air base at Novofedorovka (10th Saki Naval Aviation Brigade) surrendered. Though many serviceable aircraft had been flown to other airbases before this point, many soldiers and officers defected and surrendered the remaining military hardware and infrastructure.

Russia's 18th Motorized Rifle Brigade began shuttling across the Kerch Strait into Crimea via the captured ferry. Russian elite forces secured Ukrainian naval facilities at Novoozerne, and the port entrance was blockaded by the Black Sea fleet.

Advanced Russian Spetsnaz units then pushed onto the west coast to seize a missile depot in the town of Chornomorske. The 727th Independent Naval Infantry Battalion, 291st Artillery Brigade, and 18th Motorized Rifle Brigade were introduced to the battlespace to provide advancing elite units with heavier support and firepower.

The Crimean Referendum

At approximately 1330, a company-sized element of Russian forces (between 60 and 120 soldiers), likely from the 7th Air Assault Division of the VDV, assaulted and occupied a natural gas distribution center near Strilkove, a narrow strip of land that serves as the outside boundary of the Syvash Lake estuary, which is located on Crimea's eastern coastline with the Sea of Azov. The assault and seizure involved both helicopter gunships and armored vehicles.

The Crimean government, led by Russian puppet Sergey Aksyonov, held an informal referendum on March 16th. Selected Crimean citizens were required to cast votes under the supervision of armed KSSO operatives and without international observers present. Kremlin-approved journalists covered the proceedings for the world media. Voters were given two choices on the ballot:

Do you support the reunification of Crimea with Russia with all the rights of a federal subject of the Russian Federation?

Or:

Do you support the restoration of the Constitution of the Republic of Crimea in 1992, and the status of the Crimea as part of Ukraine?

It is worth noting that returning to the 1992 Constitution would have made Crimea a self-governing autonomous region, independent of Ukraine in all but name. Under Ukraine's 2004 Constitution, Crimea had been under the authority of Kyiv, with the President appointing a Chairman of the Supreme Council of Crimea. In effect, the choice given to the few Crimean voters who were allowed to participate in the referendum was either secede from Ukraine and be annexed by Russia or to merely secede from Ukraine.

On March 17th, Russian news outlets announced that Crimea had voted 97% in favor of annexation by Russia. The likelihood that Crimea's indigenous populations of Russians, Ukrainians, Tatars, Belarussians, Armenians, Jews, Slavs, and Muslims each with different languages, traditions, norms, values, and competing political agendas, each respectively perceived that Annexation was aligned with their interests is politically impossible in a free referendum. President Putin announced Russia's assent and annexation of Crimea soon after.

Militias claiming to be Crimean Defense Forces (likely led by Russian operatives) stormed the headquarters of the long-since surrounded Ukrainian naval base at Sevastopol on March 19th. Rear Admiral Sergey Gaiduk was arrested and later unceremoniously dropped off at the new Ukrainian border station in northern Crimea, and the Russian flag was raised over the naval base. While many sailors defected, those that chose to remain in the Ukrainian Navy had to find their own transportation back to the mainland. Many had to walk several hundred miles from Crimea to a mainland Ukrainian military base.

The Russians seized the Grisha V class frigates Ternopil and Lutsk, the Pauk class corvette Khmelnytskyi, and the Bambuk class command ship Slavutych. In addition to these four major surface combatant vessels, Russians also seized Ukraine's only submarine, the Foxtrot class Zaporizhzhia, and the ocean-going tugboat, Korets. Following this latest embarrassment, Kyiv announced that it would withdraw all forces (some 25,000 troops) from Crimea. Kyiv also announced its withdrawal from the Russian-led CIS nations.

On March 21st, the Natya class minesweeper Cherkasy attempted to break out from the Ukrainian naval base on Lake Donuzlav by tugging the scuttled blocking ships out of the way. A Russian warship moved to block this maneuver and no Ukrainian vessels were able to leave port. Final remnants of the 147th Anti-Aircraft Missile Defense Regiment, stationed at the Fiolent airbase, were overrun, and Russian forces seized the base inventory of S-300 surface-to-air missiles.

Russian Spetsnaz finally had a breakthrough with Ukraine's 1st Marine Battalion at Feodosia. Realizing the battalion was in an indefensible position with inadequate supplies and facing overwhelming firepower, the unit's commanders first attempted to negotiate with the Russians. They held out for a compromise where the garrison's 750 men would yield control of the Feodosia Naval Base but would be allowed to drive to the Ukrainian border with all their vehicles, weapons, and equipment.

Russian commanders were unwilling to allow the marines to depart fully armed. After near constant probing of the base's perimeter to identify weaknesses, the Russians ordered an assault using stun grenades and smoke, supported by BTR-82A armored personnel carriers with mounted 30mm cannons and two Mi-35M "Hind-E" gunships. With the Ukrainian marines surrounded and totally outgunned, the assault ended with no reported loss of life.

Prime Minister Dmitry Medvedev arrived in Crimea on March 31st to promise economic aid. Russian businesses were encouraged to rapidly integrate Crimea into the Russian economy. The Berkut riot police units began the gradual process of integrating into Russia's Ministry of Internal Affairs troops. Units of the Ukrainian Armed Forces that had defected were integrated into the Russian Armed Forces.

Operational and Tactical Performance

Maskirovka (Camouflage)

Russia's camouflage was complete and compelling. Neither Ukraine nor the international community was able to respond before a *fait accompli* was achieved. Russian information operations contributed to the ongoing chaos of the Euromaidan Crisis and destabilized the country. Russian intelligence operatives and special operations forces instigated riots and protests and stood up local agitators and militias, contributing to the general chaos. Russian paramilitary proxies like the Night Wolves biker club and Cossack Militias began seizing terrain inside the instigated chaos, initiating kinetic military operations without exposing Russian involvement.

Aktivnost (Activity)

Russia commissioned a wide range of activities designed to prevent Ukraine from bringing kinetic force to bear on any vital arteries of the Crimean intervention and annexation. Russian operatives bribed or blackmailed public officials to either cooperate or sit on their hands as the crisis escalated. Ukrainian military officers were offered a place in the Russian Armed Forces if they surrendered their forces, installations, or vessels. The chaos of the Euromaidan Crisis and the exile of President Yanukovych broke the chain of command from Kyiv to Ukraine's garrisons in Crimea, leaving units without orders and hesitant to exchange fire. Paramilitary groups blocked off government buildings and key roads and established improvised checkpoints at the Isthmus of Perekop along Highway E97 and the Chonhar Peninsula along M18/E105, cutting off the peninsula from mainland reinforcements.

Vnezapnost (Surprise)

The speed and surprise achieved by elite Russian Forces was leagues above and beyond what had been achieved in the Russo-Georgian War. Spearheaded by the 45th SRR and the 382nd and 727th Independent Naval Infantry Battalions, Spetsnaz and Airborne detachments moved rapidly from the Sevastopol Naval installation to seize the city center and then rapidly moved on Simferopol, Feodosia, and Kerch. The speed of the Russian advance left Kyiv reeling and achieved a *fait accompli* in less than a month. The 45th SRR infiltrated the Crimean Peninsula on approximately February 20th, and, by March 31st, Prime Minister Medvedev was giving a speech in Simferopol. Russia had completely dominated all of its operational objectives before Kyiv (or NATO) could possibly react.

Russian Ground and Special Operations Forces Performance

Russian Ground Forces demonstrated clear gains from the Serdyukov Reforms. The forces that seized Crimea were competent, professional, motivated, and precise. The chain of command from the Kremlin to the Theater Commander to the ground level officer relayed orders and information efficiently. Moreover, tactical formations maneuvered under "guidance" from operational commanders rather than under micromanagement, creating the necessary space for field commanders and junior officers to take the initiative on the battlefield under their own best judgment.

Motorized and mechanized units of Russian Ground Forces were no longer plagued with constant breakdowns of vehicles and equipment as they were in Georgia. Soldiers were equipped with the latest equipment and gear including the Ratnik combat system (consisting of body armor, night vision, communications, and IT gear). Many of the problems in battlefield communications that arose from legacy Soviet hardware and equipment during the Russo-Georgian War had been solved, allowing for excellent command and control as well as precise maneuver.

The lessons that Russia learned in Georgia regarding rapid advance and maintaining the initiative were on full display. Maneuver throughout the Crimean Peninsula was alarmingly fast and meticulously precise, having been executed by highly disciplined soldiers who avoided unnecessary violence and who understood how their demeanor complemented the propaganda campaign. These actions earned them the moniker "polite people" in Eastern press. Russian maneuver forces were so quick to seize operational objectives and so adept at maintaining the initiative that Ukrainian units capitulated without any notable resistance. By the time

Ukrainian units were able to react to the premeditated invasion, Russian forces had maneuvered into a position of such undeniable superiority that surrender or defection were the only options. Lethal force was seldom, if ever, used and the intervention itself was largely bloodless.

KSSO first debuted on the world stage in Crimea and quickly proved to the General Staff the immense value of a dedicated SMU. Their seizure of Crimean Parliament and Council of Ministers buildings in Simferopol was bloodless and highly professional. The assault was expertly planned and executed, with contingencies for a protracted siege by Ukrainian opposition forces.

KSSO's success in Crimea would justify increased funding, expansions of training facilities, and an expansion of KSSO's support elements (intelligence attachments, aviation assets, and ISR). The Crimean Referendum, though denounced as a sham by global media, went without a hitch under KSSO's protection and supervision.

Russian Air Forces Performance

The Russian Air Force did not play an offensive role in the Crimean intervention and annexation but, once again, Military Transport Aviation Command was the unsung hero of the campaign. VDV's 7th Air Assault Division, 45th SRR, KSSO, and numerous Spetsnaz elements were all flown on IL-76 transport planes and Mi-8 "Hip" transport helicopters to Crimea. The Sevastopol Naval Base and forward area airports seized by the 45th SRR, 810th NIB, or 431st MRS served as conduits for delivering additional elite forces to Crimea.

As elite forces maneuvered to secure additional terrain, transports delivered follow-on heavy forces that could entrench newly captured Russian positions. The conquest of the Crimean

Peninsula—encirclement of Ukrainian military installations, seizure of key infrastructure, capture of government buildings, establishment of border checkpoints, and shielding from intervening outside forces could not have been accomplished without dozens of round-the-clock sorties flown to forward staging areas by Russian transport aircraft. Transport aviation is an uncelebrated but key ingredient for the rapid deployment of forces.

Russian Naval Forces Performance

The primary contribution of Russia's Black Sea Fleet was blockading Ukrainian ports and naval bases to ensure Ukrainian vessels could not flee or interfere with the annexation. In this role, the Russian Navy was highly successful. Antiquated ships were scuttled at the entrance of Lake Donuzlav to seal off the Novoozerne naval base, while other bases at Sevastopol, Novofedorovka, and Feodosia were effectively blockaded by combat vessels.

Russian Naval Infantry played a leading role in the Crimean Annexation as they were an elite force already stationed at Sevastopol at the beginning of the Euromaidan Crisis. Naval Infantry units, particularly the 431st MRS, conducted AFO, preparing the battlespace for the rapid advance of elite forces.

The 810th NIB, the first elite unit to begin securing key terrain in Crimea, followed shortly by the 382nd Independent Naval Infantry Battalion from Temryuk (across the Kerch Strait), were also tasked with AFO. The 727th NIB arrived later as a component of heavier forces and entrenched these gains. Similar to the VDV's leading role in the Russo-Georgian War, Russia's Naval Infantry proved themselves to be a highly professional force, motivated enough to take the initiative within the framework of the overall campaign plan.

Taking the initiative within the commander's intent enabled them to seize objectives and identify follow-on operational imperatives without immediate guidance from higher command, and they did so with impressive speed, precision, and discretionary use of force.

Russian Proxy Forces Performance

Any celebration of Crimean militias or proxy forces (the Crimean Defense Forces) is a testament to the success of the GRU (and perhaps the FSB) in penetrating local ethnic-Russian populations so thoroughly. The 45th SRR was also highly adept at tailored messaging to these groups and quickly organized them into credible militias. What eventually coagulated into the Crimean Defense Forces began as groups of paid protestors and agitators, coordinated by intelligence operatives and Spetsnaz.

The Berkut Special Police of Ukraine's Ministry of Internal Affairs defected to the Crimean Defense Forces following their disbandment. With a little assistance from Russian operatives, Berkut became active in Crimea, establishing blocking positions on the Isthmus of Perekop along Highway E97 and the Chonhar peninsula along M18/E105. Once these checkpoints were reinforced by heavier Russian units, Crimea was effectively severed from the mainland.

The Night Wolves biker gang arrived in Simferopol to guard government buildings and block intersections, preventing Euromaidan protestors from organizing. The Night Wolves' stated purpose in the conflict was to protect voters in the Crimean Referendum. They were an effective means of prohibiting freedom of movement for the Euromaidan opposition, and they delayed the responses of Ukrainian military and police.

Cossack paramilitaries have been operating in Ukraine with Russian support since 2005. Their numbers are drawn from Cossacks living in

Russia, and they are legally authorized to defend Russian borders and national forests, train youths, and fight terrorism. Cossacks under Col Sergei Yurievich barricaded the entrances of Ukrainian bases in Sevastopol until Russian elite forces could arrive. Many of them applied to join the Russian military after the Crimean Annexation.

Chetnik Guards, led by Bratislav Zivkovic and consisting of mostly Serbian pan-Slavic ethno-nationalists, were another paramilitary group in Crimea. They closely coordinated efforts with Cossack paramilitaries but were distinguishable by their long beards and skull-and-crossbones shoulder patches.

Ukrainian Ground Forces Performance

The Ukrainian Ground Forces played no significant role in the Crimean Annexation, which may have been due to the gross lack of guidance from Ukraine's shattered political apparatus. The political leadership was left reeling after the abdication of Victor Yanukovych. Moreover, Russian operatives had deeply penetrated the officer ranks of the military and the SBU, enfeebling the chain of command of Ukraine's security apparatus. The absence of an elected President and the mass defection of all of SBU's senior staff, whole components of the navy, and dozens of army officers left Ukraine in a total leadership vacuum until the election of Petro Poroshenko on May 25, 2014.

The 56th Independent Guards Battalion was the only major Army unit stationed in Crimea and it was contained in its barracks at Sevastopol. 1st Independent Naval Infantry Battalion, stationed at Feodosia after being surrounded on base by Russian Spetsnaz, refused to surrender the post. On March 24th, Russian Spetsnaz units supported by mechanized infantry stormed the base using tear-gas and flash-bangs (non-lethal force). The 700 Ukrainian marines were rounded up, arrested, and eventually deported.

The vast majority of Ukrainian troops stationed in Crimea were naval and air force personnel. 2,500 Ministry of Internal Affairs personnel were stationed in Sevastopol and Simferopol. They originally took part in containing protests and riots but, as Russian proxies became increasingly organized and active, the troops were forced to back down. Ukraine's Ministry of Internal Affairs troops were overwhelmed and contained as Russian elite forces pushed into city centers.

Ukrainian Naval Forces Performance

The Ukrainian Navy was completely eliminated, both as a credible deterrent and as an extension of Ukrainian power into the Black Sea. 12 of its 17 major warships and the preponderance of its air assets and personnel were captured by Russian forces and added to the Russian Black Sea Fleet, including:

Grisha V class frigates the Ternopil and Lutsk

Pauk class corvette Khmelnytskyi

Bambuk class command ship Slavutych

Foxtrot class submarine Zaporizhzhia

Natya class minesweeper Cherkasy

Ropucha I class landing ship Kostiantyn Olshansky

Ocean-going tugboat Korets

At the time of the conflict, the Ukrainian Navy was staffed by approximately 15,500 sailors, marines, and officers. Over 12,000 of these men were stationed in Crimea. In three weeks, the majority had either defected to join the Russian Navy or Crimean Defense Forces, or they resigned from military service.

Kyiv is working hard to restore the Ukrainian Navy's capabilities in maritime policing, but the Navy no longer possesses any real combat power to project into the Black Sea or Sea of Azov. Without a credible Ukrainian Navy, Russia retains the ability to frustrate Ukraine's life-giving maritime commerce by throttling shipping and access to port cities at its convenience. This gives Moscow an enormous amount of leverage in diplomatic and economic negotiations with Ukraine even today.

Ukrainian Air Forces Performance

The Ukrainian Air Force did not play an air-superiority role, but the existence of surface-to-air missile systems at Ukrainian air bases, including the S-300 and Buk-M1, gave Russian military planners great pause in taking advantage of the overwhelming numerical superiority of the Russian Air Force.

These A2/AD systems also represented grave threats to transport aircraft. If Ukrainian air defenses downed a Russian IL-76 transport plane with a company of VDV troops onboard, it would not only be a tactical disaster, but it would destroy the plausible deniability of Russian involvement. Operational planners prioritized mitigating the threat by capturing the 50th, 55th, and 147th Anti-Aircraft Missile Regiments and their respective airbases.

Prominent Ukrainian Air Force Units and Air Bases Captured

Yalta Airbase (50th Anti-Aircraft Missile Regiment)

Feodosia Naval Base (55th Anti-Aircraft Missile Regiment)

Fiolent Airbase (147th Anti-Aircraft Missile Regiment)

Belbek Airbase (204th Fighter Wing surrendered 39 Mig-29 fighter jets)

Novofedorovka Naval Air Base (10th Saki Naval Aviation Brigade)

Outcomes and Conclusions

Russia maintained dominance of the Black Sea and the inherent advantages in power projection into the Mediterranean, supporting Russian foreign policy objectives in the Middle East, Africa, and even the Indian Ocean. And as Russian foreign policy became increasingly interventionist and aggressive, countries like Turkey, Israel, Egypt, Syria, Libya, Saudi Arabia, Iran, India, and Ethiopia had to invite the Kremlin to the negotiating table.

Moscow shook the world with how effortlessly it seized Crimea. In a complete reversal from the utterly brutal Chechen campaigns 15 years earlier, the Crimean Annexation was relatively bloodless. It also demonstrated to the Eastern Bloc that there are dire consequences for frustrating Moscow. Russia unveiled a dynamic modern military with professional leadership and formidable operational planning.

Russian troops were well-trained, disciplined, and motivated. Command and control was excellent. Russian coordination of logistics and supply was well-executed and kept pace with the rapid advance. New equipment proved capable and reliable on the battlefield and, unlike in Georgia, advances were not slowed by numerous armored vehicle breakdowns.

Decisions made by Russian officers reflected a thorough understanding of mission objectives and imperatives as well as discretion and an appreciation for how their interactions with locals shaped the human terrain.

The battlespace had been well-prepared through non-kinetic means including propaganda, economic and diplomatic pressure, intelligence collection, and almost ubiquitous penetration of Ukraine's political and military leadership. Russian operatives stood up proxy forces to drown the Euromaidan Movement and increase the virulence of pro-Russia protests in Sevastopol and Simferopol. These proxies also served as a force multiplier, seizing infrastructure and terrain prior to the arrival of elite forces. The elite forces (Spetsnaz, Naval Infantry, and KSSO) could advance on operational objectives extremely fast and almost without firing a shot. Over 22,000 Ukrainian soldiers, sailors, marines, and officers were surrounded and forced to either defect or surrender.

However, there was an unintended and potentially crippling consequence. The Ukrainian public united when the extent of Russian deception and influence operations came to light. The Russian-sponsored insurgency in Donbas over the summer of 2014 further anchored Ukrainian nationalist resentments against Moscow (see Chapter 8).

The Crimean Annexation precipitated a sharp rise in Ukrainian nationalism and anti-Russian sentiment. Ukraine's unity government demonstrated rare political decisiveness regarding Russian aggression by initiating highly effective military reforms.

In May 2014, the Poroshenko government reinstated military conscription. A new generation of eager, young officers began displacing the corrupt old guard, and military spending dramatically increased. The country was reorganized into military districts (similar to Russia) with a General Staff and a Chief of the General Staff answerable directly to the Minister of Defense.

The SBU was purged of Kremlin loyalists and then rebuilt under the tutelage of Western patrons. Ukraine also pivoted irrevocably toward the

E.U. and NATO, openly announcing its intent to pursue membership in both organizations.

Ultimately, the Crimean Annexation set the stage for Russia to stage an insurgency in the Donbas region of eastern Ukraine. While the Crimean Annexation was a means to ensure strategic control of the Black Sea, the insurgency was intended to prevent Ukraine from leaving Russia's orbit.

If hybrid warfare had a Woodstock, it would be the Crimean Annexation. The campaign leveraged non-military means (political, economic, and diplomatic) then non-kinetic military means (propaganda, special intelligence activities, and political coercion) to mold the circumstances and prepare the battlespace. Information dominance formed the backbone of Russian activities in Crimea and was closely coordinated with kinetic military operations.

First, proxy forces were established to support protest activity and deny freedom of movement to Ukrainian Ground Forces. Elite units then maneuvered quickly to surround Ukrainian military installations and seize the peninsula. Heavier ground forces followed shortly thereafter to entrench Russian holdings.

But what conventional war is not preceded by non-military (political, economic, and diplomatic) influences to support a favorable resolution?

What sophisticated military does not leverage information dominance, intelligence collection, covert action, or cyber activities to develop the battle space?

In both the American Gulf War and Operation Iraqi Freedom, United States Army Special Forces sponsored Kurdish proxy forces in Northern Iraq while Special Missions Units (SMUs) conducted Advanced Force Operations. Moreover, airborne infantry and special operations forces were created in World War II to seize critical terrain and infrastructure ahead of large invasions and advancing ground forces.

Western observers were deeply alarmed at Russia's guile and deception, but these were not innovations to the art of war. The Crimean Annexation, while an impressive feat of covert action and rapid maneuver, was little more than a series of well-executed preparatory activities for the introduction of heavy ground forces.

When these preparatory activities are paired with non-military influences (political, economic, and diplomatic), a unique and holistic approach to conventional warfare emerges. Once elite forces had seized their respective objectives, follow-on heavy ground forces arrived on schedule. Within these activities, the Russians applied low-intensity conflict, network-centric warfare, and reflexive control to create asymmetric advantages in a conventional military conflict. That is hybrid warfare.

---

1. Russia and Turkey have quarreled over the Crimea, the Carpathian Mountains, and strategic dominance over the Black Sea for centuries. During the Crimean War (1853-1856), Russia attempted an invasion of Ottoman territories around the Black Sea and modern-day Romania. Russia had perceived that the Ottoman Empire was declining and would not be able to muster sufficient forces to counter the invasion; however, in order to preserve the balance of power the U.K. and France intervened to assist the Turks. Russia lost over 450,000 soldiers in the bitter three-year conflict.

2. A Hetman was an eastern or central European leader. The title was political in nature, but it was usually associated with generalship and military command.

3. Commissars are officials of the Communist Party, generally associated with the former Soviet Union and Maoist China, who were responsible for political education and organization, as well as ideological enforcement.

4. The kolkhozes and sovkhozes were collectivist and state-owned farms assembled from the confiscated land.

5. The Ukrainian parliamentary coalition that emerged from the Orange Revolution, where pro-Russian Presidential candidate Viktor Yanukovych lost to Viktor Yushchenko. The new parliament was led by Prime Minister Yulia Tymoshenko.

6. Russian nationalism of emigres and ethnic-Slavs beyond Russia's borders.

7. Ethnically Turkish-Mongol peoples that live in Eastern Europe and speak dialects of the Tartar language.

Chapter Eight

An Insurgency in Donbas Initiates a Hybrid War in Eastern Ukraine

Russia Picks Up Where It Left Off in Crimea

The Euromaidan Crisis of 2013 eventually forced Russia to take the calculated risk of invading and annexing the Crimean Peninsula in February and March of 2014. Putin's national security cadre and GRU planned and executed the Crimean Annexation, demonstrating Russian hybrid warfare to a fearful world. But hybrid warfare has flaws and weaknesses.

We can draw upon an analogy to Germany's unveiling of Blitzkrieg. Planned by then General von Manstein and executed by General Heinz Guderian, an armored spearhead through the Ardennes Forest outflanked and encircled bewildered British and French Forces in 1940.[1]

Following their astounding victory, the Germans occupied Paris, France capitulated, and the British Expeditionary Force was driven back into the sea at Dunkirk. These events set the conditions for the Battle of Britain, the Battle of El Alamein, and the Battle of the Atlantic, where Germany's strategic limitations became obvious. The Luftwaffe could establish air superiority and enable armored breakouts through the lines of static forces, but it could not occupy territory or eradicate ground resistance on its own.

Armored spearheads of Blitzkrieg advance faster than supporting infantry can keep up, leaving the flanks exposed to counterattack. Blitzkrieg also tends to overextend itself, outrunning its own supply lines. The Germans made the additional discovery that Blitzkrieg could not cross the English Channel.

Similarly, Russia wielded hybrid warfare to great avail on multiple occasions, but it also struggled to deliver adequate kinetic force to achieve its goals more than once. When objectives were discrete, and the campaign to achieve them was limited in its duration and supported by a credible narrative, hybrid warfare was highly effective. But elite forces were too few to seize numerous complex objectives and too light to stand toe-to-toe with conventional ground forces in a no-holds-barred fight.

Information operations must propagate a narrative that resonates with the populace while containing competing narratives for hybrid warfare to be successful—a technique that is impossible if the narrative is tired or improbable. Extended-duration campaigns strain narratives, complicate logistics and supply, and give the enemy time to reorganize and reinforce.

The insurgency that would emerge in the Donbas region of Eastern Ukraine in 2014, centered in Donetsk and Luhansk, was entirely of Russia's making. The insurgency's independence from the Kremlin is as improbable as the independence of South Ossetia or Abkhazia (see Chapter 3). It served as a means of controlling or, at least, constraining Kyiv.

Much like the Crimean Annexation before, Russia employed a tailored array for Spetsnaz, intelligence operatives, and specialist infantry formations, insulated by a thick blanket of coercion and propaganda. But the hybrid warfare campaign that unfolded between the summer of 2014 and into the winter of 2015 stalled out, diminishing into a no-holds-barred fight reminiscent of the World Wars. The campaign also backfired against Moscow, catalyzing Ukraine's reorientation towards the West, draining precious resources in Moscow, and diplomatically isolating Russia from the larger world.

Russian Strategic Motivations

Many of the same strategic motivations underlying the Annexation of Crimea in February and March of 2014 were also at play in fueling the Donbas separatists from April 2014 forward. President Putin and his national security cadre desired to renegotiate the post-Cold War status quo and were primarily focused on dominating the former Soviet sphere of influence.

While the Crimean Annexation had a punitive aspect, its primary objective was to ensure Russia's continued dominance of the Black Sea. Once the critical strategic imperative had been satisfied, Moscow looked to ensure continued defense-in-depth through a subservient Ukraine.

When Ukraine orbited around Moscow, Russia could use the Carpathian Mountains as a strategic barrier, reducing the amount of open terrain Russia would need to defend in the event of an invasion from the West. Russia's dominance of Ukraine also ensured invading ground forces would exhaust and overextend themselves before reaching Russia itself.

Historical invaders like the French and the Germans could not continuously resupply their forward armies through increasingly long and indefensible supply lines. Nor could soldiers sustain the pace of aggressive combat operations across the vast expanses of open steppe. Firepower became impotent when it was dispersed across enormous fronts. Command and control (C2) structures fell apart when officers could not coordinate forces or fires across limitless open territory. These factors saved Russia from domination by both Adolf Hitler and Napoleon Bonaparte.

To maintain defense-in-depth, Russia could not permit Ukraine to leave its orbit economically, diplomatically, or militarily. As Russia had with Transnistria in Moldova or South Ossetia and Abkhazia in Georgia, Russian operatives laid the groundwork for sympathizers in the Donbas region of Eastern Ukraine to attempt an insurrection.

Donbas was a region in the most eastern quadrant of Ukraine that borders Russia that included the two subregions of Donetsk and Luhansk. It protruded from the rest of Ukraine, a geopolitical peninsula akin to Crimea's physical peninsula, making it easy prey for Russian intervention. Donbas was primarily ethnic-Russian, and its inhabitants spoke Russian as their first language and Ukrainian as their second.

Moscow first sought to establish "Novorossiya", a new Russia in Donbas. The Kremlin, however, refused to overtly embrace and annex the region as it had with Crimea. The point was to create leverage over Kyiv, not to secure new territories—much as Russia had with Abkhazia and South Ossetia in Georgia. Eventually, the Donetsk People's Republic and Luhansk People's Republic would emerge as separate but allied autonomous regions with Russian backing.

As this book is being written, Donetsk and Luhansk continue to give Russia leverage over the regime in Kyiv (though, following the beginning of the 2022 Russo-Ukrainian War, Moscow did finally annex these regions). But the subtext, more than Moscow's pronouncements, is most important: Russia views Ukraine as a vassal state of Russia and it cannot be allowed an independent foreign policy.

This interference by Russia prevented Ukraine from joining other international institutions like the European Union (E.U.) or NATO. The E.U., which was still reeling from the "Great Recession" of 2009 and the subsequent Greek Debt Crisis, could not permit another unstable country to join the Union. Nor would NATO admit a new member while it was already at war with Russia and its proxies. Steady hands have steered NATO away from a full-scale war with any regime in Moscow for over 70 years, and many of the member states were unclear as to how provoking Moscow by initiating Ukraine into the ranks is in the alliance's best interest.

Early Hybrid Warfare in Donbas: Non-Military Influence, Covert Action, and Unconventional Warfare

Russia walked tall after its conquest of Crimea. Russia had effectively exploited the disorder in Kyiv and secured a critical strategic asset. But the Kremlin did not consider all of the ways in which Crimea had been a unique case. Ethnic Russians in Crimea had many legitimate grievances with Kyiv, making them more susceptible to propaganda and, ultimately, a coup de main.

Additionally, Russia already had considerable combat power stationed in the region, certainly more than enough to seal off the peninsula, provided local Ukrainian Forces refused to fight back. Annexing Crimea was also very popular with the Russian public, who felt, with historical precedent from the Russian Empire and the Soviet Union, that Russia had a valid claim over Crimea.

The overall success of the Crimean Annexation in February and March of 2014 persuaded Moscow to attempt a hybrid war in Eastern Ukraine over the summer of 2014. This hybrid war began as an unconventional war (a conflict waged through local proxies) and devolved into a full conventional military intervention.[2] Moscow created and supported a separatist movement, the epicenter of which was in Donetsk and Luhansk, in breaking away from the government in Kyiv.

The goal was to compel Kyiv to accept Russian headship in the former Soviet sphere, rein in Ukrainian foreign policy, and sabotage Ukraine's pivot towards the West. Eastern Ukraine was an appealing target as it was the base of Victor Yanukovych's support and is populated by an ethnic Russian and Russian-speaking majority. The population also shared many of Crimea's same grievances with the kleptocratic regime in Kyiv.

Why Revolt?

People in Eastern Ukraine had plenty to protest about heading into the summer of 2014. The Ukrainian State itself was largely a shell for powerful political interests and oligarchs who benefitted immensely from their stewardship of state-owned industries. Political parties were already far too dependent on oligarchic contributions to institute any real reforms.

President Viktor Yanukovych's electoral power base was in Eastern Ukraine, and many people in those regions favored Russian economic ties and a proposed Russian Customs Union over the European Union. While Ukrainian exports were evenly balanced between the E.U. and Russia, Eastern Ukraine was deeply integrated into the Russian economy; especially the defense industrial sector.

The region had a lot to lose from Euromaidan's anti-Russian orientation. Russian operatives exploited these fault lines as they worked to turn out protestors in cities like Donetsk, Luhansk, Slovyansk, Kharkiv, Kramatorsk, Horlivka, Mariupol, Debaltseve, and others.

Unlike Crimea where Russian operatives directly controlled the militias, the militias in Eastern Ukraine were often operationally independent, receiving Russian support in the form of arms, supplies, indirect fires (shell artillery and rockets), and intelligence. Russian operatives were often embedded within militias but, in the beginning, they usually served more as force multipliers and communications nodes without exercising a great deal of direct control.

Once Moscow had stoked the fire of revolution, there was sufficient animus among Eastern Ukrainians for it to spread without having to fan the flames.

Russian Operatives Initiate an Unconventional War in Eastern Ukraine

Throughout March and April 2014, pro-Russian demonstrators became active in every major city in Eastern Ukraine. Both leftist and right-wing organizations chose to partake in a wave of demonstrations against the capital. While Russian intelligence operatives worked hard to spread unrest, the outcry was genuine. There were certainly paid protestors and Russian operatives amongst the populace, but most protestors were frustrated citizens. Both Acting President Oleksandr Turchynov and later President Petro Poroshenko (elected on May 25, 2014) dismissed the legitimate concerns of the populace at their peril.

The parallels to the Crimean Annexation were uncanny. GRU and FSB operatives permeated Eastern Ukraine, organizing protests and bribing (or threatening) public officials to ignore the chaos. As militias became active, they occupied key terrain.

In April 2014, the United States revealed satellite imagery of Russian supply convoys and armor moving into the Donbas Region of Eastern Ukraine, describing the activity as an invasion. The demonstrators occupied government buildings and closed off highways and city centers from Ukrainian Government Troops and police reinforcements.

On March 1, 2014, large demonstrations seized regional administrative buildings in Kharkiv and Donetsk, and Pavel Gubarev, an active member of the Progressive Socialist Party of Ukraine, was declared governor of Donetsk by a crowd in the city's Lenin Square. Gubarev was also a member of the neofascist Russian National Unity paramilitary group.

On March 3rd, Gubarev led a crowd to seize the Donetsk Regional State Administration building. In a press conference on March 6th, Gubarev declared his intent for Donetsk to hold a referendum on the territorial status of Donetsk and derecognition of the government in Kyiv. He was arrested by the SBU the same day. Gubarev was later traded back to the separatists in a prisoner exchange, though he would never again have a leading position in the movement.

On March 5, 2014, Aleksander Kharitonov, Secretary of the Progressive Socialist Party of Ukraine, was declared governor of Luhansk by a large crowd of protestors, following the example set by Pavel Gubarev. Kharitonov proposed to set up an executive committee which would oversee a referendum on appealing to President Vladimir Putin for aid.

On March 9th, protestors seized additional administrative buildings in Luhansk and escalated the crisis with calls for a referendum on Russian annexation, as had happened in Crimea. After storming the Luhansk Oblast State Administration building, Kharitonov read the resignation letter of Luhansk Governor Mykhailo Bolotskykh to a crowd. Bolotskykh was unceremoniously escorted out of the city by local militia.

On March 13th, Kharitonov was arrested by the SBU. Former paratrooper and Yanukovych ally Valeriy Bolotov replaced him to rule in Luhansk. Like his inspiration Gubarev, Kharitonov was eventually released in a prisoner exchange and became irrelevant to the movement he had helped move to violence.

On April 21, 2014, a crowd of approximately 400 demonstrators declared Vladimir Varshavskiy "people's governor" at a rally in Kharkiv. Varshavskiy was unknown and irrelevant in politics, and shortly after his "appointment" he announced that an executive committee had been formed.

It appears that Russian handlers were actually making the executive decisions in Kharkiv while Varshavskiy stood out front as a puppet.

The "people's governor" would have a moment in the sun and then, once again, become irrelevant. The actual mayor of Kharkiv, Hennadiy Kernes, was shot in the back while cycling on April 28, 2014. He would eventually recover and displace Varshavskiy. His would-be assassin was never apprehended.

Soon afterward, a deluge of like-minded "people's mayors" and de facto "governors" emerged throughout Eastern Ukraine. Many of these Russian political plants were mere criminals only hours before.

Before the insurgency, these emerging political bosses had mostly been relegated to the fringes of extreme parties on the left or right ends of the political landscape. Many had been inactive in politics prior to 2014. The fringe nature of these bosses gave credence to the speculation that most of them were discovered by GRU and FSB operatives and that the Russian intelligence services had been forced to move quickly in their vetting process.

The fact that Russian operatives, who had so expertly manipulated Crimea, could not find better puppet politicians and militia leaders indicates a lack of detailed campaign preparation prior to events in 2014. Where the actions in Crimea may be viewed as an example of Russian operations when planned in-depth, the 2014 actions in Donbas may be seen as rushed, opportunistic, and ad hoc.

On March 10th, the Ukrainian Ministry of the Internal Affairs forces and local police organized a crackdown on these self-proclaimed people's mayors and governors. The police units quickly regained control of seized administrative buildings in Kharkiv, Luhansk, and Donetsk.

The interim government in Kyiv followed through on a wider crackdown on unofficial political mobilization and illegitimate federalization. Many of the weaker "people's governors" and "popular mayors", or at least those without supporting militia, were arrested by government-loyal police.

Meanwhile, in Donbas, things escalated further. Donetsk's first self-declared governor, Gubarev, was arrested, and Aleksandr Boroday (a Russian citizen) stepped in to declare himself "people's governor". In Slovyansk, Boroday's associate Igor Girkin (who chose the more memorable and striking name "Strelkov", Russian for "shooter") took over as "people's mayor".

Strelkov moved the goal of the separatist movement from autonomy under a Kyiv-based federalist model of government to outright secession. The idea of secession was propagated through the old term "Novorossiya", referring to Ukraine's identity under the old Russian Empire. In this way, the separatists' narrative alluded to restoring past independence that had cooperative harmony with their benefactors in Moscow.

On April 6th, the main administrative building in Donetsk changed hands again to the separatists, and Strelkov made a proclamation declaring the independence of the Donetsk People's Republic (DPR). The Luhansk People's Republic (LPR) would follow suit a few weeks later.

Strelkov declared himself leader of the DPR on April 7th (he eventually relinquished the headlining political role and took the more militarily significant role of Defense Minister). This gesture was meant to motivate and unify the numerous emerging anti-Kyiv separatist movements behind a single figure.

Strelkov himself eventually took control of the South-East Army (which, despite the grandiose name, was merely a large group of disparate militias) and became the leading man in the separatist movement. But he in no way monopolized the use of force in Eastern Ukraine and many separatist leaders preferred to maintain exclusive control of their own fighting units (loosely referred to as battalions).

On April 11th, separatists overran the Ministry of Internal Affairs rapid-response force at the city's main administrative complex.

The next day, separatists seized city halls in Slovyansk, Kramatorsk, and Krasny Liman. In Donetsk, separatists seized an SBU armory and distributed 300 assault rifles and 400 handguns to local militias. Strelkov led a company-sized force of militiamen to storm Slovyansk government buildings, including the executive committee building, the police department, and the SBU office.

The Ukrainian Security Service (SBU) soon responded in force. Ukrainian Government Forces successfully restored order to cities like Odessa and Kharkiv (Varshavskiy disappeared in the chaos), but Strelkov's organized resistance in Slovyansk repelled multiple government assaults.

Strelkov had correctly assessed that Slovyansk was ideally positioned to serve as a screen between regions firmly under Kyiv's control and the Donetsk People's Republic. Capturing Slovyansk was the Ukrainian Government's key to advancing ground forces into Donbas.

In Donetsk, a militia led by Russian operatives stormed the Ministry of Internal Affairs building, forced the local chief to resign, and informed the staff they were under new leadership.

On April 16th, demonstrators captured the public administration building.

On April 27th, they captured a local TV station. Ukrainian broadcasts were immediately canceled, and Russian propaganda took over.

The Ukrainian Response Takes Form

Leaders in Kyiv moved to put down the rebellion in Donbas with far more urgency than they had in Crimea. They seemed to have learned the lesson: Russia would annex the region if they did not respond immediately.

On April 15th, the Ukrainian Army and Ministry of Internal Affairs assembled an ad hoc detachment of police and motorized infantry to put down further demonstrations, recapture government buildings, and arrest separatist leaders. These efforts would end in embarrassment after about a week as Ukrainian Government Forces were halted outside of most cities by rudimentary checkpoints or mobs of protestors.

Ukrainian commanders were trained to work operationally using the Russian language, a legacy of the Soviet Union. They were reluctant to fire on Russian-speaking peoples, even armed separatist militiamen. A detachment from the 25th Airborne Brigade allowed itself to be surrounded by a mob of GRU-organized separatists who promptly confiscated the unit's weapons and armored personnel carriers (APCs). Spetsnaz operatives replicated this tactic throughout the region: raising mobs, quietly hiding in the crowd, surrounding Ukrainian units, and emerging from within the mob to seize weapons from hesitant Ukrainian soldiers.

Defections to the DPR and LPR People's Militias among military and police personnel were also widespread. By August 2015, the Ukrainian chief military prosecutor estimated that some 5,000 police officers and 3,000 servicemen had defected.

Acting Ukrainian President Oleksandr Turchynov publicly vowed to end the separatist "terror activities" by launching a major operation in Donetsk Oblast. In Kramatorsk, Ukrainian Ground Forces recaptured the town airfield. Despite nearly constant hounding and confrontations with demonstrators (where Ukrainian troops embarrassingly backed down), they had secured the city's surrounding area by April 2nd.

On April 24th, Ukrainian troops briefly retook City Hall in Mariupol but were forced to remit it back into separatist hands when they realized that they had been cut off from follow-on support. Ukrainian airborne troops also made probing attacks around the city of Slovyansk throughout the last week of April, and, on May 2nd, they established a foothold in the city at the cost of two downed helicopters.

Anti-riot police units made a second attempt to retake Mariupol City Hall on May 7th, but separatists had regained the building by the end of the day.

On May 9th, fighting ensued over the Mariupol police station, setting the building ablaze. As sporadic fighting spread throughout the Donbas region, a telling incident occurred in which separatists attempted to disarm a convoy of Ukrainian troops near Donetsk.

The Ukrainian troops resisted by firing warning shots and maneuvering on the flanks to surround the crowd. Over 100 separatists were arrested in the incident, highlighting the outsized force that Ukrainian troops could bring to bear under competent and determined leadership.

In further brazen defiance of Kyiv, the Donetsk People's Republic and Luhansk People's Republic conducted referendums on May 11th, though these were widely denounced by international observers. The progenitors did not attempt to justify the move under either Ukrainian or international law. Unsurprisingly, the results showed that the people backed independence from Kyiv and annexation by Russia, sealing the fate of Eastern Ukraine and setting the region on an irreversible course toward open insurrection.

Drawing into focus the sharp divisions developing between Russia and Ukraine, on May 25th, Petro Poroshenko was elected President of Ukraine by a 54.7% majority, thereby avoiding a potential run-off with the next most popular candidate. Moscow objected to the legitimacy of the election, proclaiming Victor Yanukovych's government-in-exile as the rightful authority in Kyiv. Poroshenko was a Ukrainian oligarch and an advocate for E.U. integration. Among his first policies was negotiating a trade agreement with Brussels, a move that pricked Moscow in the heart.

In June 2014, the state-owned Russian energy giant Gazprom notified the Poroshenko government that, unless Ukraine satisfied its existing account balances and paid in advance for future imports, all gas pipelines into Ukraine would be shut off.

Gas supplies were shut off a few days following the notice.

Throttling energy supplies as a naked tactic of geopolitical coercion sent an eerie shudder through the E.U., particularly Germany and Poland, as continental Europe remains deeply dependent on Russian natural gas.

Information Operations

As with all Russian hybrid wars, the Donbas campaign began with Information Operations (IO). Russian messaging labeled the interim government in Kyiv, led by acting President Olexander Turchikov, a "fascist junta", and efforts to stir protests began in earnest.

Perhaps the first mistake of the campaign was how familiar Moscow's messaging was to most Ukrainians. Very similar propaganda was used in Crimea, and the narrative was tired and unbelievable. Russia always denied involvement in destabilizing Ukraine, while threatening a muscular response to outside interference.

Russia also promoted pan-Slavic nationalism and "Russkiy Mir" (Russian: Русский мир) as it had in Crimea. Messaging gave dire warnings about the creep of fascism and assaults on tradition, morals, and Russian identity. Just like in Crimea, proxy groups received targeted messaging to motivate mobilization against Kyiv. However, Russian IO had lost its plausibility to most Ukrainians, and, to the rest of the world, it was often borderline preposterous.

Eastern Ukrainians were not interested in Russian annexation or even full independence from Kyiv. They resented Kyiv for its patronage system of oligarchs, political favoritism, the political stalemate, the lack of reform, and thousands of other issues such as voting to rescind Russian as a national language.

In the eyes of most Eastern Ukrainians, such resentments were cause for protest and reform—not revolution. Many Eastern Ukrainians wanted political federalism that would have given them more autonomy to set policy within localities.[3]

Almost no one in Eastern Ukraine envisioned their local and provincial governments operating independently of Kyiv's national government. The Russian promotions of Novorossiya were an overreach that grossly overestimated its base of popular support.

Cyber Campaign

On the cyber front, Russia would also wash, rinse, and repeat. It is almost impossible to ascertain where cyber operations related to Crimea ended and where cyber operations for the war in Eastern Ukraine began. There were intermittent lulls in activity, but Crimea seems to mark the beginning of an extended cyber war on Ukraine, and the country itself became a sort of testbed for new Russian systems, tactics, methodologies, and personnel training in the cyber domain. The practice continues today (or as of the publication of this book).

It is important to note that the practice of coordinating cyberattacks with information operations only became more acute during the conflict in Donbas. Cyber tools were deployed in a similar fashion to other asymmetric tools like electronic warfare (EW).

Russian planners integrated EW functions like electronic attacks (jamming and disruption of communications) into tactics, techniques, and procedures (TTPs) executed by ground forces when they maneuver on an enemy unit or position. It seems that Russian military planners envisioned integrating cyberattacks with information operations and propaganda in a similar manner.

In October 2014, the electronic system used for compiling election results for the Rada (Ukraine's Parliament) was shut down. This forced Ukrainian authorities to manually count the ballots, undermining the credibility of the results in the eyes of the populace. CyberBerkut claimed responsibility for the attack.

On December 23, 2015, a powerful cyberattack disrupted the Ukrainian power grid. Hackers compromised the control systems of Prykarpattyaoblenergo, an energy distribution company that services Ivano-Frankivsk Oblast. 30 substations were switched off, and 230,000 people were without electricity for up to 6 hours. Chernivtsioblenergo and Kyivoblenergo, other energy distribution companies, were also affected by the attack, though on a smaller scale.

Russian Proxies:

Russian proxy forces began as semi-independent battalions, each of which operated under a War Lord Commander that, at least nominally, pledged fealty to Moscow. These separatist units were generally organized along the lines of a Russian motorized infantry battalion, with a handful of nominal officers and no sergeants, although they usually operated at only partial strength because of the difficulty in recruiting partisans to fill the ranks.

By August 2014, many of these disparate militias were increasingly integrated into battalions structured in the Russian model. Some units did continue to maintain a degree of independence; however, as Russia reinforced the insurgency and escalated the conflict into a conventional war, Moscow became more resolved to consolidate these units under its chain of command. Often, Russian BTGs leveraged these proxies as security forces to free up maneuver companies for offensive tasks. These separatist units were also frequently placed at the vanguard of assaults to reinforce the notion of Russia's distance from the conflict and ensure the most dangerous tasks were borne by cheap and expendable troops.

Ukrainian Forces Learn to Fight Russia's Proxies

The Ukrainian political apparatus was far too disorganized, and Ground Forces far too incompetently led, to initiate a full-scale offensive against the separatists at the onset of the insurgency. The Ministry of Internal Affairs special police units and the SBU were equally disheveled from the controversies of the Euromaidan Crisis and mass defections to the Russian armed forces. The SBU's entire senior leadership had been compromised by the Russian intelligence services (or, more likely, they were Russian sympathizers from their first appointments).

For all these disadvantages, Ukraine had discovered a new drive of nationalism. The Crimean Annexation February and March of 2014 had enraged much of the country. This outrage melded with the momentum of the Euromaidan movement to generate an authentic reform agenda in the Ukrainian security apparatus.

The Army restored mandatory conscription and began purging the corrupt officer corps. The SBU appointed new administrators and reoriented its collection and counterintelligence activities towards Russia. Nevertheless, the attempts to secure Eastern Ukraine started primitively with available troops and low-hanging fruit.

The Ukrainian strategy that emerged during the summer of 2014 was to press slowly toward Donetsk and Luhansk from secure provinces. Ukrainian forces brought to bear overwhelming firepower and manpower against enemy forces in the field, circumventing urban fighting in city centers while moving from town-to-town. In ideal circumstances, cities were cut-off from outside support, forcing separatist militias to withdraw eastward.

On the occasion that separatists were determined to put up a fight, cities would be peppered with field artillery and secured by pro-government volunteer forces. This practice ensured that trained combat troops did not become demoralized by heavy urban fighting, civilian deaths, and combat fatigue.

Eventually, Ukrainian commanders planned to isolate Donetsk and Luhansk from each other and maneuvered to secure the border crossings (particularly at Izvaryne) where arms, supplies, and military equipment flowed in from Russia, starving the DPR and LPR People's Militias into submission.

The First Battle of Donetsk Airport

Anticipating a separatist assault on the Donetsk Airport, Ukrainian leaders ordered the few competent troops available (elements of Ukraine's own air assault infantry and Spetsnaz) to land on the runway and secure the airport. These elite troops arrived in helicopter transport on May 25th and established a perimeter that included the tarmac, runways, and control towers.

In the early morning of May 26th, two companies worth of separatist irregulars (approximately 200 men), led by Russian GRU Spetsnaz detachments, assaulted the Donetsk Airport and captured the main terminal. They erected roadblocks to entrench their position and called on Ukrainian forces to withdraw from the surrounding area. Included in the ranks of the separatists were Vostok Battalion, Kalmius Battalion, Somali Battalion, Sparta Battalion, and Chechen irregulars.

Ukrainian National Guard troops of the Ministry of Internal Affairs issued an immediate ultimatum that the separatists surrender, which was promptly rejected. Ukrainian paratroopers and Spetsnaz then launched an assault on the airport terminal, supported by National Guard and with close air support from Su-25 fighter jets and Mi-24 attack helicopters.

Attack helicopters conducted multiple airstrikes on entrenched separatist positions and a single anti-aircraft battery. Ukrainian troops secured the airport terminal shortly thereafter. It is estimated that about 40 separatist fighters died during the engagement.

For Russian leadership, this incident marked a need to integrate operatives (Spetsnaz and agenturi) more deeply into the ranks of the separatist militias. A steady stream of artillery, mechanized equipment, armor, and anti-aircraft weaponry flowed into the Donbas region, escalating the conflict from skirmish warfare into a conventional war. Notably, following the First Battle of Donetsk Airport, Russian overseers made a point to mitigate Ukrainian air power.

Russian operatives brought in anti-access and area denial (A2/AD) systems such as the Buk-M1 and trained Donbas militias on the systems. Russian A2/AD systems took such a heavy toll on tactical and transport aviation that, by late August, the Ukrainian Air Force was effectively sidelined for the remainder of the conflict.

But there was an unfortunate and unexpected consequence to introducing advanced A2/AD systems to Donbas. As Russia increasingly tried to turn the DPR and LPR People's Militia Forces into conventional ground forces, they handed them increasingly advanced technology. On July 17, 2014, Malaysia Airlines Flight 17 was shot down. Subsequent investigations indicated that it was downed by a Buk-M1 surface-to-air missile launched from separatist-held territory in Donbas.

Separatist leaders in the DPR and LPR had no scruples over using such systems on any aircraft over Donbas airspace and had no means of reaching out to Ukrainian, Russian, or international aviation authorities to coordinate and deconflict flight paths for approaching aircraft. Seeing a large plane over Donbas (a civilian Boeing 777) and salivating over the opportunity to down IL-76 full of Ukrainian paratroopers, an unidentified separatist commander fired a Buk-M1 surface-to-air missile at the approaching plane. Though the tragedy of Flight 17 had little effect on the fighting itself, it proved to be a public relations disaster for the separatist movement and an even bigger diplomatic disaster for Russia. 298 passengers and crew died on board.

Kyiv Builds Momentum and the Unconventional Warfare Campaign Recedes

On June 3rd, Ukrainian Ground Forces assaulted and eliminated separatist positions in Semenivka and regained control of Krasnyi Lyman. Two Ukrainian soldiers were killed in the fighting and 45 were wounded.

Ukrainian officials announced on June 11th that Russia had "allowed" tanks to cross the Russo-Ukrainian border into Donbas. The tanks were a part of an armored column that included three T-64 tanks (one tank platoon), several BM-21 Grad Multiple-Launch Rocket System (MLRS) (roughly one MLRS battery or company), and other military transport vehicles.

Denis Pushilin, the new "President" of DPR, refused to comment on where the armored column originated, but claimed that the T-64s and BM-21s were sorely needed in Donetsk to defend the city from further Ukrainian assault. On June 14th, an additional two T-72 tanks entered Donetsk from Russia.

Ukrainian Government Forces recaptured the strategically important Black Sea port of Mariupol by June 12th, and the Ukrainian flag was raised over City Hall after fierce fighting. Spokesmen for the National Guard announced that the recently formed Dnepr and Azov "volunteer" units had been used in the operation in keeping with an overarching strategy of using pro-government volunteer militias to secure city centers. Using irregular units to secure urban areas allowed Ukrainian Ground Forces to stick to direct combat against heavier conventionally organized forces rather than wading into the drudgery of urban combat and guerilla warfare with local partisans.

Highlighting the increasing dangers of operating aircraft in the region, a Ukrainian Air Force IL-76 transport plane was shot down on June

14th. The plane had been planning to drop off airborne troops at the Luhansk International Airport. All 49 personnel onboard—paratroopers and crew—were lost.

The Battle of Yampil

By late June, Ukrainian Government Forces were slowly closing in on Slovyansk; a strategic imperative for forces maneuvering on Donetsk from the west. The Battle of Yampil unfolded from June 19th to the 20th. It was one of the first major engagements where large Ukrainian Ground Forces executed a preconceived operational plan and scheme of maneuver rather than simply advancing until they encountered organized resistance.

The mission was to sever the supply corridors supporting the local militias in Slovyansk by capturing key highway intersections in the vicinity of Yampil. Rather than allow themselves to be cut off, the Slovyansk militias would be forced to withdraw from the city. On June 3rd, when Ukrainian Government Forces captured Krasnyi Liman, the Highway T0514/T-513 corridor from Siversk through Yampil to Slovyansk became the only safe lifeline for the Slovyansk militia garrison.

The Ukrainian operational objectives were the intersection between Highways T-0514 and T-513 to the west of Yampil and bridges over the Siverskyi Donets River at Zakotnoe and Krivaya Luka. The Slovyansk militia garrison primarily had responsibility for protecting the vicinity of Yampil, but other units were active in the area.

Ukrainian Government Forces involved in the battle included a battalion from the 24th Mechanized Brigade, a paratrooper battalion from the 25th Airborne Brigade, 2 tank companies, supporting self-propelled howitzers, an MLRS battery, and approximately 1,500 soldiers and supporting vehicles. An assortment of militia units participated in the battle, totaling as high as 4,000 fighters.

The first assault on the militia lines to the west of Yampil lost momentum. It seized up despite overwhelming firepower and numerical superiority, likely due to the death of the commander of the mechanized battalion. The second assault scattered most of the Yampil militia garrison and captured both bridges across the Siverskyi Donets River (Zakotnoe and Krivaya Luka), cutting off avenues of retreat.

Ukrainian Government Forces surrounded the area of Yampil and Commanders emplaced a western blocking force between Yampil and Slovyansk to protect against reserves redeploying to the battle from the militia garrison. A second eastern blocking force was deployed toward the outskirts of Siversk to prevent reinforcements from arriving from the Lysychansk battalion in Luhansk.

Militia reserves were re-tasked to transit through Krivaya Luka to the south to reinforce the Yampil area. Ukrainian Government Forces had moved slowly, and evening was rapidly approaching which put eliminating the surrounded militia in the woodlands of Yampil out of reach. The Lysychansk Battalion sent further reinforcements into Siversk.

When these Lysychansk forces combined with the small local garrison, they were able to overrun the Government blocking force. Components of the Slovyansk garrison were also bleeding through the western blocking force. With the blockades failing, it became obvious that the mission was a tactical failure. Ukrainian Army HQ issued orders for forward Ukrainian Government Forces to withdraw to starting positions on the outskirts of Kransyi Lyman to the north.

Separatists Withdraw from Slovyansk

Despite the tactical failures, the Battle of Yampil demonstrated the precariousness of the separatist position in Slovyansk, and Ukrainian Government Forces still had overwhelming firepower and manpower advantages. Self-appointed Donetsk Defense Minister Igor Strelkov ordered DPR People's Militia Forces to withdraw from Slovyansk to Kramatorsk. By July 5th, separatists were also withdrawing from Kramatorsk, falling back to Donetsk.

Igor Strelkov publicly pleaded for Russian intervention, stating that his men were losing the will to fight in the face of overwhelming numbers. Ukrainian Government Forces would recapture and secure a string of cities including Druzhkivka, Kostyantynivka, and Bakhmut (Artemivsk) by mid-July, opening the approach to Donetsk. So, despite being a tactical failure, the Battle of Yampil would prove to be an operational success for Ukrainian commanders.

Following Strelkov's move, DPR People's Militia Forces fortified Donetsk and the surrounding territory, destroyed bridges, and set up barricades on major roads.

On July 10th, separatists began firing on Donetsk airport with mortars, but the government garrison repelled the following assault on the terminal.

On the same day, Ukrainian Government Forces captured the city of Siversk, once a vital supply hub for separatist forces around Slovyansk and Yampil.

The Government Offensive Comes to Luhansk

On July 11th, in part due to panic from a python-like encirclement by Ukrainian Government Forces, a Ukrainian armored column in Luhansk Oblast was attacked by separatists wielding a Grad MLRS technical (an improvised mobile rocket launcher mounted on a civilian truck) close to the town of Rovenky. After losing 23 soldiers, Ukrainian Government Forces were inflamed enough to risk losing a plane to increasingly sophisticated air defenses in order to respond to the rocket technical with an airstrike.

On July 12th, Government Air Forces executed further airstrikes across both Donetsk and Luhansk, and on July 13th, Ukrainian Government Forces broke the separatist blockade around Luhansk Airport.

On July 22nd, the city of Severodonetsk in Luhansk Oblast was recaptured by Ukrainian Government Forces, further tightening the noose on the town of Lysychansk, which is situated on the T1316 Highway and served as an outer barrier for LPR People's Militia Forces in the area and a gateway into the Luhansk Oblast region.

By July 24th, Ukrainian Government Forces had recaptured Lysychansk.

The Battle for Horlivka

On July 21st, Ukrainian Government Forces led by the 72nd Guards Mechanized Brigade reached the northern suburbs of Horlivka and maneuvered to encircle the city. As Ukrainian Government Forces cut off and slowly secured the city, partisans bitterly clung to the urban terrain. DPR People's Militia Forces also exchanged sporadic indirect fire (mostly Grad rockets and mortars) with Ukrainian Government Troops as local commanders attempted to cover their withdrawal from Horlivka.

By July 29th, much of the residential section of the town had been razed, and by August the surviving homes were without gas or electricity. Ukrainian Government Forces eliminated separatist checkpoints and blockades on the North and East sides of the city and, disregarding the practice of avoiding urban fighting with Ukrainian Regulars, they slowly attempted to move south towards the city center. Despite heavy fighting, the 72nd Guards Mechanized Brigade failed to close Highway M04 through the city, leaving an open avenue to Donetsk.

Ukrainian Government Forces would repeatedly attempt to encircle and capture Horlivka into late August, but they demonstrated a gross inability to fight in urban terrain.

The Coils Tighten Around the Donbas Region and Irregular Forces Flounder

Ukrainian Government Forces finally relieved the paratroopers and Spetsnaz who were holding the Donetsk Airport, breaking an outer cordon and blockade by DPR People's Militia Forces on July 23rd. Apart from representing a symbolic victory, the airport could also serve as a gateway for additional Ukrainian Government troops (provided A2/AD could be mitigated).

Ukrainian Government Forces pushed DPR People's Militia Forces out of the suburb Avdiivka (Bakhmut) and further advanced to the northwestern corner of Donetsk city. Igor Strelkov released a public statement that separatist forces were being withdrawn from their outer positions to fortify the Donetsk city center.

By July 28th, the strategic heights of Savur-Mohyla were under Ukrainian control. The heights over-looked Highway M03-E50 which runs from Debaltseve through Krasnyi Luch to the Russian border. The area had been exploited by separatists as an artillery and mortar position, preventing

Ukrainian Government Forces from closing this supply corridor to Debaltseve. When the DPR People's Militia Forces were forced from the Savur-Mohyla heights, Debaltseve became untenable and forced to withdraw to Donetsk.

The next day, Ukrainian troops began a brief engagement with separatists in the town of Shakhtarsk and secured the city center by late afternoon. With Debaltseve and Shakhtarsk in government possession, the vital supply corridor between Donetsk and Luhansk was cut. This put the DPR and LPR in a dire position, and defeat seemed increasingly imminent.

Igor Strelkov released an emergency statement addressing President Vladimir Putin directly. The statement read, "Losing this war on the territory that President Vladimir Putin personally named Novorossiya would threaten the Kremlin's power and personally, the power of the President." The statement was the last in a series of desperate public ploys by Strelkov to get Russia out of the cheer section and into the game.

The Kremlin had provided training, arms, and supplies and selected most of the DPR and LPR officers and politicians. But Moscow preferred working through an unseen hand, maintaining a fig leaf of rectitude. Rumor has it that President Putin was outraged that one of his automatons had called him out personally and publicly for his arms-length support—upending the Russian façade of exclusively humanitarian participation.

Up until that point, only a select few Spetsnaz detachments, VDV, and support troops had been authorized to develop the battlespace, train local forces, and conduct sabotage. These units included the 45th Special Reconnaissance Regiment, 2nd and 10th Spetsnaz Brigades, several battalion tactical grounds from the 106th Airborne Division, and the 9th and 18th MRBs.

By August 3rd, Luhansk had been completely encircled by Ukrainian Government Forces. Almost all basic services, including electricity and water, had been destroyed, and the civilian population had abandoned much of the city. Tactically, Donetsk was better insulated and protected than Luhansk, but it had been cut off from further reinforcement and supply. Donetsk's saving grace were the trains running south to Russia, which were still operational.

On August 4th, Ukrainian Government Forces pressed into Yasynuvata, a northern suburb of Donetsk, and, after brief but bitter fighting, captured the railway junction that served as Donetsk's last remaining lifeline. The move opened the door for the Ukrainian paramilitary battalions, led by Azov, to advance into Donetsk city.

But the next day, highlighting the strategic importance of the railroad junction, Russian-backed DPR People's Militia Forces surged forward to recapture the town of Yasynuvata. Despite losing control of most of the larger suburb, Ukrainian Government troops managed to hold on to the railway station, ensuring further support and supply from Russia was throttled.

On August 9th, Igor Strelkov announced that Ukrainian Government Forces had captured the town of Krasnyi Luch, another vital logistics hub between Donetsk and Luhansk that connected Debaltseve to the Russian border via Highway M03-E50. Separatist-allied Cossack militias garrisoning the town fled as it became apparent that they faced overwhelming superiority of numbers and firepower.

Highlighting the dire situation, the recently installed DPR "Prime Minister" Aleksandr Zakharchenko called for a ceasefire to prevent a "humanitarian disaster". This was an attempt to play for time and offer a political opening for Russia to lend "humanitarian assistance".

Donetsk Under Assault

In the early morning of August 10th, Ukrainian Government Forces prepared for an assault on Donetsk itself by initiating an artillery bombardment of the city. A state of panic set in amongst the DPR People's Militia Forces, and many of the militiamen began to flee the city as Strelkov's HQ was rattled by incoming artillery.

Intense shelling of Donetsk continued into August 14th, and Igor Strelkov was forced to "resign" as the DPR Defense Minister and primary commander of the DPR Militia Forces (removed by a vengeful Moscow). Strelkov was replaced by Vladimir Kononov.

Luhansk Under Assault

By August 18th, Ukrainian Government Forces had fully encircled Luhansk and were initiating an advance to clear the city block by block, led by elements of the 80th Air Assault Brigade. While intense fighting broke out on many streets, rather than risk getting bogged down or damaging morale from intensive losses, Ukrainian Government Forces relied on mortars and artillery shelling to force separatist militias to withdraw from occupied districts.

By the evening of August 20th, Ukrainian Government Forces had secured a firm foothold in Luhansk and controlled several districts.

The collapse of all separatist resistance seemed inevitable. Donetsk was cut off from resupply and was under intensive bombardment. Luhansk was surrounded and under a ground assault. To make things worse, the DPR's most experienced field commander, Igor Strelkov, had been disposed of by his Russian overseers (likely FSB) for his comments against Putin's arms-length support. Debaltseve was captured by Ukrainian Government Forces, cutting the Donbas region in half.

Separatist morale fell to an all-time low, and militiamen abandoned the ranks in droves. It is hard not to imagine the DPR leadership crowded into a dimly lit HQ, huddling over a city map, shouting desperate orders into radios as drywall rattles out of the ceiling from artillery rounds impacting nearby buildings.

The Russian Counter-Offensive: Donbas Escalates into Conventional Warfare

Throughout July and August, as Ukrainian Ground Forces secured consecutive towns in the periphery of Donetsk and Luhansk, surrounding and compressing the city centers themselves, combat forces and supplies steadily poured in from Russia. Russian Ground Forces began integrating the disparate units of the DPR and LPR People's Militia Forces into battalion tactical groups.

Within Russian BTGs, these militias were delegated basic security roles and often performed force screening. This freed up Russian line companies to maneuver to contact with the enemy under the support of the BTG's organic artillery, MLRS, EW, and support troops. Russia used Rostov-on-Don across the border as a staging area and training base for separatist militias.

Ultimately, the Kremlin did not seek to defeat Ukrainian Government Forces entirely but to keep the insurgency alive while maintaining plausible deniability. Russia only risked intervening with conventional ground forces when the separatist proxies were on the verge of total collapse, and the Kremlin vehemently denied doing so during the course of operations.

NATO officials issued warnings concerning Moscow's direct involvement, "including Russian airborne, air defense and special operations forces in Eastern Ukraine." The separatists' sudden surge in numbers, confidence, firepower, and competence quickly turned the tide against Ukrainian Government Forces.

The Battle of Ilovaisk Opens the Road to Donetsk for the Russians

Emboldened by a series of successful raids in late July to the south and east of Donetsk, particularly around the cities of Amvrosiivka and Shakhtarsk, Ukrainian Government Forces sought to secure the town of Ilovaisk. They advanced on Ilovaisk with formidable firepower including the 17th Tank Brigade, 28th Mechanized Brigade, 51st Mechanized Brigade, 92nd Mechanized Brigade, 93rd Mechanized Brigade, and the volunteer battalions Donbas, Dnipro, Azov, and Shakhtarsk (a unit named after the town).

From August 18th to the 19th, with Donbas Battalion in the lead, Ukrainian Government Forces began the frustrating process of pushing DPR People's Militia Forces (mostly Oplot Brigade and supporting Russian agenturi) out of Ilovaisk. By the end of August 19th, approximately half of the city had been secured, and the Ukrainian flag was flying over City Hall.

The early success prompted commanders to redeploy Azov and Shakhtarsk battalions to reinforce garrisons in Mariupol. Mariupol was under pressure from Russian Ground Forces in Novoazovsk and required reinforcements. Unfortunately, Ukrainian Commanders redeployed Azov and Shakhtarsk too early.

Vicious fighting took place from August 20th to the 24th, and, on the night of August 24th, heavy Russian Ground Forces were sighted crossing the border on Highway T0507, including elements of 6th Tank Brigade, 8th MRB, 18th MRB, 21st MRB, 31st Air Assault Brigade, 137th Airborne Regiment, 247th Air Assault Regiment, 331st Airborne Regiment, and 1065th Artillery Regiment.

Ukrainian Government Forces around Ilovaisk, slowed and distracted by heavy separatist resistance, were encircled before they could react. This triggered a public outcry among Euromaidan supporters of the volunteer battalions, who feared that Kyiv had effectively abandoned troops in the field.

Recognizing the direness of the situation in Ilovaisk, Ukrainian commanders assembled a relief force to break through to the town from the south. The large relief force was based on a mechanized infantry company and armored column from the 92nd Mechanized Brigade containing tanks, APCs, and IFVs. Confidence was running high that this relief force could reach Ilovaisk until the night of August 27th.

The column advanced through the city of Kalmiuske and attempted to rest in a field for the night. It became a sitting target for a devastating series of Russian artillery strikes. Infantry assaults by Russian paratroopers followed repeated artillery bombardments. Many in the relief force surrendered while remnants fled north to safety.

Ukrainian commanders in Ilovaisk requested from local separatist leaders that a corridor be opened so that Ukrainian Government Forces could withdraw from the town. On August 29th, President Vladimir Putin called for a "humanitarian corridor for besieged Ukrainian soldiers".

Yury Bereza, a commander of the Dnipro Battalion, reached an agreement with his Russian counterparts. DPR Prime Minister Alexander

Zakharchenko confirmed the agreement and a specified withdrawal route to the village of Mnohopillya. After the fact, Zakharchenko would add on the demand that withdrawing forces leave their ammunition and armored vehicles behind (something that was never agreed to).

Ukrainian Government Forces stepped off on August 29th at 0600 in a single column of approximately 60 vehicles. The column split into two separate columns that traversed separate agreed-upon routes south that would meet up again at Novokaterynivka. The Northern Column consisted of the 17th Tank Brigade and 51st Mechanized Brigade.

The Southern Column consisted of 93rd Mechanized Brigade and Donbas Battalion. Duplicitously, Russian commanders contacted the withdrawing Ukrainians and changed the terms of the agreement (according to Zakhachenko's demands) once they were already in motion.

Russian commanders demanded that the Ukrainians take a different route out of Ilovaisk, surrender all weapons, and that volunteer forces (primarily Donbas Battalion) be left behind. The Ukrainian commander for Ilovaisk, Lt. General Ruslan Khomchak, decided that the demand was preposterous and ordered the columns to proceed along the original route.

The northern column was hit first. Russian troops opened with artillery, mortars, and heavy machine guns. The column's rear-half could not advance out of the kill-box fast enough and was completely obliterated. The remnant front-half of the column surged forward to the village of Novokaterynivka. A second ambush lay in wait at the village with several dug-in tanks and IFVs. Only about 4 dozen Ukrainian troops survived and eventually returned to friendly lines.

The southern column consisted of approximately 300 soldiers and components of Dnipro and Donbas Battalion volunteer troops. It fought its way into the village of Chervonosilske, which had been pre-sighted by

Russian mortars and artillery. However, Ukrainian Government Forces were able to capture several armored vehicles and tanks as well as a half-dozen Russian paratroopers. Dnipro Battalion commander Yury Bereza parlayed the captured Russian troops for safe passage back to Ukrainian lines.

The Battle of Ilovaisk opened up a corridor to the porous Russian border. It devastated the ability of Ukrainian Government Forces to constrain supplies and reinforcements to Donetsk from the south. The Battle of Ilovaisk did not reconnect Donetsk and Luhansk, but forces and supplies could flow freely from Rostov-on-Don without the threat of Ukrainian Government Forces constricting Donetsk into submission.

The Battle of Novoazovsk: The Armored Thrust to Mariupol

On August 25th, an armored column including 10 tanks, 2 APCs, and a large assortment of military and civilian support vehicles crossed the Russo-Ukrainian border. It followed the M14/M23-E58 road from Rostov-On-Don and attempted to seize the Ukrainian border town Novoazovsk in an effort to advance on Mariupol.

Heavy artillery barrages from Russian territory rained down around Novoazovsk to drive back Ukrainian Government Forces (primarily the volunteer Dnipro and Donbas battalions) seeking to reinforce the town. Government security checkpoints had frustrated attempts at "humanitarian" supply convoys to reach separatist-controlled territories.

When reports came in from Starobesheve that a large separatist armored column (APCs, tanks, and Grad MLRS technicals) had been spotted moving south toward Novoazovsk, Ukrainian Government troops were forced to withdraw towards Mariupol. By August 27th, Russian Forces (nominally the DPR People's Militia Forces) had secured Novoazovsk.

Russian Ground Forces Relieve Luhansk

On August 14th, Ukrainian Government Forces identified and attacked a Russian military column that had passed into Ukraine through the border crossing at Izvaryne. It provided clear evidence of Russian military support for the world press, but Moscow denied any involvement or participation, calling the story a, "fantasy."

NATO Secretary General Anders Fogh Rasmussen issued a statement, "We see a continuous flow of weapons and fighters from Russia into Eastern Ukraine, and it is a clear demonstration of continued Russian involvement in its [Ukraine] destabilization."

The Russian Foreign Ministry later released a statement blaming the incident: "...Ukrainian forces with the apparent aim to stop the path, agreed on with Kyiv, of a humanitarian convoy across the Russo-Ukrainian border."

During these public denials and accusations, heavy Russian Ground Forces, led by tanks and elements of the 76th Airborne Division and supported by long-range artillery, moved quickly to relieve Luhansk and shore up floundering LPR People's Militia Forces. Ukrainian Government Forces were blind-sided by the offensive and, in the face of superior numbers and overwhelming firepower, Ukrainian Government troops were forced to withdraw from Luhansk along the same road they had arrived.

Particularly fierce fighting took place at the Luhansk Airport. Ukrainian paratroopers had occupied the airport since May, but a massive bombardment and assault by Russian tanks displaced them. The airport was razed to the ground and today remains largely a pile of scrap steel and concrete.

The Minsk Protocol is Signed

The Minsk Protocol was signed on September 5, 2014, after the Ukrainian humiliation at the Battle of Ilovaisk. Presidents Petro Poroshenko and Vladimir Putin arranged a ceasefire, which quickly became an "unofficial" ceasefire as Moscow publicly backtracked and insisted it was not a party to the conflict. The Minsk Protocol had been under negotiation with the OSCE in the background and was largely a revised version of President Poroshenko's 15 Points of Peace that were proposed in June.

Following the unofficial ceasefire, which, like the Minsk Protocol itself, was only marginally observed, all sides signed the accord to secure a more permanent cessation of hostilities. Unfortunately, Moscow realized that Donetsk and Luhansk remained in a strategically untenable position despite blunting and turning back the Ukrainian offensive. The separatists needed breathing room for open communications, restored supply lines, training, and the capability to move troops freely between each region. This meant that, despite signing on to the Minsk Protocol, Russian Ground Forces (nominally the DPR and LPR People's Militia Forces) would constantly harass Ukrainian Government Forces with artillery and skirmishes in an effort to renegotiate the peace.

Cyborgs and the Second Battle of Donetsk Airport

While Ukrainian Government Forces were falling back on both fronts in Donetsk and Luhansk, its paratroopers and other select ground forces (79th Air Assault Brigade, 80th Air Assault Brigade, 95th Air

Assault Brigade, 93rd Mechanized Brigade, 3rd Spetsnaz Regiment, and the volunteer Dnipro Battalion) held their ground at the symbolically important Donetsk Airport.

Ukrainian Government troops had used the airport as a base of operations and artillery point around Donetsk. They would come to be known as the "cyborgs" for their doggedly stubborn defense: fighting without sleep or food, fighting despite relentless artillery bombardment, fighting to the last man, fighting to the last bullet, refusing to give an inch, and repeatedly summoning the strength to counterattack.

Ultimately, the Ukrainian paratroopers and Spetsnaz were only displaced from parts of the terminal when the floor above was brought down on top of them. Even then, the Ukrainian survivors returned fire on Russian assault teams from underneath the rubble.

As soon as the ink was dry on the Minsk Protocol, Russian Ground Forces and their militia allies began skirmishing Ukrainian lines to move the ball forward.

The Russians used the aforementioned unofficial ceasefire to establish positions around the airport and, on September 28th, began peppering Government positions with artillery and Grad rockets. The Russian-backed DPR People's Militia Forces became notorious for starting artillery exchanges from positions in residential areas and in the vicinity of schools. Russian and DPR troops began to advance—supported by artillery and using UAV-based reconnaissance (very sophisticated ISR for mere militias)—on the airport with tanks and APCs along three lines of approach from the south: from Donetsk's Kyivskyi District, Kuibyshivskyi District, and the Donetsk train station.

The DPR People's Militia Forces (the Somali Battalion, the Sparta Battalion, and the Vostok Battalion) punched a hole through the

Ukrainian perimeter amidst a barrage of supporting long-range artillery and fanned out on the airport's east side. These DPR People's Militia units maneuvered slowly and methodically, seizing buildings and infrastructure to cover their advance.

By early October, the DPR People's Militia Forces had captured the hangars, fuel storage areas, and several outlying buildings.

On October 3rd, Russian and DPR Forces established a foothold in the "old" terminal, using smoke screens to cover their advance. They worked feverishly to maintain secure lines of communication and resupply to Russian-controlled rear areas and basing locations in Donetsk, enabling effective coordination of fires and allowing for the timeliness of reinforcements.

With a Russian foothold in the old terminal, the focus turned on pressuring Ukrainian Government Forces' stronghold in the "new" terminal. However, Ukrainian Government troops counterattacked, halting the advance and driving back the militias from gains in the old terminal. The Russians and DPR made another attempt to take the old terminal on October 9th but were repelled with heavy casualties.

The old and new terminal buildings began to disintegrate from the frequent artillery and mortar bombardments. Heavy fighting over the terminals caused the Ukrainian Government forces and Russian and DPR positions to wax and wane in brief surges of bitter fighting, harkening back to what the Germans called "Rattenkrieg", or war of the rats, during the Battle of Stalingrad: bitter urban engagements repeatedly fought over ruins and rubble. The runway was utterly ruined, and charred skeletons remained in the buildings.

Finally, on November 28th, realizing that the DPR People's Militia Troops could not make gains, Russian commanders brought Spetsnaz GRU and

Naval Infantry detachments forward to lead a concerted attack on the old terminal. The assault lasted three days and caused high casualties. Amazingly enough, the Government defenders were able to survive even this assault. Realizing they had too few remaining troops to hold the old terminal any longer, on December 5th, they finally withdrew to the new terminal, consolidating on the last defensible position in the airport.

Throughout December, a stalemate emerged. Russian artillery and grad rockets continuously peppered Ukrainian Government Forces' positions in the new terminal and along supply lines from the Pisky district to the west.

Russian-backed troops renewed their ground assaults on January 10, 2015 in a 3-day attack on the new terminal and control tower. The control tower finally collapsed after enduring months of sporadic bombardment.

Sensing that Ukrainian Government defenses were nearing their breaking point, on January 13th, the Russian commander issued an ultimatum for the Ukrainian Government troops to withdraw which, to his frustration, the troops promptly refused. However, the assault yielded fruit, and the Russians finally had a foothold in the new terminal. Ukrainian Government troops were pushed back to the second floor. They were increasingly bottled up and isolated from resupply and, as casualties mounted, they were unable to evacuate the wounded or the dead.

Aware that the situation was hopeless, Ukrainian Government forces committed themselves to a desperate counterattack on January 17th. They assaulted the cordon of Russian and DPR Forces, forcing Russian and DPR Forces to back in shock and disbelief. The assault gave Ukrainian Government troops enough breathing room to evacuate the dead and wounded, but it also caused Russian commanders to embrace bolder tactics. Russian Ground Force commanders dispatched two additional

Battalion Tactical Groups (approximately 600 men) to support the airport siege, complete with tanks, artillery, and MLRS. Additional GRU Spetsnaz troops accompanied these conventional troops to lead the ground assault.

By January 21st, the remaining Ukrainian defenders were cornered on the second floor of the new terminal and largely overrun. Rather than lose more troops dislodging the cornered Ukrainian Government troops, Russian Spetsnaz teams set explosives on the terminal's remaining load-bearing columns. They dropped the third floor on top of the remaining Ukrainian defenders. Over 50 Ukrainian soldiers were killed or injured in this final act, and a small remnant fled the airport in general disarray.

The Second Battle of Donetsk Airport was the cornerstone of a larger Russian winter offensive that would conclude with a Ukrainian Government Forces withdrawal from Debaltseve. The bitter engagement established the main battle line over which Ukrainian Government Forces and Russian Ground Forces (and nominal DPR and LPR People's Militia Forces) would face off.

Despite the siege ending in a Russian and DPR tactical victory, the battle became symbolic of dogged Ukrainian resistance to Russian aggression, not dissimilar to the 1836 Battle of the Alamo in Texas.[4] In that facet, Ukraine restored something more important than terrain—its national pride.

The Battle of Debaltseve

While Donetsk Airport received a great deal of media attention and proved to be a stubborn holdout against the Russian Winter Offensive, the Battle of Debaltseve was the real engagement of strategic significance. The Ukrainian Summer Offensive captured Debaltseve in late July 2014, after

Ukrainian Government Forces pushed DPR People's Militia Forces off the Savur-Mohyla heights overlooking Highway M03-E50.

Highway M03-E50 runs from Slovyansk, through Bakhmut (Artemivsk), Debaltseve, and Krasnyi Luch to the Russian border and ensured the separatist militias were well supplied from Russia. Similarly, the M04-E50 highway runs from Donetsk, through Debaltseve, to Luhansk, ensuring each stronghold can communicate with, resupply, and fortify the other.

Capturing Debaltseve severed these important communications and supply lines, preventing the cities' respective commands and militias from coordinating. Debaltseve also provided Ukrainian Government Forces a vital logistics and transit hub to quickly move its ground forces into the Donbas region's critical combat areas, while offering a direct line back to the operational headquarters in Bakhmut (Artemivsk) via Highway M03.

The Russian Fall-Winter Offensive, particularly the Battle of Ilovaisk, recaptured the critical cities of Horlivka, Krasnyi Luch, and Shakhtarsk and pushed the main line of battle north of both Donetsk and Luhansk city centers. Debaltseve became a protruding salient (a bulge in the line of contact) into separatist-held territory, simultaneously frustrating Russian Ground Force commanders and presenting them with the opportunity for an encirclement.

Russian BTGs (nominally DPR Militia Forces), the bulk of which included elements of the 8th MRB, 18th MRB, 25th Spetsnaz Regiment, 5th Guards Tank Brigade, and 232nd MRL Brigade, encircled Debaltseve and captured the M03 Highway north to Bakhmut (Artemivsk), trapping Ukrainian Government Forces in a pocket for a prolonged siege and ultimately annihilation.

The Russian BTGs along with DPR and LPR Militias were equipped with T-80 and T-90 main battle tanks and BMP-2s. They were supported by numerous BM-21 Grad MLRS, reflecting a change in the nature of the conflict from an unconventional war (guerilla or proxy war) to a full conventional war.

On the morning of January 14, 2015, Ukrainian defenders of the 128th Mountain Infantry Brigade, Ministry of Internal Affairs special police forces, and Donbas Battalion woke up to the buzz of Russian surveillance drones: ISR assets that were providing targeting information for artillery units. Conventional and rocket artillery bombardments followed minutes later, forcing Ukrainian defenders to hunker down in their trenches.

The city of Debaltseve itself was indiscriminately shelled, and over 8,000 civilians fled north in the dead of winter to Bakhmut (Artemivsk), Slovyansk, and other neighboring cities under Government control. Those that remained in the Debaltseve not only endured artillery fire, but also a lack of electricity, heat, and water due to devastated infrastructure.

By February 1st, Russian Ground Forces had pushed up to both the east and west sides of the Debaltseve salient and began skirmishing the entrenched lines around the city.

The skirmishing and artillery exchanges continued until February 9th, when Russian Ground Forces captured the town of Lohvynove, a small village is situated north of Debaltseve along the M03 Highway. Its capture severed Debaltseve's corridor of communication and resupply from higher command in Bakhmut (Artemivsk).

Once Lohvynove was under control, Russian Ground Forces initiated an assault on Debaltseve. On February 10th, Russian BTGs advanced in a pincer attack on the east and west flanks of the salient, supported by tanks, IFVs, artillery, and MLRS. Taking heavy casualties, Ukrainian Government Forces found that the Russians had captured Lohvynove, the M03 Highway had been blocked, and no further reinforcements were coming from Bakhmut (Artemivsk). And worse, Russians used their new positions north of Debaltseve to launch rocket attacks on the operations HQ in Bakhmut (Artemivsk) and the Ukrainian Army HQ in Kramatorsk.

On February 11th and 12th, Russia followed up by deploying additional forces from the Southern Military District with over 100 tanks, BMPs, and MLRS. The reinforced Russian Ground Forces then razed Debaltseve with rocket and artillery fire. Ukrainian Government Forces attempted several breakouts from the encirclement but could not get through the now-entrenched Russian positions north of Debaltseve and were repeatedly driven back.

On February 17th, a heavy assault finally broke Ukrainian resistance, and Ukrainian Government Forces requested that the Russians open a corridor for them to withdraw. Like the withdrawal from Ilovaisk, Russian separatist commanders changed the withdrawal terms after Ukrainian Government Forces had already initiated movement, forcing the remnants of the 128th Mountain Infantry Brigade, special police forces, and Donbas Battalion to conduct a fighting withdrawal while under artillery bombardment.

As the roads were largely closed off by heavy Russian Ground Forces, Ukrainian Government troops were forced to abandon their vehicles and flee over open country on foot north to friendly lines. By mid-day of February 20th, Debaltseve had been completely abandoned to DPR and LPR People's Militia Forces.

A Stalemate Emerges

The Minsk II agreement was signed on February 12th and, like its predecessor, was supposed to ultimately de-escalate the conflict. Unfortunately, Russian and separatist commanders realized that they were about to land a major strategic victory in Debaltseve, fundamentally eroding the Ukrainian Government's capacity to support combat operations in the Donbas region. Moreover, Russia never conceded in the Minsk II protocol that it was an active participant in the conflict. Moscow claimed that the ongoing Battle of Debaltseve was being waged by DPR and LPR People's Militia Forces outside of its control. Only after Russia had decimated Ukraine's offensive capability did Russian and separatist commanders observe the ceasefire.

Sporadic and frequently intense fighting continues in Donbas as this book is being written, but the Ukrainian Summer Offensive of 2014 and the Russian Fall-Winter Offensive of 2015 set the strategic status quo that continued until the 2022 Russo-Ukrainian War. Russia continues to train, arm, supply, and support the DPR and LPR People's Militia Forces and frequently commits Spetsnaz troops to deniable missions and guerilla operations.

Russia sought to build the capability of its proxies, transforming them into a fighting force that could stand on their own. In 2016, the DPR and LPR People's Militias were reorganized into the Donetsk I Army Corps and Luhansk II Army Corps. Despite the titles, both corps are brigade-sized units of about 4,500 troops. They follow the Russian organizational model but consist of several understrength motorized rifle battalions, one independent Spetsnaz battalion, one independent reconnaissance battalion, and assorted artillery, sappers, MLRS, electronic warfare, A2/AD, ISR, and support battalions. Frequently, the component units of these separatist I and II Army Corps are attached as auxiliaries to Russian BTGs.

Russia also established Internal Ministry troops for the DPR, consisting of 1,300 soldiers and special police. There is one special police "regiment", two internal troop "regiments", one special operations company, and one training battalion (indicating that these units are now conducting some level of independent training). The DPR also has a State Security Service consisting of two battalions, which likely work closely with the FSB. The DPR and LPR also share "Territorial Defense Troops" consisting of two Special Operations Battalions.

Moscow points to the DPR and LPR puppet governments and People's Militia Forces as evidence that Donbas deserves special consideration while maintaining the now preposterous claim that Russia has always been a humanitarian observer. Russia's relationship with the DPR and LPR in Ukraine is in keeping with historical practices in South Ossetia and Abkhazia in Georgia or Transnistria in Moldova. Liberating and annexing Donbas would eventually serve as a pretext to launch a full-scale invasion in the Russo-Ukrainian War.[5]

Operational and Tactical Performance

Maskirovka (Camouflage)

Russian operatives, particularly the 45th SRR and intelligence services, made a good effort in carrying forward the information operations of the Crimea Annexation. As protests and riots erupted in Donetsk, Luhansk, Slovyansk, Kharkiv, Kramatorsk, Horlivka, Mariupol, and Debaltseve, it was hard for Kyiv not to believe that Ukraine was descending into civil war. But, by mid-summer of 2014, the Russian hand had been exposed.

President Yanukovych had fled to his masters in Moscow, along with much of his senior national security cadre and intelligence staff. The seizure of Crimea so outraged the Ukrainian populace that pro-Russian narratives, no matter how carefully propagated, lost all legitimacy. Moreover, too many supply convoys had come across the Russian border.

The Kremlin excused every one of them as humanitarian aid, yet insurgents somehow acquired greater and greater stockpiles of small arms, armored vehicles, tanks, and artillery. Maskirovka was spent undermining Russia's attempt to sponsor an unconventional war in Eastern Ukraine.

Aktivnost (Activity)

The activities that Russian operatives conducted to prepare the battlespace and prevent Kyiv from bringing any real kinetic force were considerable. Apart from effectively shattering the Ukrainian political system and military chain of command during the Crimean Annexation, Russian operatives were almost immediately put to work sponsoring protests and standing up militias in every Eastern Ukrainian city center that mattered.

The protestors hounded and often surrounded Ukrainian Government troop convoys that were dispatched to quell the unrest, often forcing the convoys to turn back. However, Ukrainian Government Forces began to reorganize and build momentum. In repeated confrontations with Russian-sponsored militias, they demonstrated that they could bring superior numbers and firepower to skirmishes.

The failure of Russia's unconventional war in Donbas is largely a story of militias crumbling in the face of overwhelming force, a testament to Russia's failure to perform Aktivnost to the necessary degree.

Vnezapnost (Surprise)

Neither Russian Spetsnaz nor Russian Ground Forces achieved surprise at an operational level in either the unconventional conflict or in the later conventional war. President Poroshenko and his national defense cadre were acutely aware of Russia's role in sponsoring the insurgency in Eastern

Ukraine. Moreover, the resulting unconventional war throughout the summer of 2014 was largely a conflict of consolidation and withdrawal.

The Russian counter-offensive that began in late August was not a war of rapid maneuver, either. The fighting that took place was a slogging match of skirmishes, sieges, and devastating artillery exchanges that resulted in a slow and steady push-back of Ukrainian Government Forces. Speed and surprise were immaterial above the tactical level, as characterized by the siege warfare of Donetsk Airport or Debaltseve.

With none of hybrid warfare's characteristic conditions met, the Russian-sponsored conflict could only escalate in a brutal fashion. Russian commanders rely on these methods to create asymmetric advantages, potentially enabling Russian victory with less kinetic force and material loss. However, when Russian forces do not properly execute Maskirovka, Aktivnost, or Vnezapnost, then hybrid warfare's veneer peels away and reveals the familiar havoc of conventional warfare.

Russian Spetsnaz and Proxy Forces Performance

The initial story of Russia's involvement in Eastern Ukraine involves elite troops organizing resistance movements and covertly maneuvering to seize key terrain. And, as they did in Crimea, Spetsnaz proved to be competent, professional, politically aware, and highly aggressive in seizing the initiative.

The initial unconventional war largely consisted of Russian agenturi and Spetsnaz counterparts infiltrating Eastern Ukraine to enable an insurgency. They organized protests, paid off politicians, intimidated police forces, and led opposition rallies. One favored tactic by the Spetsnaz was instigating mobs to engulf Government troop convoys as they were dispatched to secure insurrectionist towns. Spetsnaz operatives capitalized on the soldiers' hesitancy to fire on crowds by utilizing these mobs to capture and disarm Ukrainian Government troops.

As Ukrainian Government Forces gained momentum in their 2014 summer offensive, the conflict devolved into a slugging match. Separatist battalions often contained embedded Spetsnaz troops to provide tactical-level leadership and C2.

In addition to traditional roles in ISR, Spetsnaz adopted responsibilities for organizing, training, arming, and leading insurgents, shifting the direct-action function to their proxies. It was also Spetsnaz forward observers who were most responsible for coordinating indirect fires (artillery, MLRS, and mortars) for the separatists. Neither the Crimean Annexation nor the war in Eastern Ukraine would have been within Russia's strategic grasp without the Spetsnaz.

Ultimately, the attempt at unconventional warfare in Eastern Ukraine was a failure. Russia's troops could not organize and train separatist sympathizers into competent conventional ground forces. Russia took the opposite approach, organizing militias into motorized infantry battalions and artillery batteries (under the late Soviet model) almost immediately. However, even with embedded Spetsnaz troops, the DPR and LPR People's Militia Forces crumbled in the face of Ukrainian Ground Forces, who inevitably brought superior forces and firepower to the fight.

The Russian approach of mimicking conventional military units with militia troops would never succeed without Russian Ground Forces backing the separatists directly, ultimately ensuring Russia would escalate the conflict.

Russian Ground Forces Performance

Russia demonstrated the ability to project real combat power beyond its borders by deploying, supporting, and sustaining division-level forces in the field. With the VDV in the lead, Russian Ground Forces proved themselves to be competent and motivated. They also demonstrated combined arms capabilities by maneuvering mechanized infantry and tank formations while coordinating complex and precise artillery fires.

As noted in Chapters 4 and 6, battalion tactical groups (BTGs) only have 3-4 maneuver companies (one infantry battalion) but, in Donbas, they were augmented with auxiliary attachments of militia. These auxiliaries not only added mass and basic combat power, but they were used for screening patrols, to provide basic security and outer cordon, and to maneuver to contact.

With auxiliary forces to see to the more menial infantry roles for the BTG, the Russian maneuver companies could remain engaged in strictly offensive-oriented combat tasks. BTGs frequently stationed indirect fire support, including artillery and MLRS, across the border in Russia. This kept the Russian footprint in Ukraine smaller and insulated Russian forces from retaliation while allowing Russian units to provide effective fire support to most engagements in Donbas.

Demonstrating the hybrid warfare imperatives of waging network-centric warfare and reflexive control, the C2 in Eastern Ukraine was excellent. The Russian General Staff directly controlled both non-military influence activities and regional forces from the new National Defense Control Center (located in the basement of the Ministry of Defense building).

It is important to note that, with the exception of auxiliaries attached directly to Russian BTGs, most DPR and LPR People's Militias Forces units did not fall directly under Moscow's control. Many of these units acted semi-autonomously under local commanders that shirked directives of the nominal governments in Donetsk or Luhansk (and, therefore, Moscow).

Russian units were certainly willing to "purge" particularly rebellious local commanders (Alfa, Vympel, and Wagner were typical tools for this). Moscow was also clearly willing to tolerate some degree of independence from its proxies. For Moscow, allowing its proxies some semblance of autonomy reinforced the facade that Russia was not driving the conflict.

Russian Ground Forces proved qualitatively superior in almost every major engagement with their Ukrainian counterparts. They proved to be more mobile, more flexible, and more capable of maneuver in the field. They also coordinated firepower from artillery and MLRS far better than their Ukrainian counterparts. Russian Ground Forces also effectively leveraged asymmetric capabilities such as EW and A2/AD systems, frustrating Ukrainian C2 and grounding the Ukrainian Air Force.

Russian battlefield intelligence capabilities also proved to be formidable. In most major engagements, Russian BTGs could out-maneuver their Ukrainian counterparts because they had more timely and accurate intelligence. Those BTGs in the field demonstrated the ability to integrate ISR capabilities from UAVs, reconnaissance platoons, EW, SIGINT, forward observers, and higher levels of command.

Heightened battlefield awareness for Russian commanders conveyed into superior maneuver and coordinated precision fires. The high level of performance is unsurprising, as the troops committed to the War in Donbas were from a short list of Russia's most elite combat units. While it is unlikely that the bulk of Russian Ground Forces could perform at this level, Donbas was nevertheless an impressive demonstration of combat capabilities.

Logistics cannot be overlooked. As Carl von Clausewitz aptly stated, "There is nothing more common than to find considerations of supply affecting the strategic lines of a campaign and a war."[6] Russian Ground Forces established Rostov-on-Don as a regional logistics hub, safe on the Russian side of the border. They ensured that both the separatists and Russian BTGs were well supplied from the Southern Military District.

Clear supply lines and lines of communication were consistent focus areas in Russian battleplans, as was clearly demonstrated at the Battle of Debaltseve. Russian Ground Forces zealously protected border crossings, particularly at Izvaryne, Novoazovsk, and Highway M03/E50, ensuring that supplies to forces in contact with the enemy continued to flow, usually under the pretense of humanitarian assistance.

Russian Ground Forces were highly effective in Ukraine. They had come a long way from the incompetent and lumbering ground forces that steamrolled Chechnya in the late 1990s. However, the fact that large Russian Ground Forces had to be committed to the conflict at all is evidence enough that the initial unconventional war was a failure.

Russian Aerospace Forces Performance

As in Crimea, the Russian Air Force was not a major player, but Russia's formidable capabilities in A2/AD were on full display. Russia used Eastern Ukraine as a testbed and proving ground for systems like the improved Buk-M1/M3, the Pantsir, and modernized variants of the S-300. The Ukrainian Air Force was limited to several close air support missions over the summer of 2014. It was eventually grounded as advanced Russian

A2/AD systems took a heavy toll, downing an IL-76 transport aircraft and killing 49 Ukrainian paratroopers and crew.

As in Crimea, Russian transport aviation proved to be a bright spot. Russian paratroopers were delivered to Rostov-on-Don, Crimea and, in some cases, Donbas itself on IL-76 transports. They were also frequently airlifted from the logistics hub at Rostov-on-Don to Donetsk and Luhansk via transport helicopters. Russian transport aviation remains perhaps the most reliable component of the Russian Aerospace Forces and continues to give the VDV the mobility to play a leading role in combat operations on Russia's periphery.

It is unclear to what extent Russia intentionally prioritizes operational excellence in transport aviation over the flashier fighter and bomber components, particularly because the Kremlin is spending extravagantly to increase fighter pilot numbers. But it seems that Ministry of Defense planners have concluded that the VDV is the most reliable, most competent, most aggressive component of Russian land power, and the VDV requires reliable air mobility to be effective.

Ukrainian Ground Forces Performance

The Kremlin deeply underestimated the extent to which the Crimean Annexation had reignited Ukrainian Nationalism. Nationalism's rebirth fueled previously impossible defense reforms in Ukraine. In early 2014, the Ukrainian Armed Forces were a skeleton of former Soviet-era forces, and Ukraine's security establishment was riddled with Russian agents and sympathizers.

By April, a purge and restructuring of the officer corps was underway and, by May, conscription had been reinstituted for the enlisted ranks. President Poroshenko (and before him, Acting President Oleksandr Turchynov) looked to Western militaries for models in remaking the military. A new generation of young, hungry, and patriotic officers rapidly filled vacancies in the ranks, and Kyiv began spending lavishly on its Ground Forces.

Ground Forces increased in strength throughout 2014 and 2015 and established Operational Command-East to manage the conflict in Donbas. The legacy Soviet-style chain of command was reorganized to a system where combat operations are overseen by field commanders who report to Operational Command-East, which in turn is subordinate to the General Staff. The General Staff answers to the Minister of Defense and the President.

In recognition of the extent to which Ukraine's Airborne Infantry forces showed superior fighting spirit, the Air Assault Forces became their own armed service branch apart from ground forces. Despite embarrassing early setbacks (soldiers of the 25th Airborne Brigade were disarmed by a crowd), Air Assault Forces of the 25th, 79th, 80th, 95th Independent Air Assault Brigades, and the 81st Airmobile Brigade were at the vanguard of almost all Ukrainian operations in Donbas.

The 95th Air Assault Brigade became the most prestigious unit in the Ukrainian Armed Forces, famous for a raid into separatist territory between July 19th and August 10, 2014, where they rescued several surrounded Ukrainian units and escorted them along secure corridors back to friendly lines. The 79th, 80th, and 81st Brigades became famous for the Thermopylae-like stand at the Donetsk Airport.[7]

Ukraine's Spetsnaz, eventually renamed Special Operations Forces after Western parlance, remained functionally akin to their Russian cousins. They were often deployed in direct action roles or as reliable infantry troops (in short supply). Due largely to their success in Donbas and underlying Western influence, these Spetsnaz troops were reorganized into

Ukraine's Special Operations Command in 2016, consisting of the 3rd Spetsnaz Regiment, 8th Spetsnaz Regiment, and 73rd Naval Spetsnaz Center.

Ukraine's Ground Forces began the summer offensive of 2014 demoralized and in disarray. They could only rely on superior numbers and firepower and were often pressed back by only token resistance. They struggled to coordinate basic maneuvers and instances where the Ground Forces simply stood their ground were considered victories.

As the summer dragged on, Ground Forces began to solve many of their operational deficiencies. The DPR and LPR People's Militia Forces were consistently pressed back in a series of defeats. By August, Ukrainian Ground Forces were pressing in on Donetsk and Luhansk, and Igor Strelkov begged for formal Russian assistance. Ukrainian Ground Forces won most victories by advancing steadily forward with superior firepower, paving the way for infantry to capture and hold terrain.

One of the Ground Forces' greatest deficiencies was their collective inability to win on urban terrain. Commanders chose to leave the morass of urban warfare with guerilla adversaries to volunteer units like the Donbas or Azov Battalions. Popular mobilization forces were far less likely to be demoralized by press criticism for their methods, and they were cheap, expendable, and replaceable. Moreover, Ground Forces are expensive to equip, and soldiers take time to train. Why risk them in combat tasks for which they are ill-prepared when there are credible alternatives?

Ukrainian SBU and Proxy Forces

By April 2014, the SBU was undergoing extensive re-staffing, purging its ranks of Russian sympathizers, moles, and double agents. The old SBU was a relic of the Soviet KGB, and, given the word from Moscow, the agency's entire senior leadership defected to Russia. Under exiled-President Yanukovych's orders, SBU Director Oleksandr Yakymenko emptied out the SBU's Headquarters and destroyed the administrative offices and the archives.

When Yakymenko defected, he brought all the HQ files on SBU agents abroad and cooperative activities with FSB and GRU to Moscow. The SBU's elite Alfa counter-terrorism team (established during the Cold War as a Ukrainian counterpart to its Russian big brother) was devastated with defections, losing almost a third of its strength.

The agency had to be rebuilt from the ground up while conducting counterintelligence and counter-sabotage operations. Western advisors have played a significant role in getting Ukraine's security establishment back on its feet. The SBU has had notable successes in prosecuting Russian spies and exposing operations in Donbas and throughout the country.

Recognizing the need to not only purge Russian moles but reform institutional corruption, the Ukrainian Government passed SBU Reform: Draft Law 3196-d in 2019. This reduced SBU's byzantine staffing from 27,000 to 15,000, increased civilian control, and reduced taskings to: counterintelligence, counter-reconnaissance, counter-sabotage, counterterrorism, and protection of state secrets.

Alfa was also reconstituted and played a limited role in Donbas. But, much like its Russian counterpart, Ukraine's Alfa was still tied to SBU's counterintelligence operations and would not be thrown into heavy combat with Russian BTGs in the field.

Defense Intelligence of the Ministry of Defense of Ukraine (DIU) also began to take a much more prominent role in Ukraine's national security, collecting and processing vital military intelligence to keep the Ukrainian Armed Forces abreast of Russian activities in Donetsk and Luhansk. Unlike SBU, which retained many individuals who harbored anti-Western resentments (Cold War holdovers), DIU opened itself to Western support and training with little reserve.

DIU also wielded Ukraine's special operations forces (UASOF), reforming these units to resemble their Western counterparts and practices. UASOF became increasingly sophisticated and capable of frustrating Russian military operations (conventional and otherwise). DIU also adopted a vehemently anti-Russian institutional demeanor, embedding into its emblem the Owl, a natural predator of bats: the symbol of Russian GRU Spetsnaz brigades. The Owl was depicted plunging a sword into Russia. Even the DIU motto, "the wise will rule the stars", was an insult to Russian intelligence, whose motto reads, "above us only stars".

The Ministry of Internal Affairs Troops, including the National Police Force and National Guard, played a central role in combat operations. Following the disbandment of the Russia-sympathizing Berkut riot police units (many of whose officers defected), the 30,000+ internal troops were reorganized into the National Guard. Much of the National Guard was constituted from local security troops who were charged with supporting the police and guarding government buildings and key infrastructure. The National Guard also included volunteer units that started the conflict as mere militia, including the prominent Donbas and Azov Battalions.

During the early months of instability in Donbas, the Ukrainian Armed Forces and Ministry of Internal Affairs were too disorganized and disoriented to react to the emerging separatist Movement. National defense was outsourced to Ukrainian volunteers in a grassroots movement to stand up militias. While these militias were eventually absorbed into the National Guard, they were armed with weapons, night-vision, body armor, ISR, and transportation at the expense of the volunteers.

Equipment, supplies, weapons, and uniforms were funded through crowdsourcing and donations, and the units bearing them fought tenaciously at the forefront of almost every Ukrainian operation. President Poroshenko eventually realized that allowing militias to arm themselves (or oligarchs to raise private armies) was very hazardous to the continued existence of his government in Kyiv, and he worked to integrate the volunteer units into the National Guard, where they both gained legitimacy as soldiers and came under closer control from Kyiv.

Units like the Donbas and Azov Battalions were used primarily in urban combat, saving the Regulars from fighting street to street and preserving the integrity and morale of the Ukrainian Ground Forces. Ukraine could conserve their Ground Forces for open-field fighting with heavy Russian counterparts instead of spending them on taxing exchanges with urban partisans.

Ukrainian Naval and Air Forces Performance

The Ukrainian Navy was largely irrelevant to the conflict in Donbas, except for naval infantry. Following the Crimea annexation, the singular 501st Independent Naval Infantry Battalion was reorganized into the 36th Marine Brigade and participated in the defense of Mariupol. The 35th, 37th, and 40th Marine Brigades have become active since 2014, and they are now a strictly contract force of professional Marines.

The post-Soviet Ukrainian Air Force is largely a story of managed decay. By 2014, the Ukrainian Air Force consisted of 144 aircraft, of which maybe two-thirds were airworthy. Mi-24 helicopter gunships and Su-25 fighter aircraft were used to support Ground Forces (though at considerable cost from Russian A2/AD systems). Over the summer of 2014, Ukraine lost four Mi-24s, two Mi-8 transport helicopters, six Su-25 fighters, and an assortment of air superiority and transport planes. Fortunately, Ukraine has kept Russian air assets at bay due to possessing several units of long-range S-300PS A2/AD systems (ironically of Russian origin like most Ukrainian hardware).

Outcomes and Conclusions

The Ukrainian people became united in a vehemently anti-Russian sentiment, and Ukraine economically reoriented towards the European Union.

Almost none of Russia's original strategic objectives were met. While the Donetsk and Luhansk People's Republics gave Moscow some degree of leverage over Kyiv, this leverage was not conveyed into any real material benefits for Russia. Moscow has since been unable to bind Ukrainian foreign policy to its will, and the War in Donbas severed most economic ties. This also meant that Russia lost Ukraine as a manufacturing center in its military-industrial supply chains. The Russian Ground Forces and Navy were hence denied Ukrainian steel for tanks or ships. The Russian Air Force could no longer source jet turbines and munitions from Ukraine.

Though Moscow sought to preserve its buffer by forcing Ukraine back into the fold, Russia achieved precisely the opposite. Ukraine was irrevocably reoriented to the West and became a bitter adversary on Russia's doorstep.

Russia's intransigence also inspired extensive reforms in the Ukrainian Armed Forces, overseen by Western advisors.

The Russian campaigns in Donetsk and Luhansk did not demonstrate the efficacy of hybrid warfare; nevertheless, these campaigns did use hybrid warfare's most important methodologies. The Russians waged unconventional warfare (in American lexicon) by enabling a separatist insurgency. The Russians also established reflexive control by pairing kinetic operations with non-military influence operations (particularly targeted propaganda) to gain asymmetric advantages.

The first phase (the unconventional war) was crushed under the overwhelming forces and firepower advantages of the Ukrainian Ground Forces. The second phase, a war waged between Russian and Ukrainian heavy ground forces, ended in a stalemate. Russia became stuck propping up militias that could not fight, an insurgent government that could not manage the region, a devastated regional economy, and a destitute civilian population.

Keeping the conflict in Donbas at a low boil cost Russia billions in military and economic support, denying its military modernization efforts much-needed funding, technology, production capacity, and military hardware. Russia sacrificed blood, treasure, diplomatic capital, economic partnership, and military-industrial supply chains to force Kyiv to negotiate with the proxy Donetsk and Luhansk People's Republics, neither of which Western leaders believe to be independent.

Russian hybrid warfare in Donbas suffered from four primary failures. First, Russia's information operations were largely implausible. The narrative had to be sustained for too long, and it had to be changed when support for Novorossiya failed to materialize. Moreover, after the Crimean Annexation, Ukrainians unexpectedly unified against Russian aggression. Just because propaganda had been delivered to the masses did not necessarily mean the people were receptive to it. Russia never achieved popular mobilization or broad support in Eastern Ukraine.

Second, the militias in Donetsk and Luhansk were grossly overmatched by Ukrainian Ground Forces. Spetsnaz were successful in organizing the separatists, and they outmaneuvered and frustrated larger Ukrainian Government Forces throughout the summer of 2014. Still, Ukrainian officers eventually began to organize troop movements better, and Ukrainian Government troops began to hold their ground. This evolution created a requirement for kinetic force far beyond the capabilities of Spetsnaz or the militias, which by nature must be light and maneuverable. The Donetsk and Luhansk People's Militia Forces soon collapsed, and Russian Ground Forces were forced to intervene to save the insurgency.

Third, it is not obvious that Russia identified its objectives at the operational level. The initial unconventional war relied on rapid maneuver and ambiguity, much like the Crimean Annexation. Success depended on capturing a few discrete operational objectives that, once in Russian possession, would constitute a *fait accompli*. It is not apparent that the initial campaign had clearly enumerated these objectives, so the execution was ad hoc and lacked deliberation.

The partisans that eventually solidified into the DPR and LPR People's Militia Forces were created independently within the many disconnected localities and under commanders with little initial fidelity with Russian-backed leaders in Donetsk and Luhansk themselves. These scattered and divided forces were marginally effective at capturing random villages and local administrative buildings, and simply frustrated advancing Ukrainian Government columns.

The militias of Donbas were also too incompetent and too sectarian to really stand and fight against the Ukrainian Armed Forces; executing a disciplined advance to capture enumerated objectives was simply beyond their capabilities. Russian Spetsnaz units expertly performed these tasks in Crimea and, without their direct involvement, the partisans that coagulated into the Donetsk and Luhansk People's Militia Forces were combat ineffective.

Campaign planners in the GRU may have focused on sponsoring separatist movements in each locality of Eastern Ukraine without a unifying theater plan because it met the political objective of destabilizing Ukraine with minimum exertion. But Moscow must have known that Kyiv would assemble a cohesive military response sooner or later. The lack of a clear campaign strategy was inexplicable.

The fourth failure in Donbas was that Russia's plausible deniability became entirely implausible once the Russians were forced to commit conventional Battalion Tactical Groups (BTGs) to save their crumbling separatist proxies. Neither Ukraine, the European Union, the United States, nor NATO bought that Russia was uninvolved and strictly interested in the humanitarian consequences of the conflict. And while combat losses and bad press eroded public support at home, the United States and European Union devised sanctions regimes that the Russian public would have to endure.

Hybrid warfare requires a detailed campaign plan with discrete operational objectives, highly maneuverable troops, and a cohesive IO campaign. Remove any of these elements, and hybrid warfare flounders. Ultimately, the Russian-backed insurgency digressed into a conventional military conflict and then a stalemate. Non-military political, diplomatic, and economic coercion was effective at destabilizing Kyiv's direct control over Donbas, but this did not convey into public support for Novorossiya.

Information operations, special intelligence activities, covert action, and cyberattacks were useful in sowing confusion, intimidating politicians, and frustrating Government influence; however, these tools could not stand up to the forces and fires of Ukraine's conventional combat units.

The Crimean Annexation was essentially a series of well-executed preparatory activities that outmaneuvered and pacified the enemy without a shot fired. The conventional war that emerged in Donbas was the logical result when these preparatory activities failed to achieve operational objectives. Hybrid warfare reduces to a slogging match between conventional ground forces, characterized by urban combat, mass artillery bombardments, armored advances, and costly infantry assaults. When the Russians cannot favorably shape the battlespace with non-kinetic influence and discrete force, the conflict devolves into a clash of titans.

---

1. In this case, a spearhead refers to several divisions of tanks, armored personnel carriers, and infantry fighting vehicles that are moving in an offensive thrust towards an operational objective.

2. Unconventional warfare is an American military doctrinal term that falls under the umbrella of asymmetric conflict. It is defined by the U.S. Army as, "...activities conducted to enable a resistance movement or insurgency to coerce, disrupt, or overthrow a government or occupying power by operating through or with an underground, auxiliary, and guerrilla force in a denied area."

3. Federalism is a political system with layered levels of government at the local, state or province, and national levels, with independent law-making powers and mutually exclusive responsibilities at each level of government.

4. The famous Battle of the Alamo during the Texas War of Independence (1835-1836) was a pyrrhic victory for General Santa Anna's Mexican Forces. The Battle drained his invading army of manpower and supplies, but his particularly brutal decision to kill all of the defenders to the last man galvanized the scattered and divided Texas separatists behind General Sam Houston. General Houston would go on to destroy the Mexican Army and capture Santa Ana at the Battle of San Jacinto, forcing Santa Anna to recognize the Republic of Texas in exchange for his life.

5. On February 24, 2022, President Vladimir Putin held a press conference where he announced a special military operation to de-Nazify Ukraine. He cited Ukraine's failure to implement the Minsk Protocol and claimed that the government in Kyiv was fascist. The centerpiece of the Russo-Ukrainian War would become annexing the entirety of the Donbas region and securing a land corridor between Rostov-on-Don and Crimea.

6. The famous Prussian general and military theorist who authored Vom Kreige (On War).

7. The Battle of Thermopylae is remembered as history's greatest delaying action. 300 Spartan hoplites (foot soldiers) and their Greek allies held off a Persian Army that some accounts reported to have been over 1,000,000 strong. The Spartans held this advancing force back, allowing Greek cities like Athens to be evacuated. The ancient Greeks remembered the stand with a stone marker on the site that reads, "Go tell the Spartans, stranger passerby, that here by Spartan Law we lie."

CHAPTER NINE

RISING CHALLENGES IN RUSSIA'S SECURITY ENVIRONMENT

Vladimir Putin and his national security cadre are slowly and painstakingly reshaping the Russian security environment. Moscow has taken to heart the hard lessons of two wars in Chechnya and chosen hybrid warfare as the preferred modus operandi for future conflicts because Russia is not economically, diplomatically, or culturally capable of projecting power into the world without an asymmetric means of competing with its adversaries.

Where Moscow lacks hard power, it compensates with guile, preparation of the battlespace, economic coercion, deception, propaganda, and rapid maneuver. This holistic approach to warfare could not have been timelier. In addition to great power competition with traditional rivals like the United States and NATO, rising powers such as China, Turkey, and Iran, and traditional allies like Belarus and Ukraine, are all testing the Russian security environment.

China: The Dragon Is Hungry

China is competing for influence in Central Asia, long considered a Russian domain. China has gained enormous economic clout, establishing itself as the world's manufacturing center. The Chinese system utilizes a state-driven model known for harnessing cheap labor, cheap investment capital, a deep talent pool, cooperative regulation, and economies of scale to outcompete the world's other great exporters like the United States, Germany, Japan, and India. Unfortunately, the Chinese renaissance is built on incomprehensible quantities of cheap credit, practically guaranteeing economic growth regardless of the performance of the underlying assets.

The Chinese system depends on rapid growth to paper over an immature system for pricing risk. Led by State-Owned Enterprises (SOEs), no country on Earth is more awash in bad credit and non-performing loans. The distorted banking system inflates asset bubbles and channels working capital to Chinese Communist Party favorites rather than small and mid-sized private enterprises. These firms are forced to resort to shadow banking for credit and liquidity, which regulators hesitate to crush lest they harm the productive private sector that props their system up.

This paradox has created a real estate (as well as many other asset classes) bubble that makes Lehman Brothers look tame. Evergrande, China's largest real estate investment bank, first missed payment on its bond coupons in 2021. This triggered a low-velocity, high-momentum private banking and real estate collapse, which led Evergrande to file for bankruptcy protection in the U.S. in August 2023. This slow-motion financial crisis continues in the background as China deals with many other instabilities, rivalries, and crises.

Like Russia, China is also deeply dependent on the American-sponsored global trade system. China's domestic petroleum and raw materials industries are incapable of feeding its vast industrial machine. Despite China's large population of 1.4 billion people, it lacks the young consumer base necessary to drive its own growth. Young adults aged 18-45 typically drive any country's economic demand for goods and services (consumption).

Generally, once people in developed economies age beyond 45 or 50 years, they no longer have children living with them at home, have paid off their house, are well established in their careers, and are at peak earning potential. Priorities shift at this stage, and saving for retirement becomes a much more pressing concern for the aging demographic.

In 1980, believing that China's large and expanding population might one day exceed the capacity of global agriculture to feed, the Chinese Communist Party (CCP) instituted a social engineering policy where each family was only permitted to have one child. 40 years after China instituted the "One Child Policy", China's demography has become hopelessly inverted.

China's consumer class is not large enough in proportion to the rest of the population to drive economic growth. China produces far more than it can possibly consume and is therefore overwhelmingly reliant on access to consumer markets in the United States and Europe. The American-sponsored global trade system solves these intractable problems, but the Americans now see China as a strategic competitor.

As a side effect of the One Child Policy, Chinese families have overwhelmingly favored having boys. There are horrific stories of Chinese families either aborting or abandoning their infant daughters so that the state will permit them to try again for a son. Aside from the obvious human tragedy at play here, 40 years of such practices has created a society that has millions more men than it does women.

Currently, there are 45 million more men than women in China. In Chinese schools, there are approximately 114 boys for every 100 girls. Putting the scale of this imbalance into perspective, China could fill the equivalent of seven New York Cities entirely with men who will never know female companionship. This will have dramatic repercussions in Chinese foreign policy, militaristic expansion, and internal stability.

With such population imbalances, there is very little the CCP can do but keep young men employed and busy, either by drafting them into the People's Liberation Army, or hiring them through state-owned enterprises to work on massive infrastructure projects.

Tragically, for the ethnic Uighurs of the interior province of Xinjiang, the CCP has also adopted another approach to containing civil disruption: concentration camps. Videos of Uighurs with shaved heads being herded into railroad cars destined for political reeducation facilities have emerged from Xinjiang. The CCP is neither apologetic nor repentant.

China is also economically imbalanced. The southern coastal region, along the Yangtze River and numerous tributaries of the Pearl River, has excellent geography for agriculture, industry, and export-driven commerce. It hosts approximately 350 million people who largely constitute the Chinese middle class. The region supports prosperous ultra-modern cities like Macao, Hong Kong, Shanghai, Shenzhen, Guangzhou, and Dongguan.

Alternatively, one billion people live in extreme poverty in the Chinese interior and many of these people still work in communes. The iron fist of the CCP binds these regions together from the northern political capital, Beijing.

Populist sentiments are monitored through a tech-driven social credit and surveillance system, and disruptors and community organizers are arrested or detained for resocialization. President Xi Jinping and his national security team know that the CCP is resting on top of profound internal instabilities and will do all that is necessary to maintain a unified state under Party control.

China is also attempting to erect its own global trade order through a program called the Belt and Road Initiative, also known as One Belt One Road. Belt and Road uses state-sponsored grants, private equity, and venture capital funds to invest in emerging economies across the developing world.

China channels money into port facilities, cellular data networks (China's Huawei is at the vanguard of 5G data), electrical infrastructure, airfields, rail and highway infrastructure, and foreign direct investment (FDI) in emerging technologies (5G, quantum computing, cyber security, microchips, artificial intelligence and machine learning, nanotechnology, and biotechnology).

In addition, China is developing overseas supply chains for raw materials and technologies, as well as trade-related infrastructure to feed its vast manufacturing sector. Belt and Road also intentionally builds dependencies on Chinese investment and imports within developing economies, thereby creating leverage that binds them to Beijing's policy directives.

China's Belt and Road investments into central Asian countries like Kazakhstan, Afghanistan, Pakistan, Armenia, Azerbaijan, Georgia, Kyrgyzstan, Tajikistan, and Uzbekistan, as well as traditionally Eastern Bloc countries in Europe such as Albania, Bulgaria, Estonia, Belarus, Bosnia, Hungary, Latvia, Lithuania, Moldova, Poland, Romania, and Ukraine, challenge Russian dominance in its traditional sphere of influence. Indeed, many stalwart Russian allies are finding Chinese gravity inescapable. Russia simply cannot offer developing economies FDI or infrastructure development at the same order of magnitude as China.

China is a powerful yet unstable neighbor, and there is historical precedent for animosity with Moscow. China and the Soviet Union fought an undeclared border war in 1969 over disputed regions of Xinjiang and Outer Manchuria. Beijing may one day look to the North for raw materials and petroleum to feed its growing economy. And, like Russia, China may also see a military conflict as a way to paper over internal troubles and galvanize nationalism.

China is already militarily expanding into the South China and East China Seas and frequently gets into border skirmishes with India in the Himalayas.

Since the United Kingdom released Hong Kong as a colonial possession in 1997, China had permitted the city to operate with autonomy. The establishment of English banking standards, business practices, and English Common Law in Hong Kong made it one of the great pillars of global commerce (alongside New York, London, Tokyo, and Singapore). This was very useful for channeling foreign investment into China. In negotiations with the United Kingdom, Beijing agreed to slowly integrate Hong Kong back into Mother China under the moniker of one country with two systems.

In 2019, Chief Executive Carrie Lam pushed a bill in the Legislative Council of Hong Kong that allowed citizens to be extradited to the mainland, where they would stand trial in the CCP's court system. The bill triggered widespread protests across the island and Lam was forced to withdraw the bill 6 months later. Pro-Government (pro-CCP) candidates suffered a landslide defeat in the 2019 elections.

The CCP responded to these electoral losses by passing the Law of the People's Republic of China on Safeguarding National Security in the Hong Kong Special Administrative Region. This legislation bypassed Hong Kong's internal political system entirely. Using very broad language, the Law criminalized the session of Hong Kong, subversion against the Chinese government, terrorism, and collusion with foreign forces. Its implementation effectively ended Hong Kong autonomy in spite of treaty obligations with the United Kingdom.

The public responded with desperate protests throughout the summer and fall of 2020, but leaders of the opposition were eventually rounded up. CCP loyalists were also inserted into Hong Kong's Legislative Council to ensure voters could never frustrate the CCP again, while still maintaining the illusion of democracy. China has effectively annexed Hong Kong in a ruthless coup de main. It is reasonable to expect that China will only become more bellicose in the 21st Century.

Western commentators often fret about Sino-Russian cooperation in military exports. On the surface this looks like strategic cooperation, but behind the prestigious delegations and handshaking is naked exploitation. The Kremlin has long sought to open China up as a military export market, hoping to tap into Chinese financing to keep its domestic industries running, but China's state-sponsored hackers frequently penetrate Russian state servers and steal designs to Russia's most sensitive military systems.

On the rare occasion that they cannot simply steal the plans, the Chinese PLA buys a limited production release of the desired system directly from Russia. Once the hardware is delivered, it is disassembled and studied and, within a year, China produces an unlicensed domestic copy. Notable examples of this ploy include:

J-15 fighter jet: a copy of the Su-33

J-11B and J-16 fighter jets: copies of the Su-27

Liaoning aircraft carrier: a refurbished Kuznetsov class carrier purchased from Ukraine

Shandong aircraft carrier: a larger copy of the Kuznetsov class

Shaanxi Y-8 transport plane: a copy of the Soviet-era Antonov An-12

Xian H-6 refueling plane: a copy of the Soviet-era Tupolev Tu-16

HQ-9 Surface-to-Air Missile System: a copy of the Russian S-300

HQ-22 Surface-to-Air Missile System: an iterative improvement of the S-300 and S-400

Do not be fooled by Sino-Russian cooperation in the U.N. Security Council; nor by China's assistance to Moscow in circumventing Western sanction regimes. This assistance is quid pro quo and always comes at a painful cost to Moscow. These two countries often have aligned interests, but they remain implacable strategic competitors. China's general instability will guarantee they remain competitors.

Turkey: The Return of the Ottomans

Turkey is also emerging as an implacable Russian adversary, as President Recep Tayyip Erdogan envisions restoring the Ottoman Empire. Turkey has the most dynamic economy in the Islamic world, a young consumer base to drive growth, resources to feed its economy, membership in the NATO alliance, and a sophisticated, modern military. Turkey must secure raw materials—like petroleum—to further support its economic growth and expanding population.

Concurrently, Turkey is undergoing a painful consolidation of private credit. Erdogan and his predecessors followed a debt-driven growth strategy similar to China's but, unfortunately, Ankara is not capable of pushing its credit nearly as far as Beijing. Erdogan is carrying out a campaign against Kurdish minorities in Turkey and Northern Syria specifically to distract the public from this painful debt consolidation.

Turkey is providing military assistance, training, and financing to Azerbaijan, a traditional Russian ally. In September 2020, the Azerbaijani Army began the process of annexing the disputed Nagorno-Karabakh region of the Lesser Caucasus Mountains. The region is populated by ethnic Armenians.

Armenia cannot compete with Azerbaijan on its own, so it has gone to its great protector Moscow for aid. Unfortunately, Russia does not want to get involved in a potentially expensive conflict that is not of its own making, especially not against a traditional ally like Azerbaijan. But Armenia might have begun to question its allegiances if Russia had refused to fulfill its role as a protector.

Turkey went so far as to deploy Turkish officers to lead Azerbaijani ground force units in combat. Turkey's goal was to force Moscow to choose between one of two regional allies in the Trans-Caucasus Region. Influence in Azerbaijan also gives Ankara a degree of control over oil and gas pipelines from Central Asia, jeopardizing the Russian monopoly.

After letting the Armenians get a little desperate, Russia finally intervened as a mediator in the conflict in early 2021. Moscow pledged approximately 2,000 "peacekeepers" to the Nagorno-Karabakh region to ensure Azerbaijan would not make any further territorial claims.

This brigade-sized contingent of Russian "peacekeepers" are in reality forward-staged heavy mechanized ground forces in the Trans-Caucasus, which allows Russia to keep an eye on Turkish (and Iranian) activities in a strategically important region. It is an arrangement that neither Azerbaijan, Georgia, nor Armenia would have tolerated without an open conflict festering in the region. The negotiated outcome in Nagorno-Karabakh is a good example of geopolitical judo on the Kremlin's part, but it also underlines how seriously Russia takes Turkish interference in its strategic interests.

Turkey also supports the Government of National Accord (GNA) in Libya, directly opposite Russia's deployment of Wagner to support Khalifa Haftar and the Libyan National Army (LNA). Prior to the Turkish intervention in early 2020, the Russian-sponsored LNA forces had pushed GNA territory back to Tripoli, dominating over 80% of the Libyan countryside. LNA was supported by Wagner mercenaries flying Mig-21 and Mig-23 fighter jets and Mi-24 Hind attack helicopters provided by Moscow, as well as sophisticated UAVs from the United Arab Emirates (UAE).

Turkey signed an agreement with the GNA, which was ratified by Turkish Parliament on January 2, 2020. The agreement authorized direct Turkish military support, technology transfers, and financing. During a bilateral ceasefire, the Turks deployed a series of surface-to-air missile batteries and electronic warfare (EW) systems to strategic locations around GNA territory and supplied an elite cadre of professional staff to provide intelligence, operations support, and training for GNA personnel on all of the new military hardware.

On March 25, 2020, GNA Prime Minister Sarraj announced the commencement of Operation Peace Storm, which rolled back much of the LNA territorial gains made around Tripoli. LNA's air superiority was quickly and catastrophically marginalized and GNA ground forces regained a great deal of territory previously lost to Russia's Wagner mercenaries. Libya remains in a perilous stalemate, foreshadowing Turkey's future relations with Russia closer to home.

Iran: Even A Nuclear Persia Needs Partners

Moscow would prefer to contain Iranian influence in the Trans-Caucasus Region and Syria, but it also needs junior partners with aligned interests. Iran has been slowly and steadily investing in nuclear engineering since the 1980s. The program did not really gain momentum until the late 1990s, when Tehran established a joint research group with Russian nuclear scientists who shared data and technical information.

In 2003, the International Atomic Energy Agency (IAEA) initiated an investigation into Iran's nuclear program. In 2006, a U.S. National

Intelligence Estimate (NIE) concluded that Tehran had been actively pursuing an atomic bomb up until 2003, and then, in 2011, the IAEA released a report confirming the American NIE assessment.

Experts surmised that the program had likely been shut down due to bad optics (Iran did not want to be counted as a pariah state like North Korea), while low-level research quietly continued in the background.

For Tehran, a nuclear program is extremely useful as a means of gaining concessions from the West; however, an open Iranian declaration as a nuclear power almost guarantees a first strike from Israel. It is possible that Moscow cooperated with Iran in nuclear engineering with the explicit purpose of setting Iran on a collision course with the United States and Israel.

Beyond ensuring regime survival, the Ayatollah's principle foreign policy goal is spreading the Islamic Revolution (Shi'a Islam) to the world. Iran's national security apparatchiks pursue this one guiding principle through extending influence across the Middle East, particularly in subversion of Sunni Arab rivals. Iran delivers funding, equipment, and training to Shi'ite insurgencies and militias operating in the region's most volatile areas (like Iraq, Syria, Lebanon, and Yemen) to shift the balance of power in its favor.

This makes Iran a direct competitor to Russia's continued role as the dominant power broker in Syria. Russia and Iran cooperated throughout the Syrian Civil War to prevent the collapse of the Bashar al-Assad regime and contain the Sunni-sect ISIS caliphate. The Russians provided air power and worked through the Syrian Army on the ground. Iranian-backed Shi'ite militias occupied strategically important localities that the Syrian Army could not reach, containing ISIS through control of adjacent territories.

Since stabilizing the al-Assad regime, Moscow has worked behind the scenes to marginalize Iran's influence in Syria (including permitting Israeli air strikes against Iranian-backed militias). Moscow wants to prevent Tehran from establishing the same kind of control in Syria that it already wields in Lebanon. Russia was a willing participant in the sanctions regime against Iran that was led by the Obama Administration

As the Obama Administration drew down the U.S. Combat Forces in Iraq in 2009 and 2010, the Shi'ite majority coalition (heavily influenced by Tehran) in Iraq's nascent parliament began consolidating political control and marginalizing Sunni and Kurdish rivals. Without American presence to protect them, Iraqi Sunnis looked to the remnants of al Qaeda in Iraq, which reemerged as the Islamic State of Iraq and the Levant (ISIS).

The emergence of ISIS after being bequeathed a stabilized Iraq by the Bush Administration was a black eye for the new President, so he began to consider how to withdraw U.S. troops from the region without leaving a power vacuum in their wake.

President Obama wagered that fully introducing Iran into the American-led global trade system would both moderate Iranian foreign policy and create a new regional balance of power between Iran, Israel, Turkey, and Saudi Arabia that would stabilize the region.

The agreement, termed the Joint Comprehensive Plan of Action (JCPOA), was negotiated in 2015 with support from France, the U.K., China, Russia, and Germany. The Obama Administration offered the JCPOA to the American public as a way to prevent Iran from becoming a nuclear power.

The JCPOA was not formulated by career diplomats of the U.S. State Department (most of whom supported compromise but strongly opposed the specific terms of the JCPOA), but by White House staffers in the West

Wing. Secretary of State John Kerry was ordered to sell the deal to Iran and the world without any real input from the U.S. Department of Defense, Department of Treasury, Department of Commerce, or the Intelligence Community.

This is why, at its foundation, the JCPOA assumed Iran wouldn't channel new resources into military expeditionary activities in the Levant. Institutional resistance was largely written off as political partisanship.

Israel, Turkey, Saudi Arabia, Jordan, UAE, and other regional allies were stunned when they learned the terms of the deal. Prime Minister Benjamin Netanyahu even gave a speech in the U.S. House of Representatives to galvanize resistance. The JCPOA subverted their strategic interests, recognized Iran as a threshold nuclear power, paid Tehran over $400 million in cash (most of which was funneled into Quds Force operations with Shi'ite militant groups), and introduced Iran into the global finance system.

Russian representatives capitalized on American political infighting by introducing 11th hour amendments for the sale of military weapons systems to Iran, knowing that it was now politically impossible for Secretary of State John Kerry to leave the negotiating table. Secretary Kerry capitulated.

The Administration cast the JCPOA as a choice between potential nuclear confrontation or diplomatic compromise. This failed to depolarize the issue for several reasons. First, all JCPOA prohibitions on enriching nuclear material were set to expire by 2030, clearing the way for Iran to develop a weapon anyway. Second, JCPOA enforcement largely relied on Iran self-reporting violations of the agreement. Third, the JCPOA did not address other key issues like ballistic missile development, cyberattacks, and sponsorship of Shi'ite militias (terrorism).

Knowing that the treaty would not be ratified in the U.S. Senate (which was never consulted in the drafting), Secretary Kerry took the JCPOA to the U.N. for ratification first. Even when the U.S. Senate rejected the treaty, it was de facto approved in the eyes of the world. This tactic simultaneously circumvented the President's political opposition and ensured that the JCPOA had no weight under American law; it was a mere executive nod and handshake.

The Trump Administration renewed American sanctions on Iran despite the objections of the U.N. Security Council and European allies and ruthlessly increased their precision and potency. Iranian oil exports plummeted, and military expeditionary activity decreased almost overnight. Despite Russia's desire to see Iranian influence in Syria curtailed, Moscow was furious at the Trump Administration's willingness to disregard the JCPOA, an agreement that was ratified by a full U.N. General Assembly vote.

President Biden pledged on the campaign trail to return to the JCPOA. The President spoke of the deal as both a matter of national integrity and strategic necessity, but Biden is hardly under any real pressure to return with immediate effect. On the way out the door, the Trump Administration also negotiated the diplomatic recognition of Israel by the UAE, Bahrain, Sudan, and Morocco.

Jordan and Egypt already diplomatically recognize Israel, and Saudi Arabia regularly cooperates with Israel on security issues without official recognition. An Israeli-led regional alliance against Iranian influence is clearly emerging in the Middle East and Tehran lacks the means to confront it directly. This is the regional balance of power that President Obama desired (though it was the Trump Administration who negotiated it), but it does not appear that the Biden Administration shares the same goal.

Russia is keeping a close eye on Tehran's negotiations with the Biden Administration. Russia frequently allows Israeli military aircraft into Syrian airspace in tacit recognition of its regional competition with Iran. However, there is ample opportunity for defense industrial cooperation. Iran needs advanced weapons systems, particularly as a bulwark against the Israeli Air Force and Western naval power.

Iran also needs an advocate on the U.N. Security Council and non-dollar denominated lines of credit. Russia needs defense industrial partners, oil arbitrage opportunities, and an advocate for its interests within OPEC. Moscow and Tehran are both on the receiving end of Western sanctions, and so they both have some limited means of circumventing those sanctions. Integrating some supply chains and mutually increasing trade is an intuitive pathway forward for these unlikely partners.

There's also evidence that Russia and Iran have shared interests in Venezuela. The Drug Enforcement Administration (DEA) recently discovered that Hezbollah (a Lebanese proxy of Iran's Quds Force) was trafficking Venezuelan narcotics into the United States, and then laundering the money by purchasing used cars.

These used cars were then exported to African countries and sold for cash, and the cash was routed back to financiers in Lebanon. Though this specific operation was shut down, Tehran and its acolytes see Venezuelan narcotics and oil as a means of financing covert operations abroad.

Moscow also sees Venezuelan oil arbitrage as low-hanging fruit, which is partially why Wagner was dispatched to preserve the Maduro regime. As regional ratlines for narcotics, human beings, weapons, and illicit finance are still in place, it is unlikely that Moscow and Tehran have not considered collaborating.

Belarus: Another Shield, Just Like Ukraine

Russia is also dealing with civil instability in Belarus, its most stalwart ally. Belarussian President Alexander Lukaschenko has been in power since 1994 through a series of falsified elections, term extensions, and constitutional modifications. There are dictators that seize and hold onto power because they have an ideological grand vision like Cuba's Fidel Castro and there are dictators that are in power to navigate nations through perilous waters or instability like China's Xi Jinping.

It is easy to see Lukashenko as a Russian puppet dictator, but, while he has endorsed economic cooperation and procures Russian military hardware, he has kept Moscow at arm's length. For example, Moscow has repeatedly offered defense agreements that would allow Russian Aerospace and Ground Forces to forward stage in Belarus as a shield against NATO. While President Lukashenko is a firm Russian ally, he has resisted such demands and has insisted that Belarus be permitted to chart its own course and plan its own future. The 2020 Belarussian Presidential Election finally upset the balance.

All indicators seemed to point to a closer 2020 contest for President in Belarus, but, when the polls closed on August 9, 2020, President Lukashenko had won with an 80% supermajority. The result was nearly impossible and pointed to heavy-handed ballot box stuffing. Many Western political analysts believe that Lukashenko did in fact win outright, but the brazenness of his electioneering was simply more than the Belarussian public could stomach. Protests erupted across the country and Lukashenko hunkered down to ride them out with the comforting knowledge that he had the allegiances of both the military and of Moscow.

Sviatlana Tsikhanouskaya, the Belarussian opposition candidate, at first refused to concede the election, but, after she was detained and her campaign manager Maria Moroz was arrested, Tsikhanouskaya's position began to soften. Tsikhanouskaya released a recorded public message, visibly under duress, recognizing Lukashenko's victory. She was then escorted by security service personnel to Lithuania, where she agreed to reside in exchange for the release of Maria Moroz. The West was as unconvinced of her concession as the masses of Belarus, and E.U. leaders quickly began cobbling together a regime of sanctions against Belarussian election officers.

The Kremlin learned valuable lessons in Ukraine so, as the world leaned on President Lukashenko to resign, Russia maintained an attentive but less bellicose posture. Russia publicly and diplomatically asserted that Belarus was an independent nation and outsiders did not have the right to interfere with "internal issues". But there were no overtures of protecting Russian citizens abroad or large military deployments to the Belarussian border (though they maintained a heightened readiness). Nor did the Kremlin summon ambassadors to engage in nuclear saber-rattling. Moscow simply recognized Lukashenko as President, encouraged him to keep a low profile, and maintained covert influence in Belarus (through FSB and GRU operatives).

This is the same approach Russia and Cuba used to keep Nicholas Maduro in power in Venezuela: Secure the President, Ensure the military remains loyal, Shut down national internet access to sever information flow, Push the opposition party leaders into exile, Avoid further escalation, and Wait. Protests lose momentum and die out, populists eventually exhaust themselves, and afterward, the dictator can resume business as usual. The price of Russian support was an end to Lukashenko's distancing act. Moscow now gets what it wants from Belarus, and Lukashenko is in no position to argue.

The Belarussian election protests are fascinating because it is easy to see how they could have gone down the same road as the Euromaidan Movement in Ukraine. If Lukashenko had lost his nerve, if the Belarussian generals had questioned their fealty, if the Belarussian Ministry of Interior Affairs had been less effective in suppressing opposition leaders, or had Western leaders lent more than rhetorical support, Belarus could have destabilized over the winter of 2020-2021.

Russia could have been forced to initiate an intervention similar to that of Crimea. But Belarus is a far larger, far more complex target than the tiny peninsula of Crimea. Even if much of the Belarussian military had defected (highly likely), securing Belarus would have required a full-scale Russian invasion.

Germany, France, and the rest of the E.U. would not forgive Russia yet again for such wanton disregard for international norms. This could have led to painful sanctions on Russian oil and gas exports. Even a cursory thought experiment reveals why Moscow chose to be far less visibly involved in Belarus than it was in Ukraine. Military force was a last resort here, and for good reason.

Afghanistan: The Taliban Return

Moscow is also deeply alarmed at the American withdrawal from Afghanistan. After the first few years of conflict, policy-makers began to see it as a distraction from the larger conflict in Iraq. They developed an approach of managing violence through occupation and development of indigenous institutions, rather than pacifying the insurgency through hard combat power. This was coupled with a gross failure to report the lack of true progress in constructing Afghanistan's institutions.

After 20 years, the war became seen as a distraction from countering great power competitors (the four named American competitors are China, Russia, North Korea, and Iran), and the American public was no longer invested in winning. President Trump secured a handshake agreement with the Taliban not to shelter terrorist organizations like al Qaeda (a pipe dream) and ordered a draw-down of U.S. Forces in Afghanistan. President Biden followed through, ordering a full withdrawal by August 31, 2021, and, in a matter of weeks, the Afghan Government, National Army, and police forces completely collapsed.

At the time of print, the Taliban is in control of all Afghanistan, with notable exceptions of Hazara dominated provinces tucked away in the Hindu Kush mountains. Afghan President Ashraf Ghani fled the country to Tajikistan on August 15, 2021 as the Taliban secured the capital of Kabul, effectively dissolving his government. The Taliban is slowly rounding up Afghan collaborators, especially former Afghan Commandos, Special Forces, and intelligence officers.

Following President Biden's announcement of the U.S. withdrawal, Afghan citizens flooded into Kabul's passport offices to get travel documents while Afghanistan still had an internationally recognized government. The Pentagon was forced to dispatch a quick reaction force (QRF) of 3,500 U.S. troops to protect Kabul while a broad evacuation took place on all available civilian and military transport aircraft. Desperate Afghans flooded into Kabul International Airport and, the situation became eerily reminiscent of the fall of Saigon.

Moscow is concerned that Islamists will soon come across the Afghan border into central Asian buffer states like Uzbekistan, Tajikistan, Kyrgyzstan, Kazakhstan, and Turkmenistan. Russia remembers the bitter war the Soviet Union fought in Afghanistan in the 1980s and knows that it lacks the capacity to pacify the country through military force.

Ukraine: The Bear Will Never Loosen Its Bite

The conflict in the Donbas region of Eastern Ukraine remains unresolved at the time of print. Ukraine's new President, Volodymyr Zelensky, is a self-proclaimed Europhile. Since taking office, he has pledged to apply for membership into NATO and the European Union by 2024. A comedian by trade, Zelensky was elected as a political outsider on a reform agenda. His administration has championed election reform, judicial reform, anti-corruption, and a 5% flat tax for businesses to attract foreign investment. President Zelensky described Vladimir Putin as an enemy of Ukraine, but he has expressed interest in closing out the conflict in Donbas through direct negotiations with the Kremlin.

Closing the conflict in Donbas would free Ukraine from Russia's tentacles. This is something that Moscow can never allow to happen. Ukraine, or more precisely Kyiv, is arguably the origin point of the Rus ethnicity, and it has been a shield against Western invasion for hundreds of years. Nevertheless, Ukraine will continue to push for entry into the NATO alliance and the E.U. in a desperate attempt to secure itself from Russian dominance. Moscow will do whatever it has to in order to keep Ukraine subservient.

The Ukrainian Armed Forces have come a long way under NATO tutelage, mostly from American and British military assistance programs. Kyiv is far more prepared for hostilities than it was in 2014 with fortified positions in Donbas, efficient C2, UAV-based ISR capabilities, and Buk, Tor, and S-300 A2/AD systems. Ironically, most of Ukraine A2/AD systems were purchased from Russia itself prior to 2014.

The Ukrainian Armed Forces are also far more motivated to fight than they were in 2014. Russia's meddling in Donbas and annexation of Crimea have caused a surge in patriotism that led to the rebirth of a real Ukrainian national identity, something that has been long dormant.

Ongoing skirmishes and artillery exchanges around Donetsk and Luhansk have created a vehement anti-Russian sentiment in the Ukrainian populace, even among ethnic Russians. Moscow's incessant interference has given the Ukrainian public something to unite against; something that supersedes internal squabbling amongst political factions and oligarchs.

The conflict in Donbas has also created a hardened Ukrainian soldiery and provided the impetus for real institutional reform in the officer corps. Ukraine's leading intelligence and security service SBU has also undergone a transformation. In 2019, the parliament passed SBU Reform: Draft Law 3196-d, reducing staffing from 27,000 to 15,000, which not only eliminates bloat and redundancy, but purges lingering Moscow loyalists.

The bill also reduces the number of missions SBU must support to counterintelligence, counter-reconnaissance, counter-sabotage, counterterrorism, and protection of state secrets. The military intelligence agency Defense Intelligence of the Ministry of Defense of Ukraine (DIU) is also taking a more robust role. DIU is not only providing quality military intelligence on Russian activities in Donbas but coordinating the deployment of Ukraine's Special Operations Forces (UASOF).

UASOF, created from the reformed Spetsnaz regiments, has been transformed into a highly capable and multifaceted force. The 3rd and 8th Special Purpose Regiments perform as elite light infantry units similar to the American 75th Rangers. The 73rd Maritime Special Operations Centre is a frogman unit for maritime operations. UASOF also features an elite special missions unit (SMU) called the 140th Special Operations Forces Centre, as well as the 35th Mixed Aviation Squadron. Operations in the information environment are conducted by the 16th, 72nd, 74th, and 83rd Psychological Operations Centres.

Even if it used hybrid methods to prepare the battlespace and achieved total surprise, Russia would have to seriously commit heavy ground forces in an extremely well-planned and well-executed campaign in order to expand its territorial control beyond Crimea or Donbas. Given Ukraine's importance in Russian strategic thinking, Moscow may be considering exactly that.

Sputnik V: Russia Uses Covid-19 for Leverage

Russia closely watched Covid-19 developments in continental Europe. As this book is being written, the United States and the United Kingdom are the only two Western countries that have developed reliable and exportable Covid-19 vaccines. The vaccines in continental Europe were not successful enough in human trials to bring to market, and many countries found it difficult to trust the vaccines developed in China.

Hackers stole a number of trade secrets from biolaboratories at Oxford, and U.K. cyber security experts pointed fingers at Moscow. The Kremlin has denied these accusations. Russia was, however, the first country in the world to bring a vaccine into mass production, dubbing the vaccine "Sputnik V". E.U. public health officials are insisting on thorough vetting for Russia's human trials data, but Germany, France, Italy, and Poland all negotiated to domestically produce Sputnik V under license. It is not clear what considerations are being wrung out of Europe, but it is not like Moscow to accept payment in cash alone.

NATO: Villain of the Past, Leviathan of the Present

The NATO Alliance is struggling to remain unified. NATO is the military component of an American grand strategy that was developed after World

War II. The closing pincers of Soviet and Anglo-American armies crushed Naziism, and then the United States created a global trade system in the Bretton-Woods conference of 1944.

For the first time, Europeans could truly integrate their economies and did not need to annex new territories in order to feed economic growth. The Americans then deployed permanent forces to Europe to support a collective defense against the Soviet Union. Every American Secretary of Defense dating back to George C. Marshall has complained that the Europeans do not pay their fair share in protecting the Continent.

European leaders are subject to the constraints of all democracies. If the public does not see the benefit of defense expenditures, which compete with priorities like national healthcare and pension systems, then politicians pursue them at their peril. After the fall of the Soviet Union, the threat to Europe dimmed in the public's eye and defense expenditures plummeted.

American generosity and forward thinking to preserve the European sphere of influence, which began during the Roosevelt Administration, was never going to last forever. Eventually, populist undercurrents would come to resent the massive military expenditures, the general outflow of capital, and the outsourcing of American industries to countries with cheaper labor, all of which undermine domestic wages and social initiatives. The guns and butter policies of Roosevelt, Truman, Eisenhower, Kennedy, Johnson, Nixon, Ford, Carter, Reagan, and H.W. Bush were always going to end.

Afterall, why should Americans not demand reciprocal trade agreements with sophisticated economies like Germany? Why should the United States, a country of 330 million people, not expect equal defense spending from allies in the European Union, a confederation of advanced democracies that constitutes over 450 million people?

American politicians could not provide domestic populists answers to these questions; and so, under Presidents Clinton, W. Bush, Obama, Trump, and now Biden, the United States has been slowly disengaging both from Europe and the larger world.

Europe is beginning to chart its own course, and, despite the political unity imposed by the European Union, the voters of leading nations like Germany, France, Italy, Denmark, and Poland all have radically different priorities. These diverging priorities are creating irreconcilable cracks in the E.U. framework, and as successive crises wash over Europe (the Great Recession, Syrian migrant crisis, Libyan migrant crisis, Greek Debt Crisis, Italian Debt Crisis, Polish judicial reforms, BREXIT, and Covid-19), those cracks are widening. The United Kingdom was the first to leave the European Union, but it will likely not be the last.

Moscow has much to celebrate in the emerging disunity in the E.U. and American disinterest in NATO, but this is short-sighted. Whatever security Moscow has gained from Western disunity, it has lost in the reemergence of dozens of great powers, middle powers, and lesser powers that will now each independently pursue their own foreign policy interests.

It is important to bear in mind that, while Washington was calling the shots in Europe's collective defense (especially during the Cold War), level heads prevailed and there was no great war with the regime in Moscow. The three most bitter wars in Russian history were fought with France in 1812, Germany in 1914, and Germany again in 1941. Middle powers like Poland and Turkey have fought no less than a dozen conflicts with Russia over the last 300 years.

With Washington no longer compelling cohesion between the many competing foreign policies of continental Europe, it is impossible to conceive of a future where Moscow does not come into conflict with a historical adversary. Over a 20 to 30-year horizon, powerhouse economies like Germany, immovable cultures like France, former subordinates like Poland, or neo-imperial aspirants like Turkey, will all resume the pursuit of strategic imperatives that support their respective economic and cultural development. Any or all of them may choose to act against Russian interests.

The Verdict

With all these challenges lying in wait and the numerous internal instabilities plaguing Russia, Moscow will employ the methodologies of hybrid warfare to shape its strategic environment. History has shown that, despite Russia's corrupt political apparatus, moribund economy, cultural stagnation, and numerous public health crises, Moscow always finds a way to make it work. This approach usually comes at enormous cost to the Russian people, but no people on Earth are more hardened towards making the necessary sacrifices for survival.

EPILOGUE

THE RUSSO-UKRAINIAN WAR

I must confess that the Russo-Ukrainian War, which began in 2022, took me by surprise. Conditions never seemed favorable. Moscow was unable to manage how Ukrainians, Europeans, and Americans saw the standoff. After the War in Donbas, the Ukrainian public became vehemently set against further Russian interference or dominance. The sheer size of the combat forces deployed to the Ukrainian border also squandered any element of surprise.

There were many experts in the West that simply did not believe Russia would engage in a war on such unfavorable terms. I would have expected Russia to operate on better information, not waste its strength. Russia should have waged a hybrid war or, at least, limited downside risks by waging the war through proxies, much as it had in every conflict since the 2nd Chechen War.

I considered waiting for the war to conclude before publishing and adding another case study, particularly as, in the first months of the war, Vladimir Putin's choices appeared to have broken the primary theses of this book. However, as the conflict continues to unfold, it appears that the conclusions of the previous case studies are proving to be accurate.

Recall this book's two theses:

Hybrid Warfare is a mode of conventional military conflict that holistically leverages all means of national power to efficiently achieve victory.

Russia uses Hybrid Warfare to shape the former Soviet sphere with its limited military and economic resources to create buffer states without incurring the extreme costs of a full-scale war.

Russia is clearly engaged in a full-scale conventional war to secure Ukraine as a buffer state. In this, I claim victory, as I precisely defined this strategic imperative and gave it considerable weight throughout the book. But why did Moscow not employ hybrid methods and why is Russia performing so poorly?

The Situation in Ukraine as of Winter 2021-2022

President Lukaschenko's 2021 sham reelection caused protests and riots across Belarus and Moscow backed his regime, providing intelligence and limited security assistance to ride out the populist tide. In exchange, President Lukaschenko had to authorize the forward deployment of Russian forces in Belarus.

Russia used the massive Zapad 2021 joint exercises with Belarus September 10th to September 15, 2021 to begin amassing troops on Ukraine's northern border. Heavy Russian Ground Forces began staging in Rostov-on-Don and Crimea, poised towards Donbas and Southern Ukraine. Belarus, which had not previously permitted Russia to deploy large combat formations within its borders, allowed entire Combined Arms and Tank Armies to deploy along its southern border with Ukraine.

By October 2021, it was clear that these combat formations were present to give political warnings to the West some gravity. Over Autumn, Russian leaders made diplomatic threats and aggressive gestures until December 17, 2021.

President Putin finally issued a list of demands to the United States and NATO (Ukraine and the European Union were notably excluded). The demands were:

Terminate NATO military activity in eastern Europe, especially in Ukraine, the Caucasus region, and Central Asia.

Provide legal guarantees that NATO will not accept any new members from the former Soviet sphere of influence, especially Ukraine.

The United States and Russia will mutually remove deployments of intermediate-range missiles within striking distance of each other's home territory.

NATO must terminate any military exercises of more than a single brigade in size within a mutually agreed border zone.

The United States and Russia will mutually commit not to consider each other adversaries and will resolve disputes peacefully.

Neither Russia nor the United States can deploy nuclear weapons outside their national territories.

Moscow's claims of sovereignty over the collective security policies of both former Soviet member states and old Warsaw Pact members harkened back to the Cold War, but they were no less serious. These were all buffer states captured by the armies of General Zhukov during the Second World War. Stalin's intent in installing autocratic socialist regimes in all of these countries was to ensure they would remain a potent buffer against any further aggression by the West. Russia simply wanted to reestablish this defense in depth.

By February 2022, Russia had amassed more than 200,000 troops around the border of Ukraine. All American and European diplomatic personnel were evacuated from Kyiv. It seemed as if the entire world knew that the meager Ukrainian Armed Forces would collapse in a matter of hours.

Then, on February 24th, the Russian invasion began on all fronts, and the world held its breath for the inevitable. First, heavy Russian Grounds Forces engaged the main body of the Ukrainian Armed Forces in Donbas, pinning them down. Then, elite elements of the VDV began flying sorties to drop paratroopers west of Kyiv to secure airfields. These paratroopers would be followed by Air Assault Troops that could use the airfields to stage an assault on the capitol.

Almost immediately, things began going wrong. Ukrainian A2/AD systems, mostly of Soviet origin, began shooting down IL-76 heavy transport planes loaded with Russian paratroopers. As the Russians attempted to transport Air Assault forces by helicopter to the region, small teams of Ukrainian guerillas and Special Operations Forces (SOF) used man-portable air defense systems (MANPADS) to shoot down astonishing numbers of helicopter transports.

What VDV soldiers did arrive on the battlefield safely were poorly equipped and poorly supported. It was soon clear that elite Russian troops (primarily 76th Guards Air Assault Division, 98th Guards Airborne Division, 155th Separate Marine Brigade, and select Spetsnaz battalions) had insufficient forces and firepower to rapidly secure their objectives around Kyiv.

With a 12:1 advantage in forces, Russian planners had not anticipated significant resistance in seizing Kyiv; moreover, they expected large-scale acceptance of "Russian liberation" by the indigenous population. Thus, planners chose to take the city using lighter, more mobile VDV and Spetsnaz units (preferred tools in hybrid wars).

When these elite troops floundered, Russian commanders cobbled together an ad hoc secondary ground invasion from Belarus made up of the 41st Combined Arms Army (CAA) and a few supporting brigades of the 35th (38th Motorized Rifle Brigade, 64th Motorized Rifle Brigade, 69th Fortress Brigade, 165th Artillery Brigade and 107th Rocket Brigade) and 36th CAAs (5th Tank Brigade, 37th Motorized Rifle Brigade and 103rd Rocket Brigade).

A 40-mile convoy of Russian mechanized infantry advanced south along a single highway to Kyiv. The Ukrainian 72nd Mechanized Brigade, National Guard, and local militia armed with anti-tank missiles hounded this convoy relentlessly, exacting an enormous toll. After eight days, the entire spearhead ground to a halt. The tanks and IFVs did not have sufficient fuel to continue an advance all the way to Kyiv.

Soon afterward, the Russian soldiers manning all of these tanks and IFVs exited their vehicles and walked north—all the way back to the Belarussian border. The convoy had been deployed without a logistics plan for fuel, food, and supplies, and, rather than starving in their vehicles, the soldiers simply chose to walk home.

Similar stories began emerging from Donbas and Kharkiv where the bulk of Russia's Ground Forces were engaged in fierce exchanges with the main Ukrainian Army. After the initial surge, Russian Ground Forces were unable to significantly move the line of contact more than a few miles a day, and every inch of the advance was paid for in blood.

Due to the unexpectedly fierce resistance and the utter incompetence of the 41st CAA, Russian commanders realized that they had insufficient forces in theater dedicated to capturing the Capitol. The order was given to bypass Sumy, Chernihiv, and several other cities along the line of contact.

This freed up elements of the 2nd CAA and 1st Tank Army to traverse 300 miles of hostile terrain and join the assault on Kyiv. These reinforcements arrived at Kyiv from the northeast, aiding remnants of the 41st CAA to the northwest, and the 76th Guards Air Assault Division and 98th Guards Airborne Division to the southwest in an attempt to encircle the city.

But it wasn't to be.

By late March, it was clear that the paltry few regional units fielded by the Ukrainian Armed Forces were too mobile for the Russians to pin down under one-sided artillery exchanges, and that they were bogging down Russian forward progress by hounding supply lines and shattering unprotected support units. By April 4th, remnants of Russian Ground Forces around Kyiv had been forced back to the border of Belarus in what can only be called a route.

Russian forces in Crimea fared no better in securing the coastline of the Black Sea. Though they eventually captured the coastal city of Mariupol (at enormous cost), a Ukrainian Neptune cruise missile sank the Moskva, a Slava class cruiser and flagship of the Black Sea Fleet.

Ukrainian forces also sank the Alligator class amphibious landing ship Saratov and damaged sister ships Caesar Kunikov and Novocherkassk.

By summer of 2022, Russian forces had abandoned the capture of Kyiv entirely and reconcentrated all available troops and resources in the Donbas and Crimean regions. By fall of 2022, Ukraine had initiated highly successful counter-offensives in Kherson and Kharkiv.

President Putin issued orders for a national mobilization, calling up reserve troops. Many of those troops were deployed to Ukraine to reinforce Russia's beleaguered BTGs and stabilize the lines, but many more were sent to an aggressive training camp in order to prepare for some sort of future offensive.

Mounting Losses

Russia's most elite troops, particularly the VDV, Spetsnaz Brigades, and Naval Infantry, have been entirely hollowed out of their pre-war combat potential. It appears that most of Russia's Ground Forces generals were not educated on the purpose of these elite units or how they were designed to be employed. They were regularly deployed as light infantry battalions to stabilize the lines against opposition armed with tanks, IFVs and artillery.

It will take over a decade for Moscow to rebuild these elite forces. Though it is difficult to have much confidence in public casualty reports, several outlets claimed that over 150,000 Russian soldiers were killed or wounded in the initial phases of the war. Additionally, Russia also lost at least eight generals as of August 2023, with senior officers and MoD officials continuing to be targeted by Ukrainian forces:

Lieutenant General Yakov Rezantsev (March 25, 2022)—Commander, 49th Combined Arms Army

Lieutenant General Roman Kutuzov (June 5, 2022)—Commander, 1st Army Corps, Donetsk Republic People's Militia

Major General Andrei Sukhovetsky (March 1, 2022)—Deputy Commander, 41st Combined Arms Army

Major General Sergei Goryachev (June 12, 2023)—Chief of Staff, 35th Combined Arms Army

Major General Oleg Mityaev (March 15, 2022)—Commander, 150th Motorized Rifle Division

Major General Vladimir Frolov (April 16, 2022)—Deputy Commander, 8th Guards Combined Arms Army

Major General Andrei Simonov (April 30, 2022)—Chief of Electronic Warfare Troops, 2nd Guards Combined Arms Army

Major General (ret) Kanamat Botashev (May 22, 2022)—Unit Unknown

Though the loss of so many general officers is damaging to the cohesion of the force and implementation of strategy, Russia's loss of over 200 colonels and thousands of junior officers is catastrophic.

Every brigade, regiment, and battalion in the Russian Ground Forces has lost its commanding officer and a large portion of its staff officers. Each of these units is stuck in the field against a determined enemy without leaders that have been trained in tactical maneuver, support functions, or logistics.

In addition to these egregious personnel losses, Russian Forces have lost over 2,000 tanks and 2,900 APCs and IFVs. Reliable stats on Russian Aerospace Forces remain elusive, but early losses were bad enough that most fighters, fighter-bombers, helicopters, transport aircraft, and strategic bombers have been either grounded or ordered to fire on Ukrainian targets from Russian airspace with long-range munitions in early 2023.

Ukrainian Armed Forces launched counter-offensives in Kharkiv (September 6th to October 2, 2022) and Kherson (August 29th to November 11, 2022) and captured an entire army's worth of Russian military vehicles, equipment, hardware, and ammunition. Due to these acquisitions, the Ukrainians began the 2023 fighting season better armed and supplied than at the beginning of the war.

Additionally, the Russian General Staff and Ministry of Defense have embezzled much of the money set aside to stockpile replacement equipment. In just one example of profound corruption, the Ministry of Defense had 1.5 million combat uniforms on paper, but nothing in deep storage.

Due to the sanctions regime, Russia does not have the manufacturing capacity to produce new and sophisticated military equipment. Reserve soldiers and future conscripts will likely be issued Soviet-era gear from long-term storage.

Sanctions

The United States and Europe cooperated on the strictest sanctions since the Cold War. Russian finished goods, raw materials, and services were cut off from the global banking system. Most of the Russian Central Bank's foreign currency reserves were stored in American and European banks.

Almost $600 Billion in hard currency was frozen overseas, which now prevented Russia from converting Rubles into Dollars, Yen, Euro, Pounds Sterling, Pesos, and Won. Russia responded by throttling oil and gas exports to mainland Europe.

In order to arrest a mass exodus of hard currency, the Russian Central Bank immediately initiated capital controls and seized all foreign currency within Russia's borders. Russian firms, who are paid in hard currency for services rendered abroad, were required to immediately accept a trade-in for Rubles, handing any foreign currency over to the Central Bank.

The Ruble hence rose in value, but this was artificial. Neither Russian private companies nor the national government could pay for goods and services abroad. Russia even defaulted on sovereign bond payments over the summer of 2022. The financial infrastructure was simply no longer present to move money to Western creditors.

Nevertheless, Russia retained a great deal of hard currency from oil and gas sales, primarily from India, Brazil, Argentina, and China. While Russia was moving far less volume, the global price of crude oil rose, making Moscow momentarily cash rich. Paradoxically, this increase in cash was economically meaningless because the financial infrastructure needed to spend the money on vital Western high-tech goods was turned off at the start of the war.

Another approach pioneered was to pay creditors abroad in gold. Russia was sitting on over $130 Billion in declared gold reserves, and perhaps another $100 Billion in undeclared reserves, which was useful for opening lines of credit to traditionally non-aligned trading partners in Africa and South America.

Despite extraordinary efforts by the head of the Russian Central Bank, Elvira Nabiullina, Russia was in economic decline. Official statistics conceded a nominal economic contraction but, in reality, the private sector was withering. The optimistic picture painted for the public was inflated by an influx of oil and gas revenues. This created growth on paper, but the economic contraction experienced by Russian citizens was real, measurable, and extreme.

Previous chapters have detailed the moribund nature of Russian manufacturing, the total absence of a service economy, and complete reliance on raw material exports. But now, the sanctions regime has put Russia's oil infrastructure in peril.

After the Soviet Union collapsed, Russian oil and gas production plummeted due to deteriorating and inoperable infrastructure. Rigs were shut down. Oil froze in pipes. Pipes burst. Wells locked up. These wells were re-tapped, and all of the rigs, pipelines, and refineries were rebuilt by American super-majors like Exxon, Chevron, and Shell.

Since then, the entire Russian fossil fuel ecosystem has been maintained by American service companies like Schlumberger and Halliburton. All of these firms have picked up and moved out, taking their personnel, technology, equipment, and expertise with them. Similar to Venezuela,

Russia's oil and gas production began to deteriorate over time, curtailing future revenues for Moscow and future leverage over the E.U.

Sanctions spelled bad news for the war effort. With the exception of heavy industries like steel and petrochemicals, most of Russia's military hardware required imported technology and components, especially in the case of semiconductors and software. Russia's military industrial complex was so defeated by sanctions that Moscow began partnering with the likes of Iran to produce cheap knockoff strike UAVs like the Shahed-136.

Moscow even signed a procurement contract with North Korea to replenish its depleted artillery stockpiles. After Ukrainian counter offensives in Kherson and Kharkiv captured an army's worth of equipment and supplies, re-equipping Russia's Ground Forces with modern equipment and kit was nearly impossible.

Overestimates

Media outlets and analysts have claimed that the U.S. Department of Defense, NATO, and especially the Intelligence Community, all grossly overestimated Russia's combat capabilities. Details of the accusations vary but generally devolve into something approximating the national security establishment intentionally over-estimated the Russian threat to justify larger annual budgets.

I am not sure this is correct.

I have given a detailed ground-up explanation of Russia's military reforms, particularly under Anatoly Serdyukov, as well as GPV 2020 and GPV 2027. Russia's Armed Services, especially the VDV and Ground Forces, have made enormous strides forward in modernization.

Their recent campaigns in Crimea, Donbas, and Syria each demonstrated a competent fighting force. Moreover, military planners made sure to rotate up-and-coming officers into these conflicts in order to get them real combat experience. While some scrutiny may be warranted, these anti-establishment accusations do not bear out.

Deficiencies

It is now undeniable that Russian Ground Forces are suffering from a lack of junior leadership. The technical expert approach to NCOs is not working. Russia needs to train a professional corps of NCOs to lead units below the company level.

Over 200 colonels have died.

In part, this is because officers are being forced to leave their HQs to lead unmotivated enlisted soldiers on the frontline. This is why, time and time again, the Western approach to building an NCO corps has proven effective.

Russia's nightmarish logistics have been on display during the conflict, particularly as exhibited by the 41st CAA around Kyiv. Logistics have never been a Russian strong point, but it is clear that brigade and division staff officers either did not know that the Kremlin actually planned to invade, or they were too incompetent to plan their respective pieces.

The BTG was a poorly configured combat unit. The three organic infantry maneuver companies within the formation provided insufficient protection for the enormous number of support units at its disposal. The BTG commander and his staff were also unable to coordinate and fully control a brigade's worth of fire support, ISR, and EW assets under their charge. The formation was too unwieldy and crumbled on contact with a determined adversary. Moreover, the airborne and air assault BTGs of the VDV had smaller line companies than was typical of Ground Forces infantry.

VDV companies offered a maximum of 42 dismounted soldiers (and they're often 75% manned), which means they were closer in size to a NATO rifle platoon. Especially in the case of the VDV, employing combat power through the BTG formation forced Russia's best trained, most motivated soldiers to fight with their hands tied behind their back.

It is also clear that the new National Defense Management Center (NTsUO) was incapable of efficient command and control (C2) and coordinating theater Intelligence-Surveillance-Reconnaissance (ISR) with combat operations. Defense Minister Sergey Shoygu and Chief of the General Staff Gerasimov hoped that NTsUO would give political leadership better control over combat operations, but it was a poor replacement for a trusted joint forces commander.

So Why Not Hybrid Warfare?

We can absolutely conclude that Russia has paid an egregious price for its failures in campaign planning, revealing glaring weaknesses in the Ground Forces and Aerospace Forces. But why did Moscow not attempt to mitigate these potential setbacks and losses by using a hybrid warfare methodology for the invasion of Ukraine? There are five essential points to make here.

Point #1: Attempted Hybrid Warfare

Russia did, indeed, attempt a hybrid warfare approach to the Invasion of Ukraine. All of the hybrid warfare elements were in play.

Russia deployed large conventional forces to Ukraine's border to threaten and intimidate (as during the Crimea Annexation in 2014).

Russian proxy forces in Donbas conducted demonstrations and small-scale harassing attacks (as occurred in Georgia over the summer of 2008).

GRU and FSB used decentralized networks of cyber hacktivists to execute hundreds of attacks against Ukrainian servers and websites (as they did in Georgia, Crimea, and Donbas), damaging government networks and Viasat satellite communications.

Moscow pushed an extensive propaganda campaign in Europe, the United States, Ukraine, and Russia itself, first to convey strength, then to de-legitimize President Volodymyr Zelenskyy's government in Kyiv, and then to create a narrative basis for a Russian intervention.

Russian operatives even attempted a false flag operation, creating a now-debunked video portraying Ukrainian troops conducting ethnic cleansing against Russian populations in Donbas.

Despite Moscow's best efforts, the Zelenskyy Administration, Ukrainian Armed Forces, the SBU, and the West in general all remained undisrupted by these non-kinetic influence operations (aka Russian hybrid activities). Moreover, the Ukrainian People were unmoved, unmotivated, and unconvinced by this new stream of Russian propaganda. The narrative was very similar to Russia's earlier interventions, and the public response was flat. For this reason, none of hybrid warfare's cardinal characteristics (Aktivnost, Vnezapnost, and Maskirovka) were achieved.

As was the case in earlier Ukrainian operations (Chapter 8), when hybrid warfare fails to create asymmetric advantages that translate into material gains on the battlefield, it devolves into brutal high-intensity conflict. This is exactly what happened when Russia was forced to deploy heavy ground forces to reinforce its dying insurgency in Donbas from August of 2014 on through the Battle of Debaltseve in 2015. The full-scale invasion of Ukraine posed the same problem at scale.

Point #2: Faulty Intelligence

Hybrid warfare is not possible without very accurate strategic intelligence, and it is clear that Russia's intelligence apparatus delivered false information to both policy makers and strategic planners. Recall that, in September of 2018, Vladimir Putin summoned GRU head Colonel General Igor Korobov to the Kremlin for an intense "dressing down".

Following the attempted assassination of Sergey Skripal in the U.K., 150+ career Russian diplomats and intelligence officers were expelled from the United States and Europe. The loss of strategic intelligence and diplomatic standing was incalculable. A little over a month later, Korobov collapsed at home and died. A public release claimed that his sudden death was due to "stress". This is the first key event that doomed Russia's Invasion of Ukraine on February 24, 2022.

Due to the Kremlin's lack of faith in the GRU, it was replaced by the FSB as the institution responsible for strategic planning in Ukraine. FSB Director Alexander Bortnikov (Russian: Александр Бортников) is known as a competent and conscientious manager. In 2008, he was appointed to replace ultra-nationalist Director Nikolai Patrushev (who became Secretary of the Security Council of Russia).

Over his tenure, Bortnikov attempted to reform the many different warring factions and departments within the FSB and has often expressed frustration with the seemingly irreconcilable nature of the institution.

Nevertheless, he is amongst the most influential *siloviki* in Russia, and he is one of the few officials that is truly within Putin's inner circle.

Colonel General Sergei Beseda, head of the FSB's 5th Directorate, was placed under house arrest only two weeks after the invasion of Ukraine, which is to say: it took President Putin two weeks to realize he'd been fed a stream of false information regarding Ukraine's disposition for several months (or years). The 5th Directorate is known as the Service of Operative Information and International Ties and is responsible for overseeing FSB's foreign intelligence operations.

The titles of a few of its subordinate offices (Department of Operative Information, Analysis Service, and Strategic Planning Service) reveal a little more about the 5th Directorate's role. This is the place at FSB where raw information collected by its operatives is aggregated, analyzed, vetted, and refined into validated intelligence, and the place responsible for "strategic planning" based on that intelligence. In short, despite the GRU playing a central role in previous hybrid wars, it is likely that the FSB was the institution that provided the Kremlin and General Staff with the intelligence package for the Invasion of Ukraine.

Publicly reported charges against Colonel General Beseda include misusing operational funds earmarked for subversive activities and providing poor intelligence. The meaning of "providing poor intelligence" is both self-explanatory and a gross understatement. Misusing operational funds earmarked for "subversive activities" is most likely in reference to funding that was set aside to pay Ukrainian agents or saboteurs; funding that apparently was never disbursed. Was the General enriching himself out of his own covert operations budget? It is a possibility.

Colonel General Beseda's 5th Directorate provided fabricated (or at least rose-tinted) intelligence to Director Bortnikov and the other FSB higher-ups. And Bortnikov, one of the few intelligence officials with direct access to President Putin, provided this bad intelligence to the Kremlin and General Staff.

FSB reported that Ukraine was weak and divided, that the population had a generally pro-Russian disposition, and that most anti-Russian sentiment was stoked by Western influence. FSB projected that President Zelensky's Government would crumble, that Ukrainian citizens would welcome the Russian invaders as liberators (as had happened in Crimea in 2014), and that the Ukrainian Armed Forces did not pose a significant threat.

We can only speculate how far the GRU was removed from the campaign planning process, but FSB officers have no professional experience interfacing with planners in the General Staff. The FSB's 5th Directorate produces policy recommendations for the Kremlin. Planning a scheme of maneuver and logistics for the Ground Forces' many independent divisions and brigades, across combined arms specialties, requires detailed military intelligence, driven by sophisticated collection, to meet priority information requirements (PIR). The FSB was not institutionally designed to support military intelligence so, the further the GRU was isolated from the process, the more explainable the catastrophe of Russian fires, maneuver, and logistics.

Reports have emerged that Ground Forces commanders planned for a 10-day campaign to seize all of Ukraine. This not only underlines how unrealistic intelligence assessments were, but it explains why logistics planning had been so poor. Theater generals (Defense Minister Shoygu did not appoint a single Theater Commander until April 2022) told each unit to stockpile munitions, food, and other supplies for a 2-week campaign where they would face nothing but token resistance.

Point #3: Poor Scaling

Whatever the FSB's failures, this does not exonerate the staff officers at the National Defense Management Center (NTsUO) or Russia's combined arms armies, tank armies, divisions, and brigades, all of whom were expected to turn the General Staff's invasion plan into reality. This meant planning out a combined arms scheme of maneuver to capture a chain of objectives for forces and fires across infantry, artillery, armor, sappers, electronic warfare, rocket artillery (MLRS), air defense artillery, and then coordinating re-supply through a chain of logistics hubs and support assets. This is no small feat, but this is the function of professional military officers—a function they utterly failed to perform.

Russian officers proved adept at campaign planning in Syria, Donbas, and Crimea before, but one must appreciate the difference in scale. The Syrian Intervention only required a handful of Spetsnaz units and elements of the Aerospace Forces. Russia's deployment of forces to Crimea and Donbas was confined to elite ground elements and Spetsnaz, staffed with Russia's most proficient officers. Deploying in excess of 200,000 troops to the Ukrainian border is a far more complex military operation than previous hybrid conflicts.

Rather than merely deploying premier units like the VDV and Spetsnaz, Russia mustered the full expeditionary potential of the Ground Forces. By necessity, many of the units deployed to combat were Russia's "back-water" units, staffed by the weakest officers. Many of Russia's heavy combat formations were unable to support themselves in the field due to a dearth of competent leadership.

As stated earlier, Sergey Shoygu did not appoint a single Theater Commander until April 10, 2022. Before then, the campaign was run by the General Staff through the NTsUO to generals commanding armies or divisions, and colonels commanding independent brigades. General Aleksandr Dvornikov was the first to be appointed, but once it became clear that he could not rescue the stalled offensive he was quickly replaced.

General Gennady Zhidko was appointed sometime in May. He implemented a reorientation away from capturing Kyiv and focused on securing Kharkiv, Donbas, and a land corridor from Russia to Crimea. Zhidko was not successful.

Following Zhidko's failure, General Surovikin was appointed Theater Commander on October 8, 2022. Surovikin was a bitter critic of the war strategy. Over his career he had won a reputation for being empirical, independently minded, bombastic, and utterly ruthless. In 2017, Surovikin had been appointed Commander of Russian Forces in Syria where many atrocities in targeting civilians were attributed to his leadership.

Surovikin then became the first Ground Forces officer promoted to command the VKS (Aerospace Forces) and held a dual position as Commander of the Eastern Military District. As a likely candidate for Chief of the General Staff, Moscow hoped Surovikin might give the offensive new life. Instead, Moscow began to receive a steady stream of information about the poor condition of theater equipment, morale, logistics, and supply (especially artillery munitions and fuel), as well as the precariousness of the position of Ground Forces in the Kherson region.

Surovikin advocated for a tactical withdrawal into Crimea. Though Surovikin's advice for withdrawal was heeded, Chief of the General Staff Valery Gerasimov decided to take a direct hand as Theater Commander.

General Gerasimov was a close confidant of President Putin and Defense Minister Shoygu, but it was highly unusual for any country to appoint its supreme military commander to a direct combat role, underlining

Moscow's desperation. General Surovikin focused on entrenching gains to prepare for a Ukrainian counter-offensive. He ironed out logistics problems and raised alarm bells about the short supply of fuel and artillery munitions. Gerasimov was dispatched to get Russia's Ground Forces moving forward again.

Gerasimov chose to keep General Surovikin onboard as a Deputy Commander alongside Ground Forces General Oleg Salyukov and the Deputy Chief of the General Staff Colonel General Aleksey Kim. Unfortunately, rumors percolated up from the ranks that Gerasimov, once highly respected, was increasingly viewed by subordinate officers as an incompetent political crony. He paid little attention to Russia's crippling logistics issues and continued to expend dwindling munitions supplies in engagements that moved the ball forward in strategically inconsequential localities. It is probable that, unlike Surovikin, Gerasimov was only delivering rosy reports to the Kremlin. President Putin may not have been fully apprised of the situation.

The Wagner insurrection only made Theater Command more chaotic. The Kremlin suspected that General Surovikin had prior knowledge of Prighozin's intentions. The General had been a mediator between Wagner and the MoD, and Prighozin frequently praised Surovikin on social media as the only competent general in Russia. Surovikin was placed under arrest shortly after Prighozin accepted exile to Belarus, and the Russian Government has since announced that he was released to his home (house arrest). This will probably translate into permanent retirement, depriving Russian Forces of an empirically grounded commander that both managed the details and punished incompetence.

The failure of the NTsUO to manage planning and operations in the beginning, and its replacement by a deluge of Generals, was surely a contributing factor to the non-performance of staff officers in each of

Russia's combined arms armies, tank armies, divisions, and brigades. New leaders bring new vision. New vision requires new planning and logistics before it can be implemented in operations. The constant change of command was debilitating.

Point #4: Internal Deception

The General Staff via the NTsUO may not have issued Russia's field commanders much more information than the soldiers on the line. Almost all captured Russian soldiers testified that they thought they were in a field exercise prior to the actual invasion order. There were hundreds of stories of Russia's elite VDV paratroopers boarding IL-76 transport planes, believing they were geared up for a training drop, only to be informed on the flight that they were dropping into Ukraine and going to war.

It is likely that commanders and staff officers at the division and brigade levels were only told that they were deploying for exercises on the Ukrainian border. This was the General Staff's way of maintaining strict OPSEC regarding Russia's intentions. Then, in the days leading up to February 24, 2022, Russia's line units were rapidly handed operational objectives and told to get the details in order without sufficient time to plan maneuver, fires, communications, logistics, and sustainment.

In a rushed sequence of events, President Putin pronounced that the regime in Kyiv was unacceptably fascist, Russian combat units were ordered to advance into Ukraine on February 24th, and President Putin held a press conference announcing a "Special Military Operation" to de-Nazify the country.

Point #5: A Failure to Reform

It is clear now that Sergey Shoygu has not substantively reformed the Ministry of Defense following his replacement of Anatoly Serdyukov. Recall, Anatoly Serdyukov was a determined reformer as Minister of Defense and brought a large body of tax professionals with him. These accountants made the General Staff explain every kopek in expenditures. He even established a financial control department in the Ministry of Defense to institutionalize financial accountability and curtail graft. And, as though by magic, combat units discovered that they had training budgets, and defense procurement programs began to make deliveries.

Serdyukov's reforms created powerful enemies in the General Staff and Security Council, so, when he was implicated in the Magnitsky scandal, they pounced to remove him from office. President Putin appointed Sergey Shoygu, then Minister of Emergency Situations and Governor of Moscow Oblast, as Minister of Defense in 2012.

Shoygu came to Moscow from Siberia in 1990, and, due to years of construction management experience during the Soviet-era, he was appointed to the State Architecture and Construction Committee of the Russian Federation. President Boris Yeltsin came from a similar background, and Shoygu's credentials immediately gained his trust, thereby launching Shoygu's political career.

In 1991, Yeltsin appointed Shoygu to Chairman of the State Committee of the Russian Federation for Civil Defense, Emergency Situations, and Disaster Response, which would eventually evolve into the Minister of Emergency Situations.

In 1999, Shoygu became a leader in the Unity political party, giving rise to Vladimir Putin's presidency.

Shoygu did not belong to the Saint Petersburg clique of *siloviki*, whom Putin did not wish to further empower. Moreover, Putin himself owes his rise to power to Shoygu's party leadership. After Anatoly Serdyukov became a political liability, Putin felt comfortable tapping Shoygu to take over as Minister of Defense.

While Shoygu would never leverage the military against Putin, he is one of the most corrupt officials in any government—anywhere. Since his appointment, Shoygu has extensively leveraged the Ministry of Defense finances to buy personal and political influence.

Sergey Shoygu decided to reconcile the Office of the Minister of Defense with the General Staff following the adversarial relationship with Serdyukov. He made many symbolic gestures like wearing a military uniform to show he was a team player (despite no military service or experience).

Shoygu's most meaningful (catastrophic) action was firing most of Serdyukov's tax professionals from key deputy minister positions. Shoygu then brought back individuals whom Serdyukov had fired for corruption, graft, and incompetence, and disbanded the financial control department. This is the second key event that doomed Russia's invasion of Ukraine.

To maintain the illusion of large-scale institutional reform, Shoygu followed through with the GPV 2020 and GPV 2027 procurement programs. Serdyukov's tax professionals had already negotiated many of the contracts for GPV 2020, and they had created enforcement mechanisms for contract performance and delivery.

Shoygu was able to ride on these achievements, taking delivery of new tanks, aircraft, ships, submarines, EW systems, and many other pieces of impressive military hardware. He also prioritized snap readiness drills where Ground Forces regiments often had to mobilize within 14 days, execute a long-distance movement (100+ miles) to a "combat zone" (training range), and then conduct basic maneuver drills. Any onlooker, including the Kremlin and even Western security analysts, could be forgiven for believing that the Russian Armed Services were on the rise.

Beneath the glossy finish was a rotten core. The German Institute of International and Security Affairs conducted a study in 2014, indicating that as much as 20% of the Russian Defense Budget was being embezzled. Another 40% of the remaining funds was spent on nuclear capabilities, which Moscow views as its priority strategic deterrent. Then, of course, the Russian Navy and Aerospace Forces were undergoing expensive modernizations (though the war in Ukraine revealed the Aerospace Forces to be as moribund as ever).

This was all money that did not go into building operational capability in the Ground Forces. And while Shoygu's snap readiness drills ensured proficiency in rapid mobilization, they did not require brigade, division, or army level staff officers to plan for sustained combat operations over extended periods of time and across hostile territory. They also did not inculcate soldiers with basic combat skills.

Russian soldiers learned their military specialties within their units instead of attending expensive training schools like Western militaries, but Russia did not have Western-style NCOs to manage training. Perhaps to reenforce the supremacy of Russian officers and garner favor, Shoygu went further by abolishing Warrant Officer ranks and dismissing over 140,000 such individuals. Following these changes, the only instruction soldiers of the Russian Ground Forces received came from their junior officers and peers.

Early in Shoygu's tenure as Defense Minister, Chief of the General Staff Gerasimov persistently complained that soldiers did not know how to do their jobs.

Infantrymen could not fire their weapons accurately.

Tankers did not know how to maneuver their tanks, nevertheless fire at mobile targets while on the move.

Truck drivers could not drive their transports.

Technicians could not perform basic maintenance.

Officers did not understand command and control systems.

The Invasion of Ukraine revealed that, for most of Russia's Ground Forces, little has changed since 2014. With notable exceptions in the VDV, Spetsnaz brigades, and Naval Infantry, the bulk of Russia's soldiery were never properly trained to do their jobs. When these troops were sent to real combat *en masse,* they crumbled.

The Verdict

Over time, I am certain that more details will emerge, but my supposition fits the fact pattern. Take it for what you will.

What is clear is that Russia's leading institutions are not performing their designed roles or providing accurate information to policymakers. Russia is paying in blood for these failures, and this may very well be the end of Moscow's ability to project conventional military power abroad.

Why Now?

Why would Russia decide to invade Ukraine now? The answer harkens all the way back to the Overture. Russia is facing a dire demographic collapse and a half-dozen public health crises all at the same time. The Armed

Services are finding it nearly impossible to conscript healthy young men into the force, to say nothing of finding willing volunteers.

The center of mass of the Russian workforce is aging rapidly, and there simply are not enough young people to carry the economy. This aging workforce problem plagues many advanced economies like Japan, Korea, and Germany, but they all have a highly educated workforce that can export high value-added goods and services. Russia is still an emerging economy.

As Russia stares down the barrel of an inevitable economic crisis that will create profound internal instability, the Kremlin wants to use what resources it can still muster to restore its strategic buffer: a buffer that secured the Soviet Union and the Russian Empire before it. Then, once it can shield itself from foreign interference, Russia can economically decline, and then perhaps one day renew itself. That's their hope, anyway. We'll have to watch the reality play out.

GLOSSARY

Advanced Force Operations (AFO)

U.S. Secretary of Defense-approved preparatory military action such as clandestine operations, HUMINT, deployment of enabling forces, and target-specific preparations that occur prior to an overt military operation against a specific adversary. Within the framework of OPE, AFO is conducted by SOF and SMUs that are active in the combat zone during "Phase 0" of a military campaign prior to the overt initiation of hostilities.

Agenturi

A Russian term for "agent", usually referring to operatives of the intelligence services that are responsible for HUMINT and other traditional spy craft.

Air Supremacy

A degree of air dominance or superiority where one side holds complete control of the aerial battlespace and may wield airpower over enemy forces virtually unopposed.

Aktivnost (Russian: **активность***)*

A Russian term for "activity" that refers to all measures that prevent an enemy from bringing its military power to bear, particularly on operational objectives. Aktivnost is a core component of campaign planning in hybrid warfare and includes many non-military and non-kinetic influencing measures that Russian operatives use to inhibit civil authorities from responding to the general chaos. Under Aktivnost, Russian operatives may coerce, intimidate, or blackmail key individuals in politics, law enforcement, or military command. Operatives may also organize paramilitary groups and use them to block civil authorities from containing rioters.

Anti-Access and Area Denial Systems (A2/AD)

Military hardware, such as the Russian S-400 or American Patriot systems, that are designed to prohibit the use of airspace by enemy air forces, either in air dominance roles, support to ground forces, or for military transport activities.

Anti-Submarine Warfare (ASW)

A branch of coordinated underwater warfare waged by surface vessels, aircraft, and submarines to find, track, and destroy enemy submarines using specialized tactics and equipment. ASW was first developed in World War I by the Royal Navy and honed in during World War II to combat wolf-packs of German U-Boats as they attacked allied supply convoys in the Northern Atlantic. Modern navies deploy ASW methods and technologies to protect global sea lanes, screen for carrier battle groups or task forces, and target ballistic missile submarines (boomers) operating in deep waters.

Armored Personnel Carriers (APCs)

A broad term used to describe armored military vehicles that are designed to transport personnel and equipment in combat zones. Sometimes they are called "battle taxis". Though the term "APC" has been used to describe many vehicles armed with light and heavy weaponry, the term originally described vehicles that are armored solely for defensive purposes, shielding troops as they are transported to combat. APCs have become somewhat synonymous with Infantry Fighting Vehicles (IFVs) in the modern era, and the terms are often used interchangeably.

Asymmetric Warfare (AW)

Warfare where the relative strength of belligerents is imbalanced, necessitating a strategy in which the weaker belligerent tailors its approach to enable it to engage the stronger belligerent on near-equal terms. Irregular warfare, Hybrid Warfare, unconventional warfare, and guerilla warfare are all variants of asymmetric conflict that allow small actors to engage more powerful enemies.

Ballistic Missile Submarines

Nuclear submarines that are designed to patrol in deep water, armed with Inter-Continental Ballistic Missiles (ICBMs) equipped with nuclear warheads. Also known in the submarine community as "boomers", these submarines give nations a stealthy and survivable nuclear deterrence. Any nation that fires a ballistic missile at a country with ballistic missile submarines can be assured that there will be a return volley.

Battalion Tactical Group

A Russian tactical formation that is constructed around a regiment or brigade's contract soldiers, who are concentrated into a single line or maneuver battalion (typically a motorized rifle battalion that is based on the BMP-3 or BTR-M). This single infantry battalion is complemented with up to the entire regiment's or brigade's armor, fire support, ISR, and support assets. This gives Russian Ground Forces a basic tactical unit that is legally deployable and, at least on paper, is capable of out-gunning and destroying units of much greater size by engaging their components in detail.

Blitzkrieg

A German term coined by the press during WW2 referring to the rapid advance of armored divisions to penetrate or out-flank static enemy lines. Characterized by bold flanking maneuvers and tightly coordinated close air support, Generals Heinz Guderian and Erwin Rommel became famous (or infamous) for encircling and defeating numerically superior enemy forces using Blitzkrieg tactics. The classic WW2 example of Blitzkrieg tactics was the German invasion of neutral Belgium, planned by General (later Field Marshal) Erich von Manstein and led by General Guderian in the field. France was defended by the mighty Maginot Line, which stood as a formidable obstacle to any invasion from the East, so General Guderian's panzer divisions outflanked the Maginot Line and British Expeditionary Forces in Belgium by thrusting an armored spearhead through the Ardenne Forest. The Ardenne was considered impassable for tanks, so the Wehrmacht achieved nearly total surprise. The maneuver created a breakout between the British Expeditionary Forces in Belgium and the Maginot Line in France. The encircled British Expeditionary

Forces were driven into the English Channel at Dunkirk, and then German forces wheeled around to advance on Paris. The scattered and logistically enfeebled French troops were unable to present more than token resistance to the German advance and France was forced to capitulate.

Blue Water Navy

A navy that can operate competently far from a state's own shores with a global mission and capacity for open-ocean dominance. Blue water navies are generally characterized by sophisticated deep-water vessels that can each operate as a component of a task force, often centered around an aircraft carrier or other capital ship, and an extensive network of overseas bases to support logistics and supply. The U.S. Navy is universally recognized as the world's premier blue water navy and is capable of unparalleled global reach in multiple oceans and theaters simultaneously. The Royal Navy and French Marine Nationale are also generally recognized as having true blue water navies, and they can support at least one major power projection mission across the globe at a time. The Japanese Maritime Defense Force also appears to be emerging as a true blue water navy. India, China, and Russia are also considered to have blue water navies with multi-regional capacities, although they lack real global reach.

Carpet Bombing

Also known as saturation bombing, carpet bombing is usually performed by multi-engine strategic bombers with massive payload capacity. Large area bombardments incrementally inflict damage in every part of a selected area of land. Carpet bombing was a pillar of the total war concept deployed in WW2, where the totality of a country's population, industries, and resources are mobilized to defeat other nations. Carpet bombing was used to completely destroy industries, city centers, and infrastructure in the United Kingdom, France, Germany, Japan, and the Soviet Union throughout the war.

Casus Belli

An act or event that provokes war or is used to justify war. On June 28, 1914, the assassination of Austrian Archduke Franz Ferdinand by a 19-year-old Bosnian Serb was the *casus belli* for Austria's declaration of war against Serbia. Due to the spider web of alliances between Europe's Great Powers, the assassination created a domino effect of war declarations that led to Germany's invasion of France through neutral Belgium, precipitating World War I (known as the Great War in Europe).

Clandestine Operations

Missions conducted by agents of a nation-state in a hostile or denied environment where the fact that an operation took place at all is concealed (black propaganda, sabotage, and cyber intrusions).

Close Air Support (CAS)

CAS refers to air strikes by fixed or rotary-winged aircraft against hostile targets that are in proximity to friendly forces, requiring detailed coordination of each air mission with movement and fires of the ground force component.

Combined Arms Maneuver

The application of all the elements of ground forces combat power (infantry, artillery, armor, scout or reconnaissance) in unified action to defeat enemy ground forces or to seize, occupy, and defend land areas.

Commissar

Commissars of the Soviet Union were mid-level magistrates that served as political officers to oversee the implementation of party doctrine in institutions or oversee collectivization and centralized economic planning.

Command and Control (C2)

Organizational and technical attributes and processes that employ human, physical, and informational resources to solve problems and accomplish missions. C2 generally refers to the processes wielded by a commanding officer to deploy, communicate with, and maneuver troops on the battlefield.

Command and Control Intelligence, Surveillance, Reconnaissance (C2ISR)

Command and Control measures to effectively deploy a unit's intelligence, surveillance, and reconnaissance (ISR) assets to satisfy the commander's priority information requirements (PIR). C2ISR is often used synonymously with Command, Control, Communications, Computers, Intelligence, Surveillance, and Reconnaissance (C4ISR), which simply adds the terms Communications and Computers in order to convey how effective command and control is achieved through computer network operations (CNO) on the modern battlefield.

Communications Intelligence (COMINT)

A subordinate field of SIGINT that deals with messages or voice information derived from the interception of communications signals in the electro-magnetic spectrum.

Computer Network Operations (CNO)

CNO refers to activities by militaries and intelligence services conducted through computer networks to gain informational superiority and deny the enemy information resources. Operating under the assumption that information equals power, CNO leverages sophisticate IT infrastructure to move an ever-increasing volume of relevant information in support of military decision-making through a network of computers and other electronic devices, optimizing these networks to gain informational superiority while denying the enemy this enabling capability. Computational processing is increasingly being pushed to the edge of the cloud (down to the level of the individual soldier on the battlefield) through mobile devices and portable data hubs. CNO enables the collection of enormous volumes of battlefield data and supports refining all this data into actionable intelligence.

Counterinsurgency (COIN)

Comprehensive civilian and military operations that simultaneously defeat and contain insurgencies while addressing their root causes (economic, cultural, and political). The United States conducted COIN missions in Vietnam, Afghanistan, and Iraq. COIN operations are often accompanied by military assistance to train indigenous military and police forces, counterterrorism missions, and economic aid.

Counterintelligence

Activities conducted to defend armed services or intelligence agencies from infiltration or exploitation by operatives of foreign powers. Counterintelligence prevents or disrupts not only basic information gathering, but also espionage, sabotage, assassinations, and other covert or clandestine operations conducted on behalf of foreign powers.

Counterterrorism (CT)

A mission that supports military tactics, techniques, and strategies that government, military, law enforcement, and intelligence agencies use to combat or prevent terrorism conducted by violent extremist organizations, international terrorist organizations, hostage takers, or insurgencies. Counterterrorism is often associated with direct action or counterinsurgency.

Coup d'état

The removal of an existing government from power, usually through violent means. The expression translates literally from French as "blow of state".

Coup de Main

A sudden surprise attack, especially one made by an army during war that achieves all of its objectives in a single blow. Russia's sudden invasion and annexation of Crimea, in particular the KSSO's rapid seizure of Crimean Parliament, is a good example of a *coup de main*.

Covert Action

A term used to describe deniable or non-attributable activities conducted by special operations units or intelligence operatives. Covert action is frequently used to refer to missions that nation-states cannot openly admit to conducting as their recognition could affect diplomacy or global opinion (examples include sabotage, election interference, or assassination). Covert action is also an American doctrinal term that is used to describe activities conducted by order of the President of the United States (POTUS) through a Presidential Finding that authorizes the CIA to conduct covert activities during peacetime. Operation Neptune's Spear, the mission to kill Osama bin Laden, was authorized as a covert action through a Presidential Finding.

Defense-In-Depth

A defense strategy attributed to the Middle Ages when castles had multiple concentric obstacles (a mote, outer wall, battlements, inner wall, or inner tower) for a conqueror to negotiate or bypass before the fortress could be fully secured. In modern usage, the phrase refers to the use of vast expanses of territory or open terrain to stretch out an invading army, making it impossible for the invaders to bring supplies forward or concentrate firepower, thinning them to the point of impotency. Soviet defenders stretched out the German Wehrmacht during WW2 by using defense-in-depth, ultimately breaking the German advance in the Battles of Stalingrad, Leningrad, and Moscow.

Direct Action (DA)

A special operations mission characterized by short duration strikes against limited discrete objectives and other small-scale offensive actions conducted in hostile, denied, or politically sensitive environments that employ specialized military capabilities to seize, destroy, capture, exploit, recover, or damage designated targets.

DIU or Defense Intelligence of the Ministry Defense of Ukraine (Ukrainian: **Головне управління розвідки Міністерства оборони України***)*

Defense Intelligence of the Ministry of Defense of Ukraine is the Ukrainian counterpart to the Russian GRU. Its responsibilities include: counterterrorism, counterintelligence, combating subversive activities, combating organized crime, cooperation with foreign militaries and non-state actors. Additionally, Ukraine's special operations forces are operationally controlled by DIU.

Electronic Intelligence (ELINT)

A subordinate field of SIGINT that deals in gathering non-communications related intelligence from electromagnetic emissions such as radar, surface-to-air missile systems, signal jammers, and similar capabilities.

Electronic Warfare (EW)

The deployment of measures to deny an opponent the use of the electromagnetic spectrum (EMS) for communications, radar, targeting systems, satellites, GPS, and computer hardware. Subordinate missions include Electronic Attack (EA)—the use of the EM spectrum to attack personnel, facilities, or equipment; Electronic Protection (EP)—the user of the EM spectrum to protect friendly forces and equipment from enemy attacks; and Electronic Support (ES)—the tactical use of the EM spectrum to detect, intercept, identify, locate, or localize sources of EM energy.

Fabian Strategy

Quintus Fabius Maximus Verrucosus was a Consul that consolidated and led Roman forces after Rome's disastrous defeat at Lake Trasimene at the hands of Carthaginian General Hannibal Barca during the Second Punic War. The Battle of Lake Trasimene was the latest of several catastrophic defeats suffered by the Romans, and, rather than allow the city to be seized with panic, the Senate voted emergency powers to Fabius as Dictator. Fabius needed to preserve the Roman Army to keep the Carthaginians from marching on Rome, but knew he could not defeat Hannibal in the field. Instead of seeking a decisive battle, Fabius burned fields, raided supply lines, and killed Hannibal's foraging parties—wearing the Carthaginian Army down through attrition. His critics eventually wrested power from him and pursued Hannibal into a trap at the Battle of Cannae in 216 BC. Cannae is remembered as one of history's greatest military defeats, and Rome was again seized with panic. The Roman people looked to Fabius, now a mere Senator, for a pathway forward, and, though he was never again bestowed with a military command, all of his proposals in the Senate were adopted without debate, setting Rome on the long pathway to victory over Hannibal and Carthage.

Fait Accompli

A thing that has already happened or been decided before those affected learn about it, leaving them with no option but to accept it. Russia's sudden seizure and annexation of Crimea while the Ukrainian government in Kyiv was in disarray is a recent example of a *fait accompli*.

Federation Assembly

The Federation Assembly is the Russian parliament. It is a bicameral legislature. The Duma is the lower house (similar to the U.S. House of Representatives), and the Federation Council is the upper house (similar to the U.S. Senate). The Prime Minister of Russia is the appointed leader of the majority in the Duma and is the head of Government, while the President is independently elected and is the head of State.

Fifth Generation Warfare

Fifth-generation warfare is data-driven, non-kinetic military action that leverages pre-existing cognitive biases in the population to manipulate an observer's context in order to achieve a desired outcome. Fifth-generation warfare is by nature non-attributable and is designed to create a de facto victory without the need for kinetic military force. Supporting technologies and techniques include: propaganda, cyberattacks, social engineering, social media exploitation, mass surveillance, electronic warfare.

Foreign Internal Defense (FID)

Military assistance activities, often conducted by SOF, to train foreign military and police units in stability operations, policing, or counterinsurgency. FID is usually conducted in support of a synchronized and multi-disciplinary (political, economic, cultural, security, financial, or informational) approach to combating an active or latent insurgency in a foreign state.

Forward Observers

A military artillery observer or spotter is responsible for directing artillery and mortar fire onto a target. Forward observers or Joint Terminal Attack Controllers (JTACs) may also direct close air support or naval gunfire support.

FSB (Federal Security Service) (Russian: **Федеральная служба безопасности***)*

The domestic security service, federal law enforcement, secret police, and counterintelligence service of the Russian Federation. The FSB is the Russian counterpart to the American FBI or British MI5 but has vastly more power to suppress political dissidents in Russia. The FSB also plays a role in conducting foreign intelligence operations in the Commonwealth of Independent States (CIS) under a series of diplomatic agreements. After the Soviet collapse, FSB inherited the majority of the KGB's Directorates and now plays a prominent role in Moscow as the leading special service.

Geographic Combatant Command (GCC)—United States

Also referred to as Unified Combatant Commands, GCC's are American joint military commands that cover an entire geographic theater of war and are composed of units from two or more service branches of the United States Armed Services. There are seven GCCs around the world (USNORTHCOM, USSOUTHCOM, USAFRICOM, USEUCOM, USINDOPACOM, USCENTCOM, USSPACECOM), and each are established as the highest echelons of military commands in order to provide effective command and control of all U.S. military forces within their mutually exclusive geographic jurisdictions.

Green Water Navy

A navy that is capable of operating in a state's littoral zones (seas, lakes, rivers, gulfs, bays, and ocean shoreline). Green water navies are capable of protecting a country's coastline and may be able to exert regional influence on the open ocean, but they are not capable of conducting global combat operations or ensuring access to the world's sea lanes.

GRU or Main Intelligence Directorate (Russian: **Гла́вное разве́дывательное управле́ние***)*

Now commonly referred to as the Main Directorate (GU), the GRU is Russia's military intelligence service. GRU runs many more foreign intelligence operatives than Russia's lead foreign intelligence service, the SVR, and governs the tactical collection of intelligence to support battlefield planning and C2 for the Russian Armed Services. GRU is also the lead Russian organization responsible for planning military interventions and hybrid wars.

Guerilla Warfare (GW)

Military operations conducted by small groups of combatants, characterized as paramilitaries, armed civilians, irregulars, or militia, that make use of indirect or indecisive attacks (ambushes, sabotage, raids, petty warfare, hit-and-run tactics) and mobility to fight larger and less-mobile conventional forces. Guerilla warfare closely coincides with the American doctrinal mission of unconventional warfare,

Human Intelligence (HUMINT)

A category of intelligence derived from information collected and provided by human sources. HUMINT is commonly recognized as the defining practice in traditional espionage and spy craft.

Hunter-Killer Submarines

Also known as attack submarines, hunter-killer submarines are designed to hunt down and eliminate the larger and less maneuverable "boomers", reducing the damage that a nuclear power could inflict during a nuclear confrontation. Hunter-Killer submarines are also used to hunt surface fleets and commercial shipping, denying open access to the world's oceans. The German Kriegsmarine notably used these tactics in the Battle of the Atlantic in WW2 to choke-off the United Kingdom's supplies coming from the United States and Canada.

Infantry Fighting Vehicle (IFV)

An armored combat vehicle that is designed and equipped primarily to transport an infantry squad (5-15 soldiers), armed with an integral cannon of at least 20mm caliber and sometimes an anti-tank missile launcher. Armament and a designated offensive role separate IFVs from APCs, although the terms are often used interchangeably.

Information Operations (IO)

The deployment of measures such as electronic warfare (EW), computer network operations (CNO), military information support operations (MISO or psychological operations), military deception (MILDEC), and operations security (OPSEC) to disrupt adversarial decision-making, while insulating and protecting information processes and decision-making of friendly forces.

Intelligence, Surveillance, Reconnaissance (ISR)

ISR is an umbrella term that refers to activities and systems for acquiring and processing information needed by national security decision-makers and military commanders at the strategic, operational, or tactical levels.

Intelligence, Surveillance, Targeting Acquisition, Reconnaissance (ISTAR)

ISTAR links several battlefield information collection functions together to assist a combat force in employing its sensors and managing the information they gather. Information is collected on the battlefield through observation both by deployed soldiers and a variety of electronic sensors. Surveillance, target acquisition, and reconnaissance are methods of obtaining this battlefield information. The information is then passed to intelligence personnel for analysis and then to the commander and his staff to build a target package.

Inter-Continental Ballistic Missile (ICBM)

A missile with a minimum range of 5,500 kilometers (3,400 mi), often designed for nuclear weapons delivery. They are commonly launched from silos, submarines, or mobile vehicles and follow a preset trajectory into the upper atmosphere and then down onto a target. The first ICBM was the German V-2 rocket, which was loaded with a conventional warhead and fired indiscriminately on London in order to break the British will to war. In modern times, ICBMs are the favored means of delivering a nuclear payload. Great powers retain them to maintain nuclear deterrence, which all but ensures that the regime will never be toppled by a hostile foreign power.

Irregular Warfare

An umbrella term that describes a spectrum of activities pertaining to violent struggle among state and non-state actors for legitimacy and influence over relevant populations within a strategically important region. Those activities may include but are not limited to: counterinsurgency, counterterrorism, unconventional warfare, information operations, foreign internal defense, low-intensity conflict, and asymmetric warfare.

Joint Intelligence Preparation of the Environment (JIPOE)

Intelligence collection, analysis, and dissemination to relevant decision-makers in preparation for combat operations. JIPOE is conducted by the intelligence community to support the Joint Force Commander's mission planning and decision-making process.

Joint Operations

Doctrine that integrates and deploys units of a nation's army, navy, and air force under one unified command that synchronizes and coordinates mutually supporting missions under a unified combat plan. Joint operations were first developed as a NATO operating concept, but after overwhelming victories in Operation Desert Storm and Operation Iraqi Freedom, adversarial militaries like Russia and China have begun training officers in joint operations as well. It remains unclear whether any military outside of NATO has been able to indoctrinate and train its officers to conduct joint operations.

Joint Force Commander (JFC)

A single commanding officer that oversees a joint task force of ground, air, naval, and special operations forces, coordinating capabilities of each component branch in order to achieve the greatest effect on the battlespace.

KGB or Committee for State Security(Russian: **Комитет государственной безопасности***)*

The Soviet secret police agency that eventually evolved into the primary security service and intelligence service of the Soviet Union. After the dissolution of the Soviet Union, the KGB's directorates split apart. The majority of the KGB's directorates were reorganized under the newly founded FSB, while the foreign intelligence apparatus (the 1st Chief Directorate) developed into the SVR.

Low-Intensity Conflict

Low-Intensity Conflict is conducted in hostile or denied environments where there is a nominal civil government and de facto peace. In low-intensity conflict, conventional forces conduct peacekeeping operations while SOF conduct foreign internal defense, counterinsurgency, and counterterrorism missions, in order to build out military and police capabilities while disrupting insurgency networks, funding, propaganda, and recruitment.

Maskirovka (Russian: **маскировка***)*

A Russian term for Camouflage that refers to deception efforts to hide the Russian hand instigating the conflict. Maskirovka is a core component of campaign planning in hybrid warfare, and it allows Russia to influence its strategic environment without diplomatic, economic, financial, or military reprisals, at least until after the *fait accompli*. Under Maskirovka Russia must influence the development of a crisis without the enemy detecting its signature. It is typical for Russian operatives and informants to penetrate and destabilize all levels of the target government. Russian SOF, intelligence operatives, and private military companies use working relations with local paramilitaries to employ them in seizing key objectives. When Russian Spetsnaz and SOF are deployed to secure key objectives, they operate without insignia or markings and the Kremlin denies their presence.

Mechanized Infantry

Infantry that relies on armored personnel carriers or infantry fighting vehicles for transport and mobility. In Blitzkrieg, tank battalions or brigades or divisions require a complement of mechanized infantry to protect the flanks of armored spearheads from counterattacks. Russia classifies its infantry divisions and brigades as "motorized" infantry, gaining mobility from APCs and IFVs, but by western standards this would classify them as "mechanized" infantry.

MI5 (Security Service)

The United Kingdom's domestic security and counterintelligence service. It is the British counterpart to the American FBI or Russian FSB.

MI6 (Secret Intelligence Service)

The United Kingdom's foreign intelligence service. It is the British counterpart to the American CIA or Russian SVR.

Military Assistance

A mission where military advisors are sent to train, advise, assist, or lead local indigenous forces in combat operations. Military assistance also includes providing arms, military platforms and hardware, financial support, and diplomatic assistance.

Military Deception (MILDEC)

Activities deployed to mislead adversary decision-makers into taking actions detrimental to the adversary, often achieved by amplifying the fog of war via psychological operations, visual deception, or other methods.

Military District—Russian Federation

Russian military forces are distributed between four military districts Western, Central, Eastern, Southern, with an additional district in the Northern Fleet Joint Strategic Command. Military districts are usually commanded by a Colonel General or an Admiral.

Military Industrial Complex or Defense Industrial Complex

A mutually beneficial, informal alliance between a nation's private businesses, companies, or corporations and a nation's military or policymakers to supply military weapons, hardware, equipment, systems, and platforms. The military industrial complex generally constitutes a country's standing capacity to supply military hardware and support military activity without the government having to nationalize industries specifically to meet the production requirements of an active war. In large nations, the military industrial complex is insulated from market forces and production is closely coordinated with politicians and military officers to meet the needs of the military as it conducts day-to-day operations.

Military Information Support Operations (MISO)

Also known as Psychological Operations (PSYOP), MISO refers to psychological methods to move public opinion in general, or sentiments of specific targeted groups, in a certain direction. This typically includes deploying propaganda to generate a narrative that rallies public support for military operations and reduces public support for the enemy.

Motorized Infantry

In western terminology, motorized infantry is infantry that is transported by trucks or other motor vehicles for mobility, but in Russia the term is applied to infantry that relies on armored personnel carriers or infantry fighting vehicles for transport (termed Mechanized Infantry in the West).

Multiple Independent Reentry Vehicle (MIRV)

An exo-atmospheric payload (the missile exits the atmosphere and must re-enter in order to descend on its target) on an ICBM containing multiple warheads that can each be programmed to launch from high altitude down on many independent targets. MIRV warheads were perhaps the most frightening innovation of the Cold War. Neither the United States nor the Soviet Union dared to launch an ICBM at one another in a preemptive strike because a counter-volley from even one MIRV warhead would destroy a dozen major cities and kill many millions of people

Network-Centric Warfare

Doctrine in which advanced IT capabilities, robust computer networking, and satellite communications are deployed to give geographically dispersed forces informational superiority over an adversary, enabling the Joint Force Commander to maneuver limited resources and precision fires to the points of greatest impact.

Non-Contact Warfare

Non-contact warfare is characterized both by kinetic and non-kinetic components. In the non-kinetic sense, non-contact warfare deploys EW measures, cyberattacks, and MISO to disrupt or disorient the enemy's C4ISR processes without direct contact. In the kinetic sense, non-contact warfare deploys autonomous systems, stealth aircraft, boats, and long-range precision strike munitions to strike the enemy without direct contact between each belligerent's military forces. Analysts often evoke non-contact warfare when describing fifth-generation or sixth-generation warfare.

Operational Environment (OE)

The land, sea, air, space, and cyber network environments where military forces conduct operations. It includes any adversaries, allies, neutrals, systems, and subsystems.

Operational Preparation of the Environment (OPE)

Activities that prepare the battlefield for introducing larger ground forces. Security analysts often break OPE down into three basic taskings: orientation activities, target development, and preliminary engagement. OPE can also be understood temporally as pre-crisis activities, pilot team operations, and advanced force operations (AFO). In the American conceptualization, MISO and UW are also often components of OPE.

Operational Security (OPSEC)

A process of identifying friendly critical information and employing procedures to shield it from adversarial exploitation. OPSEC tactics, techniques, and procedures are integrated into every military unit and intelligence agency in the world because of the vast potential damage an adversary could do if it had access to sensitive information.

Panzer

A German term for "tank" that was coined in the interbellum period of the 1920s and 1930s. The Germans innovated by equipping tanks with radios, removing them from an infantry support role, and concentrating them into independent divisions for armored spearheads and bold flanking maneuvers.

Pilot Team Operations

Pilot teams make contact with local allies, establish a presence, set up communications to higher command, and confirm preliminary assessments. Under the framework of OPE, pilot teams are usually the first units to infiltrate the combat zone and facilitate the introduction of SOF or SMUs and conventional forces.

Pre-Crisis Activities

Activities to prepare for a potential conflict that are performed during peacetime. They may include area assessments, infrastructure surveys, tactical training taught to host nation troops, and joint training exercises. In the American conceptualization, pre-crisis activities are defined by making friends, building relationships, and learning about the area.

Presidential Finding

The Congress requires that the President of the United States must notify the Congress if a covert action is being authorized during peacetime. The President must issue a Presidential Finding (under Title 50 Authorities) to Congress that specifies who is authorized to fund the covert action and clarifies that the action does not violate the Constitution. The Presidential Finding imposes on the President and subordinate Executive Branch agencies a requirement for a strict internal review without infringing on the Constitutional prerogatives of the President as Commander-in-Chief.

Priority Information Requirements (PIR)

Intelligence requirements for mission planning and execution that a commander has anticipated and enumerated as a priority in his task of planning and decision making. PIRs may include, but are not limited to, the location of the enemy, enemy activity, obstacles in the physical terrain, or the presence and activity of local non-combatants.

Reconnaissance

Basic taskings conducted by infantry, SOF, aerial surveillance, or scouts to observe a locality, pathway of travel, or key terrain in order to support the Commander's PIR.

Reflexive Control

A sustained information campaign that offers the enemy a narrative based on carefully selected information, either distributed as propaganda or intentionally leaked, meant to mislead the enemy. Reflexive control employs the art of deception and misinformation in order to create advantages on the battlefield and is meant to work in tandem with kinetic military operations, increasing the chances for operational success. A historical example of Reflexive Control comes from the Argentinian, Chilean, and Peruvian Chapters of the Spanish-American Wars for Independence. General Jose de San Martin was a master of reflexive control, and spent his time in Buenos Aires (where he was recruiting and training an army), sowing disinformation among Spanish Royalist Forces occupying Chile as to which passes he would take in crossing the Andes. In 1818, when General San Martin finally led his army through the Andes Mountains, his invasion achieved complete surprise and he became known as *"El Libertador de Argentina, Chile, y Peru."*

Sabotage

Activities conducted to deliberately damage, destroy, disrupt, or obstruct systems, equipment, institutions, infrastructure, or processes for military or political gain. For example, Russia may deploy agents to sabotage Ukrainian cellular infrastructure, preventing communications to or from an area where Spetsnaz units have been deployed to seize a key operational objective.

SBU or Security Service of Ukraine (Ukrainian: **Служба безпеки України***)*

SBU is the leading law enforcement agency, leading intelligence agency, and security agency of Ukraine. SBU's missions include: counterintelligence, protection of national statehood, counterterrorism, cyber security, protection of state secrets.

Security Force Assistance (SFA)

Military assistance activities that are conducted by conventional forces to train host nation field-grade officers in operations, logistics, intelligence, communications, and other functions necessary for long term sustainment of combat forces at the company (50-130 soldiers), battalion (4-6 companies or 300-800 troops), or brigade (3 to 6 battalions or 3,000-5,000 troops) level. With the necessary organizational infrastructure and leadership in place, SOF units conduct the FID mission, training soldiers and junior officers in tactical level combat tasks. SFA creates the Operational-level C2 and support to sustain combat operations, while FID (usually conducted by SOF) creates the tactical-level combat capability.

Sixth-Generation Warfare

Sixth-generation warfare deploys long-range precision-guided munitions, armed UAVs, sophisticated electronic warfare (EW) systems, and cyberattacks to disable enemy infrastructure in order to create windows of opportunity for further kinetic attacks. Sixth-generation warfare leverages technology to reduce troop exposure while delivering kinetic force against enemy forces.

Signals Intelligence (SIGINT)

A category of strategic intelligence collection characterized by the interception, decryption, and analysis of basic emissions or signals the electro-magnetic spectrum (EMS). SIGINT is generally broken down into two primary categories: communications intelligence (COMINT) and electronic intelligence (ELINT).

Siloviki (Russian: силовики́).

Russian military, diplomatic, and intelligence officials, many of whom were trained in the Soviet era, that serve as the talent pool for senior leadership and policy making positions in the Government.

Skeleton Units

Units in the Russian Ground Forces that were manned, led, and represented by real officers, but only had troops on paper. In the event of a large war, mass conscriptions would ensue, filling the skeleton unit ranks. These units were kept on the Russian registry to maintain a theoretical overmatch against NATO ground forces without having to support the staggering personnel expenses inherent in sustaining such a massive standing army.

Special Forces

An umbrella term used in Western military lexicon that generally refers to Special Operations Forces. The term Special Forces was popularized by U.S. Army Special Forces (also commonly known as the Green Berets), but the term has come to refer to SOF in a general sense.

Special Operations

NATO defines special operations as military activities conducted as, "specially designated, organized, selected, trained, and equipped forces using unconventional techniques and modes of employment." This very broad and intentionally vague definition supports missions such as direct action, special reconnaissance, foreign internal defense, hostage rescue, counterterrorism, unconventional warfare, irregular warfare, counterinsurgency, counterintelligence, civil affairs, psychological operations, counter narcotics, and counter proliferation of weapons of mass destruction (WMDs).

Special Operations Forces (SOF)

Elite forces that are specially selected, trained, equipped, and supported to perform missions of high complexity or sensitivity using unconventional tactics, techniques, and procedures in politically sensitive, hostile, or denied environments. SOF units are tasked with missions that are too specialized for an infantry unit and require personnel that have unique capabilities and training to fulfill mission requirements. SOF is sometimes characterized as a middle of the road choice between covert activities conducted by intelligence operatives in peacetime, and overt activities conducted by soldiers in war. SOF missions often straddle the watershed between traditional military fieldcraft and intelligence tradecraft (unconventional warfare, special reconnaissance, counterterrorism).

Special Services

An umbrella term that refers to departments or services of governments that have a unique or leading role in the state security apparatus or intelligence community, ostensibly with privileged access to political leadership. Examples include the British MI6, Israeli Mossad, the Russian GRU, or the American FBI.

Spetsnaz

An Eastern Bloc umbrella term that originally referred specifically to the elite units of the Soviet Ground Forces that were subordinate to the GRU, but now pertains to almost all specialized Russian military and police units.

Special Mission Unit (SMU)

The American Joint Publication 3-05.1: Joint Special Operations Task Force defines an SMU as, "a generic term to represent a group of operations and support personnel from designated organizations that is task-organized to perform highly classified activities." The term is sometimes used more broadly to refer to Special Operations Forces that are not subordinate to the regional command structure or Joint Force Commander but are directly tasked by political leadership for missions that are either highly sensitive or require extraordinary military resources and support from national-level intelligence. Plausible examples of SMUs include: British Army Special Air Service (SAS), Israeli Sayeret Matkal, and Russian KSSO.

Special Reconnaissance (SR)

A mission that is conducted by small units of highly trained military personnel in hostile, denied, or politically sensitive environments where operatives avoid direct combat or detection by the enemy and collect intelligence to satisfy the commander's PIR (enemy activity, location, movement, order of battle, target analysis, networks, logistics, area assessments, and similar information). The internationally recognized Law of War set forth in the Hague and Geneva Conventions lists SR as a legitimate military activity provided it is conducted by soldiers in uniform. The Law of War does not afford spies the same rights as soldiers, and armies are within their rights to execute enemy "spies" (provided they are given fair trial) in order to maintain OPSEC during time of war. During WW2, Adolf Hitler's infamous Commando Order decreed that all enemy soldier-commandos caught carrying out missions on the continent, either in uniform or civilian attire, were to be executed as spies. To explicitly prohibit such atrocities, the Law of War specifies that individuals in uniform apprehended performing the SR mission must be afforded the rights of soldiers as prisoners of war (POW).

Subversion

Activities conducted by intelligence operatives to undermine the power or authority of an established government or institution. Examples include bribing police officials, instigating rioting, blackmailing politicians, or deploying targeted propaganda.

SVR or Foreign Intelligence Service (Russian: **Служба внешней разведки***)*

SVR is the foreign intelligence service of the Russian Federation. It is the Russian counterpart to the American CIA, Israeli Mossad, or British M16. SVR was created from the remnants of the 1st Chief Directorate of the KGB (Russian: Пе́рвое гла́вное управле́ние, known by the English acronym PGU). The SVR is known in Russia as a chic and sophisticated intelligence service and has a reputation internationally as one of the world's most effective in collecting HUMINT. SVR deploys spies abroad under both official diplomatic sanction, and deep cover operatives from the highly secretive Department of Operations subgroup "Illegal Networks".

Tactics, Techniques, and Procedures (TTPs)

TTPs is an umbrella phrase that refer to policies, methods, and practices for integrating equipment and weapons into a human performance system. For example, soldiers have TTPs for breaching doors with explosives that integrate tactics for approaching the door, techniques for placing explosives on the door, and procedures for ensuring all personnel are beyond a minimum safe distance from the explosive blast.

Terminal Guidance

Any guidance system that is primarily or solely active during the "terminal phase" just before the weapon impacts its target. The phrase is often used to describe the role of forward observers or JTACs in guiding ordnance (missiles, bombs, and other munitions) released from aircraft onto target.

Terrorism

Terrorism constitutes a deliberate attack on a civilian population by non-state actors in order to coerce the government or specific political leaders into making extra-legal policy concessions (independence, rights, elections, monetary incentives, or trade embargos).

Theater of War

The entire land, sea, and air area that is or may become involved directly in military operations during wartime.

Title 10 Authorities

Authorities under Title 10 of the U.S. Code that specify the structure and mission of the U.S. Armed Services over which the President has Article II authority as Commander-in-Chief. Congress must declare war for the U.S. armed forces to operate in a Title 10 environment. The House Armed Services Committee and Senate Armed Services Committee share oversight of the U.S. Armed Services, particularly through control of the budget, but the President has total authority to conduct military operations with nearly all available national resources.

Title 50 Authorities

Title 50 outlines the role of War and National Defense in the U.S. Code. In relation to this text, this includes the peacetime parameters of the President's role as Commander-in-Chief. These authorities require enhanced Congressional oversight, especially in regard to the CIA's authorities to collect intelligence, counterintelligence, and conduct covert action. These activities fall under the oversight of the House Permanent

Select Committee on Intelligence and the Senate Select Committee on Intelligence.

Traditional Military Activities

Activities defined under Title 10 of the U.S. Code that are conducted by uniformed soldiers, under the direction of a military commander, and related to hostilities that involve U.S. military forces.

Ultimatum

A demand where fulfillment is requested in a specified period of time and backed up by a threat in case of non-compliance. In diplomacy, particularly in the English tradition, it is implied that non-compliance will be perceived as a hostile act, if not an open declaration of war. After the 9/11 attacks, the United States issued an ultimatum to the Taliban regime in Afghanistan to arrest and extradite Osama bin Laden.

Unconventional Warfare (UW)

Activities conducted to enable a resistance movement or insurgency to coerce, disrupt, or overthrow a government or occupying power by operating through or with an underground (partisans that serve as an insurgency's shadow government, public affairs, and information collection component), auxiliary (partisans that serve as an insurgency's means of logistics and supply component), or guerrilla force (partisans that serve as an insurgency's armed military component) in a hostile or denied area.

Unmanned Aerial Vehicle (UAV)

An aircraft or drone without a human pilot on board. UAVs require a ground-based controller and a system of communications between the two. Militaries often use UAVs as a low-cost, low-risk method of conducting intelligence, surveillance, or reconnaissance, or as a means of attacking ground targets and delivering flexible close air support to ground units.

Vnezapnost (Russian: **внезапность***)*

A Russian term that directly translates to "surprise", referring to the speedy operational deployment and maneuver of forces. Under Vnezapnost, Russian Spetsnaz, SOF, intelligence operatives conduct advanced force operations to prepare the operational environment for the introduction of heavy ground forces. Elite Russian Ground Forces rapidly maneuver to seize limited objectives such as infrastructure, thoroughfares, and government buildings. Russian air forces quickly achieve air superiority and initiate close air support operations for rapidly advancing ground forces, and large conventional ground forces reinforce and entrench Russian-held territory. The Russian advance is completed before the enemy has time to organize and react, effectively creating a *fait accompli*.

Works Cited

Chapter 1:

1. Berzins, Janis. "Current Russia Military Affairs: The Russian Way of Warfare." U.S. Army War College and Strategic Studies Institute, 2018.

2. Mastriano, Douglas, et al. "Project 1704: A U.S. Army War College Analysis of Russian Strategy in Eastern Europe, an Appropriate U.S. Response, and the Implications for U.S. Landpower." Edited by LTC Derek O'Malley. U.S. Army War College, 2015.

3. Fedyk, Nicholas. "Russian New Generation Warfare: Theory, Practice, and Lessons for U.S. Strategists." Small Wars Journal. https://smallwarsjournal.com/jrnl/art/russian-new-generation-warfare-theory-practice-and-lessons-for-us-strategists-0.

4. Friedman, George. "The Road to Four Months That Changed the World." Geopolitical Futures, November 12, 2019. https://geopoliticalfutures.com/the-road-to-four-months-that-changed-the-world/.

5. "Field Manual 100-20: Fundamentals of Low Intensity Conflict." GlobalSecurity.org.

https://www.globalsecurity.org/military/library/policy/army/fm/100-20/10020ch1.htm.

6. Gerasimov, Valery. "Contemporary Warfare and Current Issues for the Defense of the Country." Translated by Dr. Harold Orenstein. Speech, Academy of Military Sciences, March 2017.

7. Gerasimov, Valery. "Ценность науки в предвидении." Военно-промышленный курьер, February 27, 2013. http://www.vpk-news.ru/articles/14632.

8. Grau, Lester, and Charles Bartles. "Russian Aerial Operations in the Syrian War." In Russia's War in Syria: Assessing Russian Military Capabilities and Lessons Learned. Foreign Policy Research Institute, 2020.

9. Kasapoglu, Can. "Russia's Renewed Military Thinking: Non-Linear Warfare and Reflexive Control." NATO Defense College, Rome—No. 121, November 2015. http://www.ndc.nato.int/news/news.php?icode=877.

10. McDermott, Roger. "Russia's Entry to Sixth-Generation Warfare: the 'Non-Contact' Experiment in Syria." Jamestown Foundation, May 29, 2021. https://jamestown.org/program/russias-entry-to-sixth-generation-warfare-the-non-contact-experiment-in-syria/.

11. McDermott, Roger. "Russia's Network-Centric Warfare Capability." Real Clear Defense, October 31, 2018. https://www.realcleardefense.com/articles/2018/10/31/russias_network-centric_warfare_capability_113926.html.

12. McDermott, Roger. "Russia's 2015 National Security Strategy

Cements Strained Ties With U.S." The Jamestown Foundation, January 5, 2016.
https://jamestown.org/program/russias-2015-national-security-strategy-cements-strained-ties-with-us/.

13. Ministry of Defense. "Valery Gerasimov." Accessed [Date you accessed: August 25, 2023].
http://eng.mil.ru/en/management/deputy/more.htm?id=11113936@SD_Employee.

14. Radin, Andrew. "Hybrid Warfare in the Baltics: Threats and Potential Responses." Rand Corporation, 2017, 5-12.

15. Rumer, Eugene. "Current Russian Military Affairs: Russian Strategic Objectives: It's All About the State." U.S. Army War College Strategic Studies Institute, July 2018.

16. Savage, Patrick. "The Conventionality of Russia's Unconventional War." Traditional War, 2018.

17. Stent, Angela. "Current Russia Military Affairs: What Drives Russian Foreign Policy?" U.S. Army War College and Strategic Studies Institute, July 2018.

18. Stent, Angela. "Current Russia Military Affairs: What Drives Russian Foreign Policy." U.S. Army War College Strategic Studies Institute, July 2018.

19. The Radio Research Group. "An Introduction to Fifth Generation Warfare." Grey Dynamics, March 31, 2022.
https://greydynamics.com/an-introduction-to-fifth-generation-warfare/.

20. Thornton, Rod. "Current Russia Military Affairs: The Concept and Pace in Current Russian Military Thinking." U.S. Army War College and Strategic Studies Institute, July 2018.

21. U.S. Army Special Operations Command. "Little Green Men: A Primer on Modern Russian Unconventional Warfare, Ukraine 2013-2014." G-3X Sensitive Activities U.S. Army Special Operations Command, [Publication Year if Available].

22. Von Clausewitz, Carl. Vom Kriege (On War). Originally published in 1832. English translation, 1873.

23. Washington Times. "Putin Calls Collapse of the Soviet Union 'Catastrophe'." April 26, 2005. https://www.washingtontimes.com/news/2005/apr/26/20050426-120658-5687r/.

24. Wikipedia. "Charles Joseph Minard." Last modified May 10, 2023. https://en.wikipedia.org/wiki/Charles_Joseph_Minard

Chapter 2:

1. Charap, Samuel, Elina Treyger, and Edward Geist. "Understanding Russia's Intervention in Syria." Rand Corporation, 2019.

2. Encyclopedia Britannica. "Vladimir Putin, President of Russia." Last modified January 10, 2020. https://www.britannica.com/biography/Vladimir-Putin#ref330367.

3. Galeotti, Mark. Russia's Wars in Chechnya 1994-2009. Osprey Publishing, 2014.

4. Illarionov, Andrei. "The Russian Leadership's Preparation for War, 1999-2008." In The Guns of August 2008: Russia's War in Georgia, 49-84. Central Asia-Caucasus Institute of Johns Hopkins University's Paul H. Nitze School of Advanced International Studies, 2009.

5. McGrew, Isabel. "Putin: 'Managing' Democracy by Isabelle McGrew at the University of California Los Angeles." Democratic Erosion, March 15, 2018. https://www.democratic-erosion.com/2018/03/15/putin-managing-democracy-by-isabelle-mcgrew-university-of-california-los-angeles/.

6. Nilsson, Niklaus. "Russian Hybrid Tactics in Georgia." Central Asia-Caucasus Institute & Silk Road Studies Program, January 2018. https://silkroadstudies.org/resources/pdf/SilkRoadPapers/2018_01_Nilsson_Hybrid.pdf.

7. Ramani, Samuel. "Russia's New Hybrid Warfare in Africa." Italian Institute for International Political Studies, July 3, 2020. https://www.ispionline.it/en/pubblicazione/russias-new-hybrid-warfare-africa-26795.

8. Tsvetkova, Maria, and Anton Zverev. "Exclusive: Kremlin-linked contractors help guard Venezuela's Maduro." Thomson-Reuters, January 25, 2019. https://www.reuters.com/article/us-venezuela-politics-russia-exclusive/exclusive-kremlin-linked-contractors-help-guard-venezuelas-maduro-sources-idUSKCN1PJ22M?utm_source=feedburner&utm_medium=feed&utm_campaign=Feed%3A+quicksnailsfeed_simplylines+%28Simply+Lines+Drudge+RSS+Feed%29.

9. U.S. Army Special Operations Command. "Little Green Men: A Primer on Modern Russian Unconventional Warfare, Ukraine 2013-2014." G-3X Sensitive Activities, U.S. Army Special Operations Command.

Chapter 3:

1. Beehner, Lionel, Liam Collins, Steve Ferenzi, Robert Person, and Aaron Brantly. "Analyzing the Russian Way of War: Evidence from the 2008 Conflict with Georgia." Modern War Institute. March 20, 2018. https://mwi.usma.edu/wp-content/uploads/2018/03/Analyzing-the-Russian-Way-of-War.pdf.

2. Chausovsky, Eugene. "Looking Back on the Russian-Georgian War, 10 Years Later." Stratfor. August 7, 2018. https://worldview.stratfor.com/article/looking-back-russian-georgian-war-10-years-later.

3. Cohen, Ariel, and Robert Hamilton. "The Russian Military and The Georgian War: Lessons and Implications." Strategic Studies Institute. June 2011. https://ssi.armywarcollege.edu/pdffiles/pub1069.pdf.

4. Felgenhauer, Pavel. "After August 7: The Escalation of the Russia-Georgia War." In *The Guns of August 2008: Russia's War in Georgia*. Central Asia-Caucasus Institute of Johns Hopkins University's Paul H. Nitze School of Advanced International Studies, 2009.

5. Harris, Chris. "Europe's Forgotten War: The Georgian-Russian Conflict Explained a Decade On." EuroNews. July 8, 2018.

https://www.euronews.com/2018/08/07europe-s-forgotten-wa r-the-georgia-russia-conflict-explained-a-decade-on.

6. Illarionov, Andrei. "The Russian Leadership's Preparation for War, 1999-2008." In *The Guns of August 2008: Russia's War in Georgia*. Central Asia-Caucasus Institute of Johns Hopkins University's Paul H. Nitze School of Advanced International Studies, 2009.

7. Kofman, Michael. "The August War, Ten Years On: A Retrospective on The Russo-Georgian War." War On The Rocks, August 17, 2018. https://www.warontherocks.com/2018/08/the-august-war-ten-years-on-a-retrospective-on-the-russo-georgian-war.

8. Labarre, Frederic. "The Battle of Tskhinvali Revisited." The Small Wars Journal. https://smallwarsjournal.com/jrnl/art/the-battle-of-tskhinvali-r evisited.

9. Nations Online Project. "Administrative Map of Georgia." 1998-2019. https://www.nationsonline.org/oneworld/map/georgia_map2.h tm.

10. Nichol, Jim. "Russia-Georgia Conflict in August 2008: Conflict and implications for U.S. Interests." Congressional Research Service, March 3, 2009. https://www.everycrsreport.com/files/20080813_RL34618_af7 d22e7f33f1eadc090b329791f1bbc6fad71e4.pdf.

11. Nilsson, Niklaus. "Russian Hybrid Tactics in Georgia." Central Asia-Caucasus Institute & Silk Road Studies Program, January

2018.
https://silkroadstudies.org/resources/pdf/SilkRoadPapers/2018_01_Nilsson_Hybrid.pdf.

12. Popjanevski, Johanna. "From Sukhumi to Tskhinvali: The Path to War in Georgia." In *The Guns of August 2008: Russia's War in Georgia*. Central Asia-Caucasus Institute of Johns Hopkins University's Paul H. Nitze School of Advanced International Studies, 2009.

13. Pruit, Sarah. "How a Five-Day War with Georgia Allowed Russia to Reassert Its Military Might." History Stories, August 8, 2018. https://www.history.com/news/russia-georgia-war-military-nato.

14. Staff Sgt. Moor, Jonathan. "Republic of Georgia puts her best into Iraq fight." U.S. European Command, September 1, 2005. https://web.archive.org/web/20120323093954/http://www.eucom.mil/Article/21484/Republic-Georgia-puts-best-Iraq-fight

Chapter 4:

1. ArmyRecognition.com. "Russia deploys electronic warfare equipment in Arctic." TASS/Army Recognition Group SPRL, May 13, 2019. https://www.armyrecognition.com/may_2019_global_defense_security_army_news_industry/russia_deploys_electronic_warfare_equipment_in_arctic.html.

2. Bartles, Charles. "Russian Armed Forces: Enlisted Professionals." Foreign Military Studies Office, Fort Leavenworth, Kansas, March 11, 2019.

https://www.armyupress.army.mil/Journals/NCO-Journal/Archives/2019/March/Russian-NCOs/.

3. Battle Order. "The Weakness of Russian VDV Airborne Force Structure." May 10, 2022. www.youtube.com.

4. Berzins, Janis. "The Russian Way of Warfare." U.S. Army War College and Strategic Studies Institute, 2018.

5. Braun, Thomas. "The Russian Military in 2020: Russia's Way Back to Power Projection? Implications for NATO." Partnership for Peace Consortium of Defense Academies and Security Studies Institutes, Spring 2012. https://www.jstor.org/stable/10.2307/26326275.

6. Bruusgard, Kristen Ven. "Russia and Strategic Competition with the United States." U.S. Army War College and Strategic Studies Institute, 2018.

7. Bukkvoll, Tor. "Russian Special Operations Forces in Crimea and Donbas." Aleksanderi Papers, 2016. Kikimoro Publications at the Aleksanteri Institute, University of Helsinki, Finland.

8. Center for Arms Control, Energy, and Environmental Studies at MIPT. "Current Status and Future of Russian Strategic Forces." September 10, 2002. https://www.armscontrol.ru/start/rsf_now.htm.

9. Connell, George M. "The Soviet Navy in Theory and Practice: A Comparison of Gorshkov's Doctrinal Statements and Fleet Construction Programs." U.S. Army Russian Institute, May 1, 1979.

10. Connolly, Richard, and Mathieu Boulegue. "Russia's New State Armament Programme—Implications for the Russian Armed Forces and Military Capabilities to 2027." Russia and Eurasia Programme, May 2018. Chatham House—the Royal Institute of International Affairs.

11. Cooper, Julian. "Russia's State Armament Programme to 2020: A Quantitative Assessment of Implementation 2011-2015." Centre for Russian, European and Eurasian Studies, University of Birmingham, March 2016.

12. Defense-blog.com. "In Syria spotted new Russian RB-341V 'Leer-3' electronic warfare system." March 14, 2016. https://defence-blog.com/news/in-syria-spotted-new-russian-rb-341v-leer-3-electronic-warfare-system.html.

13. Field Manual 100-2-1. "Red Army Operations and Tactics." Department of the Army, July 16, 1984.

14. Field Manual 100-2-3. "The Soviet Army: Troops, Organization, and Equipment." Department of the Army, June 1991. https://fas.org/irp/doddir/army/fm100-2-3.pdf.

15. Gady, Franz-Stefan. "Russia to Test Fire RS-28 Sarmat ICBM in early 2019." The Diplomat, October 3, 2018.

16. Gady, Franz-Stefan. "Russia's Air Force to Receive First Serial-Produced Su-57 Fighter Jet by Year's End." The Diplomat, November 9, 2019. https://thediplomat.com/2019/11/russias-air-force-to-receive-first-serial-produced-su-57-fighter-jet-by-years-end/.

17. GlobalSecurity.org. "Russian Land Forces Equipment." January

5, 2016.
https://www.globalsecurity.org/military/world/russia/army-equipment.htm.

18. GlobalSecurity.org. "Soviet Air Forces."
https://www.globalsecurity.org/military/world/russia/av-main.htm.

19. GlobalSecurity.org. "Soviet Navy Ships 1945-1990."
https://www.globalsecurity.org/military/world/russia/ship-soviet-2.htm.

20. GlobalSecurity.org. "Troops of National Air Defense (PVO)." September 7, 2000.
https://fas.org/nuke/guide/russia/agency/pvo.htm.

21. Gorenburg, Dmitry. "Russia's Military Modernization Plans: 2018-2027." Russian Military Reform, November 27, 2017.

22. Grau, Lester, and Charles Bartles. "The Russian Way of War: Force Structure, Tactics and Modernization of the Russian Ground Forces." Foreign Military Studies Office, Fort Leavenworth, Kansas, 2016.

23. Grove, Thomas. "The New Iron Curtain: Russian Missile Defense Challenges U.S. Air Power." The Wall Street Journal, January 23, 2019.
https://www.wsj.com/articles/russias-missile-defense-draws-a-new-iron-curtain-against-u-s-military-11548255438.

24. Hackard, Mark. "Spy Snatchers: KGB Alpha Group." Espionage History Archive, April 9, 2015.
https://espionagehistoryarchive.com/2015/04/09/snatch-grab-t

he-kgbs-alpha/#more-109.

25. Hackard, Mark. "Vympel: The KGB's Sword Abroad." Espionage History Archive, April 2, 2015. https://espionagehistoryarchive.com/2015/04/02/vympel-kgb-spetsnaz/#more-90.

26. Harding, Joel. "Russian EW: Russian Military Unveils Revolutionary Electronic Warfare System." March 4, 2015. https://toinformistoinfluence.com/2015/03/04/russian-ew-russian-military-unveils-revolutionary-electronic-warfare-system/.

27. Harris, Catherine, and Frederick Kagan. "Russia's Military Posture: Ground Forces Order of Battle." Institute for the Study of War, March 2018.

28. Interagency Intelligence Memorandum. "Readiness of Soviet Air Forces." February 12, 1982. https://www.cia.gov/library/readingroom/docs/DOC_0000261313.pdf.

29. Joint Publication 3-13.1. "Electronic Warfare." Directed by Lt. General Walter Sharp for the Chairman of the Joint Chiefs of Staff, February 8, 2012. https://fas.org/irp/doddir/dod/jp3-13-1.pdf.

30. Klein, Margarete, and Kristian Pester. "Russia's Armed Forces on Modernization Course: Progress and Perspectives of Military Reform." Stiftung Wissenschaft und Politik—German Institute for International and Security Affairs, January 2014.

31. Lavrov, Anton. "Russian Military Reforms from Georgia to Syria." Center for Strategic International Studies (CSIS),

November 2018.
https://www.csis.org/analysis/russian-military-reforms-georgia-syria.

32. Majumdar, Dave. "Syria: Russian Vital Interests or Vital Combat Experience." June 26, 2018.
https://www.realcleardefense.com/articles/2018/06/26/syria_russian_vital_interests_or_vital_combat_experience_113556.html.

33. McDermott, Roger. "Moscow Deploys Latest Electronic Warfare Systems in Kaliningrad." Real Clear Defense, December 12, 2018.
https://www.realcleardefense.com/articles/2018/12/12/moscow_deploys_latest_electronic_warfare_systems_in_kaliningrad_114022.html.

34. McDermott, Roger. "Russian Defense Industry Creaks Under Rearmament Program." Eurasia Daily Monitor 11, no. 133, July 22, 2014. https://jamestown.org.

35. McDermott, Roger. "Russian Military Plans New NCO Training Center." Eurasia Daily Monitor 6, no. 163, September 8, 2009.
https://jamestown.org/program/russian-military-plans-new-nco-training-center/.

36. McDermott, Roger. "Russia's Armed Forces Strive for Command-and-Control Superiority in the Modern Battlespace." May 4, 2018.

37. McDermott, Roger. "Russia's Network-Centric Warfare." October 31, 2018.

38. Meakins, Joss. "The Other Side of the COIN: The Russians in Chechnya." Small Wars Journal, 2017. https://smallwarsjournal.com/jrnl/art/the-other-side-of-the-coin-the-russians-in-chechnya.

39. Myers, Steven Lee. "Hazing Trial Bares Dark Side of Russia's Military." New York Times, August 13, 2006. https://www.nytimes.com/2006/08/13/world/europe/13hazing.html.

40. Noris, Robert, and Hans Kristensen. "Nuclear U.S. and Soviet/Russian Intercontinental Ballistic Missiles, 1959-2008." January 1, 2009. https://journals.sagepub.com/doi/full/10.2968/065001008.

41. Pike, John. "Military: NCOs." GlobalSecurity.org. https://www.globalsecurity.org/military/world/russia/personnel-nco.html.

42. RussianDefense.com. "From Russia with Zaslon." December 24, 2016. http://www.russiandefence.com/from-russia-with-zaslon/.

43. Smith, Ben. "Russian Intelligence Services and Special Forces." House of Commons Library- BRIEFING PAPER Number CBP 8430, October 30, 2018. https://fas.org/irp/world/russia/CBP-8430.pdf.

44. Sukhankin, Sergey. "Continuing War by Other Means: The Case of Wagner, Russia's Premier Private Military Company in the Middle East." The Jamestown Foundation, July 13, 2018. https://jamestown.org/analyst/sergey-sukhankin/.

45. The ArchCast. "How They Fight! The Russian Battalion Tactical Group. Tactics, Equipment and Effectiveness." March 22, 2022. www.youtube.com.

46. Thornton, Rod. "Military Modernization and Russian Ground Forces." U.S. Army War College: Strategic Studies Institute, June 2011.

47. Trevithik, Joseph. "Turkey Says It Now Plans On Manufacturing Russia's S-500 Air Defense System." The Drive—The Warzone, May 20, 2019. https://www.thedrive.com/the-war-zone/28122/now-turkey-says-it-will-work-with-russia-to-build-the-s-500-air-defense-system .

48. Varfolomeeva, Anna. "Signaling strength: Russia's real Syria success is electronic warfare against the US." The Defense Post, May 1, 2018. https://thedefensepost.com/2018/05/01/russia-syria-electronic-warfare/.

49. Wiess, Michael. "Corruption and Cover-Up in the Kremlin: The Anatoly Serdyukov Case." The Atlantic, January 13, 2013. https://www.theatlantic.com/international/archive/2013/01/corruption-and-cover-up-in-the-kremlin-the-anatoly-serdyukov-case/272622/.

Chapter 5:

1. Agentura: The Secret Services Watchdog. "Foreign Intelligence Academy." Agentura.ru, 2010.

2. Agentura: The Secret Services Watchdog. "Foreign Intelligence Service the SVR." Agentura.ru, 2016. http://www.agentura.ru/english/dossier/svr/.

3. Agentura: The Secret Services Watchdog. "Structure of the FSB." Agentura.ru, 2011. http://www.agentura.ru/english/dossier/fsb/structure/.

4. Agentura: The Secret Services Watchdog. "SVR Structure." Agentura.ru, 2007. http://www.agentura.ru/english/dossier/svr/structure/.

5. Bennet, Gordon. "The SVR: Russia's Intelligence Service." Federation of American Scientists, March 2000. https://fas.org/irp/world/russia/svr/c103-gb.htm.

6. Bukkvoll, Tor. "Russian Special Operations Forces in Crimea and Donbas." In *Russian Military Power*, 2016.

7. Connolly, Richard, and Mathieu Boulegue. "Russia's New State Armament Programme—Implications for the Russian Armed Forces and Military Capabilities to 2027." Russia and Eurasia Programme, May 2018. Chatham House—the Royal Institute of International Affairs.

8. Corera, Gordon. *Russians Among Us: Sleeper Cells, Ghost Stories and the hunt for Putin's Spies*. HarperCollins Publishers, 2020.

9. Dearden, Lizzie. "Salisbury Nerve Agent Attack: Timeline of Movements By Russian 'Spies' Charged With Attempted Assassination of Sergei Skripal." *Independent*, September 5, 2018.
https://www.independent.co.uk/news/uk/crime/salisbury-ames

bury-nerve-agent-attack-novichock-timeline-russian-spies-poiso ning-a8524381.html.

10. Esch, Christian. "Doing Putin's Dirty Work: The Rise of Russia's GRU Military Intelligence Service." *Der Spiegel*, October 13, 2018.

11. EuroMaidan Press. "Putin Actively Using Cold War Stasi Agent Network in Germany, Reitschuster Says." March 9, 2018. https://www.euromaidanpress.com.

12. Faulconbridge, Guy. "What is Russia's GRU Military Intelligence Agency?" *Reuters*, October 5, 2018. https://www.reuters.com/article/us-britain-russia-gru-factbox/what-is-russias-gru-military-intelligence-agency-idUSKCN1MF 1VK.

13. Fedorov, Gleb. "GRU, Alpha and Vympel: Russia's most famous covert operators." *RBTH*, May 10, 2017. https://www.rbth.com/defence/2017/05/10/gru-alpha-vympel-russias-famous-covert-operators-759604.

14. Fitsanakis, Joseph. "FBI busts alleged Russian spy ring, 11 arrested." *intelNews.org*, June 29, 2010. https://intelnews.org/2010/06/29/02-339/.

15. Galeotti, Mark. "Russia's 'Zaslon' Military Operators Are So Shadowy They Make Ninjas Look Like Amateurs." *Business Insider: In Moscow's Shadows*, March 19, 2013. https://www.businessinsider.com/russian-zaslon-special-operati ons-2013-5.

16. Galeotti, Mark. "Russians In Syria, Zaslon, and the risks of going

native." *In Moscow's Shadows*, September 26, 2015. https://inmoscowsshadows.wordpress.com/2015/09/26/russians-in-syria-zaslon-and-the-risks-of-going-native/.

17. GlobalSecurity.org. "Alpha / Alfa / Group 'A' / Directorate A." https://www.globalsecurity.org/intell/world/russia/alpha.htm.

18. GlobalSecurity.org. "Foreign Intelligence Service (SVR) Sluzhba Vneshney Razvedki." 2019. https://www.globalsecurity.org/intell/world/russia/svr.htm.

19. GlobalSecurity.Org. "Vympel / Group 'V' / Independent Training Center." https://www.globalsecurity.org/intell/world/russia/vympel.htm.

20. Grau, Lester, and Charles Bartles. "The Russian Way of War: Force Structure, Tactics, and Modernization of the Russian Ground Forces." *Foreign Military Studies Office, Fort Leavenworth, KS.* https://www.armyupress.army.mil/Portals/7/Hot%20Spots/Documents/Russia/2017-07-The-Russian-Way-of-War-Grau-Bartles.pdf.

21. Hackard, Mark. "KGB DIRECTORATE S: TRAINING AN ILLEGAL." *Espionage History Archive*, June 3, 2016. https://espionagehistoryarchive.com/2016/06/03/kgb-directorate-s-training-an-illegal/.

22. Hackard, Mark. "KGB SPETSNAZ & WORLD WAR III." *Espionage History Archive*, April 17, 2015. https://espionagehistoryarchive.com/2015/04/17/kgb-spetsnaz-world-war-iii/.

23. Hackard, Mark. "Spy Snatchers: KGB Alpha Group." *Espionage History Archive*, April 9, 2015. https://espionagehistoryarchive.com/2015/04/09/snatch-grab-the-kgbs-alpha/#more-109.

24. Hackard, Mark. "THE ILLEGALS: RUSSIA'S ELITE SPIES." *Espionage History Archive*, July 10, 2016. https://espionagehistoryarchive.com/2010/07/10/the-illegals-russias-elite-spies-2/.

25. Hackard, Mark. "Vympel: The KGB's Sword Abroad." *Espionage History Archive*, April 2, 2015. https://espionagehistoryarchive.com/2015/04/02/vympel-kgb-spetsnaz/#more-90.

26. Hassan, Ahmed. "Meet Zaslon, Russia's Ultra-Secret Unit." *SOF REP*, February 4, 2019. https://sofrep.com/news/meet-zaslon-russias-ultra-secretive-unit/.

27. Hassan, Ahmed. "Zaslon: Russia's Most Secretive Unit." *Grey Dynamics*, January 31, 2022. https://greydynamics.com/zaslon-russias-most-secretive-unit/.

28. Lierens, Ethan. "KGB: History, Structure and Operations." *Grey Dynamics*, July 23, 2022. https://greydynamics.com/kgb-history-structure-and-operations/.

29. McKinney, Jack. "Hostages? No Problem Soviets Offer 'How-to' Lesson In Kidnapping." *Jerusalem Post*, 1986. https://web.archive.org/web/20141010144012/http://articles.philly.com/1986-01-15/news/26052630_1_hostage-crisis-soviet-c

aptives-islamic-liberation-organization.

30. Martin, Wes. "GRU Spetsnaz: The Batmen of Russia." *Grey Dynamics*, June 24, 2022. https://greydynamics.com/gru-spetsnaz-the-batmen-of-russia/.

31. Peter, Laurence. "Putin, Power and Poison: Russia's Elite FSB Spy Club." *BBC*, February 3, 2018. https://www.bbc.com/news/world-europe-42636245.

32. Pike, John. "Organization of the Main Intelligence Administration (GRU) Glavnoye Razvedyvatelnoye Upravlenie (GRU)." *Intelligence Resource Program*, November 26, 1997. http://www.fas.org/irp/world/russia/gru/org.htm.

33. Pincus, Walter, and Bill Miller. "AMES LED MULTIPLE LIVES IN CIA." *Washington Post*, March 12, 1994. https://www.washingtonpost.com/archive/politics/1994/03/12/ames-led-multiple-lives-in-cia/381c43e5-0e33-4188-ab25-e1d5276fd60e/?utm_term=.c9ce07fbdc52.

34. RIA News. "История Группы специального назначения 'Вымпел' КГБ СССР." August 19, 2011. https://ria.ru/20110819/419422103.html.

35. Schwirtz, Michael. "Top Secret Russian Unit Seeks to Destabilize Europe, Security Officials Say." *New York Times*, October 8, 2019. https://www.nytimes.com/2019/10/08/world/europe/unit-29155-russia-gru.html.

36. Seibt, Sebastian. "The GRU, Putin's not-so-secret service." *France 24*, September 9, 2018.

https://www.france24.com/en/20181009-gru-putin-russia-secret-service-spies-espionage-skripal-opcw-kgb.

37. Shapira, Ian. "'Rick is a goddamn Russian spy': Does the CIA have a new Aldrich Ames on its hands?". *Washington Post*, January 26, 2018. https://www.washingtonpost.com/news/retropolis/wp/2018/01/26/rick-is-a-goddamn-russian-spy-does-the-cia-have-a-new-aldrich-ames-on-its-hands/?noredirect=on&utm_term=.bc01449f35e4.

38. Smith, Ben. "Russian intelligence services and special forces." *House of Commons Library- BRIEFING PAPER Number CBP 8430*, October 30, 2018. https://fas.org/irp/world/russia/CBP-8430.pdf.

39. Sof, Eric. "Alpha Group." Special-ops.org. https://special-ops.org/12454/alpha-group-fsb-russia/.

40. Soldatov, Andrei, and Irina Borogan. "Mutation of the Russian Secret Services." Agentura.ru, 2007. http://www.agentura.ru/english/dosie/mutation/.

41. Soldatov, Andrei, and Irina Borogan. "Russia's Very Secret Services." *World Policy*, March 23, 2010. https://worldpolicy.org/2010/03/23/russias-very-secret-services/.

42. Soldatov, Andrei. "Putin's Secret Services: How the Kremlin Corralled the FSB." ForeignAffairs.com, May 31, 2018. https://www.foreignaffairs.com/articles/russia-fsu/2018-05-31/putins-secret-services.

43. Systemaspetsnaz.com. "Russian Spetsnaz: GRU—KGB—FSB—MVD—Alpha—Vympel." https://www.systemaspetsnaz.com/russian-spetsnaz-gru-kgb-fsb-mvd-alpha-vympel.

44. The Moscow Project. "Russia's Three Intelligence Agencies Explained." Espionage History Archive, October 12, 2018. https://themoscowproject.org/explainers/russias-three-intelligence-agencies-explained/.

45. Troianovski, Anton, and Ellen Nakashima. "How Russia's military intelligence agency became the covert muscle in Putin's duels with the West." *Washington Post*, December 28, 2018. https://www.washingtonpost.com/world/europe/how-russias-military-intelligence-agency-became-the-covert-muscle-in-putins-duels-with-the-west/2018/12/27/2736bbe2-fb2d-11e8-8c9a-860ce2a8148f_story.html?noredirect=on&utm_term=.e7a6443694a5.

Chapter 6:

1. Battle Order. "The Weakness of Russian VDV Airborne Force Structure." YouTube video. May 10, 2022. www.youtube.com.

2. Bellingcat Investigation Team. "Wagner Mercenaries With GRU-issued Passports: Validating SBU's Allegation." Bellingcat, January 30, 2019. https://www.bellingcat.com/news/uk-and-europe/2019/01/30/wagner-mercenaries-with-gru-issued-passports-validating-sbus-allegation/.

3. Boulegue, Mathieu. "Russia's Vostok Exercises Were Both

Serious Planning and a Show." Chatham House Royal Institute for International Affairs, September 17, 2018. https://www.chathamhouse.org/expert/comment/russia-s-vostok-exercises-were-both-serious-planning-and-show.

4. Bukkvoll, Tor. "Russian Special Operations Forces in Crimea and Donbas." Aleksanderi Papers. Kikimoro Publications at the Aleksanteri Institute, University of Helsinki, Finland, 2016.

5. De Faakto Intelligence Research Observatory. "Open Source Backgrounder: Russian Strategy in Sub-Sahara Africa, Military & Industrial Partnerships—What Is Russia Up To?" Small Wars Journal, 2018.

6. DIA. "Russian Military Power: Building a Military to Support Great Power Aspirations." Defense Intelligence Agency, 2017. www.dia.mil/Military-Power-Publications.

7. Embassy of the Russian Federation in Sri Lanka and to the Maldives. Facebook Post, April 11, 2020. "#OTD in 2016 Russian officer Alexander Prokhorenko was posthumously declared a Hero of Russia for courage and heroism in the performance of his military duties. Near the city of Palmyra, being surrounded by ISIS, he ordered an airstrike on his position to destroy the terrorists."

8. Fedorov, Gleb. "GRU, Alpha and Vympel: Russia's Most Famous Covert Operators." RBTH, 10 May 2017. https://www.rbth.com/defence/2017/05/10/gru-alpha-vympel-russias-famous-covert-operators-759604.

9. Fiore, Nicolas. "Defeating the Russian Battalion Tactical Group." U.S. Army, Fort Benning, 2017.

https://www.benning.army.mil/armor/earmor/content/issues/2017/spring/2Fiore17.pdf.

10. Galeotti, Mark. "The Rising Influence of Russian Special Forces." Jane's Intelligence Review, 2014. https://www.janes.com/images/assets/299/46299/The_rising_influence_of_Russian_special_forces.pdf.

11. GlobalSecurity.org. "Wagner Group Private Military Company 'Wagner', A.K.A. Chastnaya Voennaya Kompaniya 'Vagner', A.K.A. Chvk Vagner, A.K.A. PMC Wagner." GlobalSecurity.org, 19 March 2019.

12. Grau, Lester, and Bartles, Charles. "The Russian Way of War: Force Structure, Tactics, and Modernization of the Russian Ground Forces." Foreign Military Studies Office, Fort Leavenworth, KS, 2016. https://www.armyupress.army.mil/Portals/7/Hot%20Spots/Documents/Russia/2017-07-The-Russian-Way-of-War-Grau-Bartles.pdf.

13. Grove, Thomas. "Russian Special Forces Seen as Key to Aleppo Victory." Wall Street Journal, 16 December 2016. https://www.wsj.com/articles/russian-special-forces-seen-as-key-to-aleppo-victory-1481884200.

14. Kelly, Lydia. "Russia's Special Forces Officers Killed In Syria: Interfax." Thomson-Reuters, edited by Lowe, Christian and Heneghan, Tom, 24 March 2016. https://www.reuters.com/article/us-mideast-crisis-russia-death/russias-special-forces-officer-killed-in-syria-interfax-idUSKCN0WQ28Z.

15. Kofman, Michael. "Rethinking the Structure and Role of Russia's Airborne Forces." Russia Military Analysis, 30 January 2019. https://russianmilitaryanalysis.wordpress.com/2019/01/30/rethinking-the-structure-and-role-of-russias-airborne-forces/.

16. Longstreth, Samuel. "The KSSO: Russia's Special Operations Command." Grey Dynamics, 03 August 2022. https://greydynamics.com/the-ksso-russias-answer-to-special-forces/.

17. Majumdar, Dave. "Get Ready, America: Russia Has Its Own Deadly 'Delta Force'." The National Interest, 16 March 2017. https://nationalinterest.org/blog/the-buzz/get-ready-america-russia-has-its-own-deadly-delta-force-19793.

18. Marsh, Christopher. "Developments in Russian Special Operations: Russia's Spetsnaz, SOF, and Special Operations Forces Command." The CANSOFCOM Education & Research Centre, 2017.

19. McDermott, Roger. "Russia's Special Operations Forces Command and the Strategy of Limited Actions." The Jamestown Foundation, Eurasia Daily Monitor Volume: 16 Issue: 74, 21 May 2019. https://jamestown.org/program/russias-special-operations-forces-command-and-the-strategy-of-limited-actions/.

20. Savage, Patrick. "The Conventionality of Russia's Unconventional War." Traditional War, 2018.

21. Schmitt, Eric. "How a 4-Hour Battle Between Russian Mercenaries and U.S. Commandos Unfolded in Syria." New

York Times, 24 May 2018. https://www.nytimes.com/2018/05/24/world/middleeast/america-commandos-russian-mercenaries-syria.html.

22. Stewart, Will. "Trapped and Surrounded By Murderous ISIS Fighters, the Heroic Russian 'Rambo' Who Wiped Them All Out By Calling In Airstrikes on Himself." Daily Mail U.K., 29 March 2016. https://www.dailymail.co.uk/news/article-3513911/Trapped-surrounded-murderous-ISIS-fighters-heroic-Russian-Rambo-wiped-calling-airstrikes-HIMSELF.html.

23. Sukhankin, Sergey. "'Continuing War by Other Means': The Case of Wagner, Russia's Premier Private Military Company in the Middle East." The Jamestown Foundation, 13 July 2018.

24. Sukhankin, Sergey. "War, Business and 'Hybrid' Warfare: The Case of the Wagner Private Military Company (Part 1)." The Jamestown Foundation, 19 April 2018.

25. Sukhankin, Sergey. "War, Business and 'Hybrid' Warfare: The Case of the Wagner Private Military Company (Part 2)." The Jamestown Foundation, 23 April 2018.

26. The ArchCast. "How They Fight! The Russian Battalion Tactical Group. Tactics, Equipment and Effectiveness." YouTube video, 22 March 2022. www.youtube.com.

27. U.S. Army Special Operations Command. "Little Green Men: A Primer on Modern Russian Unconventional Warfare, Ukraine 2013-2014." G-3X Sensitive Activities U.S. Army Special Operations Command.

Chapter 7:

1. Angevine, Robert, John Warden, Russell Keller, and Clark Frye. "Learning Lessons from the Ukraine Conflict." Institute for Defense Analyses, May 2019.

2. Associated Press. "Pro-Russian Rally in Crimea Decries Kiev 'Bandits'." *Washington Post*, February 26, 2014. https://web.archive.org/web/20140226191043/http://www.washingtonpost.com/world/europe/ukraine-no-new-government-before-thursday/2014/02/25/44355d1e-9e00-11e3-878c-65222df220eb_story.html.

3. BBC News. "EU Signs Pacts With Ukraine, Georgia and Moldova." *BBC*, June 27, 2014. https://www.bbc.com/news/world-europe-28052645.

4. BBC News. "Ukraine Crisis: Crimea Parliament Asks to Join Russia." *BBC-Europe*, March 6, 2014. https://www.bbc.com/news/world-europe-26465962.

5. Braun, Thomas. "The Russian Military in 2020: Russia's Way Back to Power Projection? Implications for NATO." Partnership for Peace Consortium of Defense Academies and Security Studies Institutes, Spring 2014.

6. CNBC. "Ukraine Leader Seeks Cash At Kremlin To Fend Off Crisis." Thomson-Reuters, December 17, 2013. https://www.cnbc.com/2013/12/17/ukraine-leader-seeks-cash-at-kremlin-to-fend-off-crisis.html.

7. CSIS. "Ukraine Crisis Timeline: Annexation of

Crimea." Center for Strategic International Studies. http://ukraine.csis.org/crimea.htm#24.

8. Cooper, Julian. "Russia's State Armament Programme to 2020: A Quantitative Assessment of Implementation 2011-2015." Centre for Russian, European and Eurasian Studies University of Birmingham, March 2016.

9. Encyclopedia of Ukraine. "Cossack-Polish War." *Encyclopedia of Ukraine*, Vol. 1 (1984). http://www.encyclopediaofukraine.com/display.asp?linkpath=pages\C\O\Cossack6PolishWar.htm.

10. Encyclopedia of Ukraine. "Famine-Genocide of 1932-1933." *Encyclopedia of Ukraine*, 2009. http://www.encyclopediaofukraine.com/display.asp?linkpath=pages%5CF%5CA%5CFamine6Genocideof1932hD73.htm.

11. Galeotti, Mark. *Armies of Russia's War in Ukraine*. Osprey Publishing Ltd, 2019.

12. Galeotti, Mark. *Spetsnaz: Russia's Special Forces*. Osprey Publishing Ltd, 2015.

13. Geer, Kenneth. "Strategic Analysis: As Russia-Ukraine Conflict Continues, Malware Activity Rises." *FireEye: Threat Analysis*, March 28, 2014. https://www.fireeye.com/blog/threat-research/2014/05/strategic-analysis-as-russia-ukraine-conflict-continues-malware-activity-rises.html.

14. Gutterman, Steve. "Putin Puts Troops In Western Russia On Alert In Drill." *Reuters*, February 26, 2014.

https://www.reuters.com/article/us-ukraine-crisis-russia-militar y/putin-puts-troops-in-western-russia-on-alert-in-drill-idUSBRE A1P0RW20140226.

15. InfoSec Institute. "Crimea—The Russian Cyber Strategy to Hit Ukraine." March 11, 2014. https://resources.infosecinstitute.com/crimea-russian-cyber-stra tegy-hit-ukraine/#gref.

16. Kofman, Michael; Migacheva, Katya; Nichiporuk, Brian; Radin, Andrew; Tkacheva, Olesya; Oberholtzer, Jenny. *Lessons from Russia's Operations in Crimea and Eastern Ukraine*. Rand Corporation, 2017.

17. McDermott, Roger. "Brothers Disunited: Russia's Use of Military Power in Ukraine." *Foreign Military Studies Office*, U.K.

18. Miller, Christopher. "Ukraine's Top Intelligence Agency Deeply Infiltrated By Russian Spies." *Mashable*, December 30, 2014. https://mashable.com/2014/12/30/russian-vs-ukrainian-spies/.

19. Perry, Brett. "Non-Linear Warfare in Ukraine: The Critical Role of Information Operations and Special Operations." *Small Wars Journal*. https://smallwarsjournal.com/jrnl/art/non-linear-warfare-in-ukr aine-the-critical-role-of-information-operations-and-special-oper a.

20. Pravda-Ukraine. "Спікер ВР АРК вважає, що Крим може відокремитися від України." February 20, 2014. https://www.pravda.com.ua/news/2014/02/20/7015117/.

21. Ripley, Tim. "Ukrainian Navy Decimated By Russian Move into

Crimea." *IHS Jane's Defence Weekly*, March 25, 2014. https://wdsi.wordpress.com/2014/03/30/ukrainian-navy-decimated-by-russian-move-into-crimea/.

22. Schwartz, Paul. "Crimea's Strategic Value to Russia." *Center for Strategic International Studies*, March 18, 2014. https://www.csis.org/blogs/post-soviet-post/crimeas-strategic-value-russia.

23. Service, Robert. *Stalin: A Biography*. Macmillan, 2004.

24. Shuster, Simon. "The Standoff at Belbek: Inside the First Clash of the Second Crimean War." *Time Magazine*, March 5, 2014. https://time.com/12563/belbek-crimea-ukraine-russia/.

25. Smith, Jordan. "DIU: Rulers of the Stars." *Grey Dynamics*, November 11, 2022.

26. Smith, Jordan. "SBU: Protectors of the Homeland." *Grey Dynamics*, November 13, 2022. https://greydynamics.com/ukrainian-sbu-protectors-of-the-homeland/.

27. Smith-Spark, Laura; Black, Phil; Pleitgen, Frederik. "Russia Flexes Military Muscle As Tensions Rise in Ukraine's Crimea Region." *CNN*, February 27, 2014. https://edition.cnn.com/2014/02/26/world/europe/ukraine-politics/.

28. The Economist. "Edging Closer To War." *Eastern Approaches*, March 1, 2014. https://www.economist.com/eastern-approaches/2014/03/01/edging-closer-to-war.

29. Vasilyeva, Natalyia. "Russia's Conflict With Ukraine: An Explainer." *Military Times*, November 26, 2018. https://www.militarytimes.com/news/your-military/2018/11/26/russias-conflict-with-ukraine-an-explainer/.

30. U.S. Army Special Operations Command. "Little Green Men: A Primer on Modern Russian Unconventional Warfare, Ukraine 2013-2014." G-3X Sensitive Activities U.S. Army Special Operations Command.

Chapter 8:

1. Amadeo, Kimberly. "Ukraine Crisis, Summary and Explanation." *TheBalance.com*, June 25, 2019. https://www.thebalance.com/ukraine-crisis-summary-and-explanation-3970462.

2. Angevine, Robert, John Warden, Russell Keller, and Clark Frye. "Learning Lessons from the Ukraine Conflict." *Institute for Defense Analyses*, May 2019.

3. Associated Press. "At Least 7 Dead in Southeastern Ukraine Port City." *Inquirer.net*, May 10, 2014. https://newsinfo.inquirer.net/601080/at-least-7-dead-in-southeastern-ukraine-port-city.

4. BBC News. "Ukraine Conflict: Many Soldiers Dead in Rocket Strike." *BBC News*, July 11, 2014. https://www.bbc.com/news/world-europe-28261737.

5. BBC News. "Ukraine Crisis: 'Column from Russia' Crosses Border." *BBC News*, August 25, 2014.

https://www.bbc.com/news/world-europe-28924945.

6. BBC News. "Ukraine Crisis: Donetsk Rebels Call For Ceasefire." *BBC News*, August 09, 2014. https://www.bbc.com/news/world-europe-28724487.

7. BBC News. "Ukraine Crisis: Kiev Forces Win Back Mariupol." *BBC News*, June 13, 2014. https://www.bbc.com/news/world-europe-27829773.

8. BBC News. "Ukraine Crisis: Military Plane Shot Down in Luhansk." *BBC News*, June 14, 2014. https://www.bbc.com/news/world-europe-27845313.

9. BBC News. "Ukraine Crisis: Rebel Forces Abandon Slovyansk Stronghold." *BBC News*, July 05, 2014. https://www.bbc.com/news/world-europe-28174104.

10. BBC News. "Ukraine Crisis: Rebel Military Chief Strelkov Quits." *BBC News*, August 14, 2014. https://www.bbc.com/news/world-europe-28792966.

11. BBC News. "Ukraine Crisis: Troops Abandon Luhansk Airport After Clashes." *BBC News*, September 01, 2014. https://www.bbc.com/news/world-europe-29009516.

12. BBC News. "Ukraine Forces Clash with Separatists at Donetsk Airport." *BBC News*, July 10, 2014. https://www.bbc.com/news/world-europe-28255174.

13. Bender, Jeremy. "REPORT: Ukrainian Troops Attacked Russian Military Column." *Business Insider*, August 15, 2014. https://www.businessinsider.com/ukrainian-troops-attacked-ru

ssian-military-2014-8.

14. Cowan, Annie. "Daily Ukraine Crisis Updates—August 18, 2014." *EastWest Institute*, August 18, 2014. https://www.eastwest.ngo/idea/daily-ukraine-crisis-updates—august-18-2014.

15. EuromaidanPress. "In Memoriam: The Defense of Donetsk Airport (25 May 2014 to 22 January 2015)." *History, War In the Donbas*, May 27, 2017. http://euromaidanpress.com/2017/05/27/donetsk-airport-defence-in-memoriam/#!prettyPhoto.

16. Forensic Architecture. "The Battle of Ilovaisk: Mapping Russian Military Presence in Eastern Ukraine August-September 2014." https://ilovaisk.forensic-architecture.org.

17. Fox, Amos. "Battle of Debaltseve: The Conventional Line of Effort in Russia's Hybrid War in Ukraine." 2017. *Fort Benning eArmor—U.S. Army.* https://www.benning.army.mil/armor/eARMOR/content/issues/2017/Winter/1Fox17.pdf.

18. Fox, Amos. "'Cyborgs at Little Stalingrad': A Brief History of the Battles of the Donetsk Airport 26 May 2014 to 21 January 2015." May 2019. *U.S. Army Institute of Land Warfare.* https://www.ausa.org/sites/default/files/publications/LWP-125-Cyborgs-at-Little-Stalingrad-A-Brief-History-of-the-Battle-of-the-Donetsk-Airport.pdf.

19. Gordon, Michael R. "Russia Moves Artillery Units into Ukraine, NATO Says." *New York Times*, August 22, 2014. https://www.nytimes.com/2014/08/23/world/europe/russia-m

oves-artillery-units-into-ukraine-nato-says.html.

20. Grove, Thomas, and Strobel, Michael. "Special Report: Where Ukraine's Separatists Get Their Weapons." *Thompson-Reuters*, July 29, 2014. https://www.reuters.com/article/us-ukraine-crisis-arms-specialreport/special-report-where-ukraines-separatists-get-their-weapons-idUSKBN0FY0UA20140729?feedType=RSS&feedName=worldNews.

21. Grytsenko, Oksana. "Surviving Ilovaisk: Thousands of Soldiers Fought At Ilovaisk, Around a hundred Were Killed." *Kyiv Post*, April 6, 2018. https://www.kyivpost.com/thousands-russian-soldiers-fought-ilovaisk-around-hundred-killed?cn-reloaded=1.

22. Holcomb, Franklin. "The Kremlin's Irregular Army: Ukrainian Separatist Order of Battle." 2017. *The Institute for the Study of War*.

23. InfoSec Institute. "Crimea—The Russian Cyber Strategy to Hit Ukraine." March 11, 2014. https://resources.infosecinstitute.com/crimea-russian-cyber-strategy-hit-ukraine/#gref.

24. Interfax-Ukraine. "ATO Forces Take Over Debaltseve, Shakhtarsk, Torez, Lutuhyne, Fighting for Pervomaisk and Snizhne Underway—ATO Press Center." July 28, 2014. *Ukraine News Agency*. https://en.interfax.com.ua/news/general/215712.html.

25. Kunkle, Fredrick. "The Bloody Battle for Donetsk's Airport: The View From the Front Lines." *Washington Post*, May 27, 2014.

https://www.washingtonpost.com/news/worldviews/wp/2014/05/27/the-bloody-battle-for-donetsks-airport-the-view-from-the-front-lines/.

26. Kyiv Post. "Russian Troops Amass On Border as Kyiv Authorities Reformulate Operation Plans." April 24, 2014. https://www.kyivpost.com/article/content/ukraine-politics/5-dead-one-wounded-as-anti-terror-operation-continues-in-sloviansk-live-updates-344902.html.

27. Lister, Tim. "'It's hell down there:' Inside the battle for eastern Ukraine." *CNN*, June 6, 2014. https://www.cnn.com/2014/06/06/world/europe/eastern-ukraine-battle/index.html.

28. Litvinov, M.V. "Battle in Yampol—Riddles and Solutions." 2014. *Cassad LiveJournal*. https://cassad-eng.livejournal.com/5837.html.

29. Miller, Christopher. "Donetsk Faces Threat of Urban Warfare as Ukrainian Forces Move to Encircle City." *Kyiv Post*, August 4, 2014. https://www.kyivpost.com/article/content/ukraine-politics/donetsk-faces-threat-of-urban-warfare-as-ukrainian-forces-move-to-encircle-city-359270.html.

30. Morello, Carol, and DeYoung, Karen. "As Fighting Continues in East Ukraine, U.S. Releases Images Said to implicate Russia." *Washington Post*, July 27, 2014. https://www.washingtonpost.com/world/europe/fierce-battle-between-military-and-rebels-in-eastern-ukraine-halts-plane-investigation/2014/07/27/b695809c-1582-11e4-9e3b-7f2f110c6265_

story.html.

31. Park, Donghui; Summers, Julia; and Walstrom, Michael. "Cyberattack on Critical Infrastructure: Russia and the Ukrainian Power Grid Attacks." *The Henry M Jackson School of International Studies, University of Washington*, October 11, 2017. https://jsis.washington.edu/news/cyberattack-critical-infrastructure-russia-ukrainian-power-grid-attacks/.

32. Payne, Ed, and Walsh, Nick Patton. "Leading In Ukraine Election, Billionaire Petro Poroshenko Declares Victory." *CNN*, May 26, 2014. https://www.cnn.com/2014/05/26/world/europe/ukraine-crisis/index.html.

33. Shuster, Simon. "Ukraine Rebels Call Putin a Coward After Russian Inaction." *Time Magazine*, July 9, 2019. https://time.com/2969586/vladimir-putin-russia-ukraine-rebels/.

34. Smith, Jordan. "DIU: Rulers of the Stars." *Grey Dynamics*, November 11, 2022. https://greydynamics.com/ukrainian-sbu-protectors-of-the-homeland/.

35. Smith, Jordan. "SBU: Protectors of the Homeland." *Grey Dynamics*, November 13, 2022. https://greydynamics.com/ukrainian-sbu-protectors-of-the-homeland/.

36. Snyder, Xander, and Zolotova, Ekaterina. "A Top-to-Bottom Review of the Russian Economy." *Geopolitical Futures*,

November 30, 2017.
https://geopoliticalfutures.com/top-bottom-review-russian-economy/.

37. The Editorial Board. "Was the Downing of Flight MH17 State-Sponsored Murder?". *New York Times*, June 19, 2019. https://www.nytimes.com/2019/06/19/opinion/mh17-ukraine-russia-suspects.html.

38. Zoria, Yuri, and Shandra, Alya. "Everything you wanted to know about the Minsk peace deal, but were afraid to ask." *Euromaidan Press*. http://euromaidanpress.com/minsk-agreements-faq/.

Chapter 9

1. Corum, Jonathan, and Zimmer, Carl. "How Gamaleya's Vaccine Works." *New York Times*, May 7, 2021. https://www.nytimes.com/interactive/2021/health/gamaleya-covid-19-vaccine.html.

2. Ellyatt, Holly. "'It's Scientific Nonsense' Russia Denies Claims It Stole COVID Vaccine Blueprint from UK." *CNBC*, October 13, 2021. https://www.cnbc.com/2021/10/13/russia-denies-claims-it-stole-covid-vaccine-blueprint.html.

3. Friedman, George. "China's Economic Crisis and Its Foreign Policy." *Geopolitical Futures*, October 5, 2021. https://geopoliticalfutures.com/chinas-economic-crisis-and-its-foreign-policy/.

4. Friedman, George. "The Necessity of the Iraq

War." *Geopolitical Futures*, March 28, 2023. https://geopoliticalfutures.com/the-necessity-of-the-iraq-war/.

5. Geopolitical Futures Editorial Board. "Brief: Concerning China's Inequality." *Geopolitical Futures*, August 26, 2021. https://geopoliticalfutures.com/brief-concerning-chinas-inequality/.

6. Hellem, Fredrik. "Wagner: Russia's Non-State State Actor Part IV." *Grey Dynamics*, April 15, 2021. https://greydynamics.com/russias-non-state-state-actor-part-iv/#The_Libyan_Scheme.

7. Herczegh, Victoria. "A Confrontation China Can't Afford." *Geopolitical Futures*, July 27, 2022. https://geopoliticalfutures.com/a-confrontation-china-cant-afford/.

8. Herczegh, Victoria. "In China A Challenge to Xi's Power." *Geopolitical Futures*, May 23, 2022. https://geopoliticalfutures.com/in-china-a-challenge-to-xis-power/.

9. Herczegh, Victoria. "In China New Purges New Targets." *Geopolitical Futures*, August 1, 2022. https://geopoliticalfutures.com/in-china-new-purges-new-targets/.

10. Herczegh, Victoria. "Real Estate Is China's Biggest Economic Vulnerability." *Geopolitical Futures*, May 23, 2022. https://geopoliticalfutures.com/real-estate-is-chinas-biggest-economic-vulnerability/.

11. Khashan, Hilal. "Israel and Iran's Calibrated Conflict." *Geopolitical Futures*, March 9, 2023. https://geopoliticalfutures.com/israel-and-irans-calibrated-conflict/.

12. Khashan, Hilal. "Understanding Iranian Politics." *Geopolitical Futures*, November 28, 2022. https://geopoliticalfutures.com/understanding-iranian-politics/.

13. Khashan, Hilal. "What the Taliban's Resurgence Means for the Arab World." *Geopolitical Futures*, September 2, 2021. https://geopoliticalfutures.com/what-the-talibans-resurgence-means-for-the-arab-world/.

14. Orchard, Phillip. "The Trouble With China's Tech Giants." *Geopolitical Futures*. https://geopoliticalfutures.com/the-trouble-with-chinas-tech-titans/.

15. Orchard, Phillip. "Why Evergrande Is Going To Plan." *Geopolitical Futures*, October 11, 2021. https://geopoliticalfutures.com/why-evergrande-is-going-to-plan/.

16. Orchard, Phillip. "Wolf War and Peace." *Geopolitical Futures*, June 28, 2021. https://geopoliticalfutures.com/wolf-war-and-peace/.

17. Smith, Jordan. "Libyan Stability: 6 Month Outlook." *Grey Dynamics*, July 30, 2022. https://greydynamics.com/libyan-stability-6-month-outlook/.

18. Tayler, Louis. "Libyan Civil War: Shifting Balance of Power." *Grey Dynamics*, April 15, 2021. https://greydynamics.com/libyan-civil-war-shifting-balance-of-power/.

19. Tayler, Louis. "Libya: Shifting Into a Stalemated Proxy War." *Grey Dynamics*, November 27, 2019. https://greydynamics.com/libya-shifting-into-stalemated-proxy-war/

About the Author

Curtis Lee Fox is the son of a West Texas cotton farmer and a Kentucky kindergarten teacher. He was raised in Texas and Virginia, and studied Mechanical Engineering at Virginia Tech, where he lived next door to his future wife Katie.

Despite being accepted to the graduate engineering program at Virginia Tech under a research assistant-ship, Curtis chose to enlist in the Army, where he learned to speak Russian, won his Green Beret, and served in the 10th Special Forces Group.

After completing his time in service, Curtis studied at Georgetown University's McDonough School of Business, earning a Master's of Business Administration. Curtis and Katie married in June 2017, and they now reside in Northern Virginia where Curtis works as a systems engineer and project manager.

Become a -30- Press Early Reviewer

We are just getting started here at -30-, with several projects in various phases of completion set to release in subsequent years.

One of the most critical aspects of publishing is the small group of early readers who receive Advance Reader Copies (ARCs).

If you would like to be one of the lucky individuals to receive early editions of books for free in exchange for leaving an unbiased review come the launch date, then please use the QR code below, or head directly to 30press.com.

You can subscribe to one (or all) of our email lists and be the first to know about ARCs, future projects, and the inner workings of -30- Press.

https://30press.com